JOHN WILLIS

SCREEN WORLD

1985

Volume 36

Crown Publishers, Inc.

One Park Avenue

New York, New York 10016

Copyright © 1985 by John Willis. Manufactured in U.S.A.
Library of Congress Catalog Card No. 50-3023
ISBN 0-517-55821-1

TO

CLARENCE BROWN

One of Hollywood's most talented and highly respected directors. As a pioneer in both silent and talking pictures, he was influential in the development of the motion picture art form. During a distinguished 40-year career, many of his films were recognized internationally as cinematic classics.

His films: The Great Redeemer, The Last of the Mohicans (1920), The Foolish Matrons (1921), The Light in the Dark (1922), Don't Marry for Money, The Acquittal (1923), The Signal Tower, Butterfly (1924), Smouldering Fires, The Eagle, The Goose Woman (1925), Kiki (1926), Flesh and the Devil (1927), The Trail of '98, A Woman of Affairs (1928), The Wonder of Women, Navy Blues (1929), Anna Christie, Romance (1930), Inspiration, A Free Soul, Possessed (1931), Emma, Letty Lynton, The Son-Daughter (1932), Looking Forward, Night Flight (1933), Sadie McKee, Chained (1934), Anna Karenina, Ah Wilderness! (1935), Wife versus Secretary, The Gorgeous Hussy (1936), Conquest/Marie Walewska (1937), Of Human Hearts (1938), Idiot's Delight, The Rains Came (1939), Edison the Man, (1940), Come Live with Me, They Met in Bombay (1941), The Human Comedy (1943), The White Cliffs of Dover (1944), National Velvet (1945), The Yearling, Song of Love (1947), Intruder in the Dust, To Please a Lady (1950), Angels in the Outfield (1951), It's a Big Country, When in Rome, Plymouth Adventure (1952), Never Let Me Go (1953). Academy Award nominations were for Anna Christie, Romance, A Free Soul, The Human Comedy, National Velvet and The Yearling. He received a British Academy Award for Intruder in the Dust.

JUDY DAVIS and VICTOR BANERJEE
in "A Passage to India"
© *Columbia Pictures*

CONTENTS

EDITOR: JOHN WILLIS

Assistant Editor: Stanley Reeves

Staff: Joe Baltake, Marco Starr Boyajian, Terence Burk, Mark Cohen, Dick Corrigan,
Mark Gladstone, Miles Kreuger, John Sala, Tiko Vargas, Van Williams
Designer: Peggy Goddard

Acknowledgments: This volume would not be possible without the cooperation of Ward Ableson,
Gary Adelman, Lisa Agay, Tom Allen, Jane Alsobrook, Pamela Austin, Fred Baker, Amanda Barber,
Nina Baron, Jim Bertges, Liane Brandon, Joseph Brenner, Susan Brockman, Gail Brownstein, Scott
Calder, John Calhoun, Fabiano Casosa, Andy Caplan, Eileen Nad Castaldi, Philip Castanza, Cary
Chadbourne, Jerry Clark, Sandy Cobe, Anne Cochran, Arthur Cohn, Bill Coleman, Karen Cooper,
Craig Cox, Lynne Dahlgren, Alberta D'Angelo, Francene Davidoff, Josephine Dean, Cindy DePaula,
Donna Dickman, Dennis Dough, Robert Dorfman, Betty Einbinder, Helen Eisman, Bill Elson, Steve
Fagan, Suzanne Fedak, Mary Lou Finnin, Tim Fisher, Lynn Fishoff, Dom Francella, Dore Freeman,
Renee Furst, Kathryn Galan, Jess Garcia, Ted Goldberg, Joseph Green, Elissa Greer, Lisa Halliday,
Allison Hanau, Johnathan Hanna, Ron Harvey, Tom Haskins, Richard Hassanein, Gary Hertz, Dennis
Higgins, Sam Irvin, Tina Jordan, Sherry Justice, Andy Kaplan, Helen Kavanaugh, Allison Kossow,
Richard Kraft, Don Krim, Jack Kurnes, Christine LaMont, Ann Lander, Maryanne Lataif, Jack Leff,
Lloyd Leipzid, Wynn Lowenthal, Peter Lowry, Arlene Ludwig, William Lustig, Jeff Mackler, Steven
Mackler, Howard Mahler, Harold Marenstein, Priscilla McDonald, Michael Meyers, Susan Mills,
Maria Mitrione, Paul Mowry, Barbara Mudge, Steve Newman, Joanna Ney, Bill O'Connell, Sue
Oscar, Lillie Padell, Janet Perlberg, Jerry Pickman, Ed Pine, Terry Powers, Joel Preisler, John Quinn,
Gerald Rappoport, Jackie Rayanal, Ruth Robbins, Reid Rosefelt, Ed Russell, Suzanne Salter, Cheryle
Sarkin, Nicole Satescu, Eric Sawyer, Les Schecter, Barbara Schwei, Mike Scrimenti, Eve Segal,
Jacqueline Sigmund, Judy Singer, John Skouras, Stephen Soba, Fran Speelman, David Sprigle, Alicia
Springer, John Springer, Laurence Steinfeld, Stuart Strutin, Ken Stutz, Lisa Tesone, John Tilley,
Veronica Toole, Bruce Trinz, Bill Velsor, Ron Wanless, Wendy Whitescarver, Bob Winestein, Jeffrey
Wise, Christopher Wood, Loretta Woodruff, David Wright, Jane Wright, Stuart Zakim, Michael
Zuker

1. Clint Eastwood   2. Bill Murray   3. Harrison Ford   4. Eddie Murphy

5. Sally Field   6. Burt Reynolds   7. Robert Redford   8. Prince

9. Dan Aykroyd   10. Meryl Streep   11. Debra Winger   12. Sylvester Stallone

13. Tom Hanks   14. Arnold Schwarzenegger   15. Shirley MacLaine   16. Steve Martin

TOP 25 BOX OFFICE STARS OF 1984

(Tabulated by Quigley Publications)

17. Tom Cruise

18. Jack Nicholson

19. Richard Gere

20. Dolly Parton

1984 RELEASES

January 1 through December 31, 1984

21. Robert DeNiro

22. Chuck Norris

23. Kevin Bacon

24. George Burns

25. Dustin Hoffman

Faye Dunaway

Matt Dillon

Isabelle Huppert

BROADWAY DANNY ROSE

(ORION) Producer, Robert Greenhut; Direction and Screenplay, Woody Allen; Executive Producer, Charles H. Joffe; Photography, Gordon Willis; Designer, Mel Bourne; Costumes, Jeffrey Kurland; Editor, Susan E. Morse; Associate Producer, Michael Peyser; Production Manager, Fredric B. Blankfein; Assistant Directors, Thomas Reilly, James Chory; Production Manager, Ezra Swerdlow; Production Coordinator, Helen Robin; In black and white and DeLuxe Color; Rated PG; 86 minutes; January release

CAST

Danny Rose	Woody Allen
Tina Vitale	Mia Farrow
Lou Canova	Nick Apollo Forte
Themselves	Sandy Baron, Corbett Monica, Jackie Gayle, Morty Gunty, Will Jordan, Jack Rollins, Milton Berle, Joe Franklin, Howard Cosell
Ray Webb	Craig Vandenburgh
Barney Dunn	Herb Reynolds
Vito Rispoli	Paul Greco
Joe Rispoli	Frank Renzulli
Johnny Rispoli	Edwin Bordo
Johnny's Mother	Gina DeAngelis
Hood at warehouse	Peter Castellotti
Teresa	Sandy Richman
Sid Bacharach	Gerald Schoenfeld
Angelina	Olga Barbato
Phil Chomsky	David Kissell
Water Glass Virtuoso	Gloria Parker
Balloon Act	Bob and Etta Rollins
Herbie Jayson	Bob Weil
Ralph, the club owner	David Kieserman
Blind Xylophonist	Mark Hardwick
Bird Lady	Alba Ballard
Hypnotist	Maurice Shrog

and Belle Berger, Herschel Rosen, Cecilia Amerling, Maggie Ranone, Charles D'Amodio, Joie Gallo, Carl Pistilli, Lucy Iacono, Julia Barbuto, Anna Sceusa, Nicholas Pantano, Rocco Pantano, Tony Turca, Gilda Torterello, Ronald Maccone, Antoinette Raffone, Michael Badalucco, Richard Lanzano, Dom Matteo, Camille Saviola, Sheila Bond, Betty Rosotti, John Doumanian, Gary Reynolds, Sid Winter, Diane Zolten, William Paulson, George Axler, Leo Steiner

Left: Woody Allen, Nick Apollo Forte
© *Orion Pictures*

Woody Allen, Mia Farrow (also top left)

THE BUDDY SYSTEM

(20th CENTURY-FOX) Producer, Alain Chammas; Director, Glenn Jordan; Screenplay, Mary Agnes Donoghue; Photography, Matthew F. Leonetti; Designer, Rodger Maus; Editor, Arthur Schmidt; Music, Patrick Williams; Production Manager, Gordon Webb; Assistant Directors, Peter Bergquist, Chris Soldo, Leslie Jackson; Costumes, Joe Aulisi; Designers, Harold Fuhrman, Diane Wager; Special Effects, Gary Elmendorf; Production Coordinator, Kathy Herbert; In DeLuxe Color; Rated PG; 111 minutes; January release.

CAST

Joe	Richard Dreyfuss
Emily	Susan Sarandon
Carrie	Nancy Allen
Mrs. Price	Jean Stapleton
Tim	Wil Wheaton
Jim Parks	Edward Winter
Dr. Knitz	Keene Curtis
Man who gives Emily the test	Tom Lacy
Ray	Lee Weaver
Teacher	Carolyn Coates
Landlord	Milton Selzer
Frank	Todd Everett
Lawyer	F. William Parker
Woman Customer	Bianca Ferguson
Pet Shop Owner	Lew Horn
Mr. Fleeze	Frank Coppola
Man Customer	Brent Price
Potato	Jason Hervey
Indians	Scott Crow, Josh Schulman
Pilgrim	Mike Lawrence
Trees	Jason Castellano, Jimmy E. Keegan

© *20th Century-Fox*
**Top: (1) Susan Sarandon, Wil Wheaton, Richard
Dreyfuss Below: Nancy Allen, Dreyfuss,
also top right, and below with Sarandon**

Jean Stapleton, Susan Sarandon

THE LONELY GUY

(UNIVERSAL) Producer-Director, Arthur Hiller; Executive Producer, William E. McEuen; Co-Executive Producer, C. O. Erickson; Screenplay, Ed Weinberger, Stan Daniels; Adaptation, Neil Simon; Based on "The Lonely Guy's Book of Life" by Bruce Jay Friedman; Photography, Victor J. Kemper; Editors, William Reynolds, Raja Gosnell; Music, Jerry Goldsmith; Design, James D. Vance; Costumes, Betsy Cox; Sound, Larry Jost, Jimmy Sabat; Special Visual Effects, Albert Whitlock; Associate Producer, Judy Gordon; Assistant Director, Jack Roe; In Technicolor; Rated R; 93 minutes; January release.

CAST

Larry Hubbard	Steve Martin
Warren Evans	Charles Grodin
Iris	Judith Ivey
Jack Fenwick	Steve Lawrence
Danielle	Robyn Douglass
Merv Griffin	Himself
Dr. Joyce Brothers	Herself
Schneider Twins	Candi Brough, Randi Brough
Rental Agent	Julie Payne
Lonely Cop	Madison Arnold
Greeting Card Supervisor	Roger Robinson
Girl in Blood Bank	Joan Sweeny
Park Guard	Daniel P. Hannafin
Maitre d'	Nicholas Mele
Traffic Cop	Leon Jones
Raul	Richard Delmonte
Girl in bar	Leslie Wing
Woman in window	Helen Verbit
Hold Up Man	Kenneth O'Brien
Girl in bank	Erica Hiller
Couple in bar	Karyn Harrison, Hunt Block
Bookstore Man	Alan Leach

and Jerry Grayson, Michael Greer, George Saurel, Erik Holland, Hugh Douglas, Sarah Abrell, Ken Hixon, Rance Howard, Billy James, Jose Martinez, Jade Bari, Gloria Irizarry, Beau Starr, Dominic Barto, Charles DeVries, Santos Morales, Jolina Collins, Lena Pousette

Left: Steve Martin (also top),
Charles Grodin © *Universal*

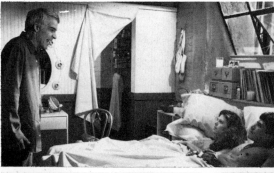

Steve Lawrence (center)

Steve Martin, Judith Ivey Above: Martin,
Robyn Douglass, Richard Del Monte

LOVE LETTERS

(NEW WORLD) Executive Producers, Mel Pearl, Don Levin; Producer, Roger Corman; Direction-Screenplay, Amy Jones; Associate Producer-Production Manager, Charles Skouras III; Photography, Alec Hirschfeld; Music, Ralph Jones; Editor, Wendy Greene; Art Director, Jeannine Oppewall; Production Coordinator, Iya Labunka; In color; Rated R; 94 minutes; January release.

CAST

Anna	Jamie Lee Curtis
Oliver	James Keach
Wendy	Amy Madigan
Danny	Bud Cort
Mr. Winter	Matt Clark
Mrs. Winter	Bonnie Bartlett
Ralph	Phil Coccioletti
Edith	Shelby Leverington
Chesley	Rance Howard
Marcia	Betsy Toll
Sally	Sally Kirkland

Top: (L) Bud Cort, Jamie Lee Curtis
(R) Jamie Lee Curtis (also below)
Center Left: James Keach, Curtis
© *New World*

Jamie Lee Curtis

FOOTLOOSE

(PARAMOUNT) Producers, Lewis J. Rachmil, Craig Zadan; Director, Herbert Ross; Screenplay, Dean Pitchford; Executive Producer, Daniel Melnick; Photography, Ric Waite; Designer, Ron Hobbs; Editor, Paul Hirsch; Choreography, Lynne Taylor-Corbett; Score Adaptation, Miles Goodman; Costumes, Gloria Gresham; Assistant Directors, L. Andrew Stone, Robert Engelman, Donald Paul Hauer; Special Effects, James W. Beauchamp; Original Songs, Dean Pitchford, Kenny Loggins, Sammy Hagar, Bill Wolfer, Jim Steinman, Michael Gore, Tom Snow, Eric Carmen; In Movielab Color and Dolby Stereo; Soundtrack Album on Columbia Records; Rated PG; 107 minutes; February release

CAST

Ren	Kevin Bacon
Ariel	Lori Singer
Rev. Shaw Moore	John Lithgow
Vi Moore	Dianne Wiest
Willard	Christopher Penn
Rusty	Sarah Jessica Parker
Woody	John Laughlin
Wendy Jo	Elizabeth Gorcey
Ethel MacCormack	Frances Lee McCain
Chuck	Jim Youngs
Burlington Cranston	Douglas Dirkson
Lulu	Lynne Marta
Wes	Arthur Rosenberg
Andy Beamis	Timothy Scott
Roger Dunbar	Alan Haufrect
Eleanor Dunbar	Linda MacEwen
Edna	Kim Jensen
Travis	Michael Telmont
Rich	Leo Geter
Jeff	Ken Kemp
Herb	Russ McGinn
Mr. Gurntz	Sam Dalton
Widdoes	H. E. D. Redford
Harvey	Jay Bernard
Team Member	David Valenza
Sarah	Meghan Broadhead
Amy	Mimi Broadhead
Bernie	Gene Pack
Virginia	Marcia Yvette Reider
Fat Cowboy	John Perryman
Mrs. Allyson	Mary Ethel Gregory
Mr. Walsh	Oscar Rowland
Mayor Dooley	J. Paul Broadhead
Elvis	John Bishop
Stunt Dancer	Peter Tramm
Girls	Carmen Trevino, Melissa Renee Graehl, Monica M. daSilva, Terri Gay Ulmer

Left: Sarah Jessica Parker, Lori Singer
Top: Lori Singer, Kevin Bacon
© Paramount Pictures

John Lithgow, Lori Singer

Dianne Wiest, John Lithgow

Kevin Bacon Above: Bacon, John Laughlin,
Christopher Penn Top: Lori Singer, Bacon

Lori Singer, Jim Youngs
Above: Lori Singer

13

SPLASH

(BUENA VISTA) Executive Producer, John Thomas Lenox; Producer, Brian Grazer; Director, Ron Howard; Screenplay, Lowell Ganz, Babaloo Mandel, Bruce Jay Friedman; Based on story by Brian Grazer; Screen Story, Bruce Jay Friedman; Music, Lee Holdridge; Photography, Don Peterman; Designer, Jack T. Collis; Editors, Daniel P. Hanley, Michael Hill; Costumes, May Routh; Production Manager, John Thomas Lenox; Assistant Directors, Jan R. Lloyd, Doug Metzger, Christopher Griffin, Hans Hanthony Beimler; Swimming Choreographer, Mike Nomad; Production Coordinator, Bobbi Kronowitz; Art Director, John B. Mansbridge; Underwater Photography, Jordan Klein; Mermaid Design, Robert Short; Special Visual Effects, Mitch Suskin; In Technicolor, Dolby Stereo; Rated PG; 111 minutes; February release

CAST

Allen Bauer	Tom Hanks
Madison	Daryl Hannah
Walter Kornbluth	Eugene Levy
Freddie Bauer	John Candy
Mrs. Stimler	Dody Goodman
Mr. Buyrite	Shecky Greene
Dr. Ross	Richard B. Shull
Jerry	Bobby DiCicco
Dr. Zidell	Howard Morris
Tim the doorman	Tony DiBenedetto
Michaelson	Patrick Cronin
His Partner	Charles Walker
Claude	David Knell
Junior	Jeff Doucette
Buckwalter	Royce D. Applegate
Augie	Tony Longo
Ms. Stein	Nora Denney
The President	Charles Macaulay
Dr. Johanssen	Ronald F. Hoiseck
Manny	Joe Grifasi
McCullough	Rance Howard
Lt. Ingram	David Lloyd Nelson
Fat Jack	Al Chesney
Stan	Lowell Ganz
TV Manager	James Ritz
TV Salesman	Maurice Rice
Rudy	Babaloo Mandel
Dr. Hess	Pierre Epstein
Sgt. Munson	Joe Cirillo
Parilli	Tom Toner
Wanda	Migdia Varela

and Cheryl Howard, Louisa Marie, Valerie Wildman, Christopher Thomas, Richard Dano, Clint Howard, Ron Kuhlman, Lori Kessler, Lee Delano, Jack Denton, Nick Cinardo, Fred Lerner, Corki Corman-Grazer, Fil Formicola, Than Wyenn, Clare Peck, Eileen Saki, Jodi Long, Victoria Lucas, Jeffrey Dreisbach, Amy Ingersoll, Daryl Edwards, Jack Hallett, Bill Smitrovich, Nancy Raffa, David Kreps, Jason Late, Shayla MacKarvich

Left: Daryl Hannah, and top with
Tom Hanks © *Buena Vista*

Tom Hanks

Daryl Hannah

Tom Hanks, Daryl Hannah
Top: Daryl Hannah

UNFAITHFULLY YOURS

(20th CENTURY-FOX) Producers, Marvin Worth, Joe Wizan; Director, Howard Zieff; Screenplay, Valerie Curtin, Barry Levinson, Robert Klane; Based on screenplay by Preston Sturges; Photography, David M. Walsh; Executive Producer, Daniel Melnick; Associate Producer, Jack B. Bernstein; Designer, Albert Brenner; Editor, Sheldon Kahn; Music, Bill Conti; Violin Solo, Pinchas Zukerman; Assistant Directors, Jerry Sobul, Hope R. Goodwin; Costumes, Kristi Zea; In DeLuxe Color; Rated PG; 97 minutes; February release

CAST

Claude Eastman	Dudley Moore
Daniella Eastman	Nastassja Kinski
Maxmillian Stein	Armand Assante
Norman Robbins	Albert Brooks
Carla Robbins	Cassie Yates
Giuseppe	Richard Libertini
Jess Keller	Richard B. Shull
Jerzy Czyrek	Jan Triska
Janet	Jane Hallaren
Bill Lawrence	Bernard Behrens
Screen Lover	Leonard Mann
Celia	Estelle Omens
Jewelry Salesgirl	Penny Peyser
Waiter	Nicholas Mele
Judge	Benjamin Rayson
Desk Sergeant	Art La Fleur
Hungarian Singer	Magda Gyenes
Elevator Operator	Frederic Franklyn
Kissing Girl	Alison Price
Kissing Man	Frank DiElsi
Lobby Attendant	Edward Zammit
Doorman	Ed VanNuys
Repairman	Tony Abatemarco
Trixie	Camille Hagen
Maitre D'	Jacque Foti

and Daniele Jaimes Worth, Alexander B. Reed, Ralph Buckley, Steven Hirsch, Murray Franklyn, Dr. Betty Shabazz, Robin Allyn, Ricky Paull Goldin, Evan Hollister Miranda, Elana Beth Rutenberg, Rochelle L. Kravit, Gabriel E. Gyorffy, Linda Stayer, Bob Larkin, Kim Leslie, Mary Alan Hokanson, Cliff Cudney, Richard Brown, Karyn Raymakers, Sorin Serene Pricopie

Left: Richard Libertini, Dudley Moore, Albert Brooks Top: Dudley Moore, Nastassja Kinski, Armand Assante © 20th Century-Fox

Armand Assante, Dudley Moore

Nastassja Kinski, Dudley Moore
Top: Armand Assante, Dudley Moore

17

RACING WITH THE MOON

(PARAMOUNT) Producers, Alain Bernheim, John Kohn; Director, Richard Benjamin; Screenplay, Steven Kloves; Photography, John Bailey; Designer, David L. Snyder; Editor, Jacqueline Cambas; Music, Dave Grusin; Costumes, Patricia Norris; Associate Producer/Production Manager, Art Levinson; Assistant Directors, William S. Beasley, Duncan S. Henderson; Set Designer, Jeannine Oppewall; In MovieLab Color; Rated PG; 110 minutes; March release

CAST

Henry "Hopper" Nash	Sean Penn
Caddie Winger	Elizabeth McGovern
Nicky	Nicolas Cage
Mr. Nash	John Karlen
Mrs. Nash	Rutanya Alda
Mr. Arthur	Max Showalter
Gatsby Boy	Crispin Glover
Gatsby Girl	Barbara Howard
Al	Bob Maroff
Soldier with Annie	Dominic Nardini
Mr. Kaiser	John Brandon
Mrs. Kaiser	Eve Brent Ashe
Sally Kaiser	Suzanne Adkinson
Gretchen	Shawn Schepps
Arnie	Charles Miller
Mrs. Spangler	Patricia Allison
Elmer	Al Hopson
Skating Soldier	Ted Grossman
Michael	Scott McGinnis
Kid in skating rink	Brian Trumbull
Mrs. Winger	Kate Williamson
Alice Donnelly	Julie Philips
Mr. Donnelly	Fielding Greaves
Tattoo Artist	Arnold Johnson
Marine	Kevin Fraser
High School Principal	Gerry Gibson
High School Girl	Page Hannah
R. D.	Shane Kerwin
Arnold Billings	Jonathan Charles Fox
Frank	Michael Madsen
Baby Face	Dana Carvey

and Victor Rendina (Luzzato), Rebecca Pollack (In Bowling Alley), Victor Paul (Pool Hall Barman), Lou Butera (Pool Player), Michael Talbott (Bill), Philip Adams, Charlie Picerni, Jr., Philip Romano (Shipmates), Arlin Miller (Voice of Minister), Jan Rabson, Walter Matthews (Voice of sailors), Sue Allen, Katherine L. Brown, Peggy Clark (Singers), Carol Kane (Annie)

Left: Sean Penn
Top: Sean Penn, Nicolas Cage
© *Paramount*

Elizabeth McGovern, Sean Penn

Nicolas Cage (c), Sean Penn (r)

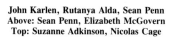

John Karlen, Rutanya Alda, Sean Penn
Above: Sean Penn, Elizabeth McGovern
Top: Suzanne Adkinson, Nicolas Cage

Sean Penn, Nicolas Cage (also top)

ROMANCING THE STONE

(20th CENTURY-FOX) Producer, Michael Douglas; Director, Robert Zemeckis; Screenplay, Diane Thomas; Photography, Dean Cundey; Design, Lawrence G. Paull; Editors, Donn Cambern, Frank Morriss; Music, Alan Silvestri; Co-Producers, Jack Brodsky, Joel Douglas; Production Manager, John Schofield; Assistant Directors, Joel Douglas, Javier Carreno; Costumes, Marilyn Vance; Art Director, Augustin Ituarte; Choreographer, Jeffrey D. Hornaday; Title Song written, produced and performed by Eddy Grant; In Dolby Stereo, Panavision and DeLuxe Color; Rated PG; 110 minutes; March release

CAST

Jack Colton	Michael Douglas
Joan Wilder	Kathleen Turner
Ralph	Danny DeVito
Ira	Zack Norman
Juan	Alfonso Arau
Zolo	Manuel Ojeda
Gloria	Holland Taylor
Elaine	Mary Ellen Trainor
Mrs. Irwin	Eve Smith
Super	Joe Nesnow
Santos	Jose Chavez
Hefty Woman	Chachita
Bus Driver	Camillo Garcia
Bad Hombre	Rodrigo Puebla
Hotel Clerk	Paco Morayta
Maitre D'	Jorge Samoro
Angelina	Kym Herrin
Jessie	Bill Burton
Grogan	Ted White
Vendors	Manuel Santiago, Ron Silver
Zolo's Men	Mike Cassidy, Vince Deadrick, Sr., Richard Drown, Joe Finnegan, Jimmy Medearis, Jeff Ramsey

Left: Michael Douglas, Kathleen Turner
© 20th Century-Fox

Kathleen Turner, Michael Douglas

Kathleen Turner, Michael Douglas Top: (l) Michael Douglas, Danny DeVito, Kathleen Turner (r) Alfonso Arau, Kathleen Turner, Michael Douglas Center: (l) Manuel Ojedo, Kathleen Turner (r) Michael Douglas, Kathleen Turner

AGAINST ALL ODDS

(COLUMBIA) Producers, Taylor Hackford, William S. Gilmore; Director, Taylor Hackford; Screenplay, Eric Hughes; Executive Producer, Jerry Bick; Photography, Donald Thorin; Art Director, Richard James Lawrence; Editors, Fredric Steinkamp, William Steinkamp; Musical Score, Michel Colombier, Larry Carlton; Associate Producer, William R. Borden; Based on film "Out of the Past" written by Daniel Mainwaring; Production Manager, Tom Joyner; Assistant Directors, Tom Mack, Bill Elvin; Costumes, Michael Kaplan; Soundtrack Album on Atlantic Records and Tapes; In MetroColor and Dolby Stereo; Rated R; 128 minutes; March release

CAST

Jessie Wyler	Rachel Ward
Terry Brogan	Jeff Bridges
Jake Wise	James Woods
Hank Sully	Alex Karras
Mrs. Wyler	Jane Greer
Ben Caxton	Richard Widmark
Tommy	Dorian Harewood
Edie	Swoosie Kurtz
Steve Kirsch	Saul Rubinek
Ed Phillips	Pat Corley
Head Coach	Bill McKinney
Bob Soames	Allen Williams
Assistant Coach	Sam Scarber
Ahmad Cooper	Jon St. Elwood
Kirsch's Girlfriend	Tamara Stafford
Ryskind	Jonathan Terry
Councilman Weinberg	Paul Valentine
Guard with dog	Ted White
Security Guard	Stone Bower
Quarterback	Mel Scott-Thomas
Receptionists	Barnetta McCarthy, Ginger LaBrie
Car Valet	David Dayan
Football Announcer	Tom Kelly
Kid Creole	August Darnell
Coconuts	Adriana Kaegi, Cheryl Poirier, Taryn Hagey
Porsche Stunt Driver	Gary Davis
Ferrari Stunt Driver	Carey Loftin
Sully Stunt Double	Carl Ciarfalio

Left: Jane Greer, Richard Widmark
Top: Jeff Bridges, Alex Karras
© Columbia Pictures

Jeff Bridges, Rachel Ward

Rachel Ward, James Woods

Rachel Ward, James Woods
Top: Rachel Ward, Jeff Bridges

HARRY & SON

(ORION) Producers, Paul Newman, Ronald L. Buck; Director, Paul Newman; Story and Screenplay, Ronald L. Buck, Paul Newman; Photography, Donald McAlpine; Music, Henry Mancini; Associate Producer, Malcolm R. Harding; Designer, Henry Bumstead; Editor, Dede Allen; Production Manager, Malcolm R. Harding; Assistant Directors, David McGiffert, Raphael Elortegui; Production Coordinator, Max Manlove; Suggested by the novel "A Lost King" by Raymond DeCapite; In Technicolor; Rated PG; 118 minutes; March release

CAST

Harry	Paul Newman
Howard	Robby Benson
Katie	Ellen Barkin
Tom	Wilford Brimley
Sally	Judith Ivey
Raymond	Ossie Davis
Siemanowski	Morgan Freeman
Nina	Katherine Borowitz
Lawrence	Maury Chaykin
Lilly	Joanne Woodward
Al	Michael Brockman
Waitress	Cathy Cahill
Andy	Robert Goodman
Jimmy	Tom Nowicki
Nurse	Claudia Robinson
Doctor	Russ Wheeler
Cop	Jerry Barrett
Max	David Mungenast
Young Men	Joseph Alva, Joe Sikorra
Construction Workers	Don Moody, Leroy Dykes, Joseph Hess
Night Watchman	Harold Bergman
Taxi Driver	Al Nesor

and Jill Selkowitz, Patricia A. Frye, Dennis W. Edwards, Jan Siegel, Suzanne M. Brierley, Will Knickerbocker, Terry Miller, Mark Anthony Wade, George E. Warren, Fred M. Wilkins, Bunny Yeager, Gilberto Costa Nunes, Jack Kassewitz, Jefferey M. Finn, Nicole Gian, Stan Barrett

Right: Robby Benson, Paul Newman
Top: Joanne Woodward, Newman, Benson,
Ellen Barkin © *Orion Pictures*

Robby Benson, Paul Newman

Joanne Woodward, Paul Newman

TANK

(UNIVERSAL) Producer, Irwin Yablans; Director, Marvin J. Chomsky; Screenplay, Dan Gordon; Photography, Don Birnkrant; Designer, Bill Kenney; Editor, Donald R. Rode; Music, Lalo Schifrin; Assistant Directors, Don Roberts, Craig West; Associate Producer-Production Manager, Richard McWhorter; Production Coordinator, Sylvia Lovegran; In Metrocolor; Rated PG; 113 minutes; A Lorimar presentation; March release.

CAST

Zack	James Garner
LaDonna	Shirley Jones
Billy	C. Thomas Howell
Elliott	Mark Herrier
General Hubik	Sandy Ward
Sarah	Jenilee Harrison
Deputy Euclid	James Cromwell
Sgt. Tippet	Dorian Harewood
Sheriff Buelton	G. D. Spradlin
Mess Sergeant	John Hancock
Sgt. Wimofsky	Guy Boyd
TV Reporters	Daniel Albright, Mark McGee, Beth Smallwood
Food Server	Gerald A. Atkins
Deputies	Ron Baskin, Wallace Merck
Motor Pool Man	Keith Jerome Brown
NCO Wenton	Robert Henry Bryant
NCO's	Frederick R. Clark, Davi J. Dominick, Doneal G. Gersh
Sgt. Majors	Alan G. Cornett, James T. Newton, Thomas P. Wann
Jackson	Bill Crabb
Gwen Tippet	T. Renee Crutcher
Radio Operator	Raymond D. Eckel
Governor Sims	J. Don Ferguson
State Trooper Commander	Bill Fleet
Reporter at State Line	Jeff Folger
Cook	Jim Jackson
School Principal	Bob Hannah

and Mickey Yablans, Larry Jordan, Bob Neal, Russ Spooner, Danny Nelson, Kathy Payne, Don Young, Joan Riordan, Larry S. Rains, Richard Lewis Smith, Andy Still, Roy Tatum, Ben Walburn, Alan Walker, Johnny Watson, Wallace Wilkinson, Laura Whyte, Kathleen L. Petro

Top: James Garner, C. Thomas Howell
Right Center: Shirley Jones, James
Garner © Universal City

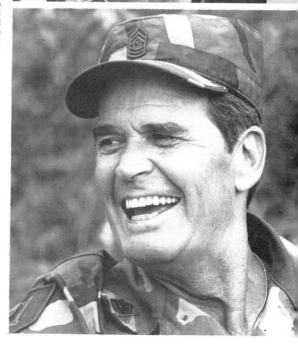

James Garner

25

THIS IS SPINAL TAP

(EMBASSY) Producer, Karen Murphy; Director, Rob Reiner; Screenplay, Christopher Guest, Michael McKean, Harry Shearer, Rob Reiner; Photography, Peter Smokler; Editors, Robert Leighton, Kent Beyda, Kim Secrist; Music and Lyrics, Christopher Guest, Michael McKean, Harry Shearer, Rob Reiner; In Dolby Stereo and color; Rated R; 82 minutes; March release

CAST

Marti DiBerti	Rob Reiner
David St. Hubbins	Michael McKean
Nigel Tufnel	Christopher Guest
Derek Smalls	Harry Shearer
Mick Shrimpton	R. J. Parnell
Viv Savage	David Kaff
Ian Faith	Tony Hendra
Tommy Pischedda	Bruno Kirby
Ethereal Fan	Jean Cromie
Heavy Metal Fans	Kimberly Stringer, Chazz Dominquez, Shari Hali

**Top: Spinal Tap: Michael McKean, R. J. Parnell,
Christopher Guest, David Kaff, Harry Shearer**
© *Embassy Pictures*

Rob Reiner

ICEMAN

(**UNIVERSAL**) Producers, Patrick Palmer, Norman Jewison; Director, Fred Schepisi; Screenplay, Chip Proser, John Drimmer; Story, John Drimmer; Photography, Ian Baker; Art Directors, Leon Ericksen, Josan Russo; Editor, Billy Weber; Music, Bruce Smeaton; Associate Producer, Charles Milhaupt; Makeup, Michael Westmore; Costumes, Rondi Johnson; Production Managers, Robert Latham Brown, Justis Greene; Assistant Directors, Jim Van Wyck, Warren Carr; Art Director, Graeme Murray; Production Coordinator, Patrice Allen; In Panavision, Technicolor, and Dolby Stereo; Rated PG; 101 minutes; April release

CAST

Dr. Stanley Shephard	Timothy Hutton
Dr. Diane Brady	Lindsay Crouse
Charlie	John Lone
Whitman	Josef Sommer
Dr. Singe	David Strathairn
Dr. Vermeil	Philip Akin
Loomis	Danny Glover
Mabel	Amelia Hall
Hogan	Richard Monette
Maynard	James Tolkan
Temp Doc	Stephen E. Miller
Scatem Doc	David Petersen
E.K.G. Doc	Judy Berlin
Technician	Paul Batten
Nurse	Lovie Eli
Lab Techs	Stephen Nemeth, Real Andrews
Helicopter Pilot	Bob Reimer
Powell	Blair Anderson
Powell's Assistant	Dave Ryder
Indian Guide	Herb (Kneecap) Nikal
Inuit Storyteller	Elizabeth Aulajut
Air Traffic Controller	Dennis Letkeman
Canuck	Paul Stanely
Stunt Doubles	Dar Robinson, V. John Wardlow, Jacob Rupp

Right: Timothy Hutton, John Lone, and above with Lindsay Crouse Top: James Tolkan, Timothy Hutton © *Universal*

John Lone

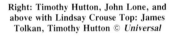

Timothy Hutton

THE STONE BOY

(20th CENTURY-FOX) Producers, Joe Roth, Ivan Bloch; Director, Chris Cain; Executive Producer, James G. Robinson; Screenplay, Gina Berriault; Photography, Juan Ruiz-Anchia; Original Music, James Horner; Associate Producers, Daniel M. Farrell, David G. Hermelin; Editor, Paul Rubell; Designer, Joseph G. Pacelli; Production Manager, Mervyn L. Edwards; Assistant Directors, Steven J. Tramz, Reuben L. Watt; Production Coordinator, Cathie Woodard; Art Director, Stephanie Wooley; Costumes, Gail Viola; An International Productions presentation in DeLuxe Color; Rated PG; 93 minutes; April release

CAST

Joe Hillerman	Robert Duvall
Andy Jansen	Frederic Forrest
Ruth Hillerman	Glenn Close
George Jansen	Wilford Brimley
Arnold Hillerman	Jason Presson
Lu Jansen	Gail Youngs
Amalie	Cindy Fisher
Nora Hillerman	Susan Blackstone
Eugene Hillerman	Dean Cain
Sheriffs	Kenneth Anderson, John L. Strandell
Sheriff McDuff	Tom Duncan
Margaret Mathews	Dana Duffy
Clint Mathews	Quentin Rhoades
Clancy Mathews	Mark Melander
Sam Sullivan	Ken Magee
Doris Simms	Mary Ellen Trainor
Amalie's Uncle	Ron Presson
Men	Cody Harvey, Buck Dear
Gary Maddox	Mayf Nutter
Casino Waitress	Sharon Thomas
Chuck	Timothy Phillips
Eva Crescent Moon Lady	Linda Hamilton
Woman at fair	Lynne Brimley
Barker	Steve Tsigonoff
Man in suit	Pat Hustis

Left: Robert Duvall, Frederic Forrest
Top: Robert Duvall, Glenn Close
© *20th Century-Fox*

Jason Presson

Wilford Brimley

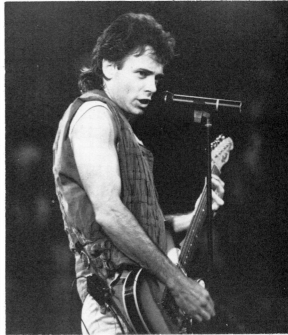

HARD TO HOLD

(UNIVERSAL) Producer, D. Constantine Conte; Director, Larry Peerce; Screenplay, Tom Hedley; Story, Tom Hedley, Richard Rothstein; Photography, Richard H. Kline; Designer, Peter Wooley; Editor, Bob Wyman; Costumes, Rosanna Norton; Associate Producers, Kurt Neumann, Dana Miller; Executive Producer, Joe Gottfried; Music, Tom Scott; Additional Music, Rick Springfield; Production Manager, Kurt Neumann; Assistant Directors, Steve Barnett, Candace Allen; Production Coordinator, Virginia Cook; Soundtrack available on RCA Records and cassettes; In Dolby Stereo and Technicolor; Rated PG; 93 minutes; April release

CAST

James Roberts	Rick Springfield
Diana Lawson	Janet Eilber
Nicky Nides	Patti Hansen
Johnny Lawson	Albert Salmi
Owen	Gregory Itzen
Casserole	Peter Van Norden
Toby	Tracy Brooks Swope
Cal Mussetter	Heather Devore-Haase
Mrs. Mussetter	Carole Tru Foster
Maitre d'	Garry Goodrow
Flower Vendor	Frank Ronzio
Punk Leader	Charles Sweigart
Mrs. Adilman	Selma Archerd
Hawker	Paul Jenkins
Cab Drivers	Warren Miller, Lew Gallo
Recording Engineer	John Blyth Barrymore
Fans	Laura Summer, Tiffany Helm
Jack	Al Hansen
Phil	Jack Stryker
Longshoremen	Brass Adams, Gino Ardito
Johnny's Friend	Don Hepner
Limo Drivers	Larry Daugherty, Harry Northup
Techie	Stu Charno
Ambulance Driver	Johnathan Findlater
Doug	Michael V. Murphy
Ethel	Cindy Pearlman
Waiter	Eddie Hice
Airline Clerk	Dale Townsend
Frank Pisani	Frank Pisani
Wives	Monique Gabrielle, Sharon Hughes, Charlene Jones

Top: (L) Rick Springfield, Albert Salmi
(R) Rick Springfield
© *Universal*

Janet Eilber, Rick Springfield
Above: Patti Hansen, Rick Springfield

29

MOSCOW ON THE HUDSON

(COLUMBIA) Producer-Director, Paul Mazursky; Screenplay, Paul Mazursky, Leon Capetanos; Photography, Donald McAlpine; Co-Producer/Designer, Pato Guzman; Editor, Richard Halsey; Costumes, Albert Wolsky; Associate Producer, Geoffrey Taylor; Music, David McHugh; Production Manager, Patrick McCormick; Assistant Directors, Alex Hapsas, Stefaan Scheider, Joseph Ray; Art Directors, Michael Molly, Peter Rothe; In MetroColor and Dolby Stereo; Rated R; 115 minutes; April release

CAST

Vladimir Ivanoff	Robin Williams
Lucia Lombardo	Maria Conchita Alonso
Lionel Witherspoon	Cleavant Derricks
Orlando Ramirez	Alejandro Rey
Boris	Savely Kramarov
Anatoly	Elya Baskin
Yury	Oleg Rudnik
Vladimir's Grandfather	Alexander Beniaminov
Vladimir's Mother	Ludmila Kramarevsky
Vladimir's Father	Ivo Vrzal
Sasha	Natalie Iwanow
Lionel's Grandfather	Tiger Haynes
Lionel's Mother	Edye Byrde
Lionel's Step-Father	Robert MacBeth
Leanne	Donna Ingram-Young
Svetlana	Olga Talyn
Leonid	Alexander Narodetzky
Young French Man	Pierre Orcel
Veronica Cohen	Stephanie Cotsirilos
Bill	Fred Strother
Male Clerk	Anthony Cortino
Bloomingdale's Manager	Betsy Mazursky
Kaity Tong	Kaity Tong
Bloomingdale's Cop	Royce Rich
Agent Ross	Christopher Wynkoop
Agent Williams	Lyman Ward
Mean Man on subway	Joe Lynn
Blanche	Joy Todd
Dave	Paul Mazursky
Korean Cab Driver	Thomas Ikeda
Mrs. Marlowe	Barbara Montgomery
Wanda	Dana Lorge
Latin Band Leader	Adelberto Santiago
Dr. Reddy	Sam Moses
Lev	Yakov Smirnoff
Panama Hat	Sam Stoneburner
Texan	Michael Greene
Judge	Rosetta LeNoire

Sal Carollo, Filomena Spanguolo, Annabella Turco, George Kelly, Yury Olshansky, Jacques Sandulescu, Emil Feist, Vladimir Tukan, Mark Rutenberg, Yury Belov, Igor Panich, Juri Gotowtschikow, Sina Kasper, Ken Fitch, Murray Grand, Ann E. Wile, Michael T. Laide, Linda Kerns, Armand Dahan, Jose Rabelo, Jim Goodfriend, Antonia Rey, James Prendergast, Brandon Rey, Paul Davidovsky, Andrei Kramarevsky, Arkady Shabashev, Donald King, David Median, Juanita Mahone, Robert Kasel, Kikue Tashiro, Joyce R. Korbin, Luis Ramos, Kim Chan

Top Left: Robin Williams
Left Center: Robin Williams
© Columbia Pictures

Robin Williams, Cleavant Derricks, Savely Kramarov

Dana Lorge, Robin Williams, Alejandro Rey,
Maria Conchita Alonso Above and Top:
Williams, Alonso

Robin Williams, Maria Conchita Alonso
Above and Top: Williams, Cleavant Derricks

31

SWING SHIFT

(WARNER BROS.) Producer, Jerry Bick; Director, Jonathan Demme; Screenplay, Rob Morton; Executive Producers, Alex Winitsky, Arlene Sellers; Photography, Tak Fujimoto; Design, Peter Jamison; Editor, Craig McKay; Music, Patrick Williams; Costumes, Joe I. Tompkins; Associate Producer/Production Manager, Charles Mulvehill; Assistant Directors, C. A. Myers, Michael Looney; Art Director, Bo Welch; In Technicolor; A Lantana Production; Rated PG; 99 minutes; April release

CAST

Kay Walsh	Goldie Hawn
Lucky Lockhart	Kurt Russell
Hazel Zanussi	Christine Lahti
Biscuits Toohey	Fred Ward
Jack Walsh	Ed Harris
Annie	Sudie Bond
Jeannie Sherman	Holly Hunter
Laverne	Patty Maloney
Violet Mulligan	Lisa Pelikan
Edith Castle	Susan Peretz
Johnny Bonnano	Joey Aresco
Clarence	Morris "Tex" Biggs
Spike	Reid Cruickshanks
Deacon	Daniel Dean Darst
Rupert George	Dennis Fimple
Lt. O'Connor	Christopher Lemmon
Moon Willens	Charles Napier
French deMille	Stephen Tobolowsky
Ethel	Laura Hawn
Rollo	Marvin Miller
Skinny	Susan Barnes
Bible Pusher	Beth Henley
M.P. at embarkation	Gene Borkan
Frankie Parker	Alana Stewart
Recruit at Egyptian	Phillip Christon
Genevieve	Penny Johnson
Documentary Narrator	Stephen Tobolowsky
Mr. MacBride	Roger Corman

and Isabell Monk, Maggie Renzi, Sandy McLeod, George Schwartz, Alan Toy, Oceana Marr, Richard K. Way, Harold Jackson, Don Carrara, Todd Allen, Gary Goetzman, Belinda Carlisle, Lissette LeCorn, Jessica Gaynes, Deena Marie, Roger Rook, Joseph Hutton, Harry Northup, David B. Carlton, Lisa Chadwick, Eddie Smith, Eugene W. Jackson, Chino "Fats" Williams, Belita Moreno

Left: Goldie Hawn, Christine Lahti
Top: Goldie Hawn, Ed Harris
© Warner Bros.

Goldie Hawn, Kurt Russell, Christine Lahti

Kurt Russell, Goldie Hawn (also top)
Above: Christine Lahti, Hawn, Russell

Goldie Hawn, Kurt Russell (also top)
Above: Belinda Carlisle, Hawn, Russell

THE KARATE KID

(COLUMBIA) Producer, Jerry Weintraub; Director, John G. Avildsen; Screenplay, Robert Mark Kamen; Executive Producer, R. J. Louis; Photography, James Crabe; Designer, William J. Cassidy; Editors, Bud Smith, Walt Mulconery, John G. Avildsen; Music, Bill Conti; Associate Producer, Bud Smith; Production Manager, Howard Pine; Assistant Directors, Clifford C. Coleman, Hope Goodwin; Martial Arts Choreography, Pat E. Johnson; Special Effects, Frank Toro; Production Coordinator, Jeannie Jeha; In Metrocolor and Dolby Stereo; Rated PG; 107 minutes; May release

CAST

Daniel	Ralph Macchio
Miyagi	Noriyuki "Pat" Morita
Ali	Elisabeth Shue
Kreese	Martin Kove
Lucille	Randee Heller
Johnny	William Zabka
Bobby	Ron Thomas
Tommy	Rob Garrison
Dutch	Chad McQueen
Jimmy	Tony O'Dell
Freddy	Israel Juarbe
Mr. Mills	William Bassett
Jerry	Larry B. Scott
Susan	Juli Fields
Barbara	Dana Andersen
Chucky	Frank Burt Avalon
Billy	Jeff Fishman
Chris	Ken Daly
Alan	Tom Fridley
Mr. Harris	Bernard Kuby
Chicken Boy	Todd Lookinland
Doctor	William Norren
Eddie	Scott Strader

Left: Ralph Macchio, Elisabeth Shue
Top: Ralph Macchio, Randee Heller
© *Columbia Pictures*

Ralph Macchio, Noriyuki "Pat" Morita

Elisabeth Shue, William Zabka
Top: "Pat" Morita, Ralph Macchio

"Pat" Morita, Ralph Macchio Above: Macchio,
Randee Heller, Elisabeth Shue Top: William
Zabka, Shue

STAR TREK III
The Search for Spock

(PARAMOUNT) Executive Producer, Gary Nardino; Produced and Written by Harve Bennett; Director, Leonard Nimoy; Based on "Star Trek" tv series created by Gene Roddenberry; Photography, Charles Correll; Editor, Robert F. Shugrue; Music, James Horner; Theme Music, Alexander Courage; Visual Effects, Kenneth Ralston; Art Director, John E. Chilberg 2nd; Production Manager, Michael P. Schoenbrun; Assistant Director, John Hockridge; Costumes, Robert Fletcher; Special Makeup, Burman Studio; Special Physical Effects, Bob Dawson; Special Sound Effects, Alan Howarth, Frank Serafine; In Dolby Stereo, Panavision and Movielab Color; Rated PG; 105 minutes; May release

CAST

Kirk	William Shatner
McCoy	DeForest Kelley
Scotty	James Doohan
Sulu	George Takei
Chekov	Walter Koenig
Uhura	Nichelle Nichols
Sarek	Mark Leonard
David	Merritt Butrick
High Priestess	Dame Judith Anderson
Saavik	Robin Curtis
Kruge	Christopher Lloyd
Capt. Styles	James B. Sikking
Alien at bar	Allan Miller
Spock	Leonard Nimoy
Cmdr. Morrow	Robert Hooks
Lieutenant	Scott McGinnis
Valkris	Cathie Shirriff
Klingon Torg	Stephen Liska
Klingon Maltz	John Larroquette
Capt. Esteban	Phillip Richard Allen
Spock at 9	Carl Steven
Spock at 13	Vadia Potenza
Spock at 17	Stephen Manley
Spock at 25	Joe W. Davis

Left: William Shatner, Robert Hooks
Top: U.S.S. Enterprise
© *Paramount*

Merritt Butrick, Robin Curtis

Cafeteria aboard Spacedock

Walter Koenig, George Takei, William Shatner, Judith Anderson, DeForest Kelley, Nichelle Nichols, James Doohan Top: (L) Christopher Lloyd, Stephen Liska, John Larroquette (R) DeForest Kelley, William Shatner Center: (L) Enterprise vs Klingon Bird of Prey (R) Landing on the planet Vulcan

SIXTEEN CANDLES

(UNIVERSAL) Executive Producer, Ned Tanen; Producer, Hilton A. Green; Direction and Screenplay, John Hughes; Photography, Bobby Byrne; Designer, John W. Corso; Editor, Edward Warschilka; Music, Ira Newborn; Associate Producers, Edward Warschilka, Michelle Manning; Production Manager, Daniel Franklin; Assistant Directors, Newton D. Arnold, James Joe Giovannetti, Jr.; Title Song performed by The Stray Cats; Soundtrack on MCA Records and Cassettes; In Technicolor; Rated PG; A Channel Production; 95 minutes; May release

CAST

Samantha	Molly Ringwald
Mike Baker	Justin Henry
Jake	Michael Schoeffling
Caroline	Haviland Morris
Long Duk Dong	Gedde Watanabe
Geek	Anthony Michael Hall
Jim Baker	Paul Dooley
Brenda Baker	Carlin Glynn
Ginny	Blanche Baker
Howard	Edward Andrews
Dorothy	Billie Bird
Helen	Carole Cook
Fred	Max Showalter
Randy	Liane Curtis
Bryce	John Cusack
Cliff	Darren Harris
Lumberjack	Deborah Pollack
Ray Gun Geek	Ross Berkson
Jimmy Montrose	Jonathan Chapin
Geek Girl	Joan Cusack
Reverend	Brian Doyle-Murray
Female D.J.	Bekka Eaton
Shower Double	Paula Elser
Robin	Jami Gertz

and Steven Farber (Geek), Frank Howard (Freshman), Cinnamon Idles (Sara), John Kapelos (Rudy), Marge Kotlisky (Irene), Tony Longo (Rock), Steve Monarque (Jock), Bill Orsi (Bruno), Beth Ringwald (Patty), Zelda Rubinstein (Organist), Dennis Vero (Bus Driver), Elaine Wilkes (Tracy)

Top: Edward Andrews, Carole Cook, Max Showalter, Billie Bird (R) Carlin Glynn, Molly Ringwald
© *Universal*

Anthony Michael Hall, Molly Ringwald Above: Michael Schoeffling, Ringwald

THE NATURAL

(TRI-STAR) Producer, Mark Johnson; Director, Barry Levinson; Associate Producer, Robert F. Colesberry; Screenplay, Roger Towne, Phil Dusenberry; Based on novel by Bernard Malamud; Executive Producers, Roger Towne, Philip M. Breen; Photography, Caleb Deschanel; Designers, Angelo Graham, Mel Bourne; Editor, Stu Linder; Music, Randy Newman; Costumes, Bernie Pollack, Gloria Gresham; Production Managers, Robert F. Colesberry, Peter Burrell, Thomas A. Razzano; Assistant Directors, Chris Soldo, Patrick Crowley, Tom Davies, Carol Smetana; In Technicolor and Dolby Stereo; Rated PG; 134 minutes; May release

CAST

Roy Hobbs	Robert Redford
Max Mercy	Robert Duvall
Iris	Glenn Close
Memo Paris	Kim Basinger
Pop Fisher	Wilford Brimley
Harriet Bird	Barbara Hershey
Judge	Robert Prosky
Red Blow	Richard Farnsworth
The Whammer	Joe Don Baker
Sam Simpson	John Finnegan
Ed Hobbs	Alan Fudge
Young Roy	Paul Sullivan, Jr.
Young Iris	Rachel Hall
Ted Hobbs	Robert Rich III
Pirates Manager	Sibby Sisti
Pitcher Vogelman	Phillip D. Rosenberg
Pitcher Youngberry	Christopher B. Rehbaum
Umpire Augie	Nicholas Koleff
Umpire Babe	Jerry Stockman
Memorial Game Umpire	James Quamo
Final Game Home Plate Umpire	Joseph Strang
Al	James Mohr
Al's Customer	Ralph Tabakin
Carnival Boy	Dennis Gould
Home Plate Photographer	Joshua Abbey
Maid	Gayle Vance
League Official	George Scheitinger
Dr. Knobb	Peter Poth
Hospital Doctor	Bernie McInerney
Stern Nurse	Elizabeth Ann Klein
Newsreel Narrator	Charles Sergis
Newsreel Presenter	Edward Walsh

and The New York Knights: Michael Madsen (Bump), John Van Ness (Dave), Mickey Treanor (Doc), George Wilkosz (Bobby), Anthony J. Ferrara (Coach), Philip Mankowski (Hank), Danny Aiello III (Emil), Joe Castellano (Allie), Eddie Cipot (Gabby), Ken Grassano (Al), Robert Kalaf (Cal), Barry Kivel (Pat), Steven Kronovet (Tommy), James Meyer (Dutch), Michael Starr (Boone), Sam Green (Murphy), Martin Grey, Joseph Mosso, Richard Oliveri, Lawrence Couzens, Duke McGuire, Steven Poliachik, Kevin Lester, Joseph Charboneau, Robert Rudnick, Ken Kamholz

Right: Richard Farnsworth, Wilford Brimley
Above: Joe Don Baker, Barbara Hershey
Top: Robert Duvall © *Tri-Star*

Glenn Close, Robert Redford

Robert Redford, Kim Basinger

INDIANA JONES AND THE TEMPLE OF DOOM

(PARAMOUNT) Producer, Robert Watts; Director, Steven Spielberg; Story, George Lucas; Screenplay, Willard Huyck, Gloria Katz; Executive Producers, George Lucas, Frank Marshall; Music, John Williams; Editor, Michael Kahn; Photography, Douglas Slocombe; Designer, Anthony Powell; Associate Producer, Kathleen Kennedy; Director Second Unit, Michael Moore; Choreography, Danny Daniels; Assistant Directors, David Tomblin, Roy Button, Steve Harding, Louis Race, Louis G. Friedman; Visual Effects, Dennis Muren; Art Directors, Alan Cassie, Roger Cain; Color by Rank Labs, DeLuxe Color; A Lucasfilm Ltd. production; Original soundtrack on Polydor Records; In Panavision and Dolby Stereo; Rated PG; 118 minutes; May release

CAST

Indiana Jones	Harrison Ford
Willie Scott	Kate Capshaw
Short Round	Ke Huy Quan
Mola Ram	Amrish Puri
Chattar Lal	Roshan Seth
Capt. Blumburtt	Philip Stone
Lao Che	Roy Chiao
Wu Han	David Yip
Kao Kan	Ric Young
Chen	Chua Kah Joo
Maitre d'	Rex Ngui
Chief Henchman	Philip Tann
Weber	Dan Aykroyd
Chinese Pilot	Akio Mitamura
Chinese Co-Pilot	Michael Yama
Shaman	D. R. Nanayakkara
Chieftan	Dharmadasa Kuruppu
Sajnu	Stany De Silva
Little Maharajah	Raj Singh
Merchants	Frank Olegario, Ahmed El-Shenawi
Eel Eater	Art Repola
Sacrifice Victim	Nizwar Karanj
Chief Guard	Pat Roach
Guards	Moti Makan, Mellan Mitchell, Bhasker Patel
Boys in cell	Arjun Pandher, Zia Gelani

1984 Academy Award for Visual Effects

Left: Kate Capshaw, and top with Harrison Ford
© Lucasfilm

Harrison Ford

Harrison Ford (extreme right)

Harrison Ford, Kate Capshaw Above: Capshaw,
Ke Huy Quan (all at top)

Harrison Ford, Kate Capshaw
Above: Ford, Ke Huy Quan
(All at top)

ONCE UPON A TIME IN AMERICA

(WARNER BROS.) Producer, Arnon Milchan; Director, Sergio Leone; Executive Producer, Claudio Mancini; Production Executive, Fred Caruso; Screenplay, Leonardo Benvenuti, Piero De Bernardo, Enrico Medioli, Franco Arcalli, Franco Ferrini, Sergio Leone; Based on novel "The Hoods" by Harry Grey; Photography, Tonino Delli Colli; Music, Ennio Morricone; Costumes, Richard Bruno, Gabriella Pescucci; Art Director, Carlo Simi; Editor, Nino Baragli; Production Supervisor, Mario Cotone; Assistant Directors, Fabrizio Sergenti Castellani, Dennis Benatar, Amy Wells; Production Coordinator, Gail Kearns; Art Director, James Singelis; Soundtrack recording on Polydor Records and tapes; A Ladd Company release in EastmanColor; Rated R; Presented by Arnon Milchan; 135 minutes; May release

CAST

Noodles	Robert De Niro
Max	James Woods
Deborah	Elizabeth McGovern
Jimmy O'Donnell	Treat Williams
Carol	Tuesday Weld
Joe	Burt Young
Frankie	Joe Pesci
Cockeye	William Forsythe
Patsy	James Hayden
Eve	Darlanne Fleugel
Fat Moe	Larry Rapp
Van Linden	Dutch Miller
Sharkey	Robert Harper
Chicken Joe	Richard Bright
Crowning	Gerard Murphy
Peggy	Amy Ryder
Woman in puppet theatre	Olga Karlatos
Mandy	Mario Brega
Trigger	Ray Dittrich
Beefy	Frank Gio
Willie the Ape	Angelo Florio
Young Noodles	Scott Tiler
Young Max/David	Rusty Jacobs
Young Patsy	Brian Bloom
Young Cockeye	Adrian Curran
Young Fat Moe	Mike Monetti
Dominic	Noah Moazezi
Bugsy	James Russo
Bugsy's Gang	Frankie Caserta, Joey Marzella
Adorable Old Man	Joey Faye

and Clem Caserta, Frank Sisto, Jerry Strivelli, Marvin Scott, Paul Herman, Ann Neville, Arnon Milchan, Bruno Iannone, Marty Licata, Marcia Jean Kurtz, Richard Foronjy, Gerritt DeBeer, Jennifer Connelly, Margherita Pace, Alexander Godfrey, Cliff Cudney, Paul Farentino, Bruce Bahrenburg, Mort Freeman, Sandra Solberg, Massimo Liti

Right: Robert DeNiro, Tuesday Weld
Above: James Woods, DeNiro, William
Forsythe, Burt Young Top: Brian Bloom, Noah
Moazezi, Scott Schutzman, Rusty Jacobs
© *The Ladd Co.*

Robert DeNiro, James Woods

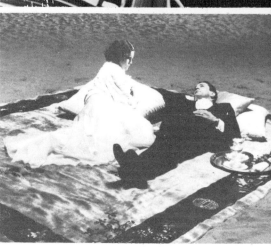

Elizabeth McGovern, Robert DeNiro

REPO MAN

(UNIVERSAL) Producers, Jonathan Wacks, Peter McCarthy; Direction and Screenplay, Alex Cox; Executive Producer, Michael Nesmith; Photography, Robby Muller, Robert Richardson; Editor, Dennis Dolan; Art Design, J. Rae Fox, Linda Burbank; Music, Tito Larriva, Steven Hufsteter; Associate Producer, Gerald Olsen; Production Manager, Allen Alsobrook; Production Coordinator, Iya Labunka; Assistant Directors, Betsy Magruder, Rip Murray, Abbe Wool; Costumes, Theda Deramus; Theme Song, Iggy Pop; In DeLuxe Color; An Edge City Production; Rated R; 94 minutes; May release

CAST

Bud	Harry Dean Stanton
Otto	Emilio Estevez
Miller	Tracey Walter
Leila	Olivia Barash
Lite	Sy Richardson
Agent Rogers	Susan Barnes
J. Frank Parnell	Fox Harris
Oly	Tom Finnegan
Lagarto	Del Zamora
Napo	Eddie Velez
Kevin	Zander Schloss
Debbi	Jennifer Balgobin
Duke	Dick Rude
Archie	Michael Sandoval
Marlene	Vonetta McGee
Plettschner	Richard Foronjy
Rev. Larry	Bruce White
Agent B	Biff Yeager
Agent E	Ed Pansullo
Agent S	Steve Mattson
Agent T	Thomas Boyd
Mr. Humphries	Charles Hopkins
Mrs. Parks	Helen Martin
Miner	Jon St. Elwood
Delilah	Kelitta Kelly
Motorcycle Cop	Varnum Honey
Sheriff	David Chung
U.F.O. Lady	Cynthia Czigeti
Old Lady	Dorothy Bartlett
Otto's Dad	Jonathon Hugger
Otto's Mom	Sharon Gregg
Peason	Dale Reynolds

and Janet Chan, Angelique Pettyjohn, Logan Carter, Laura Sorrenson, George Sawaya, Connie Ponce, Sue Kiel, Bobby Ellis, Quentin Gutierrez, The Circle Jerks, The Untouchables, Harry Hauss, Tom Musca, Terry Schwartz, Kim Williams, Michele Person, Wally Cronin, Monona Wali, Delores DeLuxe, Linda Jensen, Todd Darling, Erin Darling, Abbe Wool, Alex Cox, Peter Wacks, Cosmo Mata, Rodney Bingenheimer, Jorge Martinez

Right: Michael Sandoval, Dick Rude, Jennifer Balgobin Above: Emilio Estevez, Richard Foronjy Top: Estevez, Fox Harris
© *Universal*

Harry Dean Stanton

Steve Mattson, Susan Barnes, Biff Yeager

UNDER THE VOLCANO

(UNIVERSAL) Producers, Moritz Borman, Wieland Schulz-Keil; Director, John Huston; Screenplay, Guy Gallo; Based on novel by Malcolm Lowry; Executive Producer, Michael Fitzgerald; Music, Alex North; Editor, Roberto Silvi; Designer, Gunther Gerzso; Photography, Gabriel Figueroa; Production Supervisor, Tom Shaw; Associate Producers, Hector Lopez Lechuga, Arnold Gefsky; Production Coordinators, Anne Shaw, Luciana Cabarga; Assistant Directors, Manuel Munoz, Dennis Shaw; Art Director, Jose Rodriguez Granada; Costumes, Angela Dodson; In Technicolor; Presented by Michael and Kathy Fitzgerald; An Ithaca-Conacine production; Rated R; 112 minutes May; release

CAST

Geoffrey Firmin	Albert Finney
Yvonne Firmin	Jacqueline Bisset
Hugh Firmin	Anthony Andrews
Dr. Vigil	Ignacio Lopez Tarso
Senora Gregoria	Katy Jurado
Brit	James Villiers
Quincey	Dawson Bray
Bustamante	Carlos Requelme
Gringo	Jim McCarthy
Dwarf	Rene Ruiz
Chief of gardens	Eliazar Garcia, Jr.
Chief of stockyards	Salvador Sanchez
Chief of municipality	Sergio Calderon
Maria	Araceli Ladewuen Castelun
Diosdado	Emilio Fernandez
Cervantes	Arturo Sarabia
Few Fleas	Roberto Martinez Sosa
Sinarquista	Hugo Stiglitz
Latin Consul	Ugo Moctezuma
Chicken Lady	Isabel Vasquez
Transvestite	Gustavo Fernandez
Concepta	Irene Diaz de Davila
Matador	Alberto Olvera
Don Juan Tenerio	Eduardo Borbolla
Dona Ines	Alejandra Suarez
Bus Driver	Rodolfo De Alejandre
Passenger	Juan Angel Martinez Ramos
Dead Indian	Martin Palomares Carrion
Horsemen	Mario Arevalo, Ramiro Ramirez

**Left: Albert Finney, Gunter Meisner
Above: Finney, Katy Jurado Top: Finney,
Jacqueline Bisset, Anthony Andrews
© Universal**

Anthony Andrews, Jacqueline Bisset

Albert Finney, Rene Ruiz

RHINESTONE

(20th CENTURY-FOX) Producer, Howard Smith, Marvin Worth; Director, Bob Clark; Screenplay, Phil Alden Robinson, Sylvester Stallone; Story, Phil Alden Robinson; Based on song "Rhinestone Cowboy" by Larry Weiss; Co-Producers, Bill Blake, Richard M. Spitalny; Photography, Timothy Galfas; Designer, Robert Boyle; Editors, Stan Cole, John Wheeler; Musical Score Adapted by Mike Post; Music, Dolly Parton; Associate Producers, Linda Horner, James Brubaker; Assistant Directors, Duncan Henderson, Chris Ryan, Janet Knutsen; Costumes, Tom Bronson; Miss Parton's Costumes, Theadora Van Runkle; Art Director, Frank Richwood; Production Manager, Roger Paradiso; In Dolby Stereo, Panavision and DeLuxe Color; Rated PG; 110 minutes; June release

CAST

Nick	Sylvester Stallone
Jake	Dolly Parton
Noah	Richard Farnsworth
Freddie	Ron Leibman
Barnett	Tim Thomerson
Father	Steven Apostle Pec
Mother	Penny Santon
Elgart	Russell Buchanan
Luke	Ritch Brinkley
Walt	Jerry Potter
Billie Joe	Jesse Welles
Maurie	Phil Rubenstein
Japanese Father	Thomas Ikeda
Japanese Grandmother	Christal Kim
Japanese Mother	Arline Miyazaki
Sidney	Tony Munafo
Sid	Don Hanmer
Cowboy Doorman	Dean Smith
Countryman	David Cobb
Mr. Polk	Speck Rhodes
Wino	Guy Fitch
Street Player	Stan Yale
Esther Jean	Cindy Perlman
Photographer	Shelley Pogoda
Snorer	Laura Kingsley
Bartender	Bobby Martini

Top: Sylvester Stallone, Dolly Parton
Right center: Stallone, Penny Santon,
Parton © *20th Century-Fox*

Sylvester Stallone, Dolly Parton

GHOSTBUSTERS

(COLUMBIA) Producer-Director, Ivan Reitman; Screenplay, Dan Aykroyd, Harold Ramis; Photography, Laszlo Kovacs; Designer, John DeCuir; Editors, Sheldon Kahn, David Blewitt; Executive Producer, Bernie Brillstein; Associate Producers, Joe Medjuck, Michael C. Gross; Visual Effects, Richard Edlund; Music, Elmer Bernstein; Title Song, Ray Parker, Jr.; Costumes, Theoni V. Aldredge; Production Manager, John G. Wilson; Assistant Directors, Gary Daigler, Katterli Frauenfelder; Special Effects, Chuck Gaspar, Joe Day; Art Director, John DeCuir, Jr.; Production Coordinator, Rita Miller-Grant; Soundtrack on Arista Records; In Panavision, Metrocolor, Dolby Stereo; Rated PG; 107 minutes; June release

CAST

Dr. Peter Venkman	Bill Murray
Dr. Raymond Stantz	Dan Aykroyd
Dana Barrett	Sigourney Weaver
Dr. Egon Spengler	Harold Ramis
Louis Tully	Rick Moranis
Janine Melnitz	Annie Potts
Walter Peck	William Atherton
Winston Zeddmore	Ernie Hudson
Mayor	David Margulies
Students	Steven Tash, Jennifer Runyon
Gozer	Slavitza Jovan
Hotel Manager	Michael Ensign
Librarian	Alice Drummond
Dean Yeager	Jordan Charney
Violinist	Timothy Carhart
Library Administrator	John Rothman
Themselves	Roger Grimsby, Larry King, Joe Franklin, Casey Kasem
Fire Commissioner	Norman Matlock
Police Captain	Joe Cirillo
Police Sergeant	Joe Schmieg
Jail Guard	Reggie Vel Johnson
Real Estate Woman	Rhoda Gemignani
Man at elevator	Murray Rubin
Con Edison Man	Larry Dilg
Coachman	Danny Stone
Woman at party	Patty Dworkin
Tall Woman at party	Jean Kasem
Doorman	Lenny Del Genio
Chambermaid	Frances E. Nealy
Hot Dog Vendor	Sam Moses
TV Reporter	Christopher Wynkoop
Businessman in cab	Winston May
Mayor's Aide	Tommy Hollis
Louis's Neighbor	Eda Reiss Merin
Cop at apartment	Ric Mancini
Mrs. Van Hoffman	Kathryn Janssen
Ted Fleming	Paul Trafas
Annette Fleming	Cheryl Birchfield
Library Ghost	Ruth Oliver
Dream Ghost	Kym Herrin

Top Left: Ernie Hudson, Bill Murray, Dan Aykroyd, Harold Ramis Below: Sigourney Weaver, Bill Murray
© *Columbia Pictures*

Dan Aykroyd

Bill Murray, Dan Aykroyd, Harold Ramis (also above) and top with Ernie Hudson

Bill Murray, Dan Aykroyd Above: Sigourney Weaver, Harold Ramis

47

BACHELOR PARTY

(20th CENTURY-FOX) Producer, Ron Moler, Bob Israel; Director, Neal Israel; Screenplay, Neal Israel, Pat Proft; Story, Bob Israel; Executive Producer, Joe Roth; Associate Producer, Gautam Das; Photography, Hal Trussell; Music, Robert Folk; Production Manager, Ann Kindberg; Editor, Tom Walls; Assistant Directors, Jerry Sobul, Harvey Waldman; Art Directors, Kevin Conlin, Martin Price, Shari Adagio; Choreographer, Kathleen Knapp; Production Coordinator, Exa Durham; Additional Music, Tom Jenkins, Barry Schleifer; Raju and Sharad Patel present an Aspect Ratio/Twin Continental production in color; Rated R; 111 minutes; June release

CAST

Rick Gassko	Tom Hanks
Debbie Thompson	Tawny Kitane
Jay O'Neill	Adrian Zmed
Mr. Thompson	George Grizzard
Mrs. Thompson	Barbara Stuart
Cole Whittier	Robert Prescott
Dr. Stan Gassko	William Tepper
Dr. Tina Gassko	Wendie Jo Sperber
Rudy	Barry Diamond
Gary	Gary Grossman
Ryko	Michael Dudikoff
Brad	Bradford Bancroft
Phoebe	Marina Finch
Ilene	Deborah Harmon
Bobbi	Tracy Smith
Sister Mary Francis	Florence Schauffler
Rajah	Sumant
Milt	John Bloom
Hotel Manager	Kenneth Kimmins
Michael	Gerard Prendergast
Nick	Brett Clark
Alley Pimp	Ji-Tu Cumbuka
Kelley	Katie Mitchell
She/Tim	Christopher Morley
Desiree	Toni Alessandrini
Tracey	Monique Gabrielle
Mrs. Klupner	Angela Aames
Raul	Richard Lorenzo Hernandez
Skip	Jonathan Tyler Trevillya
Sue	Cynthia Kania
Father O'Donall	Hugh McPhillips

and Rosanne Katon, Dani Douthette, Milt Kogan, Greg Norberg, Coleen Maloney, Arlee Reed, Donald Thompson, Gregory Brown, Marcelino Razo, Pat Proft, Rebecca Perle, Elizabeth Arlen, Dorothy Bartlett, Angel and the Reruns, Annie Gaybis, Peaches Johnson, Sheri Shortt, Michael Yama, George Sasaki, Tad Horino, William T. Yamadera, Michele Starck, Renee Breault, Kim Robinson, Elizabeth Carter, Bruce Block, Paul Angelo, Lisa Purcell

Right: (clockwise) Wendy Jo Sperber, Deborah Harmon, Barbara Stuart, Martina Finch, Tawny Kitane, Tracy Smith Top: Barry Diamond, Bradford Bancroft, Tom Hanks (c), William Tepper, Michael Dudikoff, Gary Grossman © Bachelor Party Productions

Tawny Kitane, Tom Hanks

Adrian Zmed

TOP SECRET!

(PARAMOUNT) Producers, Jon Davison, Hunt Lowry; Directors, Jim Abrahams, David Zucker, Jerry Zucker; Screenplay, Jim Abrahams, David Zucker, Jerry Zucker, Martyn Burke; Photography, Christopher Challis; Designer, Peter Lamont; Editor, Bernard Gribble; Associate Producer, Tom Jacobson; Music, Maurice Jarre; Executive Producers, Jim Abrahams, David Zucker, Jerry Zucker; Choreographer, Gillian Gregory; Production Manager, Donald Toms; Assistant Director, Barry Langley; Art Directors, John Fenner, Michael Lamont; Costumes, Emma Porteous; Special Effects, Nick Allder; Score performed by Royal Philharmonic Orchestra; In MetroColor and Dolby Stereo; Rated PG; 90 minutes; June release

CAST

Cedric	Omar Sharif
Gen. Streck	Jeremy Kemp
Col. von Horst	Warren Clarke
Maj. Crumpler	Tristram Jellinek
Nick Rivers	Val Kilmer
Martin	Billy J. Mitchell
Porter	Major Wiley
Mayor	Gertan Klauber
Biletnikov	Richard Mayes
Madam Bergerone	Vyvyan Lorrayne
Pregnant Woman	Nancy Abrahams
Blindman	Ian McNeice
Maitre d'	John Sharp
Hillary Flammond	Lucy Gutteridge
Waiter	Michael Burlington
Little German	Marcus Powell
Chef	Burton Zucker
Priest	Richard Pescud
Klaus	John Carney
Student	Russell Sommers
Dr. Flammond	Michael Gough
Crying Girl	Sara Montague
Bookstore Proprietor	Peter Cushing
Young Hillary	Mandy Nunn
Young Nigel	Lee Sheward
Wagon Driver	Janos Kurucz
Du Quois	Harry Ditson
Nigel	Christopher Villiers
Deja Vu	Jim Carter
Chocolate Mousse	Eddie Tagoe
Latrine	Dimitri Andreas

**Right: Val Kilmer, Lucy Gutteridge
Above: Ian McNeice, Omar Sharif Top:
Eddie Tagoe, Gutteridge, Christopher
Villiers, Marcus Powell, Harry Ditson,
Jim Carter, Kilmer © _Paramount_**

Lucy Gutteridge, Val Kilmer

Val Kilmer

CONAN THE DESTROYER

(UNIVERSAL) Producer, Raffaella De Laurentiis; Director, Richard Fleischer; Screenplay, Stanley Mann; Story, Roy Thomas, Gerry Conway; Based on characters created by Robert E. Howard; Photography, Jack Cardiff; Executive Producer, Stephen F. Kesten; Editor, Frank J. Urioste; Music, Basil Poledouris; Designer, Pier Luigi Basile; Costumes, John Bloomfield; Art Directors, Kevin Phipps, Jose Maria Alarcon; Visual Special Effects Coordinator, Charles Finance; In J-D-C Widescreen and Technicolor; Rated PG; 103 minutes; June release

CAST

Conan	Arnold Schwarzenegger
Zula	Grace Jones
Bombaara	Wilt Chamberlain
Akjiro "The Wizard"	Mako
Malak	Tracey Walter
Queen Taramis	Sarah Douglas
Princess Jehnna	Olivia D'Abo
Man Ape/Thoth-Amon	Pat Roach
Grand Vizier	Jeff Corey
Togra	Sven Ole Thorsen
Village Heckler	Bruce Fleischer
The Leader	Ferdinand Mayne

Left: Arnold Schwarzenegger, and below with Wilt Chamberlain, Grace Jones, Olivia D'Abo, Mako, Tracey Walter © Universal

Grace Jones

Arnold Schwarzenegger, Sarah Douglas
Above: Olivia D'Abo, Wilt Chamberlain, Schwarzenegger

THE MUPPETS TAKE MANHATTAN

(TRI-STAR) Executive Producer, Jim Henson; Producer, David Lazer; Director, Oz; Screenplay, Oz, Tom Patchett, Jay Tarses; Photography, Robert Paynter; Editor, Evan Lottman; Music, Ralph Burns; Songs, Jeff Moss; Production Manager, Ezra Swerdlow; Assistant Director, Ron Bozman; Designer, Stephen Hendrickson; Art Directors, W. Steven Graham, Paul Eads; Special Effects, Faz Fazakas; Costumes, Karen Roston, Calista Hendrickson, Polly Smith; Choreography, Chris Chadman; In Technicolor and Metrocolor; Rated G; 94 minutes; July release

CAST

Jim Henson (Kermit/Rowlf/Dr. Teeth/Waldorf), Frank Oz (Miss Piggy/Fozzie/Animal), Dave Goetz (Gonzo/Chester Rat/Bill/Zoot), Steve Whitmire (Rizzo/Gil), Richard Hunt (Scooter/Statler/Janice), Jerry Nelson (Camilla/Lew Zealand/Floyd Pepper), Juliana Donald (Jenny), Lonny Price (Ronnie), Louis Zorich (Pete), Kathryn Mullen (Jill), Karen Prell (Yolanda), Brian Muehl (Tatooey Rat), Bruce Edward Hall (Masterson/Beth), and cameo appearances by Dabney Coleman, John Landis, Joan Rivers, Gregory Hines, James Coco, Art Carney, Linda Lavin, Liza Minnelli, Vincent Sardi, Elliott Gould, Mayor Ed Koch, Brooke Shields, Frances Bergen

Left: Kermit and Miss Piggy
Below: Dabney Coleman, Camilla
© *Tri-Star Pictures*

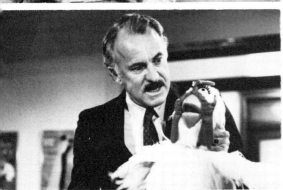

The Muppet Babies

Kermit, Miss Piggy
Above: Miss Piggy, Joan Rivers

PURPLE RAIN

(WARNER BROS.) Producers, Robert Cavallo, Joseph Ruffalo, Steven Fargnoli; Director, Albert Magnoli; Screenplay, Mr. Magnoli, William Blinn; Photography, Donald L. Thorin; Editors, Mr. Magnoli, Ken Robinson; Production Manager, Mike Frankovich, Jr.; Costumes, Marie-France, Lewis & Vaughan; Designer, Ward Preston; Music, Michel Colombier; Songs, Prince, The Time, Apollonia 6, Dez Dickerson; In Dolby Stereo and Metrocolor; Rated R; 111 minutes; July release

CAST

The Kid	Prince
Apollonia	Apollonia Kotero
Morris	Morris Day
Mother	Olga Karlatos
Father	Clarence Williams III
Jerome	Jerome Benton
Billy Sparks	Billy Sparks
Jill	Jill Jones
Chick	Charles Huntsberry
Dez	Dez Dickerson
Brenda	Brenda Bennett
Susan	Susan

Top: Prince
© *Water Productions/Warner Bros.*

1984 Academy Award for Original Song Score

Apollonia Kotero

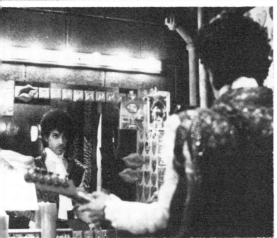

Prince (also above), Apollonia Kotero
Top: Brenda Bennett, Kotero, Susan
Moonsie

Prince Top: Jerome
Benton, Morris Day

REVENGE OF THE NERDS

(20th CENTURY-FOX) Producers, Ted Field, Peter Samuelson; Director, Jeff Kanew; Screenplay, Steve Zacharias, Jeff Buhai; Story, Tim Metcalfe, Miguel Tejada-Flores, Steve Zacharias, Jeff Buhai; Co-Producer, Peter MacGregor Scott; Executive Producers, David Obst, Peter Bart; Photography, King Baggot; Designer, James L. Schoppe; Editor, Alan Balsam; Original Score, Thomas Newman; Production Manager, Henry Kline; Assistant Directors, Terry Donnelly, James M. Freitag, Gary Law; Production Coordinator, "Pinki" Ragan; Choreographer, Dorain Grusman; In DeLuxe Color; Rated R; 90 minutes; July release

CAST

Lewis	Robert Carradine
Gilbert	Anthony Edwards
Poindexter	Tim Busfield
Wormser	Andrew Cassese
Booger	Curtis Armstrong
Lamar	Larry B. Scott
Takashi	Brian Tochi
Betty	Julie Montgomery
Judy	Michelle Meyrink
Stan	Ted McGinley
Burke	Matt Salinger
Ogre	Donald Gibb
Mr. Skolnick	Jamie Cromwell
Dean Ulich	David Wohl
Coach Harris	John Goodman
U. N. Jefferson	Bernie Casey
Mrs. Lowe	Alice Hirson
Sergeant	F. William Parker
U. N. Assistant	Roger Carter
Mrs. Wormser	Kres Mersky
Woman	Marianne Muellerleile
Suzy	Lisa Welch
Michelle	Suzanne B. Hayes
Joanne	Shawn Siqueiros
Connie	Sandra Katzel
Trainer	Henry M. Kendrick
Japanese Man	Fumio Kodama
Lamar's Date	Lance Lombardo
Tough-looking Guy	William B. Wilson
Tri-Lamb	Carl Cherry
Blond Nerd	Adam Frank
Plaid Brothers	Taylor Samuels, Bradley Grunberg

Donald Gibb, Ted McGinley, Matt Salinger, John Goodman Top Left: Anthony Edwards,
Robert Carradine Below: (front row) Brian Tochi, Curtis Armstrong, Anthony Edwards,
Andrew Cassese, Robert Carradine, Tim Busfield, Larry B. Scott

Robert Carradine, Curtis Armstrong, Brian Tochi, Anthony Edwards Top: (L) Robert
Carradine, Anthony Edwards (R) Ted McGinley, Julie Montgomery, Robert Carradine
Left Center: Andrew Cassese

BEST DEFENSE

(PARAMOUNT) Producer, Gloria Katz; Director, Willard Huyck; Screenplay, Gloria Katz, Willard Huyck; Based on novel "Easy and Hard Ways Out" by Robert Grossbach; Music, Patrick Williams; Photography, Don Peterman; Editor, Sidney Wolinsky; Production Design, Peter Jamison; Costumes, Kristi Zea; In color; Rated R; 94 minutes; July release

CAST

Wylie Cooper	Dudley Moore
Landry	Eddie Murphy
Laura	Kate Capshaw
Morgan	Michael Scalera
Loparino	George Dzundza
Clare Lewis	Helen Shaver
Frank Joyner	Peter Michael Goetz
Spy	David Rasche

Top: (L) George Dzundza, Helen Shaver, Dudley Moore
(R) Eddie Murphy (R) Center: (R) Dudley Moore,
David Rasche (L) Kate Capshaw, Dudley Moore
© *Paramount*

Eddie Murphy, Tracey Ross

THE LAST STARFIGHTER

(UNIVERSAL) Producers, Gary Adelson, Edward O. DeNault; Director, Nick Castle; Screenplay, Jonathan Betuel; Photography, King Baggot; Art Director, James D. Bissell; Designer, Ron Cobb; Editor, C. Timothy O'Meara; Associate Producer, John H. Whitney, Jr.; Costumes, Robert Fletcher; Music, Craig Safan; Production Manager, Kim C. Friese; Assistant Directors, Brian E. Franklish, Richard Denault; Production Coordinator, Debbie Smith; In Dolby Stereo, Technicolor and Panavision; Rated PG; 100 minutes; July release

CAST

Alex Rogan	Lance Guest
Grig	Dan O'Herlihy
Maggie Gordon	Catherine Mary Stewart
Jane Rogan	Barbara Bosson
Xur	Norman Snow
Centauri	Robert Preston
Enduran	Kay E. Kuter
Lord Kril	Dan Mason
Louis Rogan	Chris Hebert
Rylan Bursar	John O'Leary
Kodan Officer	George McDaniel
Rylan Sergeant	Maggie Cooper
Rylan Technician	Charlene Nelson
Rylan Sergeant	Bruce Abbott
Friendly Alien	John Maio
Underling	Robert Starr
Rylan Spy	Al Berry
Tentacle Alien	Scott Dunlop
Otis	Vernon Washington
Jack Blake	Peter Nelson
Elvira	Peggy Pope
Granny Gordon	Meg Wyllie
Clara Potter	Ellen Blake
Potter	Britt Leach
Mrs. Boone	Bunny Summers
Boone	Owen Bush
Andy	Cameron Dye
Gary	Geoffrey Blake

Right: Catherine Mary Stewart, Lance Guest
Top: Lance Guest, Dan O'Herlihy
© Universal/Lorimar

Lance Guest, Robert Preston

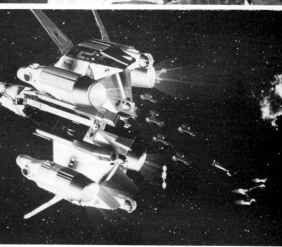

Gunstar attacking Deckfighter

THE ADVENTURES OF BUCKAROO BANZAI
Across the 8th Dimension

(20th CENTURY-FOX) Producers, Neil Canton, W. D. Richter; Director, W. D. Richter; Screenplay, Earl MacRauch; Executive Producer, Sidney Beckerman; Associate Producer, Dennis Jones; Photography, Fred J. Koenekamp; Designer, J. Michael Riva; Editors, Richard Marks, George Bowers; Music, Michael Boddicker; Assistant Directors, Gary Daigler, Katterli A. Frauenfelder; Costumes, Aggie Guerrard Rodgers; Art Directors, Richard Carter, Stephen Dane; 8th Dimension sequences by Greenlite Effects; In Panavision, Metrocolor and Dolby Stereo; Rated PG; 103 minutes; August release

CAST

Buckaroo Banzai	Peter Weller
Dr. Emilio Lizardo/Lord John Whorfin	John Lithgow
Penny Priddy	Ellen Barkin
New Jersey	Jeff Goldblum
John Bigboote	Christopher Lloyd
Perfect Tommy	Lewis Smith
John Emdall	Rosalind Cash
Prof. Hikita	Robert Ito
Reno Nevada	Pepe Serna
President Widmark	Ronald Lacey
Secretary of Defense	Matt Clark
Rawhide	Clancy Brown
General Catburd	William Traylor
John Parker	Carl Lumbly
John O'Connor	Vincent Schiavelli
John Gomez	Dan Hedaya
Senator Cunningham	Mariclare Costello
Casper Lindley	Bill Henderson
Scooter Lindley	Damon Hines
Pinky Carruthers	Billy Vera
Mrs. Johnson	Laura Harrington
Billy Travers	Michael Santoro

and Kent Perkins, Jonathan Banks, Robert Gray, Gary Bisig, Kenneth Magee, James Keane, John David Ashton, Yakov Smirnoff, Leonard Gaines, Francine Lembi, John Walter Davis, Read Morgan, James Rosin, Raye Birk, Jane Marla Robbins, Kevin Sullivan, Jessie Lawrence Ferguson, Radford Polinsky, Sam Minsky, Robert Hummer, Gerald Peterson

Left: John Lithgow, Peter Weller
© *Sherwood Productions*

Jeff Goldblum, Michael Santoro, Clancy Brown, Peter Weller, Pepe Serna, Billy Vera, Lewis Smith Top Left: Christopher Lloyd, Robert Ito, Ellen Barkin Below: Good Aliens from Planet 10

LOVE STREAMS

(CANNON) Producers, Menahem Golan, Yoram Globus; Director, John Cassavetes; Screenplay, John Cassavetes, Ted Allan; Based on play by Ted Allan; Executive Producer, Al Ruban; Costumes, Jennifer Smith-Ashley; Editor, George C. Villasenor; Music, Bo Harwood; Art Director, Phedon Papamichael; Production Managers, Chris Pearce, Al Ruban; Photography, Al Ruban; Assistant Directors, Frank Beetson, Randy Carter, Michael Lally, Eddy Donno; In MetroColor; Rated PG13; 141 minutes; August release

CAST

Sarah Lawson	Gena Rowlands
Robert Harmon	John Cassavetes
Susan	Diahnne Abbott
Jack Lawson	Seymour Cassel
Margarita	Margaret Abbott
Albie Swanson	Jakob Shaw
Agnes Swanson	Michele Conway
Stepfather Swanson	Eddy Donno
Judge Dunbar	Joan Foley
Milton Kravitz	Al Ruban
Sam the lawyer	Tom Badal
Debbie Lawson	Risa Martha Blewitt
Psychiatrist	David Rowlands
Dr. Williams	Robert Fieldsteel
Billy	Raphael DeNiro
Frank	Tony Brubaker
Ken	John Roselius
Dottie	Jessica St. John
Mrs. Kiner	Doe Avedon
Cashier	Frank Beetson
Taxi Drivers	John Finnegan, Gregg Berger, John Qualls
Phyllis George Delano	Christopher O'Neal
Jane Meadows Swift	Susan Wolf

and Alexandra Cassavetes, Dominique Davalos, Julie Allan, Renee LeFlore, Leslie Hope, Joan Dykman, Browyn Bober, Victoria Morgan, Barbara DiFrenza, Cindy Davidson, Jamie Horton, Francois Duhamel, Geraldine Hofstatter, Kathryn Donno, Carolyn Baker, William Thompson, Avram Liebman, Michael Stein, Phedon Papamichael, Jim Jones, Leonard P. Geer, Neil Bell, George Endoso, Kelly Lawrence, Logan Carter, Christopher Morley, Joe LeFlore, Michael Gallant, Dean Shindel, Al Lopez

Top: Gena Rowlands Right: John Cassavetes, Diahnne Abbott Below: Seymour Cassel, Rowlands, Risa Blewitt
© *Cannon Films*

John Cassavetes, Gena Rowlands

THE WOMAN IN RED

(ORION) Producer, Victor Drai; Direction and Screenplay, Gene Wilder; Based on French film "Un Elephant Ca Trompe Enormement"/"Pardon Mon Affair" by Jean-Loup Dabadie and Yves Robert; Executive Producer, Jack Frost Sanders; Editor, Christopher Greenburg; Designer, David L. Snyder; Associate Producers, Susan Ruskin, Xavier Gelin; Assistant Director, Michael F. Grillo; Music, John Morris; In Dolby Stereo and DeLuxe Color; Rated PG13; 87 minutes; August release

CAST

Theodore Pierce	Gene Wilder
Buddy	Charles Grodin
Joe	Joseph Bologna
Didi	Judith Ivey
Michael	Michael Huddleston
Charlotte	Kelly LeBrock
Ms. Miner	Gilda Radner
Richard	Kyle T. Heffner
Shelly	Michael Zorek

Left: Gene Wilder
© *Orion Pictures*

1984 Academy Award for Original Song

("I Just Called to Say I Love You")

Kelly LeBrock

Kelly LeBrock, Gene Wilder

CLOAK AND DAGGER

(UNIVERSAL) Producer, Allan Carr; Director, Richard Franklin; Story and Screenplay, Tom Holland; Photography, Victor J. Kemper; Designer, William Tuntke; Editor, Andrew London; Music, Brian May; Executive Producer/Production Manager, C. O. Erickson; Assistant Directors, Katy Emde, Alan Curtiss; Production Coordinator, Danis Regal; Art Director, Todd Hallowell; In Dolby Stero and Technicolor; Rated PG; 101 minutes; August release

CAST

Davey Osborne	Henry Thomas
Jack Flack/Hal Osborne	Dabney Coleman
Rice	Michael Murphy
Kim Gardener	Christina Nigra
George MacCready	John McIntire
Eunice MacCready	Jeanette Nolan
Alvarez	Eloy Casados
Haverman	Tim Rossovich
Morris	Bill Forsythe
Lt. Fleming	Robert DoQui
Marilyn Gardener	Shelby Leverington
Airport Security Chief	Linden Chiles
Murdoch	Robert Curtin
Airport Security Guards	William Marquez, Wendell Wright
Woman in cafe	Doris Hargrave
Man in cafe	Gary Moody
Woman on boat	Eleese Lester
Men on boat	John P. Edson, Jr., Steve Fromholtz
Alamo Guards	Charles Beall, Stuart MacGregor
Texan	Norman Bennett
Building Guard	Corey Rand
Taxi Driver	Nicholas Guest
Receptionist	Karen Leigh Hopkins
Check-in Clerk	Tammy Hyler
Boat Captain	Alvaro Rojas, Jr.
Ticket Agent	Robert Traynor
Bus Drivers	Berkley Garrett, Gene Ross
Navigator	Earl Houston Bullock

Top: (L) Dabney Coleman, Henry Thomas
(R) Eloy Casados, Tim Rossovich Below:
Jeanette Nolan, Thomas, John McIntire
© Universal

Henry Thomas, Christina Nigra
Above: Thomas, Dabney Coleman

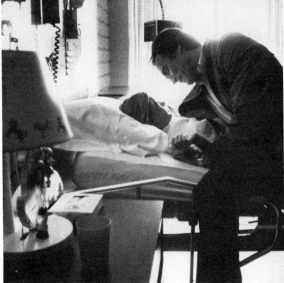

Clint Eastwood, Genevieve Bujold

TIGHTROPE

(WARNER BROS.) Producers, Clint Eastwood, Fritz Manes; Direction and Screenplay, Richard Tuggle; Designer, Edward Carfagno; Editor, Joel Cox; Music, Lennie Niehaus; Production Manager, Fritz Manes; Assistant Directors, David Valdes, Paul Moen, L. Dean Jones, Jr.; Costumes, Glenn Wright; In Panavision and Technicolor; Rated R; 111 minutes; August release

CAST

Wes Block	Clint Eastwood
Beryl Thibodeaux	Genevieve Bujold
Detective Molinari	Dan Hedaya
Amanda Block	Alison Eastwood
Penny Block	Jennifer Beck
Leander Rolfe	Marco St. John
Becky Jacklin	Rebecca Perle
Sarita	Regina Richardson
Jamie Cory	Randi Brooks
Melanie Silber	Jamie Rose
Judy Harper	Margaret Howell
Girl with whip	Rebecca Clemons
Dr. Yarlofsky	Janet MacLachlan
Luther	Graham Paul
Police Chief	Bill Holliday
Medical Examiner	John Wilmot
Mrs. Holstein	Margie O'Dair
Swap Meet Owner	Joy N. Houck, Jr.
Blond Surfer	Stuart Baker-Bergen
Shorty	Donald Barber
Lonesome Alice	Robert Harvey
Coroner	Ron Gural
Sgt. Surtees	Layton Martens
Dr. Fitzpatrick	Richard Charles Boyle
Nurse	Becki Davis
Gay Boy	Jonathan Sacher
Black Hooker	Valerie Thibodeaux
Plainclothes Gus	Lionel Ferbos
Sandoval	Eliott Keener

and Cary Wilmot Alden, David Valdes, James Borders, Fritz Manes, Jonathan Shaw, Don Lutenbacher, George Wood, Kimberly Georgoulis, Glenda Byars, John Schluter, Jr., Nick Krieger, Lloyd Nelson, Rod Masterson, David Dahlgren, Glenn Wright, Angela Hill, Ted Saari, Wayne Van Horn, George Orrison

Top: Alison Eastwood, Clint Eastwood (L) Clint Eastwood, Dan Hedaya Below: Alison Eastwood, Jennifer Beck, Clint Eastwood © Warner Bros.

THE RIVER RAT

(PARAMOUNT) Producer, Bob Larson; Executive Producer, Michael Apted; Direction and Screenplay, Tom Rickman; Photography, Jan Kiesser; Editor, Dennis Virkler; Music, Mike Post; Designer, John J. Lloyd; Costumes, Peter Saldutti; Assistant Director, L. Andrew Stone; In Technicolor; Rated PG; 93 minutes; September release

CAST

Billy	Tommy Lee Jones
Jonsy	Martha Plimpton
Doc	Brian Dennehy
Wexel	Shawn Smith
Vadie	Nancy Lea Owen
Sheriff Cal	Norman Bennett
Poley	Tony Frank
Joyce	Angie Bolling

**Right: Martha Plimpton, Tommy Lee Jones
and below with Norman Bennett
© *Paramount***

Tommy Lee Jones, Martha Plimpton, Shawn Smith,
Brian Dennehy Above: Plimpton, Jones, Nancy
Lea Owen

Martha Plimpton, Tommy Lee Jones

63

A SOLDIER'S STORY

(COLUMBIA) Producers, Norman Jewison, Ronald L. Schwary, Patrick Palmer; Director, Norman Jewison; Screenplay, Charles Fuller from his play "A Soldier's Play"; Photography, Russell Boyd; Designer, Walter Scott Herndon; Editors, Mark Warner, Caroline Biggerstaff; Associate Producer, Charles Milhaupt; Music, Herbie Hancock; Production Manager, Gerald R. Molen; Assistant Directors, Dwight Williams, Warren Gray; Executive Producer, Charles Schultz; In Metrocolor and Dolby Stereo; Rated PG; 102 minutes; September release

CAST

Captain Davenport	Howard E. Rollins, Jr.
Sergeant Waters	Adolph Caesar
Private Wilkie	Art Evans
Corporal Cobb	David Alan Grier
Private Smalls	David Harris
Captain Taylor	Dennis Lipscomb
C. J. Memphis	Larry Riley
Corporal Ellis	Robert Townsend
PFC Peterson	Denzel Washington
Private Henson	William Allen Young
Big Mary	Patti LaBelle
Lieutenant Byrd	Wings Hauser
Captain Wilcox	Scott Paulin
Sergeant Washington	John Hancock
Colonel Nivens	Trey Wilson
Ida Nivens	Patricia Brandkamp
Bus Driver	Carl Dreher
Captain Estes	Vaughn Reeves
Private Seymour	Robert Tyler
White Lieutenants	Pat Grabe, Terry Dodd
Sergeant Hooks	Warren Clements
Chaplain	James W. Bryant
Umpire	John Valentine
M.P. Sergeant	Ronald E. Greenfield
M.P. at gate	Anthony C. Sanders
M.P. at barracks	Traftin E. Thompson
Training Field Sergeant	Roy Wells
Soldier Painting	Tommy G. Liggins
Soldiers	Calvin Franklin, Kevin T. Mosley, Michael Williams, David Ashley, Thomas Howard, Bobby McGaughey, Rick Ramey, Lacarnist Hiriams

Left: Howard E. Rollins, Jr.
© *Columbia Pictures*

Art Evans (seated), William Allen Young, David Harris (standing right) Top Left: Adolph Caesar

Howard E. Rollins, Jr., Dennis Lipscomb Above: Art
Evans, Larry Riley, Adolph Caesar Top: Denzel
Washington, Larry Riley

Howard E. Rollins, Jr. (L) Above: Adolph Caesar,
Denzel Washington Top: Larry Riley, Patti LaBelle

COUNTRY

(BUENA VISTA) Producers, William D. Wittliff, Jessica Lange; Director, Richard Pearce; Screenplay, William D. Wittliff; Photography, David M. Walsh; Designer, Ron Hobbs; Editor, Bill Yahraus; Music, Charles Gross; Production Manager, William Beaudine, Jr.; Assistant Directors, Al Nicholson, Craig A. Beaudine; Additional Photography, Roger Shearman; Costumes, Tommy Welsh, Rita Salazar; Art Director, John B. Mansbridge; Production Coordinator, Sheila A. Warner; Piano Solos, George Winston; In Technicolor, and Dolby Stereo; Soundtrack available on Windham Hill Records and Tapes; Rated PG; 109 minutes; September release

CAST

Jewell Ivy	Jessica Lange
Gil Ivy	Sam Shepard
Otis	Wilford Brimley
Tom McMullen	Matt Clark
Marlene Ivy	Therese Graham
Carlisle Ivy	Levi L. Knebel
Arlon Brewer	Jim Haynie
Louise Brewer	Sandra Seacat
Fordyce	Alex Harvey
Missy Ivy	Stephanie-Stacie Poyner
Cowboy	Jim Ostercamp
Grain Elevator Operator	Robert Somers
Semi Driver	Frank Noel, Jr.
Preacher	Rev. Warren Duit
Auctioneer	Conrad Doan
Bank Officer	James Harrell
Bartender	Dean French
Secretary	Betty Smith
Longley	Vern Porter
Mrs. McAdams	Sandra J. Hughes

Left: Sam Shepard, Jessica Lange
© *Buena Vista*

Jessica Lange

Sam Shepard

Jessica Lange, and above with Wilford Brimley,
Sam Shepard, Levi L. Knebel Top: Brimley, Lange

Levi L. Knebel, Therese Graham, Jessica Lange
Top: Sam Shepard, Jessica Lange

ALL OF ME

(UNIVERSAL) Producer, Stephen Friedman; Director, Carl Reiner; Screenplay, Phil Alden Robinson; Adaptation, Henry Olek; Based on novel "Me Two" by Ed Davis; Photography, Richard Kline; Designer, Edward Carfagno; Editor, Bud Molin; Music, Patrick Williams; Associate Producer, Phil Alden Robinson; Production Manager, David Salven; Assistant Directors, Albert M. Shapiro, Marty P. Ewing; Production Coordinator, Jane Prosnit; In Technicolor; Rated PG; 93 minutes; September release

CAST

Roger Cobb	Steve Martin
Edwina Cutwater	Lily Tomlin
Terry Hoskins	Victoria Tennant
Peggy Schuyler	Madolyn Smith
Prahka Lasa	Richard Libertini
Burton Schuyler	Dana Elcar
Tyrone Wattell	Jason Bernard
Margo	Selma Diamond
Fred Hoskins	Eric Christmas
Fulton Norris	Gailard Sartain
Gretchen	Neva Patterson
Mr. Mifflin	Michael Ensign
Dr. Betty Ahrens	Peggy Feury
Divorce Lawyer	Nan Martin
Court Clerk	Basil Hoffman
Grayson	Hedley Mattingly
Judge	Harvey Vernon
Police Officer	Stu Black
Receptionist	Marilyn Tokuda
Minister	David Byrd
Hard Hat	Nick Shields
Security Guard	Bill Saito
Cabbie	Neil Elliott
Courtroom Spectator	Jillian Scott
Nurse	Judy Nagy
Cook	Ronn Wright
James Welch IV	Jim Welch

Left: Steve Martin, Lily Tomlin
© *Universal*

Dana Elcar

Richard Libertini

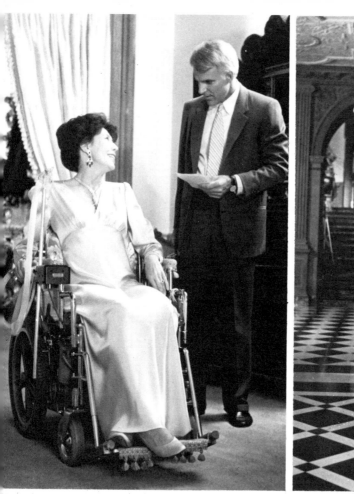

Jason Bernard Top: Lily Tomlin, Steve Martin

Lily Tomlin, also Top with Steve Martin

PLACES IN THE HEART

(TRI-STAR) Producer, Arlene Donovan; Executive Producer, Michael Hausman; Direction and Screenplay, Robert Benton; Photography, Nestor Almendros; Editor, Carol Littleton; Music, John Kander; Designer, Gene Callahan; Art Director, Sydney Z. Litwak; Costumes, Ann Roth; Assistant Director, Joel Tuber; Special Visual Effects, Bran Ferren; In Technicolor; Rated PG; 110 minutes; September release

CAST

Edna Spalding	Sally Field
Margaret Lomax	Lindsay Crouse
Wayne Lomax	Ed Harris
Viola Kelsey	Amy Madigan
Mr. Will	John Malkovich
Moze	Danny Glover
Frank	Yankton Hatten
Possum	Gennie James
Albert Denby	Lane Smith
Buddy Kelsey	Terry O'Quinn
Tee Tot Hightower	Bert Remsen
Royce Spalding	Ray Baker
W. E. Simmons	Jay Patterson

Left: Sally Field
© *Tri-Star Pictures*

***1984 Academy Awards for Best Actress
(Sally Field) and Original Screenplay***

Yankton Hatten, Gennie James, Sally Field, Danny Glover

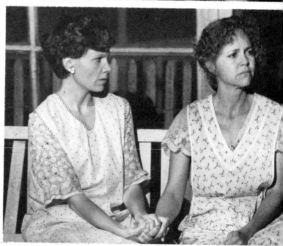

**John Malkovich Above: Yankton Hatten,
Sally Field, Gennie James Top: Terry O'Quinn,
Amy Madigan, Lindsay Crouse, Ed Harris**

Sally Field, and above
with Lindsay Crouse

GARBO TALKS

(MGM/UA) Producers, Burtt Harris, Elliott Kastner; Director, Sidney Lumet; Screenplay, Larry Grusin; Photography, Andrzej Bartkowski; Editor, Andrew Mondshein; Music, Cy Coleman; Designer, Philip Rosenberg; Costumes, Anna Hill Johnstone; Production Manager/Associate Producer, Jennifer M. Ogden; Assistant Director, Alan Hopkins; In Technicolor; Rated PG13; 105 minutes; October release

CAST

Estelle Rolf	Anne Bancroft
Gilbert Rolfe	Ron Silver
Lisa Rolfe	Carrie Fisher
Jane Mortimer	Catherine Hicks
Walter Rolfe	Steven Hill
Angelo Dokakis	Howard DaSilva
Sonya Apollinar	Dorothy Loudon
Bernie Whitlock	Harvey Fierstein
Elizabeth Rennick	Hermione Gingold
Shepard Plotnick	Richard B. Shull
Mr. Morganelli	Michael Lombard
Mr. Goldhammer	Ed Crowley
Garbo	Nina Zoe, Betty Comden

and Alice Spivak, Maurice Sterman, Antonia Rey, Court Miller, Denny Dillon, Karen Shallo, Adolph Green, Arthur Schlesinger, Jr.

Left: Anne Bancroft
Below: Dorothy Loudon, Ron Silver
© *United Artists*

Howard Da Silva, Ron Silver

Ron Silver, Hermione Gingold
Above: Harvey Fierstein, Ron Silver

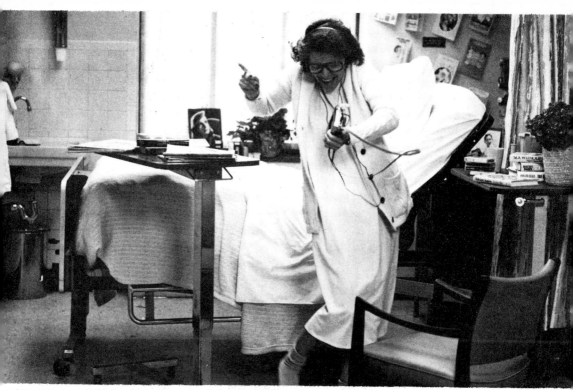

Catherine Hicks, Ron Silver
Top: Anne Bancroft

THE LITTLE DRUMMER GIRL

(WARNER BROS.) Producer, Robert L. Crawford; Director, George Roy Hill; Screenplay, Loring Mandel; Based on novel by John LeCarre; Executive Producer, Patrick Kelley; Photography, Wolfgang Treu; Designer, Henry Bumstead; Music, Dave Grusin; Editor, William Reynolds; Production Supervisor, Kieter Meyer; Assistant Directors, Don French, Peter Waller; Art Director, Helmut Gassner; Production Coordinator, Ilse Schwarzwald; In technicolor; Rated R; 131 minutes; October release

CAST

Charlie	Diane Keaton
Joseph	Yorgo Voyagis
Kurtz	Klaus Kinski
Khalil	Sami Frey
Tayeh	Michael Cristofer
Mesterbein	David Suchet
Litvak	Eli Danker
Dimitri	Ben Levine
Teddy	Jonathan Sagalle
Rose	Shlomit Hagoel
Julio	Juliano Mer
Oded	Danni Roth
Ben	Sabi Dorr
David	Doron Nesher
Toby	Smadar Brener
Rachel	Shoshi Marciano
Aaron	Philipp Moog
Raoul	Avi Keiddar
Zev	David Shalit
Udi	Dor Zweigenbom
Chairlady	Anna Massey
Ned Quilley	Thorley Walters
Young Man	Julian Firth
Ezra	Simon Osman
Green Grocer	Albert Moses
Policeman	Ben Robertson
Commander	David Cornwell

and Sebastian Graham Jones, Gawn Grainger, Michael Graham Cox, Illona Linthwaite, Irene Marot, Bill Nighy, Dee Sadler, Melanie Kilburn, Rowena Cooper, Peter Capell, Sasi Saad, Heinz Weiss, Rolf Becker, Ori Levy, Moti Shirin, Robert Pereno, Kerstin DeAhna, Yasein Shawaf, Suhiel Haddad, Dana Wheeler-Nicholson, Mohammed Kassas, Johnny Arbid, Mohammed Ali Badarni, Mahmoud Abu Elkhair, Jeff Lester, Paul Prosper, Adib Jashan, Rene Kolldehoff, Shimon Finkel, Elisabeth Neumann-Viertel, Yossi Werzansky, Aviva Joel, Noam Almaz, Dieter Augustin, Max Schillinger

Top Left: Klaus Kinski, Diane Keaton
Below: Yorgo Voyagis, Klaus Kinski
Left: Diane Keaton (C)
© *Warner Bros.*

Diane Keaton (C)

Diane Keaton, Sami Frey

Diane Keaton, Michael Cristofer
Top: (L) Diane Keaton (R) Keaton, Yorgo Voyagis

THIEF OF HEARTS

(PARAMOUNT) Producers, Don Simpson, Jerry Bruckheimer; Direction and Screenplay, Douglas Day Stewart; Photography, Andrew Laszlo; Art Director, Edward Richardson; Editor, Tom Rolf; Music, Harold Faltermeyer; Costumes, Michael Kaplan; Production Manager-Assistant Director, Michael Grillo; Production Manager-Associate Producer, Tom Jacobson; Assistant Director, Stephen P. Dunn; Additional Photography, Paul G. Ryan; Special Effects, Michael Lantieri; In Metrocolor and Dolby Stereo; Rated R; 100 minutes; October release

CAST

Scott Muller	Steven Bauer
Mickey Davis	Barbara Williams
Ray Davis	John Getz
Buddy Calamara	David Caruso
Janie Pointer	Christine Ebersole
Marty Morrison	George Wendt
Sweeney	Alan North
Nicole	Romy Windsor
Security Guard	Joe Nesnow
Parking Attendant	Gordon Pulliam
Stunt Coordinator	Walt Scott
Stunt Double for Scott	Vince Deadrick, Jr.
College Girls	Annette Sinclair, Aleana Downs
Ad-Libbers	Jane Marla Robbins, Ray Hassett, Marsha Wolfe, Brenda Currin

Left: Steven Bauer
© *Paramount Pictures*

Barbara Williams, John Getz

Barbara Williams, Christine Ebersole
Above: John Getz, George Wendt

Steven Bauer, Barbara Williams Above: Bauer,
David Caruso Top: John Getz, Williams, Bauer

Barbara Williams, Steven Bauer

FIRSTBORN

(PARAMOUNT) Producers, Paul Junger Witt, Tony Thomas; Director, Michael Apted; Executive Producers, Stanley R. Jaffe, Sherry Lansing; Co-Producer-Screenplay, Ron Koslow; Photography, Ralf Bode; Music, Michael Small; In color; Rated PG13; 105 minutes; October release

CAST

Wendy	Teri Garr
Sam	Peter Weller
Jake	Christopher Collet
Brian	Corey Haim
Lisa	Sarah Jessica Parker
Lee	Robert Downey
Adam	Christopher Gartin
Mr. Rader	James Harper
Dad	Richard Brandon
Joanne	Gayle Harbor

Left: Peter Weller, Teri Garr
Below: Sarah Jessica Parker, Christopher
Collet © *Paramount Pictures*

James Harper, Christopher Collet

Teri Garr, Corey Haim, Christopher
Collet, Richard Brandon Above:
Collet, Garr, Haim

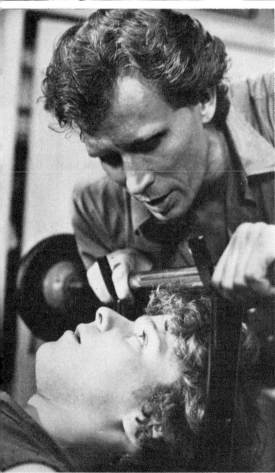

Christopher Collet, Peter Weller
Top: Collet, Teri Garr, Weller

Christopher Collet, Teri Garr

STRANGER THAN PARADISE

(SAMUEL GOLDWYN) Direction and Screenplay, Jim Jarmusch; Executive Producer, Otto Grokenberger; Photography, Tom Dicillo; Producer-Production Manager, Sara Driver; Music, John Lurie; Editors, Jim Jarmusch, Melody London; In black and white; Rated R; 95 minutes; October Release

CAST

Willie	John Lurie
Eva	Eszter Balint
Eddie	Richard Edson
Aunt Lottie	Cecillia Stark
Billy	Danny Rosen
Man with money	Rammellzee
Airline Agent	Tom Dicillo
Factory Worker	Richard Boes
Girl with hat	Sara Driver
Motel Owner	Paul Sloane
Poker Players	Rockets Redglare, Harvey Perr, Brian J. Burchill

Left: Richard Edson, Eszter Balint, John Lurie
© *Samuel Goldwyn Company*

Richard Edson, Eszter Balint, John Lurie

Eszter Balint, Richard Edson, John Lurie Top: John Lurie, Richard Edson, Cecillia Stark

BODY DOUBLE

(COLUMBIA) Producer-Director, Brian De Palma; Screenplay, Robert J. Avrech, Brian De Palma; Story, Brian De Palma; Executive Producer, Howard Gottfried; Photography, Stephen H. Burum; Designer, Ida Random; Editors, Jerry Greenberg, Bill Pankow; Costumes, Gloria Gresham; Music, Pino Donaggio; Production Manager, Ray Hartwick; Assistant Directors, Joe Napolitano, Robert Yannetti; Production Coordinator, Shari Leibowitz; In Metrocolor and Dolby Stereo; Rated R; 110 minutes; October release

CAST

Jake	Craig Wasson
Holly	Melanie Griffith
Sam	Gregg Henry
Gloria	Deborah Shelton
Jim McLean	Guy Boyd
Rubin	Dennis Franz
Drama Teacher	David Haskell
Kimberly	Rebecca Stanley
Corso	Al Israel
Video Salesman	Douglas Warhit
Douglas	B. J. Jones
Frank	Russ Marin
Billy	Lane Davies
Carol	Barbara Crampton
Assistant Director	Larry "Flash" Jenkins
Sid Goldberg	Monte Landis
Linda Shaw	Linda Shaw
Tina	Mindi Miller
Actress/Vampire Movie	Denise Loveday
Corso's Secretary	Gela Jacobson
Cops	Ray Hassett, Rick Gunderson Jerry Brutsche
Male Porno Star	Michael Kearns
Cameraman	Rob Paulsen
Theatre Director	Jeremy Lawrence

and Rod Loomis, Gary F. Griffith, Michael White, Emmett Brown, H. David Fletcher, Marcia Del Mar, Phil Redrow, Slavitza Jovan, Jack Mayhall, Alexandra Day, Pamela Weston, Brinke Stevens, Melissa Christian, Patty Lotz, Barbara Peckinpaugh, David Ursin, Casey Sander, Wes Edwards, Chuck Waters, Paul Calabria

© *Columbia Pictures*

Craig Wasson (C), Gregg Henry (R)
Top Left: Melanie Griffith, Craig Wasson

Deborah Shelton, Craig Wasson Above: Guy
Boyd, Wasson Top: Dennis Franz, Wasson,
Larry Jenkins

Craig Wasson, Melanie Griffith (also above)
Top: David Haskell, Craig Wasson

THE RAZOR'S EDGE

(COLUMBIA) Producers, Robert P. Marcucci, Harry Benn; Director, John Byrum; Screenplay, John Byrum, Bill Murray; Based on novel by W. Somerset Maugham; Executive Producer, Rob Cohen; Associate Producer, Jason Laskay; Music, Jack Nitzsche; Editor, Peter Boyle; Photography, Peter Hannan; Costumes, Shirley Russell; Designer, Philip Harrison; Production Supervisor, John Comfort; Production Managers, Serge Touboul, Sudesh Syal; Art Director, Malcolm Middleton; Assistant Directors, Ray Corbett, Laurent Bregeat, Kanwal Swaroop; In Widescreen, color and Dolby Stereo; Rated PG13; 130 minutes; October release

CAST

Larry Darrell	Bill Murray
Sophie	Theresa Russell
Isabel	Catherine Hicks
Elliot Templeton	Denholm Elliott
Gray Maturin	James Keach
Mackenzie	Peter Vaughan
Piedmont	Brian Doyle-Murray
Malcolm	Stephen Davies
Raaz	Saeed Jaffrey
Louisa Bradley	Faith Brook
Joseph	Andre Maranne
Henry Maturin	Bruce Boa
Coco	Serge Feuillard
Bob	Joris Stuyck
Red Cross Lady	Helen Horton
Tyler	Michael Fitzpatrick
Albert	Robert Manuel
Man at kissing booth	Sam Douglas
Governess	Nora Connolly
Brian Ryan	Jeff Harding
Doug Van Allen	Richard Oldfield
Doctor	Gordon Sterne
Nun	Mary Larkin
Kevin	Christopher Muncke
Lama	Kunchuck Tharching

Left: Theresa Russell, Bill Murray
© *Columbia Pictures*

Theresa Russell, Bill Murray, Catherine Hicks, James Keach, Denholm Elliott

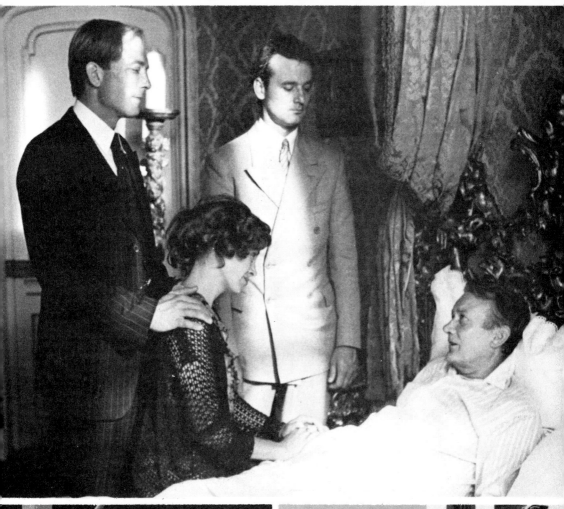

THE TERMINATOR

(ORION) Producer, Gale Anne Hurd; Director, James Cameron; Screenplay, James Cameron, Gale Anne Hurd; Executive Producers, John Daly, Derek Gibson; Photography, Adam Greenberg; Editor, Mark Goldblatt; Special Effects, Stan Winston; Production Manager, Donna Smith; Assistant Directors, Betsy Magruder, Thomas Irvine, Robert Roda; Art Director, George Costello; Production Coordinator, Anne St. Johns; Costumes, Hilary Wright; In DeLuxe Color; A Hemdale presentation of a Pacific Western production; Rated R; 108 minutes; October release

CAST

Terminator	Arnold Schwarzenegger
Kyle Reese	Michael Biehn
Sarah Connor	Linda Hamilton
Traxler	Paul Winfield
Vukovich	Lance Henriksen
Matt	Rick Rossovich
Ginger	Bess Motta
Silberman	Earl Boen
Pawn Shop Clerk	Dick Miller
Nancy	Shawn Schepps
Desk Sergeant	Bruce M. Kerner
Future Terminator	Franco Columbu
Punk Leader	Bill Paxton
Punks	Brad Reardon, Brian Thompson
Policemen	William Wisher, Jr., Ken Fritz, Tom Oberhaus
Cop in alley	Ed Dogans
TV Anchorman	Joe Farago
Anchorwoman	Hettie Lynne Hurtes
Station Attendant	Tony Mirelez
Mexican Boys	Philip Gordon, Anthony R. Trujillo
Derelict	Stan Yale
Cleaning Man	Norman Friedman
Ticket Taker	Barbara Powers
Tanker Driver	Wayne Stone
Tanker Partner	David Pierce

Left: Arnold Schwarzenegger
© *Orion Pictures*

Linda Hamilton, Arnold Schwarzenegger

Linda Hamilton, Michael Biehn
Top: (L) Arnold Schwarzenegger (R) Michael Biehn

THE RIVER

(UNIVERSAL) Producers, Edward Lewis, Robert Cortes; Director, Mark Rydell; Screenplay, Robert Dillon, Julian Barry; Story, Robert Dillon; Photography, Vilmos Zsigmond; Designer, Charles Rosen; Editor, Sidney Levin; Music, John Williams; Costumes, Joe I. Tompkins; Production Manager, Terry Carr; Assistant Directors, Jerry Ziesmer, Robert Yannetti; Art Director, Norman Newberry; Production Coordinator, Joan Wolpert; Soundtrack available on MCA Records; In Dolby Stereo and Technicolor; Rated PG13; 122 minutes; November release

CAST

Tom Garvey	Mel Gibson
Mae Garvey	Sissy Spacek
Lewis Garvey	Shane Bailey
Beth Garvey	Becky Jo Lynch
Joe Wade	Scott Glenn
Senator Neiswinder	Don Hood
Harve Stanley	Billy Green Bush
Howard Simpson	James Tolkan
Hal Richardson	Bob W. Douglas
Dave Birkin	Andy Stahl
Judy Birkin	Lisa Sloan
Rod Tessley	Larry D. Ferrell
Sally Toomey	Susie Toomey
Lisa Tessley	Kelly Toomey
Zemke	Frank Taylor
Smoot	Ivan Green
Wilderfoot	Desmond Couch
Youngdall	Charles G. Riddle
Dan Gaumer	Jim Antonio
Billy Gaumer	Samuel Scott Osborne
Betty Gaumer	Amy Rydell
Harley	David Hart
Roy	Barry Primus
Baines	Mark Erickson
Swick	Jack Starrett
Truck	Charlie Robinson
Doctor	Dean Whitworth
Fat Man	Charles S. Hanson
TV Weatherman	Ira M. Quillen II
Employees	Matt Bearson, Timothy Shadden
Secretary	Elizabeth Lane
Drifter	Gary Gershaw

Left: Scott Glenn, Sissy Spacek
Top: Mel Gibson, Shane Bailey, Sissy Spacek,
Becky Jo Lynch © *Universal*

Becky Jo Lynch, Sissy Spacek

Sissy Spacek

Mel Gibson, Sissy Spacek, Shane Bailey
Top: Mel Gibson, Sissy Spacek

Mel Gibson, Sissy Spacek (also above)

OH, GOD! YOU DEVIL

(WARNER BROS.) Producer, Robert M. Sherman; Director, Paul Bogart; Screenplay, Andrew Bergman; Executive Producer, Irving Fein; Photography, King Baggot; Designer, Peter Wooley; Editors, Randy Roberts, Andy Zall; Music, David Shire; Production Manager, William Young; Assistant Directors, Peter Bogart, Emmitt-Leon O'Neil; Special Effects, Ray Klein; In Technicolor; Rated PG; 96 minutes; November release

CAST

God/Harry O. Tophet	George Burns
Bobby Shelton	Ted Wass
Wendy Shelton	Roxanne Hart
Charlie Gray	Eugene Roche
Gary Frantz	Ron Silver
Arthur Shelton	John Doolittle
Bea Shelton	Julie Lloyd
Young Bobby	Ian Giatti
Mrs. K.	Janet Brandt
Mrs. Vega	Belita Moreno
Joey Vega	Danny Ponce
Hotel Manager	Jason Wingreen
Bellhop	Danny Mora
Widow	Jane Dulo
Louise	Susan Peretz
Waiter	Steven Dunaway
Billy Wayne	Robert Desiderio
Cap	Anthony Sgueglia
Receptionist	Cynthia Tarr
Joe Ortiz	Robert Picardo
Groupie	Christie Mellor
Houseman	Arthur Malet
Priest	James Cromwell
Shamus	Martin Garner
Preacher	Arnold Johnson
Reporter	Patricia Springer
Stage Manager	Buddy Powell
Doctor	Jim Hodge
Couple in restaurant	Tracy Bogart, Crawford Binion

Left: Ted Wass

George Burns in dual roles

Roxanne Hart, Ted Wass Top Left: George Burns, Ted Wass Right: George Burns

FALLING IN LOVE

(PARAMOUNT) Producer, Marvin Worth; Director, Ulu Grosbard; Screenplay, Michael Cristofer; Photography, Peter Suschitzky; Designer, Santo Loquasto; Editor, Michael Kahn; Music, Dave Grusin; Associate Producer, Robert F. Colesberry; Costumes, Richard Bruno; Production Manager, Mr. Colesberry; Assistant Directors, Thomas J. Mack, James Chory; Art Director, Speed Hopkins; In Technicolor; Rated PG13; 106 minutes; November release

CAST

Frank Raftis	Robert DeNiro
Molly Gilmore	Meryl Streep
Ed Lasky	Harvey Keitel
Ann Raftis	Jane Kaczmarek
John Trainer	George Martin
Brian Gilmore	David Clennon
Isabelle	Dianne Wiest
Victor Rawlins	Victor Argo
Mike Raftis	Wiley Earl
Joe Raftis	Jesse Bradford
Elevator Woman	Chevi Colton
Salesman	Richard Giza
Waitress	Frances Conroy
Cashier	James Ryan
Tow Truck Driver	Sonny Abagnale
Conductors	George Barry, L. P. McGlynn
Engineer	Paul Herman
Doctor	Kenneth Welsh
Taxi Drivers	John H. Reese, Clem Caserta
Hot Dog Vendor	Yanni Sfinias
Priest	Rev. Donald Goodness
Saleslady	Florence Anglin
First Man	Gerald M. Kline

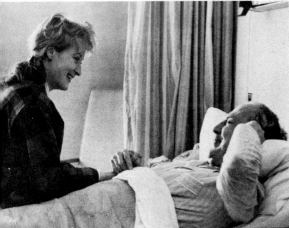

Left: Meryl Streep, George Martin
Top: Meryl Streep, Robert DeNiro
© *Paramount Pictures*

Meryl Streep, Robert DeNiro

Robert DeNiro, Meryl Streep
Above: Harvey Keitel, Robert DeNiro
Top: Meryl Streep, Dianne Wiest

Meryl Streep, Robert DeNiro
Above: Robert DeNiro, Jane Kaczmarek
Top: Meryl Streep, David Clennon

93

PARIS, TEXAS

(20th CENTURY-FOX) Executive Producer, Chris Sievernich; Producer, Don Guest; Director, Wim Wenders; Screenplay, Sam Shepard; Adaptation, L. M. Kit Carson; Photography, Robby Muller; Art Director, Kate Altman; Editor, Peter Przygodda; Music, Ry Cooder; Costumes, Birgitta Bjerke; Assistant Director, Claire Dennis; Production Manager, Karen Koch; Associate Producer, Pascale Dauman; In color; Rated R; 150 minutes; November release

CAST

Travis	Harry Dean Stanton
Gas Station Attendant	Sam Berry
Dr. Ulmer	Bernhard Wicki
Walt	Dean Stockwell
Anne	Aurore Clement
Car Rental Clerk	Claresie Mobley
Hunter	Hunter Carson
Woman on tv	Viva Auder
Carmelita	Socorro Valdez
Jane	Nastassja Kinski
Hunter (age 3)	Justin Hogg
Hunter's Friend	Edward Fayton
Screaming Man	Tom Farrell
Slater	John Lurie
Stretch	Jeni Vici
Nurse Bibs	Sally Norvell
Comedienne	Sharon Menzel
Rehearsing Band	The Mydolls

Top: Harry Dean Stanton
© *20th Century-Fox*

Nastassja Kinski, Harry Dean Stanton

Dean Stockwell, Harry Dean Stanton
(also top with Aurore Clement)

Harry Dean Stanton, Hunter Carson

NO SMALL AFFAIR

(COLUMBIA) Producer, William Sackheim; Director, Jerry Schatzberg; Screenplay, Charles Bolt, Terence Mulcahy; Story, Charles Bolt; Photography, Vilmos Zsigmond; Designer, Robert Boyle; Executive Producer, George Justin; Editors, Priscilla Nedd, Eve Newman, Melvin Shapiro; Costumes, Jo Ynocencio; Music, Rupert Holmes; Production Manager, George Justin; Assistant Directors, Chuck Myers, Michael Looney; Art Director, Frank Richwood; Production Coordinator, Judith Gill; Original Soundtrack on Atlantic Records; In MGM Color and Dolby Stereo; Rated R; 103 minutes; November release

CAST

Charles Cummings	Jon Cryer
Laura	Demi Moore
Jake	George Wendt
Leonard	Peter Frechette
Susan	Elizabeth Daily
Joan Cummings	Ann Wedgeworth
Ken	Jeffrey Tambor
Nelson	Tim Robbins
Gus Sosnowski	Hamilton Camp
Scott	Scott Getlin
Stephanie	Judy Baldwin
Mona	Jennifer Tilly
Walt Cronin	Kene Holliday
Waiter	Thomas Adams
Boy at stag party	Steven James Brown
John	Myles Berkowitz
Cafe Patron	Joe Cappetta
Bartender	Jack R. Clinton
Elderly Man	Joseph Darling
Bob	Tate Donovan

Rick Ducommun, Jan Dunn, Louis Geneva, James Guidera, Ashley Woodman Hall, Rupert Holmes, Mia Kelly, Lori Kruger, Joe Lerer, Katherine Lyons, Shermaine Michaels, Steve Monarque, George Pentecost, Maureen Ann Schatzberg, Sally Schaub, Mischa Schwartzmann, Ramona Scott, Helen Swee, Arthur Taxier, Morgan Upton, Michael Vaughn, E. F. Valderrama, Joan Valderrama, Michael David Wright

Right: Demi Moore, George Wendt
Top: Jon Cryer, Ann Wedgeworth
© *Columbia Pictures*

Demi Moore, Jon Cryer

Demi Moore, Jon Cryer

MICKI AND MAUDE

(COLUMBIA) Producer, Tony Adams; Director, Blake Edwards; Screenplay, Jonathan Reynolds; Production Manager, Alan Levine; Assistant Directors, Mickey McCardle, Joseph Paul Moore, David Kelley; Photography, Harry Stradling; Designer, Rodger Maus; Editor, Ralph E. Winters; Executive Producers, Jonathan D. Krane, Lou Antonio; Associate Producer, Trish Caroselli; Costumes, Patricia Norris; Music, Lee Holdridge; Art Director, Jack Senter; Special Effects, Roy L. Downey; Production Coordinator, Jane Prosnit; In Panavision and Metrocolor; Rated PG13; 118 minutes; December release

CAST

Rob Salinger	Dudley Moore
Maude Salinger	Amy Irving
Micki Salinger	Ann Reinking
Leo Brody	Richard Mulligan
Dr. Eugene Glztszki	George Gaynes
Dr. Elliot Fibel	Wallace Shawn
Hap Ludlow	John Pleshette
Barkhas Guillory	H. B. Haggerty
Nurse Verbeck	Lu Leonard
Diana Hutchison	Priscilla Pointer
Ezra Hutchison	Robert Symonds
Governor Lanford	George Coe
Dr. Kondoleon	Gustav Vintas
Interior Decorator	Ken Olfson
TV Cameraman	Phillippe Denham
Maude's Nurse	Emma Walton
Micki's Nurse	Ruth Silveira

and Richard Drown, Gene LeBell, Wiley Harker, Tina Theberge, Jim Giggins, Roger Rose, Tiiu Leek, Jamie Abbott, Christa Denton, Robby Kiger, Paul Bright, Robert Nadder, Hanna Hertelendy, Billy Beck, Lou Felder, Virginia Kiser, Jerry Martin, Gerry Gibson, Edith Fields, Arthur Lessac, Edward Call, Aphasia Peters, Jessica Rubin, Jaime McEnnan, Hailey McAfee, Marc Harris, Avianka Guzman, Patrick Sean Murphy, Nick Coddington, Doug Donatelli, Peter Nicholas, Joe Davis, Sam Cupae

Right: Richard Mulligan, Dudley Moore
Top: Dudley Moore, Amy Irving
© *Columbia Pictures*

**Amy Irving, Dudley Moore,
Ann Reinking**

Dudley Moore, Ann Reinking

97

THE COTTON CLUB

(ORION) Producer, Robert Evans; Director, Francis Coppola; Executive Producer, Dyson Lovell; Co-Producers, Sylvio Tabet, Fred Roos; Original Music, John Barry; Musical Re-Creations, Bob Wilber; Editors, Barry Malkin, Robert Q. Lovett; Designer, Richard Sylbert; Costumes, Milena Canonero; Photography, Stephen Goldblatt; Story, William Kennedy, Francis Coppola, Mario Puzo; Screenplay, William Kennedy, Francis Coppola; Choreographers, Michael Smuin, Henry LeTang, Gregory Hines, Claudia Asbury, George Faison, Arthur Mitchell, Michael Meacham; Production Managers, David Golden, Christopher Cronyn, Meg Hunnewell; Assistant Directors, Robert V. Girolami, Henry Bronchtein, Louis D'Esposito; Associate Producer, Melissa Prophet; Art Directors, David Chapman, Gregory Bolton; Production Supervisor, Grace Blake; Soundtrack on Geffen Records & Cassettes; In Technicolor and DeLuxe prints, and Dolby Stereo; Rated R; 127 minutes; December release

CAST

Dixie Dwyer	Richard Gere
Sandman Williams	Gregory Hines
Vera Cicero	Diane Lane
Lila Rose Oliver	Lonette McKee
Owney Madden	Bob Hoskins
Dutch Schultz	James Remar
Vincent Dwyer	Nicolas Cage
Abbadabba Berman	Allen Garfield
Frenchy Demange	Fred Gwynne
Tish Dwyer	Gwen Verdon
Frances Flegenheimer	Lisa Jane Persky
Clay Williams	Maurice Hines
Sol Weinstein	Julian Beck
Madame St. Clair	Novella Nelson
Bumpy Rhodes	Larry Fishburne
Joe Flynn	John Ryan
Irving Stark	Tom Waits
Mike Best	Ron Karabatsos
Ed Popke	Glenn Withrow
Patsy Dwyer	Jennifer Gray
Winnie Williams	Wynonna Smith
Norma Williams	Thelma Carpenter
Sugar Coates	Charles "Honi" Coles
Cab Calloway	Larry Marshall
Charles "Lucky" Luciano	Joe Dallesandro
Monk	Ed O'Ross
Sullen Man	Frederick Downs, Jr.
Gloria Swanson	Diane Venora
Kid Griffin	Tucker Smallwood
Holmes	Woody Strode
J.W.	Bill Graham
Solly	Dayton Allen
Ling	Kim Chan

and Ed Rowan (Messiah), Leonard Termo (Danny), Vince Hoods: George Cantero, Brian Tarantina, Bruce MacVittie, James Russo, Bumpy Hoods: Giancarlo Esposito, Bruce Hubbard, Rony Clanton (Holstein), Damien Leake (Jewett), Bill Cobbs (Big Joe), Joe Lynn (Flores), Oscar Barnes (Spanish Henry), Edward Zang (Clerk), Sandra Beall (Myrtle), Zane Mark (Duke Ellington), Ton Signorelli (Murdock), Paul Herman, Randle Mell (Cops), Steve Vignari (Trigger Mike), Susan Meschner (Gypsie), Gregory Rozakis (Chaplin), Marc Coppola (Husing), Norma Jean Darden (Elida), Robert Earl Jones (Stage Door Joe), Vincent Jerosa (James Cagney), Rosalind Harris (Fanny Brice)

Top Left: John Ryan, Bob Hoskins, Fred Gwynne,
James Remar Below: Lonette McKee
© Orion Pictures

Gregory Hines, Diane Lane, Richard Gere

Bob Hoskins, Fred Gwynne Above: Maurice Hines, Gregory Hines Top: Richard Gere, Diane Lane

Richard Gere, Diane Lane Above: Gregory Hines Top: Diane Lane, James Remar

STARMAN

(COLUMBIA) Producer, Larry J. Franco; Director, John Carpenter; Screenplay, Bruce A. Evans, Raymond Gideon; Executive Producer, Michael Douglas; Photography, Donald M. Morgan; Designer, Daniel Lomino; Editor, Marion Rothman; Co-producer, Barry Bernardi; Music, Jack Nitzsche; Production Manager, Tom Joyner; Assistant Directors, Larry Franco, Jeffrey Chernov; Designer, William Joseph Durrell, Jr.; Production Coordinator, Anna Zappia; Special Effects, Roy Arbogast, Bruce Nicholson, Michael McAlister; Associate Producers, Bruce A. Efans, Raynold Gideon; In Panavision, MGM color and Dolby Stereo; Rated PG; 115 minutes; December release

CAST

Starman	Jeff Bridges
Jenny Hayden	Karen Allen
Mark Shermin	Charles Martin Smith
George Fox	Richard Jaeckel
Major Bell	Robert Phalen
Sergeant Lemon	Tony Edwards
Brad Heinmuller	John Walter Davis
Deer Hunter	Ted White
Cops	Dirk Blocker, M. C. Gainey
Hot Rodder	Sean Faro
Cook	Buck Flower
Scientist	Russ Benning
Marine Lieutenant	Ralph Coshan
Fox's Assistant	David Wells
NSA Officer	Anthony Grumbach
S-61 Pilot	Jim Deeth
Gas Station Attendant	Alex Daniels
Gas Customer	Carol Rosenthal
Trucker	Mickey Jones
Roadhouse Waitress	Lu Leonard
Bus Driver	Charlie Hughes
Police Sergeant	Byron Walls
Truck Stop Waitress	Betty Bunch
Roadblock Lieutenant	Victor McLemore
Roadblock Sergeant	Steven Brennan
Bracero Wife	Pat Lee
Girl Barker	Judith Kim
Cafe Waiter	Ronald Colby
State Trooper	Robert Stein
Donnie Bob	Kenny Call
Hunters	Jeff Ramsey, Jerry Gatlin
Lettermen	David Daniell, Randy Tutton

Karen Allen, Jeff Bridges Top Left: Karen Allen Below: Richard Jaeckel
© *Columbia Pictures*

Jeff Bridges, Karen Allen
Top: Charles Martin Smith

CITY HEAT

(WARNER BROS.) Producer, Fritz Manes; Director, Richard Benjamin; Screenplay, Sam O. Brown, Joseph C. Stinson; Story, Sam O. Brown; Photography, Nick McLean; Designer, Edward Carfagno; Editor, Jacqueline Cambas; Music, Lennie Niehaus; Production Manager, Fritz Manes; Assistant Directors, David Valdes, L. Dean Jones, Jr., Matt Earl Beesley; Costumes, Norman Salling; In Technicolor and Dolby Stereo; Rated PG; 97 minutes; December release

CAST

Lt. Speer	Clint Eastwood
Mike Murphy	Burt Reynolds
Addy	Jane Alexander
Caroline Howley	Madeline Kahn
Primo Pitt	Rip Torn
Ginny Lee	Irene Cara
Dehl Swift	Richard Roundtree
Leon Coll	Tony LoBianco
Lonnie Ash	William Sanderson
Troy Roker	Nicholas Worth
Nino	Robert Davi
Dub Slack	Jude Farese
Fat Freddie	John Hancock
Tuck	Tab Thacker
Counterman Louie	Gerald S. O'Loughlin
Bruisers	Bruce M. Fischer, Art LaFleur
Aram Strossell	Jack Nance
Redhead Sherry	Dallas Cole
Referee	Lou Filippo
Vint Diestock	Michael Maurer
Keith Stoddard	Preston Sparks

and Ernie Sabella, Christopher Michael Moore, Carey Loftin, Harry Caesar, Charles Parks, Hamilton Camp, Arthur Malet, Fred Lerner, George Orrison, Beau Starr, Joan Shawlee, Minnie Lindsey, Darwyn Swalve, Tom Spratley, Bob Terhune, Holgie Forrester, Harry Demopoulos, Jim Lewis, Edwin Prevost, Alfie Wise, Hank Calia, Alex Plasschaert, Daphne Eckler, Lonna Montrose

Right: Madeline Kahn, Burt Reynolds
Top: Clint Eastwood, Jane Alexander
© *Warner Bros.*

Richard Roundtree, Irene Cara

Burt Reynolds, Clint Eastwood

PROTOCOL

(WARNER BROS.) Producer, Anthea Sylbert; Director, Herbert Ross; Executive Producer, Goldie Hawn; Screenplay, Buck Henry; Story, Charles Shyer, Nancy Meyers, Harvey Miller; Photography, William A. Fraker; Designer, Bill Malley; Editor, Paul Hirsch; Music, Basil Poledouris; Associate Producer, Lewis J. Rachmil; Costumes, Wayne A. Finkelman; Production Manager, Jack Roe; Assistant Directors, John Kretchmer, Dennis Maguire; Art Director, Tracy Bousman; Choreographer, Charlene Painter; Special Effects, Phil Cory; In Technicolor and Dolby Stereo; Rated PG; 96 minutes; December release

CAST

Sunny	Goldie Hawn
Michael Ransome	Chris Sarandon
Emir	Richard Romanus
Nawaf Al Kabeer	Andre Gregory
Mrs. St. John	Gail Strickland
Hilley	Cliff DeYoung
Crowe	Keith Szarabajka
Hassler	Ed Begley, Jr.
Vice President Merck	James Staley
Lou	Kenneth Mars
Ella	Jean Smart
Donna	Maria O'Brien
Ben	Joel Brooks
Jerry	Grainger Hines
Senator Norris	Kenneth McMillan
Mr. Davis	Richard Hamilton
Mrs. Davis	Mary Carver
Jimmy	Jack Ross Obney
Charmaine	Kathleen York
Bobbie	Georganne LaPiere
Gloria	Pamela Myers

and Joe George, Tom Spratley, Dortha Duckworth, Sally Thorner, Jeanne Mori, Elizabeth Anderson, Archie Hahn, George D. Wallace, Julie Hampton, Thom Sharp, Paul Willson, Holly Roberts, Lyman Ward, Joe Lambie, Daphne Maxwell, Michael Zand, Cece Cole, Roger Til, Marcella Saint-Amant, Ellen Tobie, Alice O'Connor, A. S. Csaky, Ken Gibbel, Ken Hill, Albert Leong, Peter Pan, Robert Donovan, Amanda Bearse, Marcie Barkin, Deborah Dutch, Lorraine Fields

Right: Goldie Hawn, Chris Sarandon
Top: Goldie Hawn, Richard Romanus
© *Warner Bros.*

Keith Szarabajka, Gail Strickland, Goldie Hawn, Andre Gregory

BEVERLY HILLS COP

(PARAMOUNT) Producers, Don Simpson, Jerry Bruckheimer; Director, Martin Brest; Screenplay, Daniel Petrie, Jr; Story, Mr. Petrie, Danilo Bach; Photography, Bruce Surtees; Designer, Angelo Graham; Editors, Billy Weber, Arthur Coburn; Associate Producer, Linda Horner; Music, Harold Faltermeyer; Costumes, Tom Bronson; Executive Producer-Production Manager, Mike Moder; Assistant Directors, Peter Bogart, Richard Graves; Art Director, James J. Murakami; In Technicolor and Dolby Stereo; Rated R; 105 minutes; December release

CAST

Axel Foley	Eddie Murphy
Det. Billy Rosewood	Judge Reinhold
Sgt. Taggart	John Ashton
Jenny Summers	Lisa Eilbacher
Lt. Bogomil	Ronny Cox
Victor Maitland	Steven Berkoff
Mikey Tandino	James Russo
Zack	Jonathan Banks
Chief Hubbard	Stephen Elliott
Inspector Todd	Gilbert R. Hill
Det. Foster	Art Kimbro
Det. McCabe	Joel Bailey
Serge	Bronson Pinchot
Jeffrey	Paul Reiser
Casey	Michael Champion
Cigarette Buyer	Frank Pesce
Truck Driver	Gene Borkan
Hotel Manager	Michael Gregory
Hotel Clerk	Alice Cadogan
Donny	Philip Levien
Maitland Receptionist	Karen Mayo-Chandler
Beverly Hills Cops	Gerald Berns, William Wallace
Room Service Waiter	Israel Juarbe
Bell Hop	Randy Gallion
Banana Man	Damon Wayans
Crate Openers	Chuck Adamson, Chip Heller
Warehouse Night Supervisor	Rick Overton
Warehouse Security Guard	Rex Ryon
Warehouse Clerks	Michael Pniewski, Douglas Warhit
Holdup Men	Paul Drake, Tom Everett
Waitress	Sally Kishbaugh
Valet	Barry Shade
Harrow Club Maitre d'	Jack Heller
Harrow Club Arresting Officer	Michael Harrington
Dispatcher	David Wells
Det. Owneby	Scott Murphy
Detroit Cops	Dennis Madden, John Achorn, John Pettis
Barmaid	Darwyn Carson
Pool Player	Mark E. Corry
Maitland Body Guard	Thomas J. Hageboek

Left: Eddie Murphy, Judge Reinhold, John Ashton
Top: Eddie Murphy, Lisa Eilbacher, Judge Reinhold
© *Paramount Pictures*

Steven Berkoff, Eddie Murphy

Michael Chapman, Eddie Murphy,
Lisa Eilbacher, Jonathan Banks

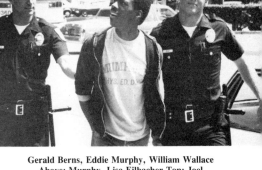

**Paul Reiser, Eddie Murphy Above: Bronson
Pinchot, Murphy Top: Mark E. Corry, Murphy**

**Gerald Berns, Eddie Murphy, William Wallace
Above: Murphy, Lisa Eilbacher Top: Joel
Bailey, Murphy, Art Kimbro**

THE FLAMINGO KID

(20th CENTURY-FOX/EDGEWOOD) Producer, Michael Phillips; Director, Garry Marshall; Screenplay, Neal Marshall, Garry Marshall; Story, Neal Marshall; Photography, James A. Contner; Designer, Ellen Mirojnick; Associate Producer, Nick Abdo; Editor, Priscilla Nedd; Production Manager, Thomas J. Kane; Assistant Directors, Stephen J. Lim, Mark McGann, Chris Griffin; Art Director, Duke Durfee; Assistant Director-Production Associate, Nan Bernstein; Presented by ABC Motion Pictures; A Mercury Entertainment production in DeLuxe Color; Rated PG13; 100 minutes; December release

CAST

Jeffrey Willis	Matt Dillon
Arthur Willis	Hector Elizondo
Ruth Willis	Molly McCarthy
Nikki Willis	Martha Gehman
Phil Brody	Richard Crenna
Phyllis Brody	Jessica Walter
Joyce Brody	Carole R. Davis
Carla Samson	Janet Jones
Steve Dawkins	Brian McNamara
Hawk Ganz	Fisher Stevens
Fortune Smith	Leon Robinson
Alfred Schultz	Bronson Pinchot
Colonel Cal Eastland	Frank Campanella
Charlie Cooper	Richard Stahl
Mario Minetta	Joe Grifasi
Pat McCarty	Ron McLarty
Jerry Berlin	Seth Allen
Big Sid	Irving Metzman
Lewis Madrone	Adam Klugman
Danny Walsh	Ray Roderick
Freddy	Googy Gress
Mrs. Unger	Sharon Thomas
Turk & Dirk	Barbarian Brothers
Dance Instructor	Christopher Chadman
Dr. Gold	Martin Chatinover
Bimbettes	Lisa Beth Ross, Laurie Stratford
Paul Hirsch	Steven Weber
Donny	Eric Douglas

and Marisa Tomei, Tracy Reiner, Kristina Kossi, Bobbie Jo Burke, Leslie S. Sachs, Michael Mahon, Lee Morey, Jillian Scharf, Carol Williard, Richard Buck, Bradley Kane, Linda Costa, Lauren Costa, Peter Costa, Scott Marshall, Blake Brocksmith, Steve Whitting, Freddy Frogs, Lee Steele, Beth Noreen Einhorn, Bo Sabato, Frances Peach, Jack Danny Foster, John Turturro, Mark Strait, Mike Markowitz, Kathi Marshall, Novella Nelson, David Berry, Mark Kaplan, George Blumenthal, Mel Allen

Left: Janet Jones, Matt Dillon
Top: Brian McNamara, Dillon, Leon
Robinson © *ABC Motion Pictures*

Richard Crenna, Jessica Walter

Richard Crenna, Matt Dillon,
Hector Elizondo

Janet Jones, Matt Dillon Above: Dillon,
Fisher Stevens, Ray Roderick, Adam Klugman
Top: Dillon, Richard Crenna

Richard Crenna, Matt Dillon
Top: Dillon, Hector Elizondo

JOHNNY DANGEROUSLY

(20th CENTURY-FOX) Producer, Michael Hertzberg; Director, Amy Heckerling; Screenplay, Norman Steinberg, Bernie Kukoff, Harry Colomby, Jeff Harris; Executive Producers, Bud Austin, Harrly Colomby; Photography, David M. Walsh; Editor, Pem Herring; Designer, Joseph R. Jennings; Choreography and Musical Staging, Tony Stevens; Title Song written and performed by "Weird Al" Yankovic; Music, John Morris; Associate Producer, Neil A. Machlis; Production Manager, Neil A. Machlis; Assistant Directors, Bill Beasley, Chris Ryan, Carol Green; Costumes, Patricia Norris; Production Coordinator, Chriss Strauss; In DeLuxe Color; Rated PG13; 89 minutes; December release

CAST

Johnny Dangerously	Michael Keaton
Vermin	Joe Piscopo
Lil	Marilu Henner
Mom	Maureen Stapleton
Dundee	Peter Boyle
Tommy	Griffin Dunne
Sally	Glynnis O'Connor
The Pope	Dom DeLuise
Maroni	Richard Dimitri
Burr	Danny DeVito
Pat	Ron Carey
Vendor	Ray Walston
Arthur	Dick Butkus
Young Johnny	Byron Thames
Desk Sergeant	Alan Hale
Charley	Scott Thomson
Cleaning Lady	Sudie Bond
Dutch	Mark Jantzen
Manny	Gary Watkins
Vito	Mike Bacarella
Mayor	Hank Garrett
Tony Scarano	Leonard Termo
Young Tommy	Troy W. Slaten
Boy in suit	Alexander Hertzberg
Young Vermin	Georg Olden
Mrs. Capone	Cynthia Szigeti
Girl on steps	Elizabeth Arlen
Woman	Doris Grossman
Prisoner #5	Richard Warwick
Blond Girl	Katie LaBourdette

and Norman Steinberg, Frank Slaten, Dean R. Miller, Mike Finneran, Neal Israel, Edward C. Short, Shelley Pogoda, Jerome Michaels, Russell Forte, Jack Nance, Joy Michael, Richard L. Rosenthal, Paul B. Brice, Carl A. Gottlieb, Paula Dell, Harvey Parry, Jeffrey Weissman, Richard A. Roth, Chuck Hicks, Bob Eubanks, Claudia Kim, Trisha Long, Hal Riddle, Will Seltzer, Mert Rich, Dick Dalduzzi, Gordon Zimmerman

Left: Maureen Stapleton, Michael Keaton
Top: Michael Keaton, Joe Piscopo

Michael Keaton

Michael Keaton and "flappers"

Joe Piscopo, Michael Keaton, Marilu Henner Top Left: Michael Keaton, Peter Boyle, Michael Hertzberg Below: Keaton, Boyle Right: Michael Keaton

DUNE

(UNIVERSAL) Producer, Raffaella DeLaurentiis; Direction and Screenplay, David Lynch; Based on novel by Frank Herbert; Photography, Freddie Francis; Designer, Anthony Masters; Editor, Antony Gibbs; Music, Toto; Special Effects, Kit West, Albert J. Whitlock; Charles L. Finance, Barry Nolan; Costumes, Bob Ringwood; Assistant Director-Associate Producer, Jose Lopez Rodero; Production Coordinator, Golda Offenheim; Art Directors, Pierluigi Basile, Benjamin Fernandez; In Todd AO and Technicolor; Soundtrack on Polydor Records; Rated PG13; 140 minutes; December release

CAST

Lady Jessica	Francesca Annis
Baron's Doctor	Leonardo Cimino
Piter DeVries	Brad Dourif
Padishah Emperor Shaddam IV	Jose Ferrer
Shadout Mapes	Linda Hunt
Thufir Hawat	Freddie Jones
Duncan Idaho	Richard Jordan
Paul Atreides	Kyle MacLachlan
Princess Irulan	Virginia Madsen
Rev. Mother Ramallo	Silvano Mangano
Stilgar	Everett McGill
Baron Vladimir Harkonnen	Kenneth McMillan
Nefud	Jack Nance
Rev. Mother Gaius Helen Mohiam	Sian Phillips
Duke Leto Atreides	Jurgen Prochnow
The Beast Rabban	Paul Smith
Gurney Halleck	Patrick Stewart
Feyd Rautha	Sting
Dr. Wellington Yueh	Dean Stockwell
Dr. Kynes	Max von Sydow
Alia	Alicia Roanne Witt
Chani	Sean Young

Left: Kyle MacLachlan, Jurgen Prochnow, Francesca Annis Top: Virginia Madsen

Sting

Kyle MacLachlan, Sean Young

**Sian Phillips, Jose Ferrer Above: Linda
Hunt Top: Patrick Stewart, Kyle MacLachlan,
Max von Sydow, Jurgen Prochnow**

Sean Young, Kyle MacLachlan Above: Brad Dourif,
Jurgen Prochnow, Kenneth McMillan Top: Prochnow,
Dean Stockwell

Zeljko Ivanek, Jack Lemmon

MASS APPEAL

(UNIVERSAL) Producers, Lawrence Turman, David Foster; Director, Glenn Jordan; Screenplay, Bill C. Davis from his play of same title; Photography, Don Peterman; Editor, John Wright; Music, Bill Conti; In color; Rated PG; 100 minutes; December release

CAST

Father Farley	Jack Lemmon
Mark Dolson	Zeljko Ivanek
Monsignor Burke	Charles Durning
Margaret	Louise Latham
Mrs. Hart	Alice Hirson
Mrs. Hart's Mother	Helene Heigh
Marion Hart	Sharee Gregory
Father De Nicola	James Ray
Mrs. Dolson	Lois De Banzie
Liz Dolson	Talia Balsam
Mr. Dolson	Jerry Hardin

Jack Lemmon (also above),
Zeljko Ivanek

Zeljko Ivanek, Jack Lemmon
Above: Charles Durning, Lemmon
Top: Louise Latham, Ivanek

Jack Lemmon, Zeljko Ivanek
Above: Ivanek, Charles Durning
Top: Ivanek, Talia Balsom

113

2010

(MGM/UA) Produced, Directed, Written and Photographed by Peter Hyams; Based on novel by Arthur C. Clarke; Visual Effects, Richard Edlund; Special Effects, Henry Millar; Editor, James Mitchell; Music, David Shire; In Panavision, color and Dolby Stereo; Rated PG; 157 minutes; December release

CAST

Heywood Floyd	Roy Scheider
Walter Curnow	John Lithgow
Tanya Kirbuk	Helen Mirren
R. Chandra	Bob Balaban
Dave Bowman	Keir Dullea
Hal 9000	Douglas Rain
Caroline Floyd	Madolyn Smith
Dimitri Moisevitch	Dana Elcar
Christopher Floyd	Taliesin Jaffe
Victor Milson	James McEachin
Betty Fernandez	Mary Jo Deschanel
Maxim Brailovsky	Elya Baskin
Vladimir Rudinko	Savely Kramarov
Vasali Oriov	Oleg Rudnik
Irina Yakunina	Natasha Schneider
Yuri Svetlanov	Vladimir Skornarovsky
Mikolai Ternovsky	Victor Steinbach
Alexander Kovalev	Jan Triska

**Left: Keir Dullea Above: Bob Balaban,
Roy Scheider, John Lithgow
© *MGM/UA Entertainment Co.***

**Victor Steinbach, Jan Triska, Oleg Rudnik, Helen Mirren, Vladimir Skomarovsky,
Elya Baskin, Savely Kramarov, Natasha Shneider**

Helen Mirren, Roy Scheider Above: (L) Leonov/Ward Room (R) Keir Dullea, Roy Scheider
Top: (L) Natasha Shneider, Roy Sheider (R) Bob Balaban

Nicolas Cage, Matthew Modine

BIRDY

(TRI-STAR) Producer, Alan Marshall; Director, Alan Parker; Executive Producer, David Manson; Screenplay, Sandy Kroopf, Jack Behr; Based on novel of same title by William Wharton; Photography, Michael Seresin; Editor, Gerry Hambling; Designer, Geoffrey Kirkland; Assistant Director, Chris Soldo; Associate Producer, Ned Kopp; Art Directors, Armin Ganz, Stu Campbell; Music, Peter Gabriel; In Metrocolor and Dolby Stereo; Rated R; 120 minutes; December release

CAST

Birdy	Matthew Modine
Al Columbato	Nicolas Cage
Dr. Weiss	John Harkins
Mr. Columbato	Sandy Baron
Hannah Rourke	Karen Young
Birdy's Father	George Buck
Birdy's Mother	Dolores Sage
Mrs. Columbato	Crystal Field
Renaldi	Bruno Kirby

Top: (L) Matthew Modine, Nicolas Cage
(R) Modine, George Buck Below: Cage, Modine
(L) Sandy Baron, Modine © Tri-Star Pictures

Matthew Modine
Top: (L) Nicolas Cage, Modine (R) Modine

MRS. SOFFEL

(MGM/UA) Producers, Edgar J. Scherick, Scott Rudin, David A. Nicksay; Director, Gillian Armstrong; Screenplay, Ron Nyswaner; Photography, Russell Boyd; Editor, Nicholas Beauman; Music, Mark Isham; Design, Luciana Arrighi; Art Director, Jacques Bradette; Associate Producer, Dennis Jones; Assistant Directors, Mark Egerton, Scott Maitland, Ron Bozman, Glenn H. Randall, Jr; In Metrocolor and Dolby Stereo; Rated PG13; 110 minutes; December release

CAST

Kate Soffel	Diane Keaton
Ed Biddle	Mel Gibson
Jack Biddle	Matthew Modine
Peter Soffel	Edward Hermann
Irene Soffel	Trini Alvarado
Margaret Soffel	Jennie Dundas
Eddie Soffel	Danny Corkill
Clarence Soffel	Harley Cross
Buck McGovern	Terry O'Quinn
Maggie	Pippa Pearthree
Guard Koslow	William Youmans
Guard Reynolds	Maury Chaykin
Matron Garvey	Joyce Ebert
Guard McGarey	John W. Carroll
Jessie Bodyne	Dane Wheeler-Nicholson
Halliday	Wayne Robson
Mr. Stevenson	Les Ruble
Mrs. Stevenson	Paula Trueman

Left: Mel Gibson, Matthew Modine
© MGM/UA Entertainment Co.

Diane Keaton

Diane Keaton, Matthew Modine, Mel Gibson
Above: Diane Keaton

SCANDALOUS (Orion) Producers, Arlene Sellers, Alex Winitsky; Director, Rob Cohen; Screenplay, Rob Cohen, John Byrum; Story, Larry Cohen, Rob Cohen, John Byrum; Co-producer, Martin C. Schute; Executive Producer, Carter DeHaven; Photography, Jack Cardiff; Music, Dave Grusin; Designer, Peter Mullins; Editor, Michael Bradsell; Art Directors, John Siddall, Brian Ackland-Snow; Assistant Directors, Derek Cracknell, Tim Reed, James Corbett; Production Manager, Ron Purdie; Title song sung by Amanda Homi; In Technicolor; Rated PG; 94 minutes; January release. CAST: Robert Hays (Frank), Ron Travis (Porno Director), M. Emmet Walsh (Simon), John Gielgud (Uncle Willie), Ed Dolan (Purser), Paul Reeve (Flight Coordinator), Alita Kennedy (Stewardess), Pamela Stephenson (Fiona), Nancy Wood (Lindsay), Kevin Elyot (Matt), Duncan Preston (Hal), Maureen Bennett (Patti), Peter Dennis (Maitre d'), Preston Lockwood (Leslie), Conover Kennard (Francine), Jim Dale (Insp. Crisp), Jim Magill (The Bobby), Mike Walling (Scotty), Stuart Saunders (Croft), Albert Moses (Vishnu), Toby Robins (Pamela), Maggie Flint (Landlady)

LOVELESS (Atlantic) Producers, Grafton Nunes, A. K. Ho; Screenplay and Direction, Kathryn Bigelow, Monty Montgomery; Photography, Doyle Smith; Editor, Nancy Kanter; In color; Rated R; 84 minutes; January release. CAST: J. Don Ferguson (Tarver), Willem Dafoe (Vance), Marin Kanter (Telena), Robert Gordon (Davis), Tina L. Hotsky (Debbie), Lawrence Matarese (LaVille), Daniel Rosen (Ricky), Philip Mont Kimbrough (Hurley), Ken Call (Buck)

HOT DOG (MGM/UA) Producer, Edward S. Feldman; Director, Peter Markle; Screenplay, Mike Marvin; Photography, Paul G. Ryan; Editor, Stephen Rivkin; Music, Peter Bernstein; In color; Rated R; 96 minutes; January release. CAST: David Naughton (Dan), Patrick Houser (Harkin), Tracy N. Smith (Sunny), John Patrick Reger (Rudi), Frank Koppola (Squirrel), James Saito (Kendo), Shannon Tweed (Sylvia), George Theobald (Slasher), Marc Vance (Heinz), Erik Watson (Fergy), Lynn Wieland (Michelle)

ANGEL (New World) Producers, Roy Watts, Don Borchers; Director, Robert Vincent O'Neil; Screenplay, Mr. O'Neil, Joseph M. Cala; Photography, Andy Davis; Editors, Charles Bornstein, Will Henderson; Music, Craig Saffin; In color; Rated R; 93 minutes; January release. CAST: Donna Wilkes (Angel/Molly), Rory Calhoun (Kit), John Diehl (Billy Boy), Cliff Gorman (Lt. Andrews), Dick Shawn (Mae), Susan Tyrrell (Mosler)

SURF II (International Film) Producers, George G. Braunstein, Ron Hamady; Direction-Screenplay, Randall Badat; Executive Producers, Frank D. Tolin, Lou George; Photography, Alex Phillips, Jr.; Editor, Jackie Cambas; Assistant Director, D. Scott Easton; Art Director, Jeff Staggs; Costumes, Carin Berger; In DeLuxe Color; Rated R; 91 minutes; January release. CAST: Eddie Deezen (Menlo), Linda Kerridge (Sparkel), Cleavon Little (Daddy), Peter Isacksen (Breaker), Lyle Waggoner (Chief), Eric Stoltz (Chuck), Jeffrey Rodgers (Bob), Ruth Buzzi (Chuck's Mother), Carol Wayne (Jocko's Mother), Terry Kiser (Jocko's Father), Tom Villard (Jocko), Corinne Bohrer (Cindy Lou), Lucinda Dooling (LindySue)

NIGHT OF THE ZOMBIES (MPM) Director, Vincent Dawn; Screenplay, Claudio Fragasso, J. M. Cunilles; Photography, John Cabrera; Music, Goblin; In color; Not rated; January release. CAST: Margit Evelyn Newton, Frank Garfield, Selan Karay, Robert O'Neil, Luis Fonoll, Gaby Renom, Ester Mesina, Victor Israel

PORTRAIT OF A HITMAN (Wildfire) Producers, James R. Rokos, Andrej Krakowski; Director, Allan A. Buckhantz; Screenplay, Yabo Yablonsky; In color; Rated R; 85 minutes; January release. CAST: Jack Palance (Jimbuck), Bo Svenson (Michael), Richard Roundtree (Coco), Ann Turkel (Cathy), Rod Steiger (Max), Richard Ahn (Wong), Herb Jeffries (Charlie), Conrad Bachmann (George), John Dresden (Volsted), Ed Ness (Capt. Ed), Garrison True (Joe), Carla Haley (Della), Gloria Lynn Dyer (Nurse Gregg), Monica Peterson (Mrs. Roberts), Robert Starks (Louie)

GOODBYE PORKPIE (New Zealand) Director, Geoff Murphy; In color; Rated R; January release. CAST: Kelly Johnson (Gerry), Tony Barry (John), Claire Oberman (Shirl)

MARVIN AND TIGE (Major Films) Producer, Wanda Dell; Executive Producers, Wanda Dell, Frank Menke; Director, Eric Weston; Screenplay, Dell and Weston; Based on novel by Frankcina Glass; Photography, Brian West; Editor, Fabien Dahlen Tordjmann; Music, Patrick Williams; Art Directors, Paul Rhudy, Frank Blair; Costumes, Cheryl Kilborn, Christine Goluding; Associate Producer, Elayne Ceder; Assistant Director, Joan Feinstein; In DeLuxe Color; Rated PG; 104 minutes; January release. CAST: John Cassavetes (Marvin), Billy Dee Williams (Richard), Denise Nicholas-Hill (Vanessa), Gibran Brown (Tige), Fay Hauser (Brenda), Georgia Callen (Carrie)

Kathleen Sullivan, Clayton Day
in "Deep in the Heart"
© Warner Bros.

DEEP IN THE HEART (Warner Bros.) Produced, Directed and Written by Tony Garnett; Co-Producer, David Streit; Music, Mike Post; Photography, Charles Stewart; Editor, William Shapter; Designer, Lilly Kilvert; Supervisor, Pat Churchill; Assistant Directors, John Colwell, Forrest Murray; Costumes, Janet Lawler; Production Coordinator, Karen Avila; In DuArt Color; Rated R; 99 minutes; January release. CAST: Karen Young (Kathleen Sullivan), Suzie Humphreys (Nancy), Helena Humann (Miss Davis), Clayton Day (Larry), Ben Jones (Chuck), Jane Abbott, Jane Simoneau, Peggy Akin (Ladies), Joe Bowman (Trick Shooter), John Tufts, Jr. (Tranquilizer Man), Norine Williams (Student with baby), Kitty Harlen (Mrs. Sullivan), Jim Harlen (Mr. Sullivan), Sam Shipp, Gary Richardson, Vincent G. Zubras, Jr. (Lawyers), Glenda Standifer (Barmaid), Barbara Woodard (Boxing MC), Robert Hibbard (Detective), William Brantley (Desk Sgt.), Steve Chambless (Doctor), Michael O'Shea (Priest), Maggie Attaway (Hairdresser), Larry Corwin (Jim), Kenneth Garner (Masters), Bob Rankin (Knife Expert), Iris Dodd (Woman Deputy), Ray Brantley (Gun Salesman), Gordon Fox (Survivalist), Raymond Rios (Announcer), Holly Woods (Holly), Stephanie Thomas (Stephanie)

THE POWER (Film Ventures International) Producer, Jeffrey Obrow; Direction, Screenplay, Editing, Jeffery Obrow, Stephen Carpenter; Associate Producer, Stacey Giachino; Story, Jeffrey Obrow, Stephen Carpenter, John Penney, John Hopkins; Photography, Stephen Carpenter; Music, Chris Young; Design, Chris Hopkins; Assistant Director, John Hopkins; Production Manager, Samson Aslanian; Color by Getty Film Lab; Rated R; 84 minutes; January release. CAST: Susan Stokey (Sandy), Warren Lincoln (Jerry), Lisa Erickson (Julie), Chad Christian (Tommy), Ben Gilbert (Matt), Chris Morrill (Ron), Rod Mays (Lee), J. Dinan Myrtetus (Francis), Jay Fisher (Raphael), Costy Basile (Jorge), Juan Del Valle (Jeep Driver), Alice Champlin (Roxanne), Gabe Cohen (Marty), Milton Robinson (Jack), Steve Nagle (Driver), Barbara Murray (Tommy's Mother), Joseph Scott (Doctor), Richard Cowgill (Cemetery Guard)

SOLE SURVIVOR (International Film) Producer, Don Barkemeyer; Executive Producer, Sal Romeo; Direction/Screenplay, Thom Eberhardt; Photography, Ross Carpenter; In CFI color; Rated R; 90 minutes; January release. CAST: Anita Skinner, Kurt Johnson, Caren Larkey

Robert Hays, John Gielgud
in "Scandalous" © Orion Pictures

"In Our Hands"
© *Almi Pictures*

Valerie Harper, Michelle Johnson, Demi Moore,
Joseph Bologna, Michael Caine in "Blame It on
Rio" © *Sherwood Productions*

SAHARA (MGM/UA) Producers, Menahem Golan, Yoram Globus; Executive Producer, Teri Shields; Director, Andrew V. McLaglen; Screenplay, James R. Silke; Photography, David Gurfinkel; Designer, Luciano Spadoni; Music, Ennio Morricone; Associate Producer, Rony Yacov; Production Manager, Omri Maron; In color; Rated PG; 104 minutes; January release. CAST: Brooke Shields (Dale), Lambert Wilson (Jaffar), Horst Buchholz (von Glessing), John Rhys-Davies (Rasoul), Ronald Lacey (Beg), John Mills (Cambridge), Steve Forrest (R. J.), Perry Lang (Andy), Cliff Potts (String), Terence Hardiman (Browne)

THE PRODIGAL (World Wide) Producer, Ken Wales; Direction and Screenplay, James F. Collier; Executive Producer, William F. Brown; Music, Bruce Broughton; Photography, Frank Stanley; In color; Rated PG; January release. CAST: John Hammond, Hope Lange, John Cullum, Morgan Brittany, Ian Bannen, Joey Travolta, Arliss Howard

O'HARA'S WIFE (Enfield) Producers, Peter S. Davis, William N. Panzer; Executive Producer, Michael Timothy Murphy; Director, William S. Bartman; Screenplay, James Nasella, Mr. Bartman; Based on story by Mr. Bartman and Joseph Scott Kierland; Photography, Harry Stradling; Editors, George Berndt, James A. Borgardt; Music, Artie Butler; Lyrics, Molly-Ann Leikin; Art Director, Robert Zentis; Costumes, Madeline Ann Graneto; Assistant Director, Richard Luke Rothschild; In DeLuxe Color; Not rated; 87 minutes; January release. CAST: Edward Asner (Bob O'Hara), Mariette Hartley (Harry O'Hara), Jodie Foster (Barbara), Perry Lang (Rob), Tom Bosley (Fred), Ray Walston (Walter Tatum), Allen Williams (Billy), Mary Joe Catlett (Gloria), Nelson Welch (Nelson), Richard Schaal (Jerry), Nehemiah Persoff (Dr. Fischer), Kelly Bishop (Beth), Eric Kilpatrick (Policeman)

SACRED GROUND (Pacific International) Producer, Arthur R. Dubs; Direction, Screenplay, Photography, Charles B. Pierce; Music, Gene Kauer, Don Bagley; Editors, David E. Jackson, Steven L. Johnson, Lynne Southerland; In CFI Color; Rated PG; 100 minutes; January release. CAST: Tim McIntire (Matt), Jack Elam (Witcher), L. Q. Jones (Tolbert), Mindi Miller (Wannetta), Eloy Phil Casados (Prairie Fox), Serene Hedin (Little Doe), Vernon Foster (Wounded Leg), Lefty Wild Eagle (Medicine Man), Larry Kenoras (Brave Beaver)

IN OUR HANDS (Libra Cinema 5) Producers, Robert Richter, Stanley Warnow; Associate Producer, Jacqueline Leopold; Editors, Stanley Warnow, Sharon Sachs, Anthony Forma, Donald Blank, Gloria Williams, Joan Morris; Production Manager, Robert Nickson; Coordinating Producer, Nina Streich; Executive Producer, Leon Falk; In color; Not rated; 90 minutes; February release. Appearing in the film: James Taylor, Holly Near, Rita Marley, Pete Seeger, Carly Simon, Peter, Paul and Mary, John Hall, Lucy Simon, House of the Lord Choir, Fred Moore, Are & Be Ensemble, Judy Gorman Jacobs, Meryl Streep, Roy Scheider, John Shea, Ellen Burstyn, Kathryn Walker, Bob Balaban, Orson Welles, Jerry Stiller, Anne Meara, Dr. Helen Caldicott, Dr. Benjamin Spock, Rev. William Sloan Coffin, Randall Forsburg, Rep. Edward Markey, Maibritt Thorin, Rev. Roy Nichols, Jack Sheinkman, Cleveland Robinson, atomic bomb survivors from Hiroshima and Nagasaki

DEATHSTALKER (New World) Producer, James Sbardellati; Co-producers, Hector Olivera, Alex Sessa; Director, John Watson; Screenplay, Howard Cohen; Photography, Leonardo Rodriguez Solis; Editors, John Adams, Silvia Ripoli; Art Director, Emilio Basaldua; Music, Oscar Cardozo Ocampo; Costumes, Maria Julia Bertott; Associate Producer, Frank Isaac; Assistant Director, Amerik Von Zaratt; In color; Rated R; 80 minutes; February release. CAST: Richard Hill (Deathstalker), Barbi Benton (Codille), Richard Brooker (Oghris), Lana Clarkson (Kaira), Victor Bo (Kang), Bernard Erhard (Munkar), August Larreta (Salmaron), Lillian Ker (Toralva), Marcos Woinsky (Gargit)

THE HOUSE WHERE DEATH LIVES (New American Films) Executive Producer, John Cofrin; Producers, Alan Beattie, Peter Shanaberg; Director, Alan Beattie; Screenplay, Jack Viertel from story by Mr. Beattie; Photography, Stephen Posey; Editor, Robert Leighton; Music, Don Peake; Art Director, Steven Legler; Assistant Director, David Blocker; Associate Producers, David Charles Thomas, Thomas Viertel; In Metrocolor; Rated R; 82 minutes; February release. CAST: Patricia Pearcy (Meredith), David Hayward (Jeffrey), John Dukakis (Gabriel), Joseph Cotten (Ivar), Leon Charles (Phillip), Alice Nunn (Duffy), Patrick Pankhurst (Wilfred), Simone Griffeth (Pamela)

CHORDS OF FAME (Pretty Smart) Executive Producer, David Sternburg; Producers, Sternburg, Mady Schutzman, Michael Korolenko; Director, Michael Korolenko; Written by Mady Schutzman; Photography, John Newby; Editor-Associate Producer-Co-director, John Bloomgarden; Assistant Director, Randy Sabasala; Music, Mady Schutzman; In DeLuxe Color; Not rated; 88 minutes; February release. A documentary portrait of folksinger Phil Ochs.

Mary Travers, Paul Stookey
"In Our Hands" © *Almi Pictures*

Phil Ochs
in "Chords of Fame"

**Aidan Quinn, Daryl Hannah
in "Reckless" © MGM/UA Entertainment**

**The Beatles in "The Compleat Beatles"
© Teleculture**

BURROUGHS (Citifilmworks) Producers, Howard Brookner, Alan Yentob; Director, Howard Brookner; Photography, Richard L. Camp, Mike Southon, James Lebovitz, Tom Dicillo, Howard Brookner, Cathy Dorsey, Larry Shlu, Anthony Balch; Editors, Scott Vickrey, Ben Morris; In color; Not rated; 86 minutes; February release. A documentary on the life of William S. Burroughs.

RECKLESS (MGM/UA) Producers, Edgar J. Scherick, Scott Rudin; Director, James Foley; Screenplay, Chris Columbus; Photography, Michael Balhaus; Editor, Albert Magnoli; Music, Thomas Newman; In Dolby Stereo and color; Rated R; 90 minutes; February release. CAST: Aidan Quinn (Johnny), Daryl Hannah (Tracey), Kenneth McMillan (John Rourke, Sr.), Cliff DeYoung (Phil), Lois Smith (Mrs. Prescott), Adam Baldwin (Randy), Dan Hedaya (Peter), Billy Jacoby (David), Toni Kalem (Donna), Jennifer Grey (Cathy)

BLAME IT ON RIO (20th Century-Fox) Producer-Director, Stanley Donen; Screenplay, Charlie Peters, Larry Gelbart; Executive Producer, Larry Gelbart; Photography, Reynaldo Villalobos; Associate Producer, Production Manager, Robert E. Relyea; Editors, George Hively, Richard Marden; Assistant Directors, Scott Easton, Jose Joaquin Salles; Art Director, Marcos Flaksman; In Metrocolor; Rated R; 110 minutes; February release. CAST: Michael Caine (Matthew), Joseph Bologna (Victor), Valerie Harper (Karen), Michelle Johnson (Jennifer), Demi Moore (Nicole), Jose Lewgoy (Eduardo), Lupe Gigliotti (Signora Botega), Michael Menaugh (Peter), Ana Lucia Lima, Maria Helena Velasco (Macumba Ladies), Zeni Pereira (Mother of the bride), Eduardo Conde (Singer in club), Betty Von Wien (Isabella), Nelson Dantas (Doctor), Thomas Lee Mahon (Lorenzo), Victor Haim (Bernardo), Jane Duboc (Singer in cafe), Romulo Arantes (Diego), Giovanna Sodre (Astrid), Grupo Senzala (Capoeirista), Angelo Mattos (Dancer)

WEEKEND PASS (Crown International) Producer, Marylin J. Tenser; Direction and Screenplay, Lawrence Bassoff; Co-producer, Michael D. Castle; Photography, Bryan England; Editor, Harry B. Miller III; Art Director, Ivo G. Cristante; Assistant Director, Dan Dugan; Music, John Baer; In DeLuxe Color; Rated R; 92 minutes; February release. CAST: D. W. Brown (Paul), Peter Ellenstein (Lester), Patrick Hauser (Webster), Chip McAllister (Bunker), Pamela G. Kay (Tina) Hilary Shapiro (Cindy), Graem McGavin (Tawny), Daureen Collodel (Heidi), Annette Sinclair (Maxine)

IN SEARCH OF A GOLDEN SKY (Comworld) Director, Jefferson Richard; Screenplay, John Goff, Buck Flower; Executive Producer, James G. Robinson; Music, Bob Summers; An I.P.I. Genaric Film in color; Rated PG; February release. CAST: Charles Napier, George "Buck" Flower, Cliff Osmond

THE COMPLEAT BEATLES MOVIE (TeleCulture) Director, Patrick Montgomery; Written by David Silver; Narrated by Malcolm McDowell; Editor, Pamela Page; Producers, Patrick Montgomery, Stephanie Bennett; A Delilah Film production in Dolby Stereo and color; Not rated; 120 minutes; February release. A documentary on the group's rise and subsequent evolution.

RUNNING HOT (New Line Cinema) Producer, David Calloway; Co-producer, Zachary Feuer; Direction-Screenplay, Mark Griffiths; Executive Producer, Dimitri T. Skouras; Photography, Tom Richmond; Editor, Andy Blumenthal; Music, Al Capps; Production Manager, Dennis Hoffman; Assistant Directors, Steve Buck, Ron Hacohen; Production Coordinator, Deborah Brinkley; Art Director, Anthony Cowley; Designer, Katherine Vallin; Costumes, Jane E. Anderson; In color; Rated R; 95 minutes; February release. CAST: Eric Stoltz (Danny), Stuart Margolin (Trent), Virgil Frye (Pimp), Richard Bradford (Tom), Monica Carrico (Charlene), Louise Baker (Shane), Joe George (Derman), Laurel Patrick (Angie), Sorrells Pickard (Ex-Con), Ben Hammer (Danny's Father), Juliette Cummins (Jenny), Lesley Woods (Charlene's Mother), Bob Carroll (Harry), Clark Howatt (Judge), Geno Havens (Foreman), Seth Kaufman (Bailiff), Dickie Walsh (Dickie)

STUCK ON YOU (Troma) Producers, Lloyd Kaufman, Michael Herz; Directors, Michael Herz, Samuel Weil; Screenplay, Stuart Strutin, Warren Leight, Don Perman, Darren Kloomok, Melanie Mintz, Anthony Gittleson, Duffy Caeser Magesis, Michael Herz, Lloyd Kaufman; Editors, Darren Kloomok, Richard Haines; In color; Rated R; 90 minutes; February release. CAST: Prof. Irwin Corey (Judge), Virginia Penta (Carol), Mark Mikulski (Bill), Albert Pia (Artie), Norma Pratt (Bill's Mother), Daniel Harris (Napoleon), Denise Silbert (Cavewoman), Eddie Brill (Caveman), June Martin (Eve), John Gibham (Adam), Robin Burroughs (Isabella), Carl Sturmer (Columbus), Julie Newdow (Pocahontas), Pat Tallman (Guinevere), Mr. Kent (King Arthur), Barbie Kiellan (Josephine), Louis Homyak (Lance), Ben Kellman (Indian Chief)

**Patrick Houser, Chip McAllister, D. W. Brown,
Peter Ellenstein in "Weekend Pass"
© Crown International**

**Eric Stoltz (R) in "Running Hot"
© New Line Cinema**

Tom Selleck, Jane Seymour
in "Lassiter" © *Pan-Pacific/Warner Bros.*

Tom Selleck, Lauren Hutton
in "Lassiter" © *Pan-Pacific/Warner Bros.*

ANDROID (Island Alive) Producer, Mary Ann Fisher; Executive Producer, Rupert Harvey; Associate Executive Producer, Barry Opper; Director, Aaron Lipstadt; Screenplay, James Reigle, Don Opper; Based on idea by Will Reigle; Photography, Tim Suhrstedt; Art Directors, K. C. Scheibel, Wayne Springfield; Editors, R. J. Kizer, Andy Horvitch; Music, Don Preston; Costumes, Merril Greene, Audrey Kasoff; Production Manager, Charles P. Skouras III; Assistant Directors, Matia Karrell, Stephen Buck; Production Coordinator, Iya Labunka; In color; Rated PG; 81 minutes; February release. CAST: Klaus Kinski (Dr. Daniel), Don Opper (Max), Brie Howard (Maggie), Norbert Weisser (Keller), Crofton Hardester (Mendes), Kendra Kirchner (Cassandra), Gary Corarito, Mary Ann Fisher, Darrel Larson, Ian Scheibel (Terrapol: Neptune), Wayne Springfield, Julia Gibson (Terrapol: Minos), Randy Connor, Roger Kelton, Rachel Talalay, Johanne Todd (Terrapol Landing Party)

CRACKERS (Universal) Producers, Edward Lewis, Robert Cortes; Director, Louis Malle; Screenplay, Jeffrey Fiskin; Photography, Laszlo Kovacs; Designer, John J. Lloyd; Editor, Suzanne Baron; Music, Paul Chihara; Assistant Directors, James Quinn, Carol Green; In Technicolor; Rated PG; 92 minutes; February release. CAST: Donald Sutherland (Weslake), Jack Warden (Garvey), Sean Penn (Dillard), Wallace Shawn (Turtle), Larry Riley (Boardwalk), Trinidad Silva (Ramon), Christine Baranski (Maxine), Charlaine Woodard (Jasmine), Tasia Valenza (Maria), Irwin Corey (Lazzarelli), Edouard DeSoto (Don Fernando), Anna Maria Horsford (Slam Dunk), Mitchell Lichtenstein (Artiste), Marjorie Eaton (Mrs. O'Malley), Edward Call (Darney), Joseph Hindy (Ronnie), Charles Bouvier (Cable Man), Ed Corbett (Kurnitz), Maria Alcorcha (Mama), Raymond Rios (Painter), Elba Montes (Market Woman)

AMERICAN TABOO (Lustgarten) Producers, Steve Lustgarten, Sali Borchman, Ron Schmidt; Director, Lustgarten; Photography, Lee Nesbit, Lustgarten, Eric Edwards, Mark Whitney; Editors, Lustgarten, Schmidt; Music, Dana Libonati, Dan Brandt; In color; Not rated; February release. CAST: Jay Horenstein (Paul), Nicole Harrison (Lisa), Mark Rabiner (Michael), Katherine King (Maggie), Ki Skinner, Suzette Taylor (Models), Dorothy Anton (Lisa's Mother)

GORE VIDAL: THE MAN WHO SAID NO (Alcon) Produced, directed, photographed and edited by Gary Conklin; No other credits; 99 minutes; February release. A documentary depicting Vidal the private man and the literary personality.

LASSITER (Warner Brothers) Producer, Albert S. Ruddy; Director, Roger Young; Screenplay, David Taylor; Executive Producers, Raymond Chow, Andre Morgan; Photography, Gil Taylor; Designer, Peter Mullins; Editor, Benjamin A. Weissman; Associate Producer, Frederick Muller; Production Coordinator, Marilyse Morgan; Assistant Directors, Patrick Clayton, Chris Brock, Callum McDougall; Art Directors, Alan Tomkins, Brian Ackland-Snow; Costumes, Barbara Lane; Choreography, Eleanor Fazan; In Technicolor; Rated R; 100 minutes; February release. CAST: Tom Selleck (Lassiter), Jane Seymour (Sara), Lauren Hutton (Kari), Bob Hoskins (Becker), Joe Regalbuto (Breeze), Ed Lauter (Smoke), Warren Clarke (Max), Edward Peel (Allyce), Paul Antrim (Askew), Christopher Malcolm (Quaid), Barri Houghton (Eddie), Peter Skellern (Pianist), Harry Towb (Roger), Belinda Mayne (Helen), Morgan Sheppard (Sweeney), Brian Coburn (Burto), Jane Wood (Mary), Tristram Jellinek (Phipps), David Warbeck (Agent), Michael Howarth (Commander), Nicholas Bond-Owen (Boy), Eleanor Fazan (Choreographer), George Malpas (Old Man), Fanny Carby (Old Lady), Desmond Barrit, Terence Mountain (Cops)

FIRST CONTACT (Filmakers Library) Produced and Directed by Bob Connolly, Robin Anderson; Photography, Dennis O'Rourke, Tony Wilson; Editors, Stewart Young, Martyn Down; Music, Ron Carpenter; In color, black and white; Not rated; 58 minutes; March release. A record of the 1930 visit of the Leahy brothers to the interior of New Guinea, and their confrontation with thousands of Stone Age people.

MUSICAL PASSAGE (Films Inc.) Producers, Jim Brown, David Karpoff, Ginger Turek; Director, Jim Brown; Photography, Jim Brown; Editor, Paul Barnes; In color; Not rated; 76 minutes; March release. A documentary on the Soviet Emigre Orchestra and its founder Lazar Gosman.

THE ICE PIRATES (MGM/UA) Producer, John Foreman; Director, Stewart Raffill; Screenplay, Mr. Raffill, Stanford Sherman; Photography, Matthew F. Leonetti; Editor, Tom Walls; Music, Bruce Broughton; In color; Rated PG; 96 minutes; March release. CAST: Robert Urich (Jason), Mary Crosby (Princess Karina), Michael D. Roberts (Roscoe), Anjelica Huston (Maida), John Matuszak (Killjoy), Ron Perlman (Zeno), John Carradine (Supreme Commander), Natalie Core (Nanny), Jeremy West (Zorn), Bruce Vilanch (Wendon), Alan Caillou (Count Paisley)

Sean Penn, Larry Riley, Irwin Corey, Donald
Sutherland in "Crackers" © *Universal*

Robert Urich, Mary Crosby in "The Ice
Pirates" © *MGM/UA Entertainment Co.*

Paul Winfield, Debra Winger in "Mike's Murder" © *The Ladd Co.*

"The Secret Agent"

MIKE'S MURDER (Warner Bros.) Executive Producer, Kim Kurumada; Direction and Screenplay, James Bridges; Music, John Barry; Additional Music, Joe Jackson; Photography, Reynaldo Villalobos; Designer, Peter Jamison; Editors, Jeff Gourson, Dede Allen; Associate Producer, Jack Larson; Production Manager, Kim Kurumada; Assistant Directors, Albert Shapiro, Marty Ewing; Art Director, Hub Braden; Production Coordinator, Penny McCarthy; A Skyeway Production in Technicolor; A Ladd Company release; Rated R; 109 minutes; March release. CAST: Debra Winger (Betty), Mark Keyloun (Mike), Paul Winfield (Phillip), Darrell Larson (Pete), Brooke Alderson (Patty), Robert Crosson (Sam), Daniel Shor (Richard), William Ostrander (Randy), Gregory Hormel (Kid Drug Buyer), John Michael Stewart, Victor Perez (Tough Guys), Mark High (Ben), Ken Y. Namba (Sushi Chef), Ruth Winger (Betty's Mother), April Ferry (Boss Lady), Randy White (Boss Man), Robert Kincaid (Bodyguard), Kym Malin, Lori Butler, Dawn Abraham (Beautiful Girls), Freeman King, Alphonse Walter (Killers), James Carrington (Jim), Rebecca Marder, Bruce Marder (Cafe Workers), Sarah Zinsser (Girl in video tape), James Dale Ryan, Robert Johnstreet, Gordon Hoban (Police Technicians), Javier Jose Gonzalez (Bus Stop Boarder), Cliff Jenkins (Bus Boarder), Aurelia Gallardo (Pancho's Waitress), Frank Cavestani (Charles), Spazz Attack (Himself), Johnny B. Frank, MariSol Garcia (Blonde Punkers), Jennifer Dixon, Steve Solberg, Annie Jones, Michael Uhlenkot (Party Goers)

MISUNDERSTOOD (MGM/UA Entertainment) Producer, Tarak Ben Ammar; Director, Jerry Schatzberg; Screenplay, Barra Grant; Based on novel by Florence Montgomery; Executive Producers, Keith Barish, Craig Baumgarten; Associate Producer, Mark Lombardo; Photography, Pasqualino DeSantis; Designer, Joel Schiller; Editor, Marc Laub; Costumes, Jo Ynocencio; Production Manager, Umberto Sambuco; Assistant Directors, Bernard Farrel, Mohamed Ali El Okby, Hanane Ben Mahmoud; In Color; Rated R; 101 minutes; March release. CAST: Gene Hackman (Ned), Henry Thomas (Andrew), Rip Torn (Will), Huckleberry Fox (Miles), Maureen Kerwin (Kate), Susan Anspach (Lily), June Brown (Mrs. Paley), Helen Ryan (Lucy), Nadim Sawalha (Ahmed), Nidal Ashkar (Mrs. Jallouli), Khaled Akrout (Electronic Salesman), Rajah Gafsi (Cafe Owner), Moheddine Mrad (Kassir), James R. Cope (Mr. Grace), Halima Daoud (Aisha), Raad Rawi (Doctor), Habiba (Girl), Fathia Boudabous (Woman in Red Light District), Nabil Massad (Jallouli), Anick Allieres (Marie), Mohamed

Ben Othman (Chocolate Merchant), Abdellatif Hamrouni (Holy Man), Salah Rahmouni (Rachid), Mohamed Dous (Judo Instructor), Tarak Sancho (Ned's Driver), Hattab Dhib (Kassir's Driver), Andre Valiquette (Bob), Dirk Holzapfel (Lucien)

THE SECRET AGENT (First Run Features) Producer, Daniel Keller, Jacki Ochs; Director, Jacki Ochs; Editor, Daniel Keller; Narrator, Max Gail; Score, Country Joe McDonald; A Green Mountain Post Film/Human Arts Association Production; Not rated; 56 minutes; March release with SL-1 (Direct Cinema); Produced, Directed, Written, Photographed and Edited by Diane Orr, C. Larry Roberts; Music, Brian Eno, Popol Vuh; A Beecher Films Production; Not rated; 60 minutes; March release.

CHILDREN OF THE CORN (New World) Producers, Donald P. Borchers, Terrence Kirby; Director, Fritz Kiersch; Screenplay, George Goldsmith; Based on story by Stephen King; Photography, Raoul Lomas; Editor, Harry Keramidas; Music, Jonathan Elias; In color; Rated R; 93 minutes; March release. CAST: Peter Horton (Dr. Stanton), Linda Hamilton (Vicky), R. G. Armstrong (Diehl), John Franklin (Isaac), Courtney Gains (Malachai), Robby Kiger (Job), AnneMarie McEvoy (Sarah), Julie Maddalena (Rachel), Jonas Marlowe (Joseph), John Philbin (Amos), Dan Snook (Boy), David Cowan (Dad), Suzy Southam (Mom), D. G. Johnson (Hansen).

CIRCLE OF POWER (Televicine International) Producer, Gary L. Mehlman; Director, Bobby Roth; Screenplay, Beth Sullivan, Stephen Bello, suggested by book by Gene Church, Conrad D. Carnes; Photography, Alfonso Beato; Editor, Gail Yasunaga; Music, Richard Markowitz; In color; Not rated; 97 minutes; March release. CAST: Yvette Mimieux (Blanca), Christopher Allport (Jack), Cindy Pickett (Lyn), John Considine (Jordan), Walter Olkewicz (Buddy), Leo Rossi (Chris), Scott Marlowe (Ted), Carmen Argenziano (Tony), Mary McCusker (Jean), Denny Miller (Uwe), Hugh Gillin (Ben)

KADDISH (First Run Features) Directed, Produced and Edited by Steve Brand; Associate Producer, Robert Rosenberg; Photography, Robert Achs; Music, Andy Statman; A Ways and Means Production in color; Not rated; 92 minutes; March release. A documentary on the effects of the Holocaust on a Hungarian-born survivor and his American-born son.

Henry Thomas, Gene Hackman in "Misunderstood" © *MGM/UA Entertainment*

"Kaddish" © *First Run Features*

Karin Mani in "Alley Cat"
© Film Ventures International

"The Good Fight"
© Robert Capa

ALLEY CAT (Film Ventures International) Producers, Robert E. Waters, Victor Ordonez; Director, Edward Victor; Screenplay, Robert E. Waters; Associate Producer, David A. Gronsky; Photography, Howard Anderson III; Editor, Robert Ernst; Music, Quito Colayco; Designer, Robert Lee; Production Manager, Mark Defrain; Assistant Directors, Mary Ellen Woods, Adolfo Lopez; Assistant Producer, Bruce M. Mannis; Color by United Color Lab; A Dragonfly Production presented by Edward L. Montoro; Rated R; 89 minutes; March release. CAST: Karin Mani (Billie), Robert Torti (Johnny), Britt Helfer (Hooker), Michael Wayne (Scarface), Jon Greene (Boyle), Jay Fisher (Charles), Claudia Decea (Rose), Tim Cutt (Thomas), Jay Walker (Judge), Moriah Shannon (Sam), Marla Stone (Karen), Kevin Velligan (Gouger), Tony Oliver (Bob), Victoria Shea (Police Lady), Bob Baisa (Capt. Smith), Tom Bismark (Thug), Robert Dennis (Strickland), Peter Furman (Grossman), Mark Zaslove (Bailiff), Mark Defrain, Dennis Keep (Toughs), Gino Valenti (Sgt.), Mark Bradford (Switchboard), Bois Elwell (Director), John Cardona (Bondsman), Rose Dreifus (Kate), Rosemary Patterson (Admitting Clerk), Edward Archer (Accompanist), Dolores Waggoner (Matron), Adolfo Lopez (Gonzales), Robert Noonoo, Ashok Mukhey (Attorneys), Barry Jamesby (Doctor), Patricia Heald (Nurse), Suzan Stadner, Charon Heuer, Beth Staeheli (Guards), Cynthia Helferstay, Roxanne Duvall, Vanessa McCabe, Tracy O'Brien, Irene Waters, Diane Stroebel (Prisoners)

THE GOOD FIGHT (First Run Features) Produced and Directed by Noel Buckner, Mary Dore, Sam Sills; Editor, Noel Buckner; Narrated by Studs Terkel; In color, black and white; Not rated; 98 minutes; March release. A documentary featuring the testimony of 11 veterans of the Lincoln Brigade who went to Spain to fight for the Loyalist cause from 1936–39.

THE HOTEL NEW HAMPSHIRE (Orion) Producer, Neil Hartley; Director, Tony Richardson; Screenplay, Mr. Richardson from novel by John Irving; Photography, David Watkin; Editor, Robert K. Lambert; Music, Offenbach; In Dolby Stereo and color; Rated R; 110 minutes; March release. CAST: Rob Lowe (John), Jodie Foster (Franny), Paul McCrane (Frank), Beau Bridges (Father), Lisa Banes (Mother), Jennie Dundas (Lillie), Seth Green (Egg), Wallace Shawn (Freud), Matthew Modine (Chip Dove), Wilford Brimley (Iowa Bob), Cali Timmins (Bitty), Dorsey Wright (Junior), Anita Morris (Ronda), Nastassja Kinski (Susie), Amanda Plummer (Miss Miscarriage), Matthew Modine (Ernst), Gayle Garfinkle (Screaming Annie)

POLICE ACADEMY (Warner Bros.) Producer, Paul Maslansky; Director, Hugh Wilson; Screenplay, Neal Israel, Pat Proft, Hugh Wilson; Story, Neal Israel, Pat Proft; Photography, Michael D. Margulies; Designer, Trevor Williams; Editors, Robert Brown, Zach Staenberg; Music, Robert Folk; Production Manager, Jim Margellos; Assistant Directors, Michael Zenon, Allan Harmon; Costumes, Christopher Ryan; Production Coordinator, Suzanne Lore; Color by Medallion Labs; A Ladd Company release; Rated R; 101 minutes; March release. CAST: Steve Guttenberg (Carey), Kim Cattrall (Karen), G. W. Bailey (Lt. Harris), Bubba Smith (Moses), Donovan Scott (Leslie), George Gaynes (Commandant Lassard), Andrew Rubin (George), David Graf (Tackleberry), Leslie Easterbrook (Sgt. Callahan), Michael Winslow (Larvell), Debralee Scott (Mrs. Fackler), Bruce Mahler (Doug Fackler), Ted Ross (Capt. Reed), Scott Thompson (Chad), Brant Van Hoffman (Kyle), Marion Ramsey (Laverne), Doug Lennox (Bad Guy), George R. Robertson (Chief Hurnst), Don Lake (Mr. Wig), Bill Lynn (Parking Lot Mgr.), Michael J. Reynolds (Office Executive), Joyce Gordon (Mrs. Thompson), Don Payne (Barber), Bruce McFee (Supply Clerk), Beth Amos (Old Lady), Araby Lockhart (Mrs. Lassard), Barry Greene (Cadet), Gary Farmer (Sidewalk Store), Josef Field, Gary Colwell (Dancers), Jim Bearden (Driver), Fred Brigham (Punk), Marco Bianco, Ted Hanlan, Braun McAsh, Rob Watson (Toughs), Roger Dunn (Booking Sgt.), Wally Bondarenko, J. Winston Carroll, David Clement, George Zeeman (Officers), Gino Marrocco (Arresting Cop), Gene Mack (Thug), Bob Collins (Drill Instructor), Danny Pawlick (Pool Hall Man), Ruth Sisberg (Mayor), Peter Cox, Danny Lima, Dwayne McLean, Brent Meyers, Carole Alderson, Suzanne Barker, Kimberley Foorman, Jayne Broughton, Julie McLeod, Karen Robyn, Joe Dunne

ROTWEILER: DOGS OF HELL (E.O. Corp) Producer, Earl Owensby; Director, Worth Keeter III; Screenplay, Tom McIntyre; In color and 3D; Rated R; March release. CAST: Earl Owensby

THE WORLD OF TOMORROW (Direct Cinema) Produced and Directed by Tom Johnson and Lance Bird in association with the TV Lab at WNET/13; Written by John Crowley; Narrated by Jason Robards; Edited by Kate Hirson; Project Director, Gerald O'Grady; In color, black and white; Not rated; 78 minutes; March release. A documentary of original materials from the 1939 NY World's Fair.

Nastassja Kinski, Rob Lowe, Jodie Foster
in "Hotel New Hampshire" © Orion Pictures

Scott Schwartz, Tristine Skyler, Cinnamon
Idles, Elizabeth Gorcey in "Kidco"
© 20th Century-Fox

KILLPOINT (Crown International) Producers, Frank Harris, Diane Stevenett; Executive Producers, Roger Jacobson, Dana J. Welch; Direction-Screenplay, Frank Harris; Music, Herman Jeffreys, Daryl Stevenett; Assistant Director-Production Manager, Diane Stevenett; Art Director, Larry Westover; In Metrocolor; Rated R; 89 minutes; March release. CAST: Leo Fong (Lt. Long), Richard Roundtree (Bryant), Cameron Mitchell (Marks), Stack Pierce (Nighthawk), Hope Holiday (Anita), Diana Leigh (Candy)

THE HOUSE OF GOD (United Artists) Producers, Charles H. Joffe, Harold Schneider; Direction-Screenplay, Donald Wrye; Based on novel by Samuel Shem; Photography, Gerald Hirschfeld; Editors, Bob Wyman, Billy Weber; Music, Basil Poledouris; Design, Bill Malley; Associate Producer, John Lugar; Assistant Director, Jerry Bellew; In Technicolor; Not rated; 108 minutes; March release. CAST: Tim Matheson (Dr. Basch), Charles Haid (Fats), Michael Sacks (Dr. Potts), Lisa Pelikan (Jo), Bess Armstrong (Dr. Worthington), George Coe (Dr. Leggo), James Cromwell (Officer Quick), Ossie Davis (Dr. Sanders), Howard Rollins, Jr. (Chuck)

THE DORM THAT DRIPPED BLOOD (New Image) Producer, Jeffrey Obrow; Directors, Mr. Obrow, Stephen Carpenter; Screenplay, Obrow, Carpenter, Stacey Giachino; Photography, Stephen Carpenter; Music, Chris Young; Assistant Director, Jon Hopkins; Production Manager, Samson Asianian; Art Director, Charlotte Grant; In Getty color; Rated R; 85 minutes; March release. CAST: Laurie Lapinski (Joanne), Stephen Sachs (Craig), David Snow (Brian), Pamela Holland (Patti), Dennis Ely (Bobby), Woody Roll (John), Daphne Zuniga, Jake Jones, Robert Frederick, Chris Morrill

NEW YORK NIGHTS (Bedford Entertainment) Produced and Written by Roman Vanderbes; Director, Simon Nuchtern; Loosely based on Arthur Schnitzler's play "Reigen"; Photography, Alan Doberman; Editor, Victor Zimet; Music, Linda Schreyer; Art Directors, Fran Boros, Patrick Mann; Assistant Director, Keven Dowd; Production Manager, William Milling; Costumes, Donna Williams; Associate Producer, John Maddocks; In Technicolor; Rated R; 102 minutes; March release. CAST: Corinne Alphen (Brooke), George Ayer (Jesse), Bobbi Burns (Lenore), Peter Matthey (Werner), Missy O'Shea (Chris), Nicholas Cortland (Harris), Marcia McBroom (Nicki), Cynthia Lee (Margo), William Dysart (Owen)

BOARDINGHOUSE (Coast Films) Producer, Peter Baahlu; Director, John Wintergate; Screenplay, Jonema; Photography, Jan Lucas, Obee Ray; Music, Kalassu, 33½ and Jonema; Assistant Director, Lanny Williamson; In color; Rated R; 89 minutes; March release. CAST: Hawk Audley (Jim/Gardener), Kalassu (Victoria), Alexandra Day, Joel McGinnis Riordan, Brian Bruderlin, Tracy O'Brian, Belma Kura, Mary McKinley, Rosane Woods, Elizabeth Haill, A'Ryen Winter

FORCED ENTRY (Century International) Producers, Jim Sotos, Henry Scarpelli; Director, Jim Sotos; Screenplay, Henry Scarpelli; Photography, Aaron Kleinman; Editors, Felix di Leone, Jim Markovic, Drake Silliman; Music, Tommy Vig; Assistant Director, Katherine Connolly; Associate Producer, Sandy Charles; In Getty Color; Not rated; 83 minutes; March release. CAST: Tanya Roberts, Ron Max, Nancy Allen, Robin Leslie, Michelle Miles

SLAPSTICK OF ANOTHER KIND (International Film) Executive Producers, Hank Paul, Larry Sugar, Dan Murphy; Direction-Screenplay, Steven Paul; Based on novel "Slapstick" by Kurt Vonnegut; Photography, Anthony Richmond; Editor, Doug Jackson; Music, Morton Stevens; Assistant Director, Benjamin Legrand; Designer, Joel Schiller; Associate Producer, Murray Schwartz; In MGM Color; Rated PG; 87 minutes; March release. CAST: Jerry Lewis (Wilbur/Caleb), Madeline Kahn (Eliza/Letitia), Marty Feldman (Sylvester), John Abbott (Dr. Frankenstein), Jim Backus (U.S. President), Samuel Fuller (Col. Sharp), Merv Griffin (Amchorman), Pat Morita (Ambassador Fong), Orson Welles (Alien Father), Virginia Graham, Ben Frank, Cherie Harris, Robert Hackman, Eugene Choy, Ken Johnson, Peter Kwong, Steven Paul, Patrick Wright, Steve Aaron, Richard Lee-Sung

THE BLACK ROOM (CI Films) Executive Producer, Douglas P. Cronin; Producer, Aaron C. Butler; Directors, Elly Kenner, Norman Thaddeus Vane; Screenplay, Vane; Photography, Robert Harmon; Editor, David Kern; Music, Art Podell, James Achley; Designer, Yoram Barzilai; In Color; Rated R; 87 minutes; March release. CAST: Stephen Knight (Jason), Cassandra Gaviola (Bridget), Jim Stathis (Larry), Clara Perryman (Robin), Geanne Frank (Sandy), Charlie Young (Lisa), Christopher McDonald (Terry), Linnea Quigley (Milly)

ANOTHER STATE OF MIND (Coastline Films) Produced, Written and Directed by Adam Small, Peter Stuart; No other credits; In color; Not rated; 78 minutes. A documentary on the hardcore punk-rock scene.

KIDCO (20th Century-Fox) Producers, Frank Yablans, David Niven, Jr.; Director, Ronald F. Maxwell; Screenplay, Bennett Trainer; Production Manager, Marty Katz; In color; Rated PG; 105 minutes; April release. CAST: Scott Schwartz (Dickie Cessna), Cinnamon Idles (Nene Cessna), Tristine Skyler (Belle Cessna), Elizabeth Gorcey (June Cessna)

"Preppies"

PREPPIES (Platinum) Producer-Director, Chuck Vincent; Associate Producer, Bill Slobodian; Photography, Larry Revene; Production Manager, Per Sjostedt; Screenplay, Rick Marx, Chuck Vincent; Editor, Clement Barclay; Music, Ian Shaw; Art Director, George C. Brown; Costumes, Robert Pusilo; Assistant Directors, Josh Andrews, Don Reed; Rated R; 83 minutes; April release. CAST: Dennis Drake (Chip), Steven Holt (Bayard), Peter Brady Reardon (Marc), Nitchie Barrett (Roxanne), Cindy Manion (Jo), Katie Stelletello (Tip), Katt Shea (Margot), Lynda Wiesmeier (Trini), Jo Ann Marshall (Suzy), Paul Sutton (Dick), Leonard Haas (Blackwel), Anthony Matteo (Louie), Leslie Barrett (Dean), Wayne Franson (Binki), Myra Chasen (Corki), Lara Berk (Kiki), William Hardy (Boobie), William Soso (Mickey), Robert Poletick (Terry), Mark Cronogue (Bosco), Jack Mead (Mechanic), Virgil Roberson (Foreman), Beverly Brown (Tanya), Lynette Sheldon (Saleswoman), Jack Burkhard (Roxanne's Father), Perry Rosen (Mike), Dayton Callie, Bruce Smolanoff (Break Dancers), Jerry Winsett (Waiter), Joe Geschwind (Cop), Craig Horrall (Barman), Samuelle Easton (Waitress), Jim Bonney (Guard), Phil LoPresti (Singer), James Louis Fleming (Snob)

SUBURBIA (New Horizons) formerly "The Wild Side"; Producer, Bert Dragin; Direction-Screenplay, Penelope Spheeris; Photography, Timothy Suhrstedt; Art Director, Randy Moore; Editor, Ross Albert; Production Manager, Gordon Wolf; Assistant Directors, Eric Jewett, James "Rip" Murray; Production Coordinator, Sherry Waters; In color; Rated R; 99 minutes; A Roger Corman/Bert Dragin Production; April release. CAST: Chris Pederson (Jack), Bill Coyne (Evan), Jennifer Clay (Sheila), Timothy Eric O'Brien (Tom), Michael Bayer (Razzle), Wade Walston (Joe), Andrew Pece (Ethan), Grant Miner (Keef), Dee Waldron (DeGenerate), Maggie Ehrig (Mattie), Christina Beck (T'resa), Andre Boutilier (Peg Leg), Robert Peyton (Jim), Jeff Prettyman (Bob), Donald V. Allen (Rennard), Joe Battenberg (Bates), Dorlinda Griffin (Mother), Robert Griffin (Baby), Donna La Manna (Tina), Julie Winchester (Blonde), John McCormack (Bouncer), Gavin Courtney (Joe's Father), Robert A. Van Senus (Joe's Father's Friend), Larry Wiley (Camp Buyer), Marlena Brause (Mrs. Triplett), Ron Hugo (Rev. Farrell), Jerry Madison (Dawson), J. Dinan Myrtetus (Sheila's Father), Barbara Benham (Mrs. Martin), Ed Mertens (Cop), Barbara Doyle, Arvid Blomberg, Ray Lawrence

"Suburbia"
© *New World Pictures*

Sybil Danning, Eric Brown in
"They're Playing with Fire"
© *New World Pictures*

Stephen Furst, Tim Matheson, Dan Monahan,
Sandy Helberg in "Up the Creek"
© *Orion Pictures*

CAGED FURY (Saturn International) Producer, Emily Blas; Director, Cirio H. Santiago; Screenplay, Bobby Greenwood; Music, Ernani Cuenco; In color; Rated R; 84 minutes; April release. CAST: Bernadette Williams, Jennifer Laine, Taffy O'Connell, Catherine Barch, S. P. Victoria, Mari Karen Ryan, Ken Metcalf

TEX AVERY CLASSICS (MGM/UA Classics) Directed by Tex Avery; In color; 96 minutes; April release. A selection of Mr. Avery's cartoons, produced between 1938 and 1952.

THEY'RE PLAYING WITH FIRE (New World) Produced and Written by Howard Avedis, Marlene Schmidt; Director, Howard Avedis; Associate Producers, Ernest Kaye, Tim Siu; Music, John Cacavas; Photography, Gary Graver; Editor, Jack Tucker; In color; Rated R; 96 minutes; A Hickmar Production; April release. CAST: Sybil Danning (Diane), Eric Brown (Jay), Andrew Prine (Michael), Paul Clemens (Bird), K. T. Stevens (Lillian), Gene Bicknell (George), Curt Ayers (Bartender), Dominick Brascia (Glenn), Bill Conklin (Preacher), Terese Hanses (Singer), Greg Kaye (Dale), Suzanne Kennedy (Janice), Violet Manes (Jenny), Alvy Moore (Jimbo), Joe Portaro (Prof.), Beth Schaffel (Cynthia), Margaret Wheeler (Lettie)

FRIDAY THE 13th-THE FINAL CHAPTER (Paramount) Producer, Frank Mancuso, Jr.; Director, Joseph Zito; Screenplay, Barney Cohen; Story, Bruce Hidemi Sakow; Music, Harry Manfredini; In color; Rated R; 91 minutes; April release. CAST: Kimberly Beck (Trish), Corey Feldman (Tommy), E. Erich Anderson (Rob), Peter Barton (Doug), Barbara Howard (Sara), Crispin Glover (Jimmy), Lawrence Monoson (Ted), Ted White (Jason), Antony Ponzini (Vincent), Frankie Hill (Lainie), Bruce Mahler (Axel), Lisa Freeman (Nurse Morgan), Alan Hayes (Paul), Judie Aranson (Samantha), Bonnie Hellman (Fat Girl), Camilla More (Tina), Carey More (Terri)

WHERE THE BOYS ARE '84 (TriStar) Producer, Allan Carr; Director, Hy Auerbach; Screenplay, Stu Krieger, Jeff Burkhart; Photography, James A. Contner; Editors, Melvin Shapiro, Bobbie Shapiro; Music, Sylvester Levay; In Dolby Stereo and color; Rated R; 97 minutes; April release. CAST: Lisa Hartman (Jennie), Russell Todd (Scott), Lorna Luft (Carole), Wendy Schaal (Sandra), Howard McGillin (Chip), Lynn-Holly Johnson (Laurie), Louise Sorel (Barbara), Alana Stewart (Maggie), Christopher McDonald (Tony), Daniel McDonald (Camden)

UP THE CREEK (Orion) Producer, Michael L. Meltzer; Director, Robert Butler; Executive Producers, Samuel Z. Arkoff, Louis S. Arkoff; Screenplay, Jim Kouf; Photography, James Glennon; Editor, Bill Butler; Co-Producer, Fred Baum; Designer, William E. Hiney; Assistant Director, Daniel McCauley; Music, William Goldstein; In DeLuxe Color; Rated R; 99 minutes; April release. CAST: Tim Matheson (Bob), Jennifer Runyon (Heather), Stephen Furst (Gonzer), Dan Monahan (Max), Sandy Helberg (Irwin), Jeff East (Rex), Blaine Novak (Braverman), James B. Sikking (Tozer), John Hillerman (Dean), Mark Andrews (Rocky), Will Bledsoe (Roger), Grant Wilson (Reggie), Julie Montgomery (Lisa), Jeana Tomasina (Molly), Romy Windsor (Cork)

HELL'S KITCHEN CHRONICLE (Lightworks) Co-Producers-Directors, Maren Erskine, Reed Erskine; Edited and Narrated by Maren Erskine; In color; Not rated; 60 minutes; April release. A documentary on New York City's Hell's Kitchen district.

PURPLE HEARTS (Warner Bros.) Producer-Director, Sidney J. Furie; Screenplay, Rick Natkin, Sidney J. Furie; Photography, Jan Kiesser; Editor, George Grenville; Production Supervisor, Kevin Elders; Associate Producer, Rick Natkin; Music, Robert Folk; Production Manager, Joe Constantino; Assistant Directors, Jun Amazan, Ricardo De Guzman; Art Director, Francisco Balangue; Special Effects, Danilo Dominguez; A Ladd Company release in Panavision, Technicolor and Dolby Stereo; Rated R; 116 minutes; May release. CAST: Ken Wahl (Don), Cheryl Ladd (Deborah), Stephen Lee (Wizard), Annie McEnroe (Hallaway), Paul McCrane (Brenner), Cyril O'Reilly (Zuma), David Harris (Hanes), Hillary Bailey (Jill), Lee Ermey (Gunny), Drew Snyder (Lt. Col. Larimore), Lane Smith (Cmdr. Markel), James Whitmore, Jr. (Bwana), Kevin Elders (CIA Driver), Sydney Squire (Nurse), David Bass (Lt. Grayson), Bruce Guilchard (Jackson), Rod Birch, Joel Escamilla (Patients), Helen McNeely (Chief of Nursing), Steve Rosenbaum (Schoenblum), Steven Rodgers (August), Adam Rice (Mail Clerk), Rudy Nash (Hartman), John Smith (Dr. Altman), Paul Williams (MP Jeep), Koko Trinidad (Black Marketer), Paul Anderson (Marine Capt.), Chuck Dougherty (Cmdr. Norbitt), Ted Thomas (R & R Sgt.), Claude Wilson (CIA Man), Richard Bean (Recon Sgt.), Rick Natkin (Hospital MP), Don Tamuty (Kevin's Father), Art Thompson (Soldier in warehouse), Hugh Gillam (Dr. Weymuth)

Lorna Luft (c) in "Where the Boys
Are '84" © *Tri-Star Pictures*

Ken Wahl, Cheryl Ladd in
"Purple Hearts" © *Warner Bros.*

Diane Lane, Amy Madigan, Michael Pare
in "Streets of Fire" © *Universal*

Maura Ellyn, Allan Nicholls, Roland Caccavo,
Lucille Rivin in "Home Free All" © *Almi*

STREETS OF FIRE (Universal) Producers, Lawrence Gordon, Joel Silver; Director, Walter Hill; Screenplay, Walter Hill, Larry Gross; Photography, Andrew Laszlo; Designer, John Vallone; Editors, Freeman Davies, Michael Ripps; Executive Producer, Gene Levy; Costumes, Marilyn Vance; Choreography, Jeffrey Hornaday; Music, Ry Cooder; Associate Producer, Mae Woods; Production Manager, Gene Levy; Assistant Directors, David Sosna, Deborah Love, Rob Corn; Art Directors, James Allen, Tony Brockliss; In Dolby Stereo, Panavision and Technicolor; Rated PG; 100 minutes; May release. CAST: Michael Pare (Tom), Diane Lane (Ellen), Rick Moranis (Billy), Amy Mafigan (McCoy), William Dafoe (Raven), Deborah Van Valkenburgh (Reva), Richard Lawson (Ed Price), Rick Rossovich (Cooley), Bill Paxton (Clyde), Lee Ving (Greer), Stoney Jackson (Bird), Grand Bush (Reggie), Robert Townsend (Lester), Mykel T. Williamson (B. J.), Elizabeth Daily (Baby Doll), Lynne Thigpen (Motorwoman), Marine Jahan (Dancer), Ed Begley, Jr. (Ben), John Dennis Johnston (Pete), Harry Beer (Squirt), Olivia Brown (Addie), Kip Waldo (Waldo), Peter Jason (Harry), Matthew Laurance (Cop), Sarah Marten, Tamu Blackwell, Ric Moreno, Antonie Becker, Elizabeth Jordan, Susan Cheung, Vicki McCarty, John Hateley, Rock Walker

FIRESTARTER (Universal) Producer, Frank Capra, Jr.; Director, Mark L. Lester; Screenplay, Stanley Mann; Based on novel of same title by Stephen King; Associate Producer, Martha Schumacher; Photography, Guiseppe Ruzzolini; Art Director, Giorgio Postiglione; Music, Tangerine Dream; Production Manager, Don Goldman; Editors, David Rawlins, Ron Sanders; Assistant Directors, David Whorf, Ric Kidney, Glenn Randall, Jr., Nikita Knatz; Production Coordinator, Janis Rockwell-Strong; In J-D-C Widescreen and Technicolor; Rated R; 116 minutes; May release. CAST: David Keith (Andrew), Drew Barrymore (Charlie), Freddie Jones (Dr. Wanless), Heather Locklear (Vicky), Martin Sheen (Capt. Hollister), George C. Scott (John Rainbird), Art Carney (Irv), Louise Fletcher (Norma), Moses Gunn (Dr. Pynchot), Antonio Fargas (Taxi Driver), Drew Synder (Orville), Curtis Credel (Bates), Keith Colbert (Mayo), Richard Warlock (Knowles), Jeff Ramsey (Steinowitz), Jack Manger (Young Serviceman), Lisa Anne Barnes (His Girl), Larry Sprinkle (Guard), Cassandra Ward-Freeman (Woman in stall), Scott R. Davis (Bearded Student), Nina Jones (Grad Student), William Alspaugh (Proprietor), Laurens Moore (Old Man), Anne Fitzgibbon (Old Lady), Steve Boles (Mailman), Stanley Mann (Motel Owner), Carole Francisco (Joan), Wendy Womble (Josie), John Sanderford (Albright), Carey Fox (Agent)

HOME FREE ALL (Almi) Executive Producer, Steven P. Reifman; Producer, Stewart Bird, Peter Belsito; Direction and Screenplay, Stewart Bird; Photography, Robert Levi; Editor, Daniel Loewenthal; Designer, Mischa Petrow; Music, Jay Chattaway; Presented by Albert Schwartz, Michael Landes; In color; Not rated; 93 minutes; May release. CAST: Allan Nicholls (Barry), Roland Caccavo (Roland), Maura Ellyn (Cathy), Shelley Wyant (Rita), Lucille Rivin (Lynn), Lorry Goldman (Marvin), Janet Burnham (Chastity), Jose Ramon Rosario (Carlos), Daniel Benzalli (Therapist), Melanie Bradshaw (Melanie), Francesca Valerio (Samantha), Joyce Sozen (Mildred), Elizabeth Burkland (Cathy's Friend), John Hallow (Investor), Mark Urman (Edmonds), Sam Rubinsky (Cabbie), Mike Alpert (Picketer), Steve Powers (Reporter), Chazz Palminteri (Hijacker), Tom Kopache (Truck Driver), Harve Soto, Mario Todisco, Joe Lisi (Thugs), Geoffrey Ewing, Pura Bobe (Tenants at meeting), Jimmy Adler (Clown), Rose Geffen (Customer)

DARK CIRCLE (New Yorker) Producer, Ruth Landy; Written, Directed, Photographed and Edited by Chris Beaver, Judy Irving; Co-produced and Narrated by Judy Irving; Associate Producer, Judith Lit; Music, Gary S. Remal, Bernard L. Krause, Pat Metheny and Lyle Mays, Eberhard Weber; In color; 82 minutes; Not rated; May release. A documentary look at what life holds for people in and around the Rocky Flats Nuclear Weapons Facility near Denver, Colorado.

HARDBODIES (Columbia) Producers, Jeff Begun, Ken Dalton; Director, Mark Griffiths; Story, Steve Greene, Eric Alter; Screenplay, Greene, Alter, Mark Griffiths; Photography, Tom Richmond; Editor, Andy Blumenthal; Associate Producer, Judy Mooradian; Assistant Directors, Eric M. Breiman, Daniel Eisenberg; Designer, Gregg Fonseca; Production Coordinators, Kate McMahon, Rob Roda; Music Director, Vic Caesar; Choreographer, Randy DiGrazio; A Chroma III production in DeLuxe color; Rated R; 88 minutes; May release. CAST: Grant Cramer (Scotty), Teal Roberts (Kristi), Gary Wood (Hunter), Michael Rapport (Rounder), Sorrells Pickard (Ashby), Roberta Collins (Lana), Cindy Silver (Kimberly), Courtney Gaines (Rag), Kristi Somers (Michelle), Crystal Shaw (Candy), Darcy DeMoss (Dede), Antony Ponzini (Rocco), Marvin Katzoff (Dorky Geek), Kip Waldo (Head Geek), Michael Miller (Landlord), Chuck Hart (Young Geek), Kane Hodder (Old Geek)

Art Carney, Louise Fletcher, Drew Barrymore,
David Keith in "Firestarter" © *Universal*

Grant Cramer, Teal Roberts in
"Hardbodies" © *Columbia Pictures*

Judd Nelson, Jonna Lee, Scott McGinnis
in "Making the Grade" © *MGM/UA-Cannon*

Michael "Shrimp" Chambers, Adolfo "Shabba-Doo"
Quinones in "Breakin'" © *Cannon Films*

SILENT MADNESS (Almi Pictures) Producer-Director, Simon Nuchtern; Executive Producer, Gregory Earls; Producer, William P. Milling; Screenplay, Robert Zimmerman, William P. Milling; Photography, Gerald Feil; Production Manager, Robert Zimmerman; In color; Rated R; 82 minutes; May release. CAST: Belinda Montgomery (Dr. Joan Gilmore), Viveca Lindfors (Mrs. Collins), Solly Marx (Howard Johns), David Greenan (Mark McGowan), Sydney Lassick (Sheriff), Roderick Cook (Dr. Kruger)

RENT CONTROL (Group S Films) Producer, Benni Korzen; Director, Gian L. Polidoro; Screenplay, John Menegold, Sherill Tippins; Photography, Benito Frattari; Editors, Ed Orshan, Jim Cookman; Music, Oscar De Mejo, Ian North; In color; Not rated; 86 minutes; May release. CAST: Brent Spiner (Leonard), Elizabeth Stack (Anne), Leonard Melfi (Milton), Jeanne Ruskin (Margaret), Annie Korzen (Nancy), Leslie Cifarelli (Barbara), Charles Laiken (Jim), Roy Brocksmith (Stan), Anita Bosic (Mrs. Spovic), Robin Pogrebin (Shelley), Abigail Pogrebin (Sharon), Kimberly Stern (Jeanne)

MAKING THE GRADE (MGM/UA/Cannon) Produced and Written by Gene Quintano; Story, Mr. Quintano, Charles Gale; Photography, Jacques Haitkin; Editor, Dan Wetherbee; Music, Basil Poledouris; In Dolby Stereo and color; Rated R; 105 minutes; May release. CAST: Judd Nelson (Eddie), Ionna Lee (Tracey), Gordon Jump (Harriman), Walter Olkewicz (Coach), Ronald Lacey (Nicky), Dana Olsen (Palmer), Carey Scott (Rand), Scott McGinnis (Bif), Andrew Clay (Dice), John Dye (Skip), Daniel Schneider

FLESHBURN (Crown International) Producer, Beth Gage; Director, George Gage; Screenplay, Beth and George Gage; Based on book "Fear in a Handful of Dust" by Brian Garfield; Photography, Bill Pecchi; Editor, Sonya Sones; Music, Arthur Kempel; In color; Rated R; 90 minutes; May release. CAST: Steve Kanaly (Sam), Karen Carlson (Shirley), Macon McCalman (Earl), Robert Chimento (Jay), Sonny Landham (Calvin), Robert Alan Browne (Jim), Duke Stroud (Smyley), Larry Vigus (Sgt.), Newton John Skinner (Chris)

FINDERS KEEPERS (Warner Bros.) Producers, Sandra Marsh, Terence Marsh; Director, Richard Lester; Screenplay, Ronny Graham, Terence Marsh, Charles Dennis; Photography, Brian West; Editor, John Victor Smith; Music, Ken Thorne; In color; Rated R; 96 minutes;

May release. CAST: Michael O'Keefe (Michael), Beverly D'Angelo (Standish), Louis Gossett, Jr. (Century), Pamela Stephenson (Georgiana), Ed Lauter (Josef), David Wayne (Stapleton), Brian Dennehy (Mayor), Jack Riley (Ormond)

COLD FEET (Cinecom International) Producer, Charles Wessler; Direction and Screenplay, Bruce van Dusen; Photography, Benjamin Blake; Editor, Sally Joe Menke; Music, Todd Rundgren; In color; Not rated; 96 minutes; May release. CAST: Griffin Dunne (Tom), Marissa Chibas (Marty), Blanche Baker (Leslie), Mark Cronogue (Bill), Kurt Knudson (Louis), Joseph Leon (Harold), Marcia Jean Kurtz (Psychiatrist), Peter Boyden (Dr. Birbrower), Dan Strickler, John Jellison (Executives), Mary Fogarty (Susan)

BREAKIN' (MGM/UA/Cannon) Producers, Allen DeBevoise, David Zito; Director, Joel Silberg; Screenplay, Charles Parker, Allen DeBevoise, Gerald Scalfe; Story, Mr. Parker, Mr. DeBevoise; Photography, Hanania Beer; Music, Gary Remal, Michael Boyd; Editors, Larry Boch, Gib Jaffe, Vincent Sklena; In Dolby Stereo and color; Rated PG; 90 minutes; May release. CAST: Lucinda Dickey (Kelly), Adolfo Quinones (Ozone), Michael Chambers (Turbo), Ben Lokey (Franco), Christopher McDonald (James), Phineas Newborn 3d (Adam)

ALPHABET CITY (Atlantic) Producer, Andrew Braunsberg; Director, Amos Poe; Screenplay, Gregory Heller, Amos Poe; Photography, Oliver Wood; Editor, Grahame Weinbren; Music, Nile Rodgers; In color; Rated R; 85 minutes; May release. CAST: Vincent Spano (Johnny), Kate Vernon (Angie), Michael Winslow (Lippy), Zohra Lampert (Mama), Jami Gertz (Sophia), Laura Carrington (Louisa), Raymond Serra (Gino), Daniel Jordano (Juani), Kenny Marino (Tony)

THE FINAL TERROR (Aquarius) Presented by Samuel Arkoff; Producer, Joe Roth; Co-Producer, J. Stein Kaplan; Associate Producers, Gary Shusett, Anthony J. Ridio; Director, Andrew Davis; Screenplay, Jon George, Neill Hicks, Ronald Shusett; Photography, Andreas Davidescu; Editors, Paul Rubell, Erica Flaum; Music, Susan Justin; Assistant Director, Luca Kouimelis; Production Manager, Jim Dennett; In DeLuxe Color; Rated R; 82 minutes; May release. CAST: John Friedrich (Zorich), Adrian Zmed (Cerone), Daryl Hannah (Windy), Rachel Ward (Margaret), Mark Metcalf (Mike), Ernest Harden Jr., Akosua Busia, Lewis Smith, Cindy Harrell, Joe Pantoliano

Louis Gossett, Jr., Beverly D'Angelo, Michael
O'Keefe in "Finders Keepers" © *CBS*

Vincent Spano in "Alphabet City"
© *Atlantic Releasing Corp.*

Kelly Reno, John Savage in "Brady's Escape"
© *Satori Entertainment*

Mickey Rourke, Daryl Hannah, Eric Roberts
in "The Pope of Greenwich Village" © *UA Corp.*

JOINT CUSTODY: A NEW KIND OF FAMILY (New Day Films)
Producer-Director, Josephine Hayes Dean; Editor, Marian Hunter; Photography, Stuart Math, John Hazard; Music, Peter Fish; Executive Producer, Kathy Kline; In color; Not rated; 85 minutes; May release. A documentary about divorced parents who live split weeks with parents.

STACY'S KNIGHTS (Crown International) Previously "Double Down"; Executive Producers, David L. Peterson, Jim Wilson; Producers, Joann Locktov, Freddy Sweet; Director, Jim Wilson; Screenplay, Michael Blake; Photography, Raul Lomas; Editor, Bonnie Koehler; Music, Norton Buffalo; Art/Set Direction, Florence Fellman; Production Manager-Assistant Director, Jacqueline Zambrano; In DeLuxe Color; Rated PG; 95 minutes; May release. CAST: Andra Millian (Stacy), Kevin Costner (Will), Eve Lilith (Jean), Mike Reynolds (Shecky), Garth Howard (Mr. C), Ed Semenza (The Kid)

HOLLYWOOD HIGH PART II (Lone Star) Executive Producers-Directors, Caruth C. Byrd, Lee Thornburg; Producers, Cotton Whittington, Colleen Meeker; Screenplay, Thornburg, Byrd, Whittington, Meeker; Photography, Gary Graver; Editor, Warren Chadwick; Music/Songs, Doug Goodwin; In CFI Color; Rated R; 85 minutes; May release. CAST: April May (Bunny), Brad Cowgill (Rocky), Donna Lynn (Kiki), Drew Davis (Jock), Bruce Dobos (Skip), Camille Warner (Ginger), Alisa Ann Hull (Chessie), Angela Field, Anne Morris

CHESTY ANDERSON—U.S. NAVY (Coast Films) Executive Producer, Philip Hacker; Producer, Paul Pompian; Director, Ed Forsyth; Screenplay, H. F. Green, Paul Ponpian; Photography, Henning Schellerup; Assistant Director, Arello Blanton; Production Manager, John Burrows; In color; Rated R; 89 minutes; May release. CAST: Shari Eubank (Chesty), Dorrie Thomson (Tina), Rosanne Katon (Coco), Marcie Barkin (Pucker), Fred Willard (Peter), Frank Campanella (Baron), George Cooper (Senator), John Davis Chandler (Don), Scatman Crothers, Mel Carter, Constance Marie, Dyanne Thorne, Betty McGuire, Brenda Fogerty, Joyce Gibson, Uschi Digard, Pat Parker, Betty Thomas

BEAT STREET (Orion) Producers, David V. Picker, Harry Belafonte; Director, Stan Lathan; Screenplay, Andy Davis, David Gilbert, Paul Golding; Story, Steven Hager; Photography, Tom Priestly, Jr.; Editor, Dov Hoenig; Music, Harry Belafonte, Arthur Baker; Designer, Patrizia Von Brandenstein; Costumes, Kristi Zea; Choreographer, Lester Wilson; Associate Producer, Mel Howard; In Dolby Stereo and

DeLuxe Color; Rated PG; 105 minutes; June release. CAST: Rae Dawn Chong (Tracy), Guy Davis (Kenny), John Chardiet (Ramon), Leon Grant (Chollie), Robert Taylor (Lee), Dean Elliott (Henri), Franc Reyes (Luis), and New York City Breakers, Rock Steady, Magnificent Force, Grand Master Melle Mel & The Furious Five, Afrika Bambaataa & The Soul Sonic Force, The System, Brenda K., Us Girls, Tina B., Jazzy Jay

BRADY'S ESCAPE (Satori) Producer, Robert Halmi; Executive Producer, Jozsef Marx; Director, Pal Gabor; Screenplay, William W. Lewis; Story, Pal Gabor; Photography, Elemer Ragalyi; Music, Charles Gross; Art Director, Jozsef Romvari; Editor, Norman Gay; Associate Producer, Robert Halmi, Jr.; In color; Not rated; 96 minutes; June release. CAST: John Savage (Brady), Kelly Reno (Miki), Ildiko Bansagi (Klara), Laszlo Mensaros (Dr. Dussek), Ferenc Bacs (Wortman), Dzsoko Rosic (Csorba), Laszlo Horvath (Moro), Matyas Usztics (Sweede)

THE POPE OF GREENWICH VILLAGE (MGM/UA) Producer, Gene Kirkwood; Director, Stuart Rosenberg; Screenplay, Vincent Patrick from his novel of same title; Photography, John Bailey; Editor, Robert Brown; Music, Dave Grusin; In color; Rated R; 122 minutes; June release. CAST: Eric Roberts (Paulie), Mickey Rourke (Charlie), Daryl Hannah (Diane), Geraldine Page (Mrs. Ritter), Kenneth McMillan (Barney), Tony Musante (Pete), M. Emmet Walsh (Burns), Burt Young (Bedbug Eddie), Jack Kehoe (Bunky), Philip Bosco (Paulie's Father), Val Avery (Nunzi)

GREMLINS (Warner Bros.) Producer, Michael Finnell; Director, Joe Dante; Screenplay, Chris Columbus; Photography, John Hora; Editor, Tina Hirsch; Music, Jerry Goldsmith; Presented by Steven Spielberg; In Dolby Stereo and color; Rated PG; 111 minutes; June release. CAST: Zach Galligan (Billy), Phoebe Cates (Kate), Hoyt Axton (Rand), Frances Lee McCain (Lynn), Polly Holliday (Mrs. Deagle), Keye Luke (Grandfather), John Louie (Chinese Boy), Dick Miller (Futterman), Jackie Joseph (Mrs. Futterman), Scott Brady (Sheriff), Harry Carey, Jr. (Anderson), Don Steele (Rockin' Ricky Rialto), Corey Feldman (Pete), Arnie Moore (Pete's Father), Glynn Turman (Roy), Belinda Balaski (Mrs. Yarris), Judge Reinhold (Gerald), Jonathan Banks (Deputy), Joe Brooks (Santa), Edward Andrews (Corben), Chuck Jones (Jones), Kenny Davis (Dorry), Jim McKrell (Lew)

Leon Grant, Jon Chardiet, Guy Davis
in "Beat Street" © *Orion Pictures*

Zach Galligan, Frances Lee McCain, Hoyt
Axton in "Gremlins" © *Warner Bros.*

Dom DeLuise, Burt Reynolds, Shirley MacLaine,
Marilu Henner, Dub Taylor in "Cannonball Run II"
© *Arcafin B.V./Claridge Pictures*

CANNONBALL RUN II (Warner Bros.) Producer, Albert S. Ruddy; Director, Hal Needham; Screenplay, Mr. Needham, Albert S. Ruddy, Harvey Miller; Based on characters created by Brock Yates; Photography, Nick McLean; Editors, William Gordean, Carl Kress; Music, Al Capps; In color; Rated PG; 108 minutes; June release. CAST: Burt Reynolds (J.J.), Dom DeLuise (Victor), Dean Martin (Blake), Sammy Davis, Jr. (Fenderbaum), Jamie Farr (Sheik), Marilu Henner (Betty), Telly Savalas (Hymie), Shirley MacLaine (Veronica), Susan Anton (Jill), Catherine Bach (Marcie), Foster Brooks, Louis Nye, Sid Caesar (Fishermen). Jackie Chan (Jackie), Tim Conway (C.H.P.1), Ricardo Montalban (King), Jim Nabors (Homer), Molly Picon (Mrs. Goldfarb), Charles Nelson Reilly (Don), Alex Rocco (Tony), Henry Silva (Slim), Frank Sinatra (Himself)

THE EXECUTIONER PART II (21st Century) Producer, Renee Harmon; Director, James Bryant; In Pacific Color; Rated R; 85 minutes; June release. CAST: Christopher Mitchum (Lt. O'Malley), Aldo Ray (Police Commissioner), Antoine John Mottet (Mike), Renee Harmon (Celia Amherst), Dan Bradley, Jim Draftfield

HOT AND DEADLY (Arista) Formerly "The Retrievers"; Executive Producer, Lou George; Producer-Director, Elliot Hong; Screenplay-Co-producer, Larry Stamper; Photography, Stephen Kim; Editor, Rob Smith; Music, Ted Ashford, Paul Fontana; Assistant Director, Bill Poplar; Production Manager, Brandock Oaha; In United Color; Rated R; 90 minutes; June release. CAST: Max Thayer (Tom), Shawn Hoskins (Janice), Randy Anderson (Trigger), Lenard Miller (Danny), Bud Cramer (Philip)

THE ALIEN FACTOR (Cinemagic) Written and Directed by Donald M. Dohler; Photography, Britt McDonough; Editors, Dohler, Dave Ellis; Music, Kenneth Walker; Assistant Director, Anthony Malanowski; Special Effects, Larry Schlechter, John Cosentino; In Quality Color; Not rated; 80 minutes; June release. CAST: Don Leifert (Ben), Tom Griffith (Sheriff), Richard Dyszel (Mayor), Mary Martens (Edie), Richard Geiwitz (Pete), George Stover (Steven), Eleanor Herman (Mary Jane), Anne Frith (Dr. Sherman), Christopher Gummer (Clay), Don Dohler (Ernie), Dave Ellis (Rich), Johnny Walker (Rex), Tony Malnowski (Ed)

Sheila Kennedy in "Ellie"
© *R. S. Releasing*

RARE BREED (New World) Producer, Jack Cox; Director, David Nelson; Screenplay, Gardner Simmons; Photography, Darryl Cathcart; Assistant Director, Worth Keeter; In color; Rated PG; 94 minutes; June release. CAST: George Kennedy (Nathan Hill), Forrest Tucker (Jess Cutler), Tom Hallick (Lou Nelson), Don Defore (Frank Nelson), Tracy Vaccaro (Anne Cutler)

MYSTERY MANSION (Pacific International) Producer, Arthur R. Dubs; Director, David E. Jackson; Screenplay, Jack Duggan, Arn Wihtol; Photography, Milas C. Hinshaw; Editor, Stephen Johnson; Music, William Loose, Jack K. Tillar, Marty Wereski; Assistant Director, Zachari Brown; Production Manager, William Humphrey; In CFI Color; Rated PG; 95 minutes; June release. CAST: Dallas McKennon (Sam), Greg Wynne (Gene), Jane Ferguson (Mary), Randi Brown (Susan), Lindsay Bishop (Billy), David Wagner (Johnny), Barry Hostetler (Fred), Joseph D. Savery (Willy)

BLIND DATE (New Line) Producer-Director, Nico Mastorakis; Screenplay, Mastorakis, Fred C. Perry; Associate Producers, J. D. Corins, Michael Rich; Executive Producer, Demetri T. Skouras; Songs, John Kongos; Music, Stanley Myers; Photography, Andrew Bellis; Editor, George Rosenberg; An Omega production in Technicolor and Dolby Stereo; Rated R; 102 minutes; June release. CAST: Joseph Bottoms, Kirstie Alley, James Daughton, Lana Clarkson, Keir Dullea

SPLITZ (Film Ventures) Producers, Kelly Van Horn, Stephen Low; Director, Domonic Paris; Screenplay, Domonic Paris, Bianca Littlebaum, Harry Azorin, Kelly Van Horn; Art Director, Tom Allen; Photography, Ronnie Taylor; Choreography, Matthew Diamond; Composer, George Small; In color; Not rated; 83 minutes; June release. CAST: Robin Johnson (Gina), Patti Lee (Joan), Chuck McQuary (Chuck), Barbara M. Bingham (Susie), Shirley Stoler (Dean Hunta), Raymond Serra (Vito), Martin Rosenblatt (Louie), Sal Carollo (Tony)

ELLIE (Film Ventures) Producer, Francine Roudine; Director, Peter Wittman; Screenplay, Glenn Allen Smith; Photography, George Tirl; Editor, John Davis; Music, Bob Pickering; Performed by Atlanta, Charlie Pride; In Dolby Stereo and Eastmancolor; Not rated; 88 minutes; June release. CAST: Sheila Kennedy (Ellie), Shelley Winters (Cora), Edward Albert (Tom), Pat Paulsen (Sheriff), George Gobel (Preacher)

A BREED APART (Orion) Producers, John Daly, Derek Gibson; Associate Producer, Dan Allingham; Director, Philippe Mora; Screenplay, Paul Wheeler; Photography, Geoffrey Stephenson; Editor, Chris Lebenzon; Art Director, Bill Barclay; Music, Maurice Gibb; In Metrocolor; Not rated; 101 minutes; June release. CAST: Rutger Hauer (Jim Malden), Powers Boothe (Michael Walker), Kathleen Turner (Stella), Donald Pleasance (J.P.), John Dennis Johnston (Charlie), Brion James (Hughie), Adam Fenwick (Adam), Jayne Bentzen (Amy)

THE NAKED FACE (MGM/UA) Producers, Menahem Golan, Yoram Globus; Direction and Screenplay, Bryan Forbes; Based on novel by Sidney Sheldon; Associate Producer, Rony Yacov; Photography, David Gurfinkel; Design, William Fosser; Editor, Philip Shaw; Music, Michael J. Lewis; In Metrocolor; Not rated; June release. CAST: Roger Moore (Dr. Judd Stevens), Rod Steiger (Lt. McGreavy), Elliott Gould (Angeli), Art Carney (Morgens), Anne Archer (Ann Blake), David Hedison (Dr. Hadley), Deanna Douglas (Mrs. Hadley), Ron Parady (Cortini)

GIRLS NITE OUT (Aries International) formerly "The Scaremaker"; Executive Producers, Kevin Kurgis, Richard Barclay; Producer, Anthony N. Gurvis; Director, Robert Deubel; Screenplay, Gil Spencer, Jr., Joe Bolster, Kevin Kurgis; Photography, Joe Rivers; Editor, Arthur Ginsberg; Designer, Howard Cummings; Production Manager, Patrick McCormick; In TVC Color; Rated R; 96 minutes; June release. CAST: Julie Montgomery, James Carroll, Suzanne Barnes, Rutanya Alda, Hal Holbrook, David Holbrook, Lauren-Marie Taylor, Al McGuire, Matthew Dunn, Paul Christie, Richard Bright

MY FRIENDS NEED KILLING (Nick Felix) Producer, Jack Marshall; Director, Paul Leder; Photography, Parker Bartlett; Editor, Paul Leder; Music, Mark Bucci; In color; Rated R; 72 minutes; June release. CAST: Greg Mullavey (Gene), Meredith MacRae (Laura), Clayton Wilcox (Gil), Carolyn Ames (Susan), Elaine Partnow (Audrey), Roger Cruz, Laurie Burton, Bill Michael, Savannah Bently, Eric Morris

SPLATTER UNIVERSITY (Troma) Producers, Richard W. Haines, John Michaels; Associate Producer, Miljan Peter Ilich; Director, Richard W. Haines; Photography, Fred Cohen, Jim Grib; Music, Chris Burke; Songs, The Pedestrians; An Aquifilm picture in color presented by Lloyd Kaufman and Michael Herz; Rated R; 77 minutes; July release. CAST: Francine Forbes, Cathy Lacommare, Dick Biel, Denise Texeira

"First Turn On"
© *Grande Co./Troma Inc.*

C. Thomas Howell, Jamie Lee Curtis, Patrick
Swayze in "Grandview U.S.A." © *CBS Inc.*

SECRET HONOR (Sandcastle 5) Executive Producer, Scott Bush-nell; Producer-Director, Robert Altman; Screenplay, Donald Freed, Arnold M. Stone from their solo-drama; Photography, Pierre Mignot; Music, George Burt; Art, Stephen Altman; Editor, Juliet Weber; Associate Director, Robert Harders; In Movielab Color; Not rated; 85 minutes; July release. CAST: Philip Baker Hall (Richard M. Nixon).

THE FIRST TURN-ON! (Troma) Producers, Lloyd Kaufman, Michael Herz; Executive Producers, William E. Kirksey, Spencer A. Tandy; Directors, Michael Herz, Samuel Weil; Screenplay, Stuart Strutin; Additional Material, Mark Torgl, Georgia Harrell, Lloyd Kaufman, Michael Herz; Photography, Lloyd Kaufman; Editor, Richard Haines; Editors, Adam Fredericks, Richard King; Special Effects, Les Larrain; Art Director, Ellen Christiansen; Costumes, Danielle Brunon; Associate Producer, Stuart Strutin; Production Supervisor, Nelson Vaughn; Assistant Director, Ilan Cohen; Production Manager, Jill Boniske; In color by Guffanti Film Labs; Rated R; 85 minutes; July release. CAST: Georgia Harrell (Michele), Michael Sanville (Mitch), Googy Gress (Henry), John Flood (Danny), Heidi Miller (Annie), Al Pia (Alfred), Betty Pia (Mrs. Anderson), Gilda Gumbo (Mme. Gumbo), Lara Grills (Lucy), Kristina Marie Wetzel (Barbara), Frank Trent Saladino (Jeff), David Berardi (Johnny), Ted Henning (Ted), Donna Winter (Mona), Sheila Kennedy (Dreamgirl)

GRANDVIEW, U.S.A. (CBS Theatrical Films) Director, Randal Kleiser; Producers, William Warren Blaylock, Peter W. Rea; Screenplay, Ken Hixon; Executive Producers, Jonathan Taplin, Andrew Gellis; Photography, Reynaldo Villalobos; Designer, Jan Scott; Score, Thomas Newman; Editor, Robert Gordon; Production Manager, Tom Joyner; Assistant Directors, Donald Heitzer, Roger J. Pugliese; Costumes, Wayne Finkelman; Choreography, Lisa Niemi, Patrick Swayze; Production Coordinator, Judith Pritchard; In Dolby Stereo and Astro Color; Rated R; 97 minutes; July release. CAST: Jamie Lee Curtis (Michelle/"Mike"), C. Thomas Howell (Tim), Patrick Swayze (Ernie/ "Slam"), Troy Donahue (Donny), Jennifer Jason Leigh (Candy), William Windom (Bob), Carole Cook (Betty), M. Emmet Walsh (Clark), Ramon Bieri (Pearson), Elizabeth Gorcey (Bonnie), John Philbin (Cowboy), John Cusack (Johnny), Joan Cusack (Mary), Camilla Hawk (Mrs. Pearson), Melissa Domke (Susan), Jason Court (Benny), Tim Gamble (Larry), Fred Lerner (Tucker), Larry Brandenburg (Mickey), Taylor Williams (Fleming), Kathryn Joosten (Mrs. Clark), Fern Persons (Teacher), Bruno Aclin (Foreman), Steve Dahl (Moose), Tony Lincoln (Kutch), George Womack (Whitewood), Frank T. Panno (Pettiman), Bob Swan (Fire Chief), Michael Winslow (Spencer), Donald Bernardi (Randy)

GO TELL IT ON THE MOUNTAIN (Learning in Focus) Producer, Calvin Skaggs; Executive Producer, Robert Geller; Director, Stan Lathan; Screenplay, Gus Edwards, Leslie Lee; Based on novel by James Baldwin; Photography, Hiro Narita; Editor, Jay Freund; Music, Webster Lewis; Design, Charles Bennett; Costumes, Bernard Johnson; Assistant Director, Herb Gains; In TVC Color; Not rated; 96 minutes; July release. CAST: Paul Winfield (Gabriel), Rosalind Cash (Aunt Florence), James Bond 3d (John), Roderic Winberly (Roy), Olivia Cole (Elizabeth), Ving Rhames (Young Gabriel), Alfre Woodard (Esther), C. C. H. Pounder (Deborah), Linda Hopkins (Sister McCandless)

HOLLYWOOD HOT TUBS (Manson International) Producer, Mark Borde; Director, Chuck Vincent; Screenplay, Borde, Craig McDonnell; Photography, Larry Revene; Editor, Michael Hoggan; Art, Loma Lee Brookbank; Music, Joel Goldsmith; In color; Rated R; 102

minutes; July release. CAST: Donna McDaniel (Leslie), Michael Andrew (Jeff), Paul Gunning (Eddie), Katt Shea (DeeDee), Edy Williams (Desire), Jewal Shepard (Crystal)

I'M ALMOST NOT CRAZY: John Cassavetes—the Man and His Work (Cannon Group) Producers, Menahem Golan, Yoram Globus; Direction and Screenplay, Michael Ventura; Photography, Gideon Porath; Editor, Daniel Wetherbee; In Metrocolor; Not rated; 60 minutes; July release. A documentary on the personal and creative life of John Cassavetes, with clips from his films.

MEATBALLS PART II (Tri-Star) Producers, Stephen Poe, Tony Bishop; Executive Producer, Lisa Barsamian; Director, Ken Wiederhorn; Screenplay, Bruce Singer; Story, Martin Kitrosser, Carol Watson; Photography, Donald M. Morgan; Editor, George Berndt; Music, Ken Harrison; Designer, James William Newport; Costumes, Sandi Love; Assistant Director, Robert P. Cohen; In Movielab Color; Rated PG; 97 minutes; July release. CAST: Archie Hahn (Jamie), John Mengatti (Flash), Tammy Taylor (Nancy), Kim Richards (Cheryl), Ralph Seymour (Eddie), Richard Mulligan (Giddy), Hamilton Camp (Hershey), John Larroquette (Meathead), Paul Reubens (Albert)

THE CENSUS TAKER (Seymour Borde) Producer, Robert Bealmer; Director, Bruce Cook; Executive Producer, Gordon Smith; Screenplay, Bruce Cook, Gordon Smith; Story, Tim Jewett; Music, Jay Seagrave; Editor, Bruce Cook; In color; Not rated; 95 minutes; July release. CAST: Garrett Morris (Harvey), Greg Mullavey (George), Meredith MacRae (Martha), Austen Taylor (Eva), Timothy Bottoms (Pete)

LAST NIGHT AT THE ALAMO (Cinecom) Producers, Kim Henkel, Eagle Pennell; Director, Eagle Pennell; Screenplay, Kim Henkel; Photography, Brian Huberman, Eric Edwards; Music, Chuck Pennell, Wayne Bell; In color, black and white; Not rated; 82 minutes; July release. CAST: Sonny Davis (Cowboy), Lou Perry (Claude), Steve Matilla (Ichabod), Tina Hubbard (Mary), Doris Hargrave (Janice), J. Michael Hammond (Steve), Amanda LaMar (Lisa), Peggy Pennell (Ginger), David Shied (Poke), George Pheneger (Skipper), Henry Wideman (Willie), John Heaner (Wayne), Ernest Huerta (Hector), Pam Feight (Connie), Henry Kana (Ray), Sarah Hudgins (Darla), Jeanette Wiggins (Lois), Judie Stephens (Mavis), Hi Bice (Slim), Kim Henkel (Lionel), Eagle Pennell (Bo)

John Mengatti, Richard Mulligan, Paul Rubens,
Blackie Dammett, Donald Gibbs in "Meatballs II"
© *Tri-Star Pictures* **133**

Judge Reinhold, Willem Dafoe, Kaaren Lee,
Kate Vernon in "Roadhouse 66"
© *Atlantic Releasing Corp.*

Richard "Cheech" Marin, Tommy Chong in
"The Corsican Brothers" © *Orion Pictures*

ROADHOUSE 66 (Atlantic) Producers, Scott M. Rosenfelt, Mark Levinson; Executive Producers, Thomas Coleman, Michael Rosenblatt; Director, John Mark Robinson; Screenplay, Galen Lee, George Simpson; Story, Galen Lee; Photography, Tom Ackerman; Editor, Jay Lash Cassidy; Music, Gary Scott; Designer, Chester Kaczenski; Assistant Director, Mary Ellen Woods; In United Color; Rated R; 90 minutes; July release. CAST: Willem Dafoe (Johnny), Judge Reinhold (Beckman), Kaaren Lee (Jesse), Kate Vernon (Melissa), Stephen Elliott (Sam), Alan Autry (Hoot), Kevyn Major Howard (Dink), Peter Van Norden (Moss), Erica Yohn (Thelma)

SCREAM FOR HELP (Lorimar) Producer-Director, Michael Winner; Executive Producer, Irwin Yablans; Screenplay, Tom Holland; Photography, Robert Paynter; Editor, Arnold Ross; Music, John Paul Jones; Art Director, Tony Reading; In color; Rated R; 88 minutes; July release. CAST: Rachael Kelly (Christie), Marie Masters (Karen), David Brooks (Paul), Lolita Lorre (Brenda), Rocco Sisto (Lacey), Corey Parker (Josh), Sandra Clark (Janey), Tony Sibbald (Bob)

THE PHILADELPHIA EXPERIMENT (New World) Executive Producer, John Carpenter; Producers, Douglas Curtis, Joel B. Michaels; Director, Stewart Raffill; Screenplay, William Gray, Michael Janover; Story, Wallace Bennett, Don Jakoby; Photography, Dick Bush; Editor, Neil Travis; Associate Producer, Pegi Brotman; Art Director, Chris Campbell; Production Manager, Billy Ray Smith; Production Coordinator, Coni Lancaster; Assistant Directors, Pat Kehoe, Gail Fortmuller; Visual Effects Director, Max Anderson; In color; Rated PG; 102 minutes; August release. CAST: Michael Pare (David), Nancy Allen (Allison), Eric Christmas (Longstreet), Bobby Di Cicco (Jim), Kene Holliday (Clark), Debra Troyer (Young Pamela), Gary Brockette (Andrews), Pamela Brull (Doris), James Crittenden (Cowboy), Pamela Doucette (Nurse), Robin Krieger (Technician), Clayton Wilcox (Young Man), Rudy Daniels (Cop), Don Dolan (Driver), Glenn Morshower (Mechanic), Stephen Tobolowsky (Barney), Ed Bakey, Vivian Brown (Pa and Ma Willis), Jim Edgecomb (Boyer), Louise Latham (Mature Pamela), Steve Sachs, Harry Beer (Sailors), Anthony R. Nuzzo (Technician), Joe Moore, Andrew Bracken, Pat Dasko, Brent S. Laing, Kerry Maher, Charles Hall, Raymond Kowalski, Bo Parham, Lawrence Doll, Bill Smillie, Ralph Manza, Stephanie Faulkner, Michael Villani, Michael Currie, Lawrence Lott, Mary Lois Grantham, Sharon Doss

CHEECH AND CHONG'S THE CORSICAN BROTHERS (Orion) Producer, Peter MacGregor-Scott; Director, Thomas Chong; Screenplay, Cheech Marin, Thomas Chong; Photography, Harvey Harrison; Editor, Tom Avildsen; Music, Geo; In color and Dolby Stereo; Rated PG; 90 minutes; July release. CAST: Cheech Marin, Thomas Chong (Corsican Brothers), Roy Dotrice (Queen's Adviser/Old Jailer), Shelby Fiddis (Princess I), Rikki Marin (Princess II), Edie McClurg (Queen), Robbi Chong (Princess III), Rae Dawn Chong (Gypsy), Simono (Waiter), Kay Dotrice (Midwife), Martin Pepper (Martin)

SCARRED (Seymour Borde) Producers, Marie Turko, Mark Borde; Co-Producer, Dan Halperin; Executive Producer, Seymour Borde; Directed, Written and Edited by Marie Turko; Photography, Michael Miner; Art Director, Cecilia Rodarte; Assistant Director, Alex Cox; In DeLuxe Color; Rated R; July release. CAST: Jennifer Mayo (Ruby), Jackie Berryman (Carla), David Dean (Easy), Rico L. Richardson (Jojo), Debbie Dion (Sandy), Lili (Rita), Randolph Pitts, Walter Klenhard (Tricks), Haskell Anderson, Andre Waters (Pimps), Eddie Pansullo (Porno Producer)

JOY OF SEX (Paramount) Producer, Frank Konigsberg; Director, Martha Coolidge; Screenplay, Kathleen Rowell, J. J. Salter; Based on book of same title; Photography, Charles Correll; Art Director, Jim Murakami; Editors, Allan Jacobs, William Elias, Ned Humphreys, Eva Gardos; Music, Bishop Holiday; Scott Lipster, Harold Payne; Assistant Directors, Tony Brown, Don Heitzer, Irwin Marcus; In Movielab Color; Rated R; 93 minutes; August release. CAST: Cameron Dye (Alan), Michelle Meyrink (Leslie), Colleen Camp (Liz), Ernie Hudson (Porter), Lisa Langlois (Melanie), Charles Van Eman (Max), Joanne Baron (Miss Post), Darren Dalton (Ed), Heidi Holicker (Candy), Cristen Kauffman (Sharon), David H. MacDonald (Ernie), Paul Tulley (Ted), Joe Unger (Ranada), Christopher Lloyd (Coach), Connie Marie Brazelton (Allison), D. W. Brown (Dinko), Randolph Dreyfuss (Mushroom), Ellen Gerstein (Nurse), Eugene Robert Glazer (Dr. Fox), Sharee Gregory, Laura Harrington (Pretty Girls), Peter MacPherson (Earl), DeVera Marcus (Mrs. Fish), Nancy Neuman (Inga), Miguel A. Nunez, Jr., Jason Planco (Jocks), Robert Prescott (Tom/Richard), Danton Stone (Farouk), Jan Stratton (Miss Bismark), Sherry Unger (Mrs. Holt), Perry Van Soest (Student), Terry Wagner-Otis (Jenny), Carole Ita White (Roberta), Marlon Whitfield (Punk)

Nancy Allen, Michael Pare, Eric Christmas
in "The Philadelphia Experiment"
© *New World Pictures*

Cameron Dye, Michelle Meyrink, Charles Van Eman,
Lisa Langlois in "Joy of Sex"
© *Paramount Pictures*

Blaine Novak, Victoria Tennant, Peter Coyote in "Strangers Kiss" © *Orion Classics*

Kate Capshaw, Dennis Quaid in "Dreamscape" © *Chevy Chase Films*

STRANGERS KISS (Orion Classics) Producer, Douglas Dilge; Director, Matthew Chapman; Screenplay, Blaine Novak, Matthew Chapman; Story, Blaine Novak; Executive Producer, Michael White; Co-Producer, Hercules Bellville; Associate Producer, Sean Ferrer; Photography, Mikhail Suslov; Editor, William Carruth; Costumes, Tracy Tynan; Music, Gato Barbieri; Art Director, Ginny Randolph; In color; Rated PG; 93 minutes; August release. CAST: Peter Coyote (Director), Victoria Tennant (Carol/Betty), Blaine Novak (Stevie/Billy), Dan Shor (Farris/Producer), Richard Romanus (Frank Silva), Linda Kerridge (Shirley), Carlos Palomino (Estoban), Vincent Palmieri (Scandelli), Jay Rasumny (Jimmy), Jon Sloan (Mikey), Arthur Adams (Hanratty), Joseph Nipote (Tony), Jeannette Joseph (Miss Stein), Cecil Hill (Manager), Frank Moon (Rich Man), Larry Dilg (Clapper Man)

OVER THE BROOKLYN BRIDGE (Cannon/MGM/UA) Producers, Menahem Golan, Yoram Globus; Director, Menaham Golan; Screenplay, Arnold Somkin; Associate Producer, Christopher Pearce; Photography, Adam Greenberg; Music, Pino Donaggio; Editor, Mark Goldblatt; Art Director, John Lawless; Assistant Director, David Womark; In MetroColor; Rated R; 108 minutes; August release. CAST: Elliot Gould (Alby), Margaux Hemingway (Elizabeth), Sid Caesar (Uncle Ben), Burt Young (Phil), Shelley Winters (Becky), Carol Kane (Cheryl), Robert Gosset (Eddie), Karen Shallo (Mariena), Jerry Lazarus, Francine Beers, Leo Postrel, Rose Arrick, Matt Fischel, Lynnie Greene, Amy S. Ryder, Sal Richards, Leib Lensky, Lou David, Tom McDermott, Zvee Scooler

THE SEVEN MAGNIFICENT GLADIATORS (Cannon) Executive Producer, Alexander H. Cohen; Producers, Menahem Golan, Yoram Globus; Director, Bruno Mattei; Screenplay, Claudio Fragasso; Music, Ennio Morricone; Photography, Silvano Ippolitti; Art Director, Amedeo Mellone; Costumes, Pierro Rizzo; Production Manager, Marcello Berni; Assistant Directors, Claudio Fragasso, Domenico B. Attista, Remo Odevaine; Rated PG; In color; 83 minutes; August release. CAST: Lou Ferrigno (Gan), Brad Harris (Scipio), Sybil Danning (Julia), Dan Vadis (Nicerote), Carla Ferrigno (Pandora), Mandy Rice-Davies (Lucilla), Yehuda Erfoni (Emperor), Emillia Messina (Golia), Sal Borghese (Glafiro), Marina Rocchi (Cornelia), Antonella Giacomini (Fabia), Cesarina Tacconi (Morena), Franco Daddi (Neomio), Mark Urban (Dario), Kendal Kaldwell (Anacora), Kim McKay (Livia), Raul Cabrera (Elenio), Omero Capanna (Elios), Renata Roggero (Mora), Roberto Mura (Vendrix)

DREAMSCAPE (20th Century-Fox) Producer, Bruce Cohn Curtis; Director, Joseph Ruben; Screenplay, David Loughery, Chuck Russell, Joseph Ruben; Co-Producer, Jerry Tokofsky; Executive Producers, Stanley R. Zupnik, Tom Curtis; Photography, Brian Tufano; Editor, Richard Halsey; Visual Effects, Peter Kuran; Music, Maurice Jarre; Associate Producer, Chuck Russell; Production Coordinator, Julie Bilson Ahlberg; Assistant Directors, Michael Daves, Thomas Lofaro, Bob Doherty, Jerry Ketcham; Art Director, Jeff Staggs; Costumes, Linda M. Bass; Special Photography, Kevin Kutchaver; Chief Animator, Edward Manning; In Dolby Stereo and CFI Color; A Zupnik-Curtis Enterprises presentation; Rated PG13; 98 minutes; August release. CAST: Dennis Quaid (Alex), Max von Sydow (Paul), Christopher Plummer (Bob), Eddie Albert (President), Kate Capshaw (Jane), David Patrick Kelly (Tommy Ray), George Wendt (Charlie), Larry Gelman (Webber), Larry Cedar (Snakeman), Cory Yothers (Buddy), Redmond Gleeson (Snead), Peter Jason (Babcock), Chris Mulkey (Finch), Jana Taylor (Mrs. Webber), Madison Mason (Fred), Kendall Carly Browne (Mrs. Matusik), Kate Charleson (President's Daughter), Eric Gold (Tommy's Father), Virginia Kiser (President's Wife), Carl Strano (Edward), Brian Libby (McClaren), Bob Terhune (Dobbs), Fred M. Waugh (Hardy), Timothy Blake (Mrs. Blair), Carey Fox, Marii Mak, Claudia Lowe (Tech Aides), Anna Chavez (Newswoman), Ben Kronen (Conductor), John Malone (Trolley Conductor), Mindi Iden (Waitress), Betty Kean (Grandma), Trent Dolan (Guard), Andrew Boyer (Webber's Brother), George Caldwell (Buddy's Father), Ernest Harada (Gardener), Tin Greenberg (Nurse), Alan Buchdahl (Announcer)

BOLERO (Cannon) Producer, Bo Derek; Direction-Screenplay, John Derek; Executive Producers, Menahem Golan, Yoram Globus; Photography, John Derek; Music, Peter Bernstein; Love scenes scored by Elmer Bernstein; Associate Producer, Rony Yacov; Designer, Alan Roderick-Jones; Assistant Directors, Yousaf Bokhari, Alfredo Berlinchon; In Dolby Stereo and color; Not rated; 106 minutes; August release. CAST: Bo Derek (Ayre McGillvary), George Kennedy (Cotton Gray), Andrea Occhipinti (Angel Contreras), Ana Obregon (Catalina Terry), Olivia d'Abo (Paloma), Greg Bensen (Shiek), Ian Cochrane (Robert Stewart), Mirta Miller (Evita), Mickey Knox (Guide), Paul Stacey, James Stacey (Young Valentinos)

Margaux Hemingway, Elliott Gould in "Over the Brooklyn Bridge" © *Cannon Films*

Bo Derek, Andrea Occhipinti in "Bolero" © *Cannon Productions*

Neill Barry, Rainbow Harvest, Sarah Boyd
in "Old Enough" © Orion Classics

Lillian Gish, Timothy Bottoms, Anne Lockhart
in "Hambone and Hillie" © Sandy Howard/Adams Apple

SHEENA (Columbia) Producer, Paul Aratow; Director, John Guillermin; Screenplay, David Newman, Lorenzo Semple, Jr.; Story, David Newman, Leslie Stevens; Executive Producer, Yoram Ben-Ami; Photography, Pasqualino De Santis; Designer, Peter Murton; Editor, Ray Lovejoy; Music, Richard Hartley; Associate Producers, Christian Ferry, Alan Rinzler; Costumes, Annalisa Nasalli-Rocca; Art Director, Malcolm Middleton; Assistant Directors, Pat Clayton, Bill Mizel, Callum McDougall, Tom Mwangi; Production Coordinator, Liz Kerry; Special Effects, Peter Hutchinson, Bob Nugent; In Panavision, Metrocolor and Dolby Stereo; Rated PG; 117 minutes; August release. CAST: Tanya Roberts (Sheena), Ted Wass (Vic), Donovan Scott (Fletcher), Elizabeth of Toro (Shaman), France Zobda (Countess), Trevor Thomas (Prince), Clifton Jones (King), John Forgeham (Jorgensen), Errol John (Bolu), Sylvester Williams (Juka), Bob Sherman (Grizzard), Michael Shannon (Philip), Nancy Paul (Betsy), Kathryn Gant (Child Sheena), Kirsty Lindsay (Young Sheena), Nick Brimble (Wadman), Paul Gee (Blau), Dave Cooper (Anders), Tim Ward-Booth (Pilot)

OLD ENOUGH (Orion Classics) Producer, Dina Silver; Direction-Screenplay, Marisa Silver; Photography, Michael Ballhaus; Designer, Jeffrey Townsend; Editor, Mark Burns; Music, Julian Marshall; Costumes, Teri Kane; In color; Rated PG; 91 minutes; August release. CAST: Sarah Boyd (Lonnie), Rainbow Harvest (Karen), Neill Barry (Johnny), Danny Aiello (Bruckner), Susan Kingsley (Mrs. Bruckner), Roxanne Hart (Carla), Fran Brill (Mrs. Sloan), Gerry Bamman (Sloan), Alyssa Milano (Diane), Anne Pitoniak (Katherine), Charlie Willinger (Danny), Michael Monetti (Mikey), Manny Jacobs (Jimmy), Gina Batiste (Marlene), Tristine Skyler (Sarah), Al Israel (Bodega Owner), Paul Butler (Guard), Primy Rivera (Spanish Boy)

RED DAWN (MGM/UA) Producers, Buzz Feitshans, Barry Beckerman; Director, John Milius; Screenplay, Kevin Reynolds, John Milius; Photography, Ric Waite; Editor, Thom Noble; Music, Basil Poledouris; In color and Dolby Stereo; Rated PG13; 114 minutes; August release. CAST: Patrick Swayze (Jed), C. Thomas Howell (Robert), Lea Thompson (Erica), Charlie Shee (Matt), Darren Dalton (Daryl), Jennifer Grey (Toni)

FLASHPOINT (Tri-Star) Producer, Skip Short; Director, William Tannen; Screenplay, Dennis Shryack, Michael Butler; Photography, Peter Moss; Editor, David Garfield; Music, Tangerine Dream; In color; Rated R; 94 minutes; August release. CAST: Kris Kristofferson

SAM'S SON (Invictus) Producer, Kent McCray; Direction-Screenplay, Michael Landon; Photography, Ted Voightlander; Music, David Rose; Art Director, George Renne; Editor, John Loeffler; In color; Rated PG; 104 minutes; August release. CAST: Eli Wallach (Sam Orowitz), Anne Jackson (Harriet Orowitz), Timothy Patrick Murphy (Gene Orowitz), Hallie Todd (Cathy), Alan Hayes (Robert), Jonna Lee (Bonnie), Michael Landon (Gene Orman), Howard Witt (Cy), William Boyett (Coach), John Walcutt (Ronnie), David Lloyd Nelson (Lonnie), William H. Bassett (Turner), Harvey Gold (Jake), James Karen (Collins)

BODY ROCK (New World) Producer, Jeffrey Schechtman; Co-Executive Producers, Jon Feltheimer, Phil Ramone, Charles J. Weber; Director, Marcelo Epstein; Screenplay, Desmond Nakano; Associate Producer, Chuck Russell; Designer, Guy Comtois; Assistant Directors, Leon Dudevoir, Gerald Fleck; Photography, Robby Muller; Editor, Richard Halsey; Art Director, Craig Stearns; Choreographer, Susan Scanlan; Costumes, Marlene Stewart; Production Coordinator, Rebecca Greeley; In color and Dolby Stereo; Soundtrack available on EMI America Records and Tapes; Rated PG13; 93 minutes; September release. CAST: Lorenzo Lamas (Chilly D), Vicki Frederick (Claire), Cameron Dye (E-Z), Michelle Nicastro (Darlene), Ray Sharkey (Terrence), Grace Zabriskie (Chilly's Mother), Carole Ita White (Carolyn), Joseph Whipp (Donald), Oz Rock (Ricky), LaRon A. Smith (Magick), Rene Elizondo (Snake), Seth Kaufman (Jama), Russell Clark (Jay), Robin Menken (Jodie), Tony Ganios (Big Mac), Shashawnee Hall (Theo), Barbara Beaman (Cashier), Mimi Kinkade (Little Freak), Ellen Gerstein (Secretary), Mark Sellers (D. J.), Ken Powell (Fred), Dark Hoffman, James Greene (Chilly's Friends), Robert Kessler (Doctor)

IMPULSE (20th Century-Fox) Producer, Tim Zinneman; Director, Graham Baker; Screenplay, Bart Davis, Don Carlos Dunaway; Music, Paul Chihara; Photography, Thomas Del Ruth; Editor, David Holden; In color; Rated R; 91 minutes; September release. CAST: Tim Matheson (Stuart), Meg Tilly (Jennifer), Hume Cronyn (Dr. Carr), John Karlen (Bob), Bill Paxton (Eddie), Amy Stryker (Margo), Claude Earl Jones (Sheriff), Robert Wightman (Howard), Lorinne Vozoff (Mrs. Russell)

NIGHT SHADOWS (Film Ventures International) also released as "Mutant"; Executive Producers, Edward L. Montoro, Henry Fownes; Producer, Igo Kantor; Director, John "Bud" Cardos; Associate Producer/Production Manager, Nathaniel J. Dunn; Screenplay, Peter Z.

Treat Williams (L) in "Flashpoint"
© Tri-Star Pictures

Patrick Swayze, C. Thomas Howell, Charlie Sheen
in "Red Dawn" © MGM/UA Entertainment

**Michelle Nicastro, Lorenzo Lamas in
"Body Rock" © New World Pictures**

**Meg Tilly, Tim Matheson, Hume Cronyn
in "Impulse" © ABC Motion Pictures**

(Logan), Treat Williams (Ernie), Rip Torn (Sheriff), Tess Harper (Ellen), Jean Smart (Doris)

HAMBONE AND HILLIE (New World) Executive Producers, Mel Pearl, Don Levin; Producers, Gary Gillingham, Sandy Howard; Co-Producer, Roger LaPage; Associate Producers, Michael Murphey, Joel Soisson; Director, Roy Watts; Screenplay, Sandra K. Bailey, Michael Murphey, Joel Soisson; Based on story by Ken Barnett; Photography, Jon Kranhouse; Assistant Directors, Jay Kamen, Scott White; Production Coordinator, Pam Knapp; Costumes, Kathy Estocin; Art Director, Helena Rubinstein; Editor, Robert J. Kizer; Music, George Garavarentz; In Astral Bellevue Pathe Color, Dolby Stereo; CAST: Lillian Gish (Hillie), Timothy Bottoms (Michael), Candy Clark (Nancy), O. J. Simpson (Tucker), Robert Walker (Wanderer), Jack Carter (Lester), Alan Hale (McVicker), Anne Lockhart (Roberta), William Jordan (Bert), Paul Koslo (Jere), Nancy Morgan (Ellen), Arnie Moore (Dognapper), Sidney Robin Greenbush (Amy), Maureen Quinn (Edna), Mark Bentley (Danny), Nicole Eggert (Marci)

THE ACT (Film Ventures) Previous title "Bless 'Em All"; Executive Producer, Ron Gorton; Producers, David Greene, Sig Shore; Director, Sig Shore; Screenplay, Robert Lipsyte; Photography, Benjamin Davis; Editor, Ron Kalish; Music, John Sebastian, Phil Goldston; Design, Steve Wilson; Assistant Director, Mike Shore; Production Manager, Ron Gorton, Jr.; In Technicolor; Rated R; 94 minutes; August release. CAST: Robert Ginty (Don), Sarah Langenfeld (Leslie), Nick Surovy (Julian), John Aprea (Ron), John Tripp (Dixie), Eddie Albert (Harry), James Andronica (Mickey), John Cullum (President), Roger Davis (Police Chief), Pat Hingle (Frank), David Huddleston (Corky), Jill St. John (Elise), Arika Wells (Hooker), Tom Hunter (The John)

MIRRORS (First American) Formerly "Marianne"; Producers, John T. Parker, Stirling W. Smith; Director, Noel Black; Screenplay, Sidney L. Stebel; Photography, Michael D. Murphy; Editor, Robert Estrin; Music, Stephen Lawrence; Assistant Director, Michael Daves; Design, Ronald Weinberg; Art Director, Ray Kutos; Associate Producer, Daniel Bossier; Assistant Producer, Jack Boasberg; In CFI color; Rated PG; 88 minutes; August release. CAST: Kitty Winn (Marianne), Peter Donat (Dr. Godard), William Swetland (Charbonnet), Mary-Robin Redd (Helene), William Burns (Gary), Lou Wagner (Chet), Don Keefer (Peter), Vanessa Hutchinson (Marie)

Orton, Michael Jones, John C. Kruize; Music, Richard Band; Story, Michael Jones, John C. Kruize; Photography, Al Taylor; Production Coordinator, Enid Kantor; Art Director, Tony Kupersmith; Editor, Michael Duthie; Assistant Directors, Mel Bishop, Bruce Simon; Color by TVC Labs; In Dolby Stereo; Rated R; 99 minutes; September release. CAST: Wings Hauser (Josh), Bo Hopkins (Sheriff), Jody Medford (Holly), Lee Montgomery (Mike), Marc Clement (Albert), Cary Guffey (Billy), Jennifer Warren (Dr. Tate), Danny Nelson (Jack), Mary Nell Santacroce (Mrs. Mapes), Stuart Culpepper (Mel), Johnny Popwell, Sr. (Dawson), Ralph Redpath (Vic), Larry Quackenbush (Harve), Ralph Pace (Art), Wallace Wilkinson (Mitchell), Charles Franzen (E.P.A. Man), Lit Cannah (Mrs. Miller), Pat Moss (Penelope), Tina Kincaide (Judy), Albert's Gang: Jerry Rushing, Chester Clark, Joshua Lee Patton

VAMPING (Atlantic) Producers, Howard Kling, Stratton Rawson; Executive Producers, Nathan Boxer, Patrick Duffy, Frederick King Keller; Director, Frederick King Keller; Screenplay, Michael Healy; Additional Material, Robert Seidman; Story, Mr. Keller; Photography, Skip Roessel; Design, Howard Kling, Karen Morse, Stratton Rawson; Music, Ken Kaufman; Editor, Darren Kloomok; Costumes, Elizabeth Haas; Production Manager, Laurie Dann; Assistant Directors, Tom Trovato, Robert Sherman; In color; Rated R; 107 minutes; September release. CAST: Patrick Duffy (Harry), Catherine Hyland (Diane), Rod Arrants (Raymond), Fred A. Keller (Fat Man), David Booze (Benjamin), Jed Cooper (Lennie), Steve Gilborn (Jimmy), John McCurry (Sam), Wendel Meldrum (Rita), Henry Stram (Deacon), Nataljia Nogulich (Julie), Raymond Fleszar, Frank O'Hara (Old Men), Isabel Price, Sally Birkhead (Matrons), Lambros Touris (Huge Man), Elizabeth Klein (Shopping Cart Lady)

UNTIL SEPTEMBER (MGM/UA) Producer, Michael Gruskoff; Director, Richard Marquand; Screenplay, Janice Lee Graham; Photography, Philippe Weit; Editor, Sean Barton; Music, John Barry; In color; Rated R; 100 minutes; September release. CAST: Karen Allen (Mo), Johanna Pavils (Marcia), Marie-Catherine Conti (Isabelle), Thierry Lhermitte (Xavier), Tiphanie Spencer (Laurence), Oliver Spencer (David), Rochelle Robertson (Carol), Raphaeile Spencer (Jenny), Hutton Cobb (Andrew), Christopher Cazenove (Philip), Steve Gadler (Carry), Edith Perret (Mme. Durand), Nitza Saul (Sylvia), Helene Desbiez (Sophie)

**Jody Medford, Wings Hauser in "Night Shadows"
© Film Ventures International**

**Karen Allen, Christopher Cazenove, Thierry
Lhermitte in "Until September" © United Artists**

Drew Barrymore, Shelley Long, Ryan O'Neal in
"Irreconcilable Differences" © *Warner Bros.*

Kate Capshaw, John Shea in "Windy City"
© *CBS Inc.*

THE WILD LIFE (Universal) Producers, Art Linson, Cameron Crowe; Director, Art Linson; Screenplay, Cameron Crowe; Photography, James Glennon; Designer, William Sandell; Editor, Michael Jablow; Costumes, Marilyn Vance; Co-Producer, Don Phillips; Executive Producer, C. O. Erickson; Original Music, Edward Van Halen, Donn Landee; Assistant Directors, Albert Shapiro, Marty Ewing; Production Coordinator, Danis Regal; Soundtrack available on MCA Records and Cassettes; In Dolby Stereo and Technicolor; Rated R; 96 minutes; September release. CAST: Christopher Penn (Tom), Ilan Mitchell-Smith (Jim), Eric Stoltz (Bill), Jenny Wright (Eileen), Lea Thompson (Anita), Brin Berliner (Tony), Rick Moranis (Harry), Hart Bochner (David), Susan Blackstone (Donna), Cari Anne Warder (Julie), Robert Ridgely (Craig), Jack Kehoe (Parker), Jennifer White (Brenda), Beth McKinley (Robin), Michael Bowen (Vince), Angel Salazar (Benny), Randy Quaid (Charlie), Dick Rude (Eddie), Robert Chestnut (Eddie's Friend), Reginald Farmer (Reggie), Sherilyn Fenn (Penny), Leo Penn (Tom's Dad), Hildy Brooks (Mrs. Conrad), Lee Ving (Installer), William Bramley, Dean Devlin, Brynja Willis, Leigh Lombardi, Rande Worcester, Kim Vignal, Nancy Wilson, Ben Stein, Tommy Swerdlow, Paul Wiggins

C.H.U.D. (New World) Executive Producer, Larry Abrams; Producer, Andrew Bonime; Director, Douglas Cheek; Screenplay, Parnell Hall; Music, Cooper Hughes; Photography, Peter Stein; Designer, William Bilowit; Production Manager, Robert Bordiga; Assistant Directors, Lewis Gould, Stephen Wertimer; Special Makeup, John Caglione, Jr.; Associate Producer, Thomas H. Field; Art Director, Jorge Luis Toro; Associate Producer, Alphonso Tafoya; Color by TVC Labs; Rated R; 90 minutes; September release. CAST: Laure Mattos (Flora), John Heard (George), Kim Greist (Lauren), Brenda Currin (Francine), Justin Hall (Justin), Christopher Curry (Capt. Bosch), Michael O'Hare (Fuller), Cordis Heard (Sanderson), Vic Polizos (Hays), Eddie Jones (Chief O'Brien), Sam McMurray (Crespi), Frak Adu (Cop), Ruth Maleczech (Mrs. Monroe), J. C. Quinn (Murphy), Patricia Richardson (Ad Woman), Raymond Baker (Ad Man), Daniel Stern (Reverend), Beverly Bentley (Doris), Graham Beckel (Val), Gene O'Neill (Jackson), Peter Michael Goetz (Gramps), George Martin (Wilson), John Bedford-Lloyd (Shadow), John Ramsey (Commissioner), Henry Yuk (Coroner)

WINDY CITY (Warner Bros.) Producer, Alan Greisman; Direction and Screenplay, Armyan Bernstein; Photography, Reynaldo Villalobos; Editor, Clifford Jones; Music, Jack Nitzsche; In color; Rated R; 105 minutes; September release. CAST: John Shea (Danny), Kate Capshaw (Emily), Josh Mostel (Sol), Jim Borrelli (Mickey), Jeffrey DeMunn (Bobby), Eric Pierpoint (Pete), Lewis J. Stadlen (Marty), James Sutorius (Eddie), Niles McMaster (Michael), Lisa Taylor (Sherry), Nathan Davis (Jones), Louie Lanciloti (Ernesto)

THE BROTHER FROM ANOTHER PLANET (Cinecom International) Producers, Peggy Raiski, Maggie Renzi; Written, Directed and Edited by John Sayles; Photography, Ernest Dickerson; Music, Mason Daring; In color; Not rated; release. CAST: Joe Morton (The Brother), Darryl Edwards (Fly), Steve James (Odell), Leonard Jackson (Smokey), Bill Cobbs (Walter), Maggie Renzi (Noreen), Men in black: John Sayles, David Strathairn

IRRECONCILABLE DIFFERENCES (Warner Bros.) Producers, Arlene Sellers, Alex Winitsky; Director, Charles Shyer; Screenplay, Mr. Shyer, Nancy Meyers; Photography, William A. Fraker; Editor, John F. Burnett; Music, Paul DeSenneville, Oliver Toussaint; In color; Rated PG; 114 minutes; September release. CAST: Ryan O'Neal (Albert Brodsky), Shelley Long (Lucy), Drew Barrymore (Casey), Sam Wanamaker (David Kessler), Allen Garfield (Phil), Sharon Stone (Blake), Hortenzia Colorado (Maria Hernandez), Colleen Devine (Nurse)

THE EVIL THAT MEN DO (Tri-Star) Producer, Pancho Kohner; Director, J. Lee Thompson; Screenplay, David Lee Henry, John Crowther; Based on novel by R. Lance Hill; Music, Ken Thorne; In color; Rated R; 90 minutes; September release. CAST: Charles Bronson (Holland), Theresa Saldana (Rhiana), Joseph Maher (Moloch), Jose Ferrer (Lomelin), Rene Enriquez (Max), John Glover (Briggs), Raymond St. Jacques (Randolph), Antoinette Bower (Claire), Enrique Lucero (Aristos), Jorge Luke (Cillero), Mischa Hausserman (Karl), Roger Cudney (Cannell)

CRIMES OF PASSION (New World) Producer, Barry Sandler; Director, Ken Russell; Screenplay, Mr. Sandler; Photography, Dick Bush; Editor, Brian Tagg; Music, Rick Wakeman; In color; Rated R; 102 minutes; September release. CAST: Bruce Davison (Hopper), John Laughlin (Grady), Anthony Perkins (Shayne), Annie Potts (Amy), Kathleen Turner (Joanna/China Blue)

John Heard, Kim Greist in "Chud"
© *New World Pictures*

Kathleen Turner, Anthony Perkins in "Crimes of
Passion" © *New World Pictures*

Imogene Coca, Zach Galligan in "Nothing
Lasts Forever" © *MGM/UA Classics*

Joe Morton, Dee Dee Bridgewater in "The Brother
from Another Planet" © *CineCom International*

OUT OF ORDER (First Run Features) Produced, Directed and Edited by Diane Christian and Bruce Jackson; Photography, Bruce Jackson; In color; Not rated; 89 minutes; September release. A documentary concerning six dropout nuns and why they left.

NOTHING LASTS FOREVER (MGM/UA) Producer, Lorne Michaels; Direction and Screenplay, Tom Schiller; Photography, Fred Schuler; Editors, Kathleen Dougherty, Margot Francis; Art Director, Woods MacKintosh; Co-Producer, John Head; In black and white and Technicolor; Rated PG; 82 minutes; September release. CAST: Zach Galligan (Adam), Apollinia van Ravenstein (Mara), Lauren Tom (Ely), Dan Aykroyd (Buck), Imogene Coca (Daisy), Anita Ellis (Aunt Anita), Eddie Fisher (Himself), Sam Jaffe (Father Knickerbocker), Paul Rogers (Hugo), Mort Sahl (Uncle Mort), Jan Triska (Architect), Rosemary DeAngelis (Helen), Clarice Taylor (Lu), Bill Murray (Cruise Director)

HEARTBREAKERS (Orion) Producers, Bob Weis, Bobby Roth; Executive Producers, Lee Muhl, Harry Cooper, Joseph Franck; Direction and Screenplay, Bobby Roth; Photography, Michael Ballhaus; Editor, John Carnochan; Music, Tangerine Dream; Costumes, Betsy Jones; Associate Producer, Cass Coty; Assistant Director, Jack Baran; In Dolby Stereo and DeLuxe Color; Rated R; 98 minutes; September release. CAST: Peter Coyote (Arthur), Nick Mancuso (Eli), Carole Laure (Liliane), Max Gail (Charles), James Laurenson (Terry), Carol Wayne (Candy), Jamie Rose (Libby), Kathryn Harrold (Cyd), George Morfogen (Max), Jerry Hardin (Warren)

JAWS OF SATAN (United Artists) formerly "King Cobra"; Producer, Bill Wilson; Director, Bob Claver; Screenplay, Gerry Holland from story by James Callaway; Photography, Dean Cundey; Editor, Len Miller; Music, Roger Kellaway; Art Director, Robert Topol; Production Manager-Associate Producer, Joel Douglas; In Technicolor; Rated R; 92 minutes; September release. CAST: Fritz Weaver (Father Farrow), Gretchen Corbett (Dr. Sheridan), Jon Korkes (Paul), Norman Lloyd (Monsignore), Diana Douglas (Evelyn), Bob Hannah (Matt), Nancy Priddy (Elizabeth), Christina Applegate (Kim), John McCurry (Sheriff), Jack Gordan (Mayor)

ALMOST YOU (20th Century-Fox) Producer, Mark Lipson; Executive Producers, Charles C. Thieriot, Sandy Climan, Stephen J. Levi; Director, Adam Brooks; Screenplay, Mark Horowitz from a story by Adam Brooks; Photography, Alexander Gruszynski; Editor, Mark Burns; Art Director, Nora Chavoosian; Music, Jonathan Elias; Assistant Director, Craig Laurence Rice; In color; Not rated; 96 minutes; September release. CAST: Brooke Adams (Erica), Griffin Dunne (Alex), Karen Young (Lisa), Marty Watt (Kevin), Christine Estabrook (Maggie), Josh Mostel (David), Laura Dean (Jeannie), Dana Delany (Susan), Miguel Pinero (Ralph), Joe Silver (Uncle Stu), Joe Leon (Uncle Mel), Daryl Edwards (Sal), Suzzy Roche (Receptionist)

MASSIVE RETALIATION (One Pass-Hammermark) Producer-Director, Thomas A. Cohen; Executive Producer, Steve Michelson; Screenplay, Larry Wittnebert, Richard Beban; Photography, Richard Derner; Editor, B. J. Sears; Music, Harn Soper, Paul Potyen; Production Manager-Assistant Director, Geoffrey de Valois; In color; Not rated; 90 minutes; September release. CAST: Tom Bower (Kirk), Karlene Crockett (Marianne), Peter Donat (Lee), Marilyn Hassett (Lois), Susan O'Connell (Jackie), Michael Pritchard (Harry), Jason Gedrick (Eric), Mimi Farina (Susie)

THE WARRIOR AND THE SORCERESS (New World) Producers, Frank Isaac, John Broderick; Direction and Screenplay, John Broderick; Story, John Broderick, William Stout; Music, Louis Saunders; Editor, Silvia Ripoll; Photography, Leonard Solis; Co-Producers, Hector Olivera, Alex Sessa; Art Director, Emmett Baldwin; Production Manager, Alex Plowing; Costumes, Mary Bertram; Assistant Directors, Andrew Sargent, Charles Ritter, Nick Salter; Production Coordinator, Ginny Nugent; A New Horizons production in color; Rated R; 81 minutes; October release. CAST: David Carradine (Kain), Luke Askew (Zeg), Maria Socas (Naja), Anthony DeLongis (Kief), Harry Townes (Bludge), William Marin (Bal Caz), Arthur Clark (Burgo), Daniel March (Blather), John Overby (Gabble), Richard Paley (Scarface), Mark Welles (Burgo's Captain), Cecilia North (Exotic Dancer), Ned Ivers (Slave), Lillian Cameron (Drowning Slave), Eve Adams (Woman at well), Zeg's Guards: Dylan Williams, Herman Cass, Joe Cass, Arthur Neal, Michael Zane, Herman Gere, Gus Parker

THE TIME OF HARVEY MILK (Teleculture) Producers-Directors, Robert Epstein, Richard Schmiechen; Editors, Deborah Hoffmann, Robert Epstein; Associate Producer, Greg Bex; Narrator, Harvey Fierstein; Music, Mark Isham; Photography, Frances Reid; Art Director, Michael McNeil; Narration Writers, Judith Coburn, Carter Wilson; Coordinating Producer, Kathy Kline; Executive Producer, David Loxton; In color; Not rated; 87 minutes; October release. A documentary on the life and death of Harvey Milk in San Francisco.

TEACHERS (MGM/UA) Producer, Aaron Russo; Director, Arthur Hiller; Screenplay, W. R. McKinney; Editor, Don Zimmerman; In color; Rated R; 120 minutes; October release. CAST: Nick Nolte (Alex), JoBeth Williams (Lisa), Judd Hirsch (Roger), Ralph Macchio (Eddie), Allen Garfield (Rosenberg), Lee Grant (Dr. Burke), Richard Mulligan (Herbert), Royal Dano (Ditto), William Schallert (Horn)

TERROR IN THE AISLES (Universal) Producers, Stephen J. Netburn, Andrew J. Kuehn; Director, Mr. Kuehn; Screenplay, Margery Doppelt; Photography, John A. Alonzo; Music, John Beal; Editor, Gregory McClatchy; Clip Research, John JB Wilson; In color, black and white; Rated R; 85 minutes; October release. Film clips from some 75 horror and suspense movies.

Nick Nolte, JoBeth Williams in "Teachers"
© *United Artists Corp.*

139

Genevieve Bujold, Lesley Ann Warren
in "Choose Me" © *Island Alive*

Talking Heads, Alex Weir in "Stop
Making Sense" © *Island Alive/Cinecom*

WHEN NATURE CALLS (Troma) Producers, Frank Vitale, Charles Kaufman; Director, Charles Kaufman; Executive Producer, Susan Thomases; Story and Screenplay, Charles Kaufman, Straw Weisman; Photography, Mike Spera; Editor, Michael Jacobi; Art Director, Susan Kaufman; Music, Arthur Custer; Assistant Directors, Rex A. Piano, Per Sjostedt; Costumes, Ellen Lutter; In color; Rated R; 88 minutes; October release. CAST: David Orange (Greg), Barbara Marineau (Barb), Nicky Beim (Little Billy), Tina Marie Staiano (Bambi), David Strathairn (Weejun), Silas Davis (O'Malley), Mike Brancato (Milos), Patricia Clement (Cleaning Lady), Scott Perrin (Little Timmy), Ted Brooks (Parking Attendant), Amy Miller (Millie), Willie Mays, Morey Amsterdam, Fred Blassie, Myron Cohen, Stanley Siegel, John Cameron Swayze, G. Gordon Liddy, Sture M. Sjostedt, Thomas MacGregor Vitale (Baby Bullets), Stanley Kaufman (Official), Frank Vitale (Interrogator), Timmy Leight (Bag Lady), Lanc Acktiv, Anthony Cala, Ed Sato (Gangsters), John Hays (Bobby), Matthew Adams (Marty), Kristin Walker (Maria), Cheryl McFadden (Gena), Bill C. W. Long (Blind-o-vision Man), Ric Braun (Jacques Perrier), Bill Smith (Husband)

FAR FROM POLAND (Film Forum) Producer-Director, Jill Godmilow; In collaboration with Susan Delson, Mark Magill, Andrzej Tymowski; Photography, Jacek Laskus; Piano, Michael Sahl; In color, black and white; Not rated; 106 minutes; October release. CAST: Ruth Maleczech (Anna Walentynowicz), Mark Margolis (Adam Zarewski), John Perkins (Gen. Jaruzelski), William Raymond (K-62), David Warrilow (Voice of Gen. Jaruzelski)

NOT FOR PUBLICATION (Samuel Goldwyn) Producer, Anne Kimmel; Director, Paul Bartel; Executive Producer, Mark Forstater; Screenplay, John Meyer, Paul Bartel; Associate Producer, Lynwood Spinks; Associate Producer/Assistant Director, Jack Cummins; Photography, George Tirl; Designer, Robert Schulenberg; Art Director, Michael O'Sullivan; Editor, Alan Toomayan; Costumes, Rondi Hilstrom-Davis; Choreographer, Utah Ground; Music, John Meyer; A Thorn Emi Screen entertainment presentation in color; Rated R; 88 minutes; October release. CAST: Nancy Allen (Lois), David Naughton (Barry), Laurence Luckinbill (Mayor Franklyn), Alice Ghostley (Doris), Richard Paul (Troppogrosso), Barry Dennen (Senor Woparico), Cork Hubbert (Odo), Richard Blackburn (Jim), Robert Ahola (Signore Scoppi), Jeanne Evan (Helen), J. David Moeller (Duffy), Michael O'Sullivan (Eddie), Hart Sprager (Gene)

STOP MAKING SENSE (Cinecom International) Producer, Gary Goetzman; Director, Jonathan Demme; Photography, Jordan Cronenweth; Editor, Lisa Day; In color, black and white; Not rated; 88 minutes; October release. A performance film of Talking Heads.

SAVAGE STREETS (Motion Picture Marketing) Producer, John C. Strong; Director, Danny Steinmann; Screenplay, Norman Yonemoto, Danny Steinmann; Photography, Stephen L. Posey; Editor, Bruce Stubblefield, John O'Connor; Music, Michael Lloyd, John D'Andrea; In color; Rated R; 93 minutes; October release. CAST: Linda Blair (Brenda), John Vernon (Underwood), Robert Dryer (Jake), Johnny Venocur (Vince), Sal Landi (Fargo), Scott Mayer (Red), Debra Blee (Rachel), Lisa Freeman (Francine), Marcia Karr (Stevie), Luisa Leschin (Maria)

CHOOSE ME (Island Alive) Producers, Carolyn Pfeiffer, David Blocker; Direction and Screenplay, Alan Rudolph; Photography, Jan Kiesser; Editor, Mia Goldman; In color; Rated R; 114 minutes; October release. CAST: Genevieve Bujold (Nancy), Keith Carradine (Mickey), Lesley Ann Warren (Eve), Patrick Bauchau (Zack), Rae Dawn Chong (Pearl), John Larroquette (Billy), Edward Ruscha (Ralph), Gailard Sartain (Mueller), Robert Gould (Lou), John Considine (Dr. Greene), Jodi Buss (Babs)

A BIGGER SPLASH (Buzzy Enterprises) Producer-Director, Jack Hazan; Screenplay, Mr. Hazan, David Mingay; Photography, Jack Hazan; Editor, David Mingay; Music, Patrick Gowers, Greg Bailey; In color; Not rated; October release. CAST: David Hockney (Painter), Peter Schlesinger (Painter's Friend), Ossie Clark (Dress Designer), Celia Birtwell (Designer's Wife), Mo McDermott (Friend), Henry Geldzahler (Collector), Kasmin (Dealer)

AMERICAN DREAMER (Warner Bros.) Executive Producer, Barry Krost; Director, Rick Rosenthal; Screenplay, Jim Kouf, David Greenwalt; From story by Ann Biderman; Photography, Giuseppe Rofumo; Music, Lewis Furey; Costumes, Michael Kaplan; Designer, Brian Eatwell; Editor, Anne Goursaud; In color; Rated PG; 105 minutes; October release. CAST: JoBeth Williams (Cathy), Tom Conti (Alan), Giancarlo Giannini (Victor), Coral Browne (Margaret), James Staley (Kevin Palmer), C. B. Barnes (Kevin Palmer, Jr.), Huckleberry Fox (Karl), Jean Rougerie (Don Carlos), Pierre Santini (Ins. Klaus), Leon Zitrone (Russian Ambassador)

Nancy Allen, David Naughton in "Not for
Publication" © *Samuel Goldwyn Co.*

JoBeth Williams, Tom Conti in
"American Dreamer" © *Warner Bros.*

Willie Nelson, Lesley Ann Warren
in "Songwriter" © *Tri-Star Pictures*

"Nicaragua: No Pasaran"
© *New Yorker Films*

THE BEAR (Embassy) Producer, Larry Spangler; Executive Producer, James Hearn; Director, Richard C. Sarafian; Screenplay, Michael Kane; Photography, Laszlo George; Editor, Robert Florio; Designer, George Costello; Music, Bill Conti, Charles Koppelman, Martin Bandier; Costumes, Ron Talsky; Assistant Director, Buck Edwards; In DeLuxe Color; Rated PG; 112 minutes; October release. CAST: Gary Busey (Paul "Bear" Bryant), Cynthia Leake (Mary Harmon Bryant), Harry Dean Stanton (Coach Thomas), Jon-Erik Hexum (Pat Trammell), Carmen Thomas (Mae Martin Bryant), Cary Guffey (Grandson Marc), Steve Greenstein (Joe Namath), D'Urville Martin (Billy), Eric Hipple (Tony Easton)

SONGWRITER (Tri-Star) Producer, Sydney Pollack; Director, Alan Rudolph; Screenplay, Bud Shrake; Executive Producer-Production Manager, Mike Moder; Photography, Matthew Leonetti; Designer, Joel Schiller; Editor, Stuart Pappe; Songs, Willie Nelson, Kris Kristofferson, Larry Cansler; Assistant Directors, David McGiffert, Pamela Eilerson; Editors, Stephen Lovejoy, George A. Martin; Production Coordinator, Janis Benjamin; In Dolby Stereo and color; Rated R; 94 minutes; October release. CAST: Willie Nelson (Doc Jenkins), Kris Kristofferson (Blackie Buck), Melinda Dillon (Honey), Rip Torn (Dino), Lesley Ann Warren (Gilda), Mickey Raphael (Arly), Rhonda Dotson (Corkie), Richard C. Sarafian (Rodeo Rocky), Robert Gould (Ralph), Sage Parker (Pattie), Shannon Wilcox (Anita), Jeff MacKay (Hogan), Gailard Sartain (Mulreaux), Stephen Bruton (Sam), Glen Clark (Paul), Cleve Dupin (Road Manager), B. C. Cooper (Cooper), Poodie Locke (Purvis), Joe Keyes (Eddie), Amanda Bishop, Kristin Renfro, Sammy Allred, Bill Boyd, Steve Fromholtz, Johnny Gimble, Eloise Schmitt, Kate Cadenhead

BAD MANNERS (New World) previously titled "Growing Pains"; Producer, Kim Jorgensen; Director, Bobby Houston; Screenplay, Bobby Houston, Joseph Kwong; Executive Producer, Amy Rabins; Music, Ron Mael, Russell Mael, Michael Lewis; Art Director, Jim Dulz; Photography, Jan De Bont; Production Manager, Alan Blomquist; Assistant Directors, Eric Jewett, Roger Duvall; Costumes, Linda Bass, Jack Buehler; Editor, Barry Zetlin; Production Coordinators, Jeannie Issacs, Renee Armalin; In Metrocolor; Rated R; 85 minutes; November release. CAST: Karen Black (Gladys), Martin Mull (Warren), Anne De Salvo (Sister Serena), Murphy Dunne (Kurtz), Pamela Segall (Girl Joey), Georg Olden (Piper), Michael Hentz (Mouse), Joey Coleman (Whitey), Christopher Brown (Blackie), Steve Stucker (Dr. Bender),

Kimmy Robertson (Sarah), John Paul Lussier (Garth), Edy Williams (Mrs. Slatt), Hy Pike (Slatt), Gertrude Flynn (Mother Celestina), Lark Hackshaw (Nurse Bates), Bill Quinones (Pepe), Seth Wagerman (Professor), Thomas Stokes (Chubby), Michelle Cundey (Suzy), Marshall Effron (Cabbie), Susan Ruttan (Biker), Richard Deacon (Ticket Salesman), Bridget Sienna (Carnation), Barry Cutler (Pizza Man), Steve Lalande (Gay Guy), Rex Ryon (Cop), Bobby Houseon (Retard), Drew Davis (Teenage Samurai)

A NIGHTMARE ON ELM STREET (New Line Cinema) Producer, Robert Shaye; Direction and Screenplay, Wes Craven; Co-producer, Sara Risher; Executive Producers, Stanley Dudelson, Joseph Wolf; Associate Producer, John Burrows; Music, Charles Bernstein; Photography, Jacques Haitkin; Designer, Greg Fonesca; Special Effects, Jim Doyle; In color; Rated R; 91 minutes; November release. CAST: John Saxon (Lt. Thompson), Ronee Blakley (Marge), Heather Langenkamp (Nancy), Amanda Wyss (Tina), Nick Corri (Rod), Johnny Depp (Glen), Charles Fleischer (Dr. King), Joseph Whipp (Sgt. Parker), Lin Shaye (Teacher), Robert Englund (Fred)

OBSERVATIONS UNDER THE VOLCANO (TeleCulture) Produced, Directed and Photographed by Christian Blackwood; Editor, Ned Bastille; Production Coordinator, Lisa Tesone; In color; Not rated; 82 minutes; November release. A documentary observing John Huston as he directs the making of Malcolm Lowry's novel "Under the Volcano" shot on location in Cuernavaca, Mexico, with stars Albert Finney, Jacqueline Bisset, Anthony Andrews.

NICARAGUA: NO PASARAN (New Yorker) Producer-Director, David Bradbury; Editor, Stewart Young; Photography, Geoffrey Simpson; Associate Producer, Leah Cocks; In color; Not rated; 74 minutes; November release. A documentary on the human face of a troubled revolution.

ZOMBIE ISLAND MASSACRE (Troma) Producer, David Broadnax; Director-Editor, John N. Carter; Executive Producer, Michael Malagiero; Screenplay, William Stoddard, Logan O'Neill; Based on story by David Broadnax, Logan O'Neill; Music, Harry Manfredini; Associate Producers, Dennis Stephenson, Umberto DiLeo; Special Effects, Dennis Eger; In color; Rated R; 95 minutes; November release. CAST: David Broadnax, Rita Jenrette, Tom Cantrell, Diane Clayre Holub, Ian MacMillan, George Peters, Dennis Stephenson

Martin Mull, Karen Black, Anne DeSalvo
in "Bad Manners" © *New World Pictures*

David Broadnax (L) in "Zombie Island
Massacre" © *Troma Inc.*

Steve Bond, Debbie Thurseon in "The Prey"
© *New World Pictures*

Eddie Deezen, Peter Scolari in "The Rosebud
Beach Hotel" © *Almi*

THE PREY (New World) Executive Producer, Joe Steinman; Producer, Summer Brown; Director, Edwin Scott Brown; Co-Producer, Randy Rovins; Screenplay, Summer Brown, Edwin Scott Brown; Photography, Teru Hayashi; Music, Don Peake; Editor, Michael Barnard; Art Director, Roger Holzberg; Costumes, Julie Dresner; Production Manager, D. K. Miller; Assistant Director, Jenny Townsend; An Essex International production in color; Rated R; 80 minutes; November release. CAST: Debbie Thureson (Nancy), Steve Bond (Joel), Lori Lethin (Bobbie), Robert Wald (Skip), Gayle Gannes (Gail), Philip Wenckus (Greg), Carl Struycken (The Giant), Jackson Bostwick (Mark), Jackie Coogan (Lester), Ted Hayden (Frank), Connie Hunter (Mary), Garry Goodrow (Cop)

SKI COUNTRY (Warren Miller) Produced, Directed and Written by Warren Miller; Photography, Don Brolin, Fletcher Manley, Gary Nate, Gary Capo, Lex Fletcher, Gary Bigham, Fletcher Anderson, Brian Sissleman, Karl Herrimann, Warren Miller; Editors, Michael Usher, Ray Laurent, Kim Schneider, Robert Knop, Hamilton Camp; In color; Rated G; 93 minutes; November release. CAST: Greg Smith, Hans Fahlen, Lhasa Fahlen, Gunner Moberg, Pierre Vuarnet, John Low, Fred Noble, Otto Lang, Scott Brooksbank, Mike Chew, Judy McClintock, Jeff Sanders, Glenn Thurlow

JUST THE WAY YOU ARE (MGM/UA) Producer, Leo L. Fuchs; Director, Edouard Molinaro; Screenplay, Allan Burns; Photography, Claude Lecomte; Editors, Claudio Ventura, Georges Klotz; Music, Vladimir Cosma; In color; Rated PG; 94 minutes; November release. CAST: Kristy McNichol (Susan), Michael Ontkean (Peter), Kaki Hunter (Lisa), Andre Dussollier (Francois), Catherine Salviat (Nicole), Robert Carradine (Sam), Alexandra Paul (Bobbie), Lance Guest (Jack), Timothy Daly (Frank), Patrick Cassidy (Steve)

NIGHT OF THE COMET (Atlantic) Producers, Andrew Lane, Wayne Crawford; Direction and Screenplay, Thom Eberhardt; Photography, Arthur Albert, Editor, Fred Stafford; In color; Rated PG13; 100 minutes; November release. CAST: Catherine Mary Stewart (Regina), Kelli Maroney (Samantha), Robert Beltran (Hector), Geoffrey Lewis (Carter), Mary Woronov (Audrey), John Achorn (Oscar), Sharon Farrell (Doris), Michael Bowen (Larry), Ivan Roth (Willy), Raymond Lynch (Chuck), Janice Kawaye (Sarah), Chance Boyer (Brian), Bob Perlow (Reporter)

THE ROSEBUD BEACH HOTEL (Almi) Producers, Irving Schwartz, Harry Hurwitz; Director, Harry Hurwitz; Executive Producers, Michael Landes, Stephen Chrystie; Associate Producer, William Tasgal; Screenplay, Harry Narunsky, Irving Schwartz, Thomas Rudolph; Photography, Joao Fernandes; Music, Jay Chattaway; Editor, Daniel Lowenthal; In color; Rated R; 105 minutes; November release. CAST: Colleen Camp (Tracy), Peter Scolari (Elliot), Christopher Lee (King), Fran Drescher (Linda), Eddie Deezen (Sydney), Chuck McCann (Dorfman), Hank Garrett (Kramer), Hamilton Camp (Matches), Jonathan Schmock (Dennis), Jim Vallely (Leonard), Marie Currie Lukather (Marie), Cherie Currie (Cherie)

THE GOODBYE PEOPLE (Embassy) Producer, David V. Picker; Associate Producer, Mel Howard; Direction and Screenplay, Herb Gardner, based on his stage play of same title; Photography, John Lindley; Editor, Rick Shaine; Designer, Tony Walton; In DeLuxe Color; Rated PG; 104 minutes; November release. CAST: Judd Hirsch (Arthur Korman), Martin Balsam (Max Silverman), Pamela Reed (Nancie "Shirley" Scot), Ron Silver (Eddie Bergson), Michael Tucker (Michael Silverman), Gene Saks (Marcus Soloway)

DADDY'S DEADLY DARLING (Aquarius) Previously "The Pigs" and "Daddy's Girl"; Executive Producer, Donald L. Reynolds; Producer-Director, Marc Lawrence; Screenplay, F. A. Foss (Lawrence); Photography, Glenn Roland, Jr.; Editor, Irvin Goodnoff; Music, Charles Bernstein; Production Manager, Bill Bushnell; In CFI Color; Rated R; 83 minutes; November release. CAST: Toni Lawrence (Lynn), Marc Lawrence (Zambrini), Jesse Vint (Sheriff), Walter Barnes (Doctor), Katherine Ross (Miss Macy), Jim Antonio, Erik Holland, Paul Hickey, Iris Korn, William Michael

BLAME IT ON THE NIGHT (Tri-Star) Producer-Director, Gene Taft; Executive Producer, Tony Wade; Screenplay, Len Jenkin; Photography, Alex Phillips; Editor, Ted Haworth; Assistant Director, Jerry Ballew; Associate Producer, Rhonda Rosen-Lipnick; Music, Ted Neeley; In Dolby Stereo and Technicolor; Rated PG13; 85 minutes; November release. CAST: Nick Mancuso (Chris), Byron Thames (Job), Leslie Ackerman (Shelly), Dick Bakalyan (Manzini), Leeyan Granger (Melanie), Rex Ludwick (Animal), Melissa Prophet (Charlotte), Sandy Kenyon (Coloneo), Themselves: Merry Clayton, Billy Preston, Ollie E. Brown

Sharon Farrell, Raymond Lynch in "Night of
the Comet" © *Atlantic Releasing Corp.*

Byron Thames, Nick Mancuso in "Blame It on
the Night" © *Tri-Star Pictures*

NIGHT PATROL (New World) Producer, Bill Osco; Directed, Co-produced, Edited by Jackie Kong; Screenplay, Murray Langston, Bill Levey, Bill Osco, Jackie Kong; Photography, Jurg Walthers, Hanania Baer; Art Directors, Jay Burkhardt, Bob Danyla; Costumes, Terry Roop; Associate Producer, Jay Koiwai; Assistant Directors, Koiwai, Paul Leclair, Tom Jon; In color; Rated R; 82 minutes; November release. CAST: Linda Blair (Sue), Pat Paulsen (Kent), Jaye P. Morgan (Kate), Jack Riley (Dr. Ziegler), Billy Barty (Capt. Lewis), Murray Langston (Melvin), Pat Morita (Rape Victim)

INVISIBLE STRANGLER (Seymour Borde) Producer, Earle Lyon; Executive Producer, Fred Jordan; Director, John Florea; Screenplay, Arthur C. Pierce from story by Lyon and Pierce; Photography, Alan Stensvold; Editor, Bud S. Isaacs; Music, Richard Hieronymous, Alan Oldfield; Assistant Director, Joseph Wonder; Special Effects, Roger George; Associate Producer, Robert Fitzgerald; In color; Rated PG; 85 minutes; November release. CAST: Robert Foxworth (Lt. Charles Barrett), Stefanie Powers (Candy), Elke Sommer (Chris), Sue Lyon (Miss DeLong), Leslie Parrish (Coleen), Mariana Hill (Bambi), Mark Slade, Frank Ashmore, Alex Dreier, Percy Rodriguez, Jo Anne Meredith, Cesare Danova, John Hart

WHAT YOU TAKE FOR GRANTED (Iris Feminist Collective) Produced, Directed, Written and Edited by Michelle Citron; Photography, Frances Reid; Production Manager, Eileen Fitzpatrick; Music, Karen Pritikin; In color; Not rated; 75 minutes; November release. CAST: Belinda Cloud (Doctor Dianna), Donna Blue Lachman (Truck Driver/Anna), Mosetta Harris (Cable Splicer), Fran Hart (Philosophy Professor), Helen Larimore (Sculptor)

SILENT NIGHT, LONELY NIGHT (Tri-Star) Producer, Ira Richard Barmak; Director, Charles E. Sellier, Jr.; Screenplay, Michael Hickey; Based on story by Paul Caimi; Co-Executive Producers, Scott J. Schneid, Dennis Whitehead; Photography, Henning Schellerup; Editor, Michael Spence; Music, Perry Botkin; Designer, Dian Perryman; Special Effects, Rick Josephson; Production Manager, Bart Foster; Assistant Directors, Denis Stewart, Perry Husman; Production Coordinator, Janet Johnson; In color; Rated R; 79 minutes; November release. CAST: Lilyan Chauvin (Mother Superior), Gilmer McCormick (Sister Margaret), Toni Nero (Pamela), Robert Brian Wilson (Billy at 18), Britt Leach (Sims), Nancy Borgenicht (Mrs. Randall), H. E. D. Redford (Capt. Richards), Danny Wagner (Billy at 8), Linnea Quigley (Denise), Leo Geter (Tommy), Randy Stumpf (Andy), Will Hare (Grandpa), Tara Buckman (Mother/Ellie), Charles Dierkop (Father/Jim), Eric Hart (Levitt), Jonathon Best (Billy at 5), A. Madeline Smith (Sister Ellen), Amy Stuyvesant (Cindy), Max Robinson (Barnes), Oscar Rowland (Dr. Conway)

LOVELINES (Tri-Star) Producers, Hal Taines, Michael Lloyd; Director, Rod Amateau; Screenplay, Chip Hand, William Hillman; Story, Chip Hand, Michael Lloyd, William Hillman; Photography, Duke Callaghan; Art Director, Robert K. Kinoshita; Editors, David Bretherton, Fred A. Chulack; Music, Michael Lloyd; Associate Producers, Chip Hand, Gary Hudson; Production Manager, Gilles A. DeTurenne; Assistant Directors, Laura Andrus, Nicholas Batchelor; Soundtrack on MCA/Curb Records; Underwater Photography, Alan Gornick, Jr.; Production Coordinator, Robin Birnie; In Metrocolor and Dolby Stereo; Rated R; 93 minutes; November release. CAST: Greg Bradford (Rick), Mary Beth Evans (Piper), Michael Winslow (J.D.), Don Michael Paul (Jeff), Tammy Taylor (Priscilla), Stacey Toten (Cynthia), Robert Delapp (Beagle), Frank Zagarino (Godzilla), Todd Bryant (Hammer), Jonna Lee (Lisa), Robin Watkins (Theresa), Claudia Cowan (Brigit), Lynn Cartwright (Mrs. Woodson), Albert Szabo (Prof. Fromawitz), David Jolliffe (Tongue), Miguel Ferrer (Dragon), Sherri Stoner (Suzy), Sarah Buxtom (Cathy), Joyce Jamison (Mary), Shecky Greene (M.C.), Paul Valentine (Vandermeer), Gary Morgan, Marguerite Kimberly, Kelley Jean Browser, Michael Lloyd, Conrad Palmisario, Robert Fiacco, James Davis Trenton, Ernest Robinson, Aimee Eccles

PERFECT STRANGERS (New Line) Formerly "Blind Alley"; Executive Producer, Carter DeHaven; Direction-Screenplay, Larry Cohen; Producer, Paul Kurta; Photography, Paul Glickman; Editor, Armond Lebowitz; Songs, Michael Minard; Music, Dwight Dixon; A Helmdale presentation in color; Rated R; 94 minutes; November release. CAST: Anne Carlisle, Brad Rijn, John Woehrle, Matthew Stockley, Stephen Lack

YELLOW HAIR AND THE FORTRESS OF GOLD (Crown International) Producers, John Ghaffari, Diego G. Sempre; Director, Matt Cimber; Screenplay, John Kershaw, Matt Cimber; Photography, John Cabrera; Based on characters and story by Matt Cimber; Editor, Claudio Cutry; Music, Franco Piersanti; Executive Producer, Jose Truchado Reyes; Special Effects, Carlo DeMarchis; Costumes, Augustin Jimenez; Assistant Directors, Tony Tarruella, Yousaf Bokhari; In Metrocolor and Dolby Stereo; Rated R; 102 minutes; November release. CAST: Laurene Landon (Yellow Hair), Ken Roberson (Pecos Kid), John Ghaffari (Shayowteewah), Luis Lorenzo (Col. Torres), Claudia Gravi (Grey Cloud), Aldo Sambrel (Flores), Eduardo Fajardo (Man-Who-Knows), Ramiro Oliveros (Tortuga), Suzannah Woodside

Mary Beth Evans, Greg Bradford in "Lovelines" © *Tri-Star Pictures*

(Rainbow), Concha Marquez Piquer, Tony Tarruella (Gambling Couple), Daniel Martin (1st Comanche), Mario de abros (Deputy), Roman Ariz-Navarreta, Pablo Garcia Ortega (Machine Gunners), Joaquin Lopez (Fighting Indian), Juan Gomez Fernandez (Young Soldier), Paloma Gomez, Jose Truchado Jr. (Newlyweds), Juan Garcia Delgado (Barman), Alfonso Maria Delgado (Waiter)

SPECIAL EFFECTS (New Line Cinema) Producer, Paul Kurta; Executive Producer, Carter DeHaven; Direction and Screenplay, Larry Cohen; In color; Rated R; 93 minutes; November release. CAST: Zoe Tamerlis (Andrea/Elaine), Eric Bogosian (Neville), Brad Rijn (Keefe), Kevin O'Connor (Delroy)

LUST IN THE DUST (Fox Run) Executive Producers, James C. Katz, Robert Raymond; Director, Paul Bartel; Screenplay, Philip Taylor; Photography, Paul Lohmann; Editor, Alan Toomayan; Music, Peter Matz; Songs, Karen Hart; Art Director, Walter Pickette; Costumes, Dona Granata; Assistant Director, Michael Schroeder; In CFI Color; Rated R; 87 minutes; November release. CAST: Tab Hunter (Abel), Divine (Rosie), Lainie Kazan (Marguerita), Geoffrey Lewis (Hard Case), Henry Silva (Bernardo), Cesar Romero (Father Garcia), Gina Gallego (Nifa), Courtney Gains (Red Dick), Woody Strode (Black Man), Pedro Gonzalez-Gonzalez (Mexican), Daniel Firshman (Clarence), Ernie Shinagawa (Chang)

THE INITIATION (New World) Executive Producers, Bruce Lansbury, Jock Gaynor; Producer, Scott Winant; Director, Larry Stewart; Screenplay, Charles Pratt, Jr.; Production Manager/Assistant Director, John M. Colwell; Production Coordinator, Samai Brown; Special Effects, Jack Bennett; In Movielab Color; Rated R; 97 minutes; December release. CAST: Vera Miles (Frances), Clu Gulager (Dwight), Daphne Zuniga (Kelly), James Read (Peter), Marilyn Kagan (Marcia), Patti Heider (Nurse), Robert Dowdell (Jason), Frances Peterson (Megan), Deborah Morehart (Alison), Patti Heider (Nurse), Robert Stroud (Ralph), Peter Malof (Andy), Christopher Bradley (Chad), Joy Jones (Heidi), Mary Davis Duncan (Gwen), Rusty Meyers (Nightwatchman), Christi Michelle Allen (Kelly at 9), Dan Dickerson (Detective), Ronald M. Hubner (Cop), Jerry L. Clark (Orderly), Kathy Lee Kennedy (Nurse), Sorority Girls: Cheryl Foster, Diane Page, Traci Odom, Melissa Toomin, Jennifer Suttles; Students: Lance Funston, Andrea Vaccarello

Patrick Cassidy, Kristy McNichol in "Just the Way You Are" © *MGM/UA Entertainment*

BLESS THEIR LITTLE HEARTS (Black Independent Features)
Produced, Directed and Edited by Billy Woodberry; Screenplay and
Photography, Charles Burnett; In black and white; Not rated; 80
minutes; December release. CAST: Nate Hardman (Charlie Banks),
Kaycee Moore (Andais Banks), Angela, Ronald and Kimberly Burnett
(Banks Children)

MISSING IN ACTION (Cannon) Producers, Menahem Golan,
Yoram Globus; Director, Joseph Zito; Screenplay, James Bruner;
Story, John Crowther, Lance Hool; Based on characters created by
Arthur Silver, Larry Levinson, Steve Bing; Executive Producer, Lance
Hool; Music, Jay Chattaway; Editors, Joel Goodman, Daniel Loewen-
thal; Photography, Joao Fernandes; Associate Producer, Avi Klein-
berger; Production Manager, Pieter Jan Brugge; Assistant Director,
Gidi Amir; Art Director, Ladi Wilheim; Costumes, Nancy Cone; Co-
Associate Producer, Ken Metcalfe; Production Supervisor, Lope V.
Juban, Jr.; Production Coordinator, Ricardo de Guzman; Art Director,
Toto Castillo; In Metrocolor; Rated R; 101 minutes; December release.
CAST: Chuck Norris (Braddock), M. Emmett Walsh (Tuck), David
Tress (Senator), Lenore Kasdorf (Ann), James Hong (Gen. Tran),
Ernie Ortega (Vinh), Pierrino Mascarino (Jacques), E. Erich Anderson
(Masucci), Joseph Carberry (Carter), Avi Kleinberger (Dalton), Willy
Williams (Randall), Ric Segreto (G.I.), Bella Flores (Madame Pearl),
Gil Arceo, Roger Dantes (Vietnamese Businessmen), Sabatini Fernan-
dez (Dinh), Renato Morado (Mike), Jim Crumrine (Gibson), Jeff
Mason (Barnes), Stephen Barbers (Moore)

RUNAWAY (Tri-Star) Producer, Michael Rachmil; Direction and
Screenplay, Michael Crichton; Photography, John A. Alonzo; Editor,
Glenn Farr; Music, Jerry Goldsmith; In color, Panavision and Dolby
Stereo; Rated PG13; 100 minutes; December release. CAST: Tom
Selleck (Ramsay), Cynthia Rhodes (Karen), Gene Simmons (Luther),
Kirstie Alley (Jackie), Stan Shaw (Marvin), G. W. Bailey (Chief), Joey
Cramer (Bobby), Chris Mulkey (Johnson), Anne-Marie Martin
(Hooker)

BREAKIN' 2: ELECTRIC BOOGALOO (Tri-Star) Producers,
Menahem Golan, Yoram Globus; Director, Sam Firstenberg; Screen-
play, Jan Ventura, Julie Reichert; Photography, Hanania Baer; Editors,
Sally Allen, Bert Glatstein, Bob Jenkis, Barry Zetlin; Music, Russ
Regan; In color and Dolby Stereo; Rated PG; 94 minutes; December
release. CAST: Lucinda Dickey (Kelly), Adolfo Quinones (Ozone),
Michael Chambers (Turbo), Susie Bono (Rhonda), Harry Caesar
(Byrone), Jo de Winter (Mrs. Bennett), John Christy Ewing (Mr.
Bennett), Steve Notario (Strobe)

TIGER TOWN (Buena Vista) Producer, Susan B. Landau; Direction
and Screenplay, Alan Shapiro; Photography, Robert Elswit; Music,
Eddy L. Manson; Editors, Richard A. Harris, John F. Link; Designer,
Neil J. Spisak; Costumes, Gary Jones; In color; Not rated; 96 minutes;
December release. CAST: Roy Scheider (Billy Young), Justin Henry
(Alex), Noah Moazezi (Alex's Father), Bethany Carpenter (Alex's
Mother)

SAFARI 3000 (MGM/UA) Previously titled "Rally" and "Two in the
Bush"; Producers, Jules V. Levy, Arthur Gardner; Director, Harry
Hurwitz; Screenplay, Michael Harreschou; Photography, Adam
Greenberg; Editor, Samuel E. Beetley; Music, Ernest Gold; Assistant
Director, Cedric Sundstrom; Art Director, Peter Williams; Associate
Producer, Robert Levy; In Panavision and Technicolor; Rated PG; 91
minutes; December release. CAST: David Carradine (Eddie), Stockard
Channing (J.J.), Christopher Lee (Lorenzo), Hamilton Camp (Feodor),
Ian Yule (Freddie), Hugh Rouse (Hawthorne), Mary Ann Berold (Vic-
toria)

R.S.V.P. (Platinum) Executive Producer, Chuck Vincent; Producer,
John Amero; Director, Lem Amero; Photography, Larry Revene; Pro-
duction Manager, John Amero; Screenplay, LaRue Watts; Editor, Lem
Amero; Costumes-Art Directors, LaRue Watts, Fabian Stuart; Music,
Ian Shaw; In color; Rated R; December release. CAST: Adam Mills
(Toby), Lynda Wiesmeier (Jennifer), Veronica Hart (Ellen), Ray Col-
bert (Bill), Harry Reems (Grant), Katt Shea (Rhonda), Lola Mason
(Polly), Allene Simmons (Patty), Dustin Stevens (Jonathan), Carey
Hayes (Bernie), Judith Cassmore (Evelyn), Paul Coufos (Senator),
Robert Pinkerton (Lance), Steve Nave (Herb), Bob Gorman (Fr. Wil-
liams), Jimmy Jue (Delivery Boy), Arlene Stege (Carrie), Laurie Senit
(Sherry), Tamara Landry (Vicki), Cindy Kirby (Sally), Derek Partridge
(Governor), Ted Chapman (Judge), Michael Pataki (Rex), Dulcie Jor-
dan (Monique), Jeff Eagle, Volker, Ritchie Montgomery, Ralph Doug-
las, Suzanne Remey Lawrence, Richard Guthrie, Cal Bedford, Laine
Jastram

HOT MOVES (Cardinal) Producer-Director, Jim Sotos; Screenplay,
Larry Anderson, Peter Foldy; Assistant Director, Donald Newman;
Photography, Eugene Shugleit; Editor, Drake P. Silliman; Art Direc-
tor, George Costello; Costumes, Phillip Herzog Richards; Choreogra-
phy, Andrea Muller; In CFI Color; Rated R; 86 minutes; December
release. CAST: Michael Zorek, Adam Silbar, Jeff Fishman, Johnny
Timko, Jill Schoelen, Debi Richter, Virgil Frye, Tami Holbrook,
Monique Gabrielle, David Christopher

Lucinda Dickey (c) in "Breakin' 2"
© *Tri-Star* Top: Chuck Norris in "Missing
in Action" © *Cannon Productions*

"R.S.V.P." © *Platinum Pictures*
Top: Cynthia Rhodes, Tom Selleck in
"Runaway" © *Tri-Star Pictures*

DREW BARRYMORE

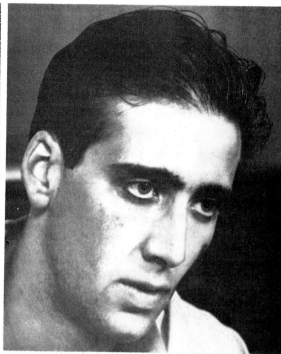

NICOLAS CAGE

ROB LOWE

KIM BASINGER

LINDSAY CROUSE

RALPH MACCHIO

JOHN MALKOVICH

DARYL HANNAH

KELLY McGILLIS

SEAN PENN

ERIC STOLTZ

MOLLY RINGWALD

AMADEUS

(ORION) Producer, Saul Zaentz; Director, Milos Forman; Screenplay, Peter Shaffer from his play of same title; Photography, Miroslav Ondricek; Executive Producers, Michael Hausman, Bertil Ohlsson; Editors, Nena Danevic, Michael Chandler; Costumes, Theodor Pistek; Art Director, Karel Cerny; Opera Sets, Josef Svoboda; Production Design, Patrizia Von Brandenstein; Choreography/Opera Staging, Twyla Tharp; Music Coordinator, John Strauss; Assistant Director, Michael Hausman; In Panavision, Technicolor, and Dolby Stereo; Rated PG; 158 minutes; September release

CAST

Antonio Salieri	F. Murray Abraham
Wolfgang Amadeus Mozart	Tom Hulce
Constanze Mozart	Elizabeth Berridge
Emanuel Schikaneder	Simon Callow
Leopold Mozart	Roy Dotrice
Katerina Cavalieri	Christine Ebersole
Emperor Joseph II	Jeffrey Jones
Count Orsini-Rosenberg	Charles Kay
Parody Commendatore	Kenny Baker
Papagena	Lisabeth Bartlett
Frau Weber	Barbara Bryne
Young Salieri	Martin Cavani
Count Von Strack	Roderick Cook
Karl Mozart	Milan Demjanenko
Francesco Salieri	Peter DiGesu
Father Vogler	Richard Frank
Kappelmeister Bonno	Patrick Hines
Archbishop Colloredo	Nicholas Kepros
Salieri's Servant	Philip Lenkowsky
Priest	Herman Meckler
Baron Van Swieten	Jonathan Moore
Lorl	Cynthia Nixon
Hospital Attendant	Brian Pettifer
Salieri's Valet	Vincent Schiavelli
Count Arco	Douglas Seale
Young Mozart	Miroslav Sekera
Conductor	John Strauss
Wig Salesman	Karl-Heinz Teuber

Left: F. Murray Abraham
© *The Saul Zaentz Co.*

1984 Academy Awards for Best Picture, Actor (F. Murray Abraham), Director, Screenplay Adaptation, Art Direction, Costumes, Sound, Makeup

Tom Hulce

Elizabeth Berridge

BEST PICTURE OF 1984

Tom Hulce, F. Murray Abraham Top: (L) Tom Hulce, Elizabeth Berridge (R) Tom Hulce
Below: (L) Tom Hulce (R) F. Murray Abraham

F. MURRAY ABRAHAM in "AMADEUS"

© The Saul Zaentz Company

1984 ACADEMY AWARD FOR BEST ACTOR

SALLY FIELD in "PLACES IN THE HEART"
© Tri-Star Pictures

1984 ACADEMY AWARD FOR BEST ACTRESS 151

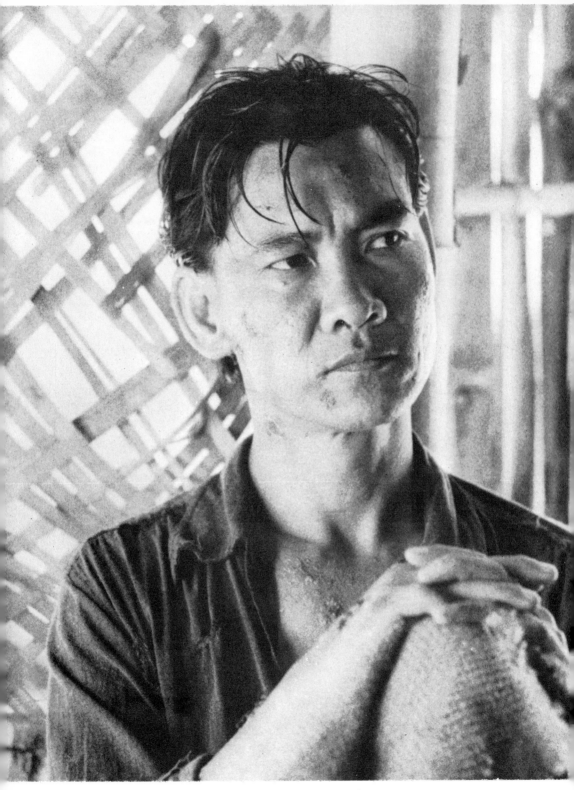

HAING S. NGOR in "THE KILLING FIELDS"
© Warner Bros.

1984 ACADEMY AWARD FOR BEST SUPPORTING ACTOR

PEGGY ASHCROFT in "A PASSAGE TO INDIA"

© *Columbia Pictures*

1984 ACADEMY AWARD FOR BEST SUPPORTING ACTRESS

DANGEROUS MOVES

Producer, Arthur Cohn; Direction and Screenplay, Richard Dembo; Photography, Raoul Coutard; Editor, Agnes Guillemot; Sound, Alex Compte; Production Managers, Martine Marignac, Ruth Waldburger; Design, Ivan Maussion; Costumes, Pierre Albert; Music, Gabriel Yared; Chess games created by Nicolas Giffard; In color; Not rated.

CAST

Liebskind	Michel Piccoli
Marina	Liv Ullmann
Henia	Leslie Caron
Fromm	Alexandre Arbatt
Tac-Tac	Daniel Olbrychski
Kerossian	Michel Aumont
Fadenko	Serge Avedikian
Yachvili	Pierre Michael
Heller	Pierre Vial
Felton	Wojtek Pszoniak
Miller	Jean-Hugues Anglade
Foldes	Hubert Saint-Macary
Puhl	Bernhard Wicki
Barrabal	Benoit Regent
Stuffli	Jacques Boudet
Carsen	Jean-Paul Eydoux
Dalcroze	Albert Simono
Judge Dombert	Sylvie Granotier
Dr. Randelier	Alain Rimoux
Prof. Polotin	Willy Nicoidsky
Colonel of the KGB	Constantin Melnik

Right: Alexandre Arbatt, Liv Ullmann
Below: Michel Piccoli (L), Arbatt (R)
© *Arthur Cohn Productions*

1984 ACADEMY AWARD FOR BEST FOREIGN LANGUAGE FILM

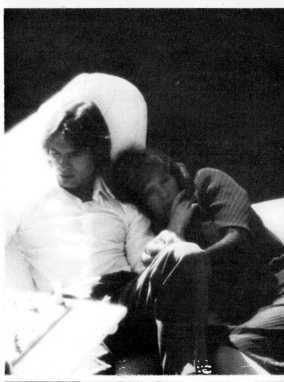

Alexandre Arbatt

Michel Piccoli, Leslie Caron

1984 ACADEMY AWARD FOR BEST FOREIGN LANGUAGE FILM

THE TIMES OF HARVEY MILK

(TELECULTURE) Producer, Richard Schmiechen; Director, Robert Epstein; Editors, Deborah Hoffmann, Robert Epstein; Associate Producer, Greg Bex; Assistant Editor, Thomas O'Shea; Narrated by Harvey Fierstein; Original Music composed and performed by Mark Isham; Photography, Frances Reid; Sound, Dan Gleich; Graphic Art Director, Michael McNeil; Narration Writers, Judith Coburn, Carter Wilson; Photo Research, Wendy Zheutlin; Print Media Archivist, Robert Hawk; Sound Editor, John Benson; Coordinating Producer, Kathy Kline; Executive Producer, David Loxton; In color; Not rated; 87 minutes; October release. A documentary on the life and death of Harvey Milk in San Francisco, California.

1984 ACADEMY AWARD FOR BEST FEATURE DOCUMENTARY

1984 ACADEMY AWARD FOR BEST FEATURE-LENGTH DOCUMENTARY

| Fred Astaire | Julie Andrews | Red Buttons | Olivia DeHavilland | Ernest Borgnine | Joan Fontaine |

PREVIOUS ACADEMY AWARD WINNERS

(1) Best Picture, (2) Actor, (3) Actress, (4) Supporting Actor, (5) Supporting Actress, (6) Director, (7) Special Award, (8) Best Foreign Language Film

1927–28: (1) "Wings," (2) Emil Jannings in "The Way of All Flesh," (3) Janet Gaynor in "Seventh Heaven," (6) Frank Borzage for "Seventh Heaven," (7) Charles Chaplin.

1928–29: (1) "Broadway Melody," (2) Warner Baxter in "Old Arizona," (3) Mary Pickford in "Coquette," (6) Frank Lloyd for "The Divine Lady."

1929–30: (1) "All Quiet on the Western Front," (2) George Arliss in "Disraeli," (3) Norma Shearer in "The Divorcee," (6) Lewis Milestone for "All Quiet on the Western Front."

1930–31: (1) "Cimarron," (2) Lionel Barrymore in "A Free Soul," (3) Marie Dressler in "Min and Bill," (6) Norman Taurog for "Skippy."

1931–32: (1) "Grand Hotel," (2) Fredric March in "Dr. Jekyll and Mr. Hyde" tied with Wallace Beery in "The Champ," (3) Helen Hayes in "The Sin of Madelon Claudet," (6) Frank Borzage for "Bad Girl."

1932–33: (1) "Cavalcade," (2) Charles Laughton in "The Private Life of Henry VIII," (3) Katharine Hepburn in "Morning Glory," (6) Frank Lloyd for "Cavalcade."

1934: (1) "It Happened One Night," (2) Clark Gable in "It Happened One Night," (3) Claudette Colbert in "It Happened One Night," (6) Frank Capra for "It Happened One Night," (7) Shirley Temple.

1935: (1) "Mutiny on the Bounty," (2) Victor McLaglen in "The Informer," (3) Bette Davis in "Dangerous," (6) John Ford for "The Informer," (7) D. W. Griffith.

1936: (1) "The Great Ziegfeld," (2) Paul Muni in "The Story of Louis Pasteur," (3) Luise Rainer in "The Great Ziegfeld," (4) Walter Brennan in "Come and Get It," (5) Gale Sondergaard in "Anthony Adverse," (6) Frank Capra for "Mr. Deeds Goes to Town."

1937: (1) "The Life of Emile Zola," (2) Spencer Tracy in "Captains Courageous," (3) Luise Rainer in "The Good Earth," (4) Joseph Schildkraut in "The Life of Emile Zola," (5) Alice Brady in "In Old Chicago," (6) Leo McCarey for "The Awful Truth," (7) Mack Sennett, Edgar Bergen.

1938: (1) "You Can't Take It with You," (2) Spencer Tracy in "Boys' Town," (3) Bette Davis in "Jezebel," (4) Walter Brennan in "Kentucky," (5) Fay Bainter in "Jezebel," (6) Frank Capra for "You Can't Take It with You," (7) Deanna Durbin, Mickey Rooney, Harry M. Warner, Walt Disney.

1939: (1) "Gone with the Wind," (2) Robert Donat in "Goodbye, Mr. Chips," (3) Vivien Leigh in "Gone with the Wind," (4) Thomas Mitchell in "Stagecoach," (5) Hattie McDaniel in "Gone with the Wind," (6) Victor Fleming for "Gone with the Wind," (7) Douglas Fairbanks, Judy Garland.

1940: (1) "Rebecca," (2) James Stewart in "The Philadelphia Story," (3) Ginger Rogers in "Kitty Foyle," (4) Walter Brennan in "The Westerner," (5) Jane Darwell in "The Grapes of Wrath," (6) John Ford for "The Grapes of Wrath," (7) Bob Hope.

1941: (1) "How Green Was My Valley," (2) Gary Cooper in "Sergeant York," (3) Joan Fontaine in "Suspicion," (4) Donald Crisp in "How Green Was My Valley," (5) Mary Astor in "The Great Lie," (6) John Ford for "How Green Was My Valley," (7) Leopold Stokowski, Walt Disney.

1942: (1) "Mrs. Miniver," (2) James Cagney in "Yankee Doodle Dandy," (3) Greer Garson in "Mrs. Miniver," (4) Van Heflin in "Johnny Eager," (5) Teresa Wright in "Mrs. Miniver," (6) William Wyler for "Mrs. Miniver," (7) Charles Boyer, Noel Coward.

1943: (1) "Casablanca," (2) Paul Lukas in "Watch on the Rhine," (3) Jennifer Jones in "The Song of Bernadette," (4) Charles Coburn in "The More the Merrier," (5) Katina Paxinou in "For Whom the Bell Tolls," (6) Michael Curtiz for "Casablanca."

1944: (1) "Going My Way," (2) Bing Crosby in "Going My Way," (3) Ingrid Bergman in "Gaslight," (4) Barry Fitzgerald in "Going My Way," (5) Ethel Barrymore in "None but the Lonely Heart," (6) Leo McCarey for "Going My Way," (7) Margaret O'Brien, Bob Hope.

1945: (1) "The Lost Weekend," (2) Ray Milland in "The Lost Weekend," (3) Joan Crawford in "Mildred Pierce," (4) James Dunn in "A Tree Grows in Brooklyn," (5) Anne Revere in "National Velvet," (6) Billy Wilder for "The Lost Weekend," (7) Walter Wanger, Peggy Ann Garner.

1946: (1) "The Best Years of Our Lives," (2) Fredric March in "The Best Years of Our Lives," (3) Olivia de Havilland in "To Each His Own," (4) Harold Russell in "The Best Years of Our Lives," (5) Anne Baxter in "The Razor's Edge," (6) William Wyler for "The Best Years of Our Lives," (7) Laurence Olivier, Harold Russell, Ernst Lubitsch, Claude Jarman, Jr.

1947: (1) "Gentleman's Agreement," (2) Ronald Colman in "A Double Life," (3) Loretta Young in "The Farmer's Daughter," (4) Edmund Gwenn in "Miracle On 34th Street," (5) Celeste Holm in "Gentleman's Agreement," (6) Elia Kazan for "Gentleman's Agreement," (7) James Baskette, (8) "Shoe Shine."

1948: (1) "Hamlet," (2) Laurence Olivier in "Hamlet," (3) Jane Wyman in "Johnny Belinda," (4) Walter Huston in "The Treasure of the Sierra Madre," (5) Claire Trevor in "Key Largo," (6) John Huston for "The Treasure of the Sierra Madre," (7) Ivan Jandl, Sid Grauman, Adolph Zukor, Walter Wanger, (8) "Monsieur Vincent."

1949: (1) "All the King's Men," (2) Broderick Crawford in "All the King's Men," (3) Olivia de Havilland in "The Heiress," (4) Dean Jagger in "Twelve O'Clock High," (5) Mercedes McCambridge in "All the King's Men," (6) Joseph L. Mankiewicz for "A Letter to Three Wives," (7) Bobby Driscoll, Fred Astaire, Cecil B. DeMille, Jean Hersholt, (8) "The Bicycle Thief."

1950: (1) "All about Eve," (2) Jose Ferrer in "Cyrano de Bergerac," (3) Judy Holliday in "Born Yesterday," (4) George Sanders in "All about Eve," (5) Josephine Hull in "Harvey," (6) Joseph L. Mankiewicz for "All about Eve," (7) George Murphy, Louis B. Mayer, (8) "The Walls of Malapaga."

1951: (1) "An American in Paris," (2) Humphrey Bogart in "The African Queen," (3) Vivien Leigh in "A Streetcar Named Desire," (4) Karl Malden in "A Streetcar Named Desire," (5) Kim Hunter in "A Streetcar Named Desire," (6) George Stevens for "A Place in the Sun," (7) Gene Kelly, (8) "Rashomon."

1952: (1) "The Greatest Show on Earth," (2) Gary Cooper in "High Noon," (3) Shirley Booth in "Come Back, Little Sheba," (4) Anthony Quinn in "Viva Zapata," (5) Gloria Grahame in "The Bad and the Beautiful," (6) John Ford for "The Quiet Man," (7) Joseph M. Schenck, Merian C. Cooper, Harold Lloyd, Bob Hope, George Alfred Mitchell, (8) "Forbidden Games."

1953: (1) "From Here to Eternity," (2) William Holden in "Stalag 17," (3) Audrey Hepburn in "Roman Holiday," (4) Frank Sinatra in "From Here to Eternity," (5) Donna Reed in "From Here to Eternity," (6) Fred Zinnemann for "From Here to Eternity," (7) Pete Smith, Joseph Breen.

1954: (1) "On the Waterfront," (2) Marlon Brando in "On the Waterfront," (3) Grace Kelly in "The Country Girl," (4) Edmond O'Brien in "The Barefoot Contessa," (5) Eva Marie Saint in "On the Waterfront," (6) Elia Kazan for "On the Waterfront," (7) Greta Garbo, Danny Kaye, Jon Whitely, Vincent Winter, (8) "Gate of Hell."

1955: (1) "Marty," (2) Ernest Borgnine in "Marty," (3) Anna Magnani in "The Rose Tattoo," (4) Jack Lemmon in "Mister Roberts," (5) Jo Van Fleet in "East of Eden," (6) Delbert Mann for "Marty," (8) "Samurai."

Charlton Heston	Shirley Jones	Gene Kelly	Sophia Loren	Ray Milland	Rita Moreno

1956: (1) "Around the World in 80 Days," (2) Yul Brynner in "The King and I," (3) Ingrid Bergman in "Anastasia," (4) Anthony Quinn in "Lust for Life," (5) Dorothy Malone in "Written on the Wind," (6) George Stevens for "Giant," (7) Eddie Cantor, (8) "La Strada."

1957: (1) "The Bridge on the River Kwai," (2) Alec Guinness in "The Bridge on the River Kwai," (3) Joanne Woodward in "The Three Faces of Eve," (4) Red Buttons in "Sayonara," (5) Miyoshi Umeki in "Sayonara," (6) David Lean for "The Bridge on the River Kwai," (7) Charles Brackett, B. B. Kahane, Gilbert M. (Bronco Billy) Anderson, (8) "The Nights of Cabiria."

1958: (1) "Gigi," (2) David Niven in "Separate Tables," (3) Susan Hayward in "I Want to Live," (4) Burl Ives in "The Big Country," (5) Wendy Hiller in "Separate Tables," (6) Vincente Minnelli for "Gigi," (7) Maurice Chevalier, (8) "My Uncle."

1959: (1) "Ben-Hur," (2) Charlton Heston in "Ben-Hur," (3) Simone Signoret in "Room at the Top," (4) Hugh Griffith in "Ben-Hur," (5) Shelley Winters in "The Diary of Anne Frank," (6) William Wyler for "Ben-Hur," (7) Lee de Forest, Buster Keaton, (8) "Black Orpheus."

1960: (1) "The Apartment," (2) Burt Lancaster in "Elmer Gantry," (3) Elizabeth Taylor in "Butterfield 8," (4) Peter Ustinov in "Spartacus," (5) Shirley Jones in "Elmer Gantry," (6) Billy Wilder for "The Apartment," (7) Gary Cooper, Stan Laurel, Hayley Mills, (8) "The Virgin Spring."

1961: (1) "West Side Story," (2) Maximilian Schell in "Judgment at Nuremberg," (3) Sophia Loren in "Two Women," (4) George Chakiris in "West Side Story," (5) Rita Moreno in "West Side Story," (6) Robert Wise for "West Side Story," (7) Jerome Robbins, Fred L. Metzler, (8) "Through a Glass Darkly."

1962: (1) "Lawrence of Arabia," (2) Gregory Peck in "To Kill a Mockingbird," (3) Anne Bancroft in "The Miracle Worker," (4) Ed Begley in "Sweet Bird of Youth," (5) Patty Duke in "The Miracle Worker," (6) David Lean for "Lawrence of Arabia," (8) "Sundays and Cybele."

1963: (1) "Tom Jones," (2) Sidney Poitier in "Lilies of the Field," (3) Patricia Neal in "Hud," (4) Melvyn Douglas in "Hud," (5) Margaret Rutherford in "The V.I.P's," (6) Tony Richardson for "Tom Jones," (8) "8½."

1964: (1) "My Fair Lady," (2) Rex Harrison in "My Fair Lady," (3) Julie Andrews in "Mary Poppins," (4) Peter Ustinov in "Topkapi," (5) Lila Kedrova in "Zorba the Greek," (6) George Cukor for "My Fair Lady," (7) William Tuttle, (8) "Yesterday, Today and Tomorrow."

1965: (1) "The Sound of Music," (2) Lee Marvin in "Cat Ballou," (3) Julie Christie in "Darling," (4) Martin Balsam in "A Thousand Clowns," (5) Shelley Winters in "A Patch of Blue," (6) Robert Wise for "The Sound of Music," (7) Bob Hope, (8) "The Shop on Main Street."

1966: (1) "A Man for All Seasons," (2) Paul Scofield in "A Man for All Seasons," (3) Elizabeth Taylor in "Who's Afraid of Virginia Woolf?," (4) Walter Matthau in "The Fortune Cookie," (5) Sandy Dennis in "Who's Afraid of Virginia Woolf?," (6) Fred Zinnemann for "A Man for All Seasons," (8) "A Man and A Woman."

1967: (1) "In the Heat of the Night," (2) Rod Steiger in "In the Heat of the Night," (3) Katharine Hepburn in "Guess Who's Coming to Dinner," (4) George Kennedy in "Cool Hand Luke," (5) Estelle Parsons in "Bonnie and Clyde," (6) Mike Nichols for "The Graduate," (8) "Closely Watched Trains."

1968: (1) "Oliver!," (2) Cliff Robertson in "Charly," (3) Katharine Hepburn in "The Lion in Winter" tied with Barbra Streisand in "Funny Girl," (4) Jack Albertson in "The Subject Was Roses," (5) Ruth Gordon in "Rosemary's Baby," (6) Carol Reed for "Oliver!," (7) Onna White for "Oliver!" choreography, John Chambers for "Planet of the Apes" make-up, (8) "War and Peace."

1969: (1) "Midnight Cowboy," (2) John Wayne in "True Grit," (3) Maggie Smith in "The Prime of Miss Jean Brodie," (4) Gig Young in "They Shoot Horses, Don't They?," (5) Goldie Hawn in "Cactus Flower," (6) John Schlesinger for "Midnight Cowboy," (7) Cary Grant, (8) "Z."

1970: (1) "Patton," (2) George C. Scott in "Patton," (3) Glenda Jackson in "Women in Love," (4) John Mills in "Ryan's Daughter," (5) Helen Hayes in "Airport," (6) Franklin J. Schaffner for "Patton," (7) Lillian Gish, Orson Welles, (8) "Investigation of a Citizen above Suspicion."

1971: (1) "The French Connection," (2) Gene Hackman in "The French Connection," (3) Jane Fonda in "Klute," (4) Ben Johnson in "The Last Picture Show," (5) Cloris Leachman in "The Last Picture Show," (6) William Friedkin for "The French Connection," (7) Charles Chaplin, (8) "The Garden of the Finzi-Continis."

1972: (1) "The Godfather," (2) Marlon Brando in "The Godfather," (3) Liza Minnelli in "Cabaret," (4) Joel Grey in "Cabaret," (5) Eileen Heckart in "Butterflies Are Free," (6) Bob Fosse for "Cabaret," (7) Edward G. Robinson, (8) "The Discreet Charm of the Bourgeoisie."

1973: (1) "The Sting," (2) Jack Lemmon in "Save the Tiger," (3) Glenda Jackson in "A Touch of Class," (4) John Houseman in "The Paper Chase," (5) Tatum O'Neal in "Paper Moon," (6) George Roy Hill for "The Sting," (8) "Day for Night."

1974: (1) "The Godfather Part II," (2) Art Carney in "Harry and Tonto," (3) Ellen Burstyn in "Alice Doesn't Live Here Anymore," (4) Robert DeNiro in "The Godfather Part II," (5) Ingrid Bergman in "Murder on the Orient Express," (6) Francis Ford Coppola for "The Godfather Part II," (7) Howard Hawks, Jean Renoir, (8) "Amarcord."

1975: (1) "One Flew over the Cuckoo's Nest," (2) Jack Nicholson in "One Flew over the Cuckoo's Nest," (3) Louise Fletcher in "One Flew over the Cuckoo's Nest," (4) George Burns in "The Sunshine Boys," (5) Lee Grant in "Shampoo," (6) Milos Forman for "One Flew over the Cuckoo's Nest," (7) Mary Pickford, (8) "Dersu Uzala."

1976: (1) "Rocky," (2) Peter Finch in "Network," (3) Faye Dunaway in "Network," (4) Jason Robards in "All the President's Men," (5) Beatrice Straight in "Network," (6) John G. Avildsen for "Rocky," (8) "Black and White in Color."

1977: (1) "Annie Hall," (2) Richard Dreyfuss in "The Goodbye Girl," (3) Diane Keaton in "Annie Hall," (4) Jason Robards in "Julia," (5) Vanessa Redgrave in "Julia," (6) Woody Allen for "Annie Hall," (7) Margaret Booth (film editor), (8) "Madame Rosa."

1978: (1) "The Deer Hunter," (2) Jon Voight in "Coming Home," (3) Jane Fonda in "Coming Home," (4) Christopher Walken in "The Deer Hunter," (5) Maggie Smith in "California Suite," (6) Michael Cimino for "The Deer Hunter," (7) Laurence Olivier, King Vidor, (8) "Get Out Your Handkerchiefs."

1979: (1) "Kramer vs. Kramer," (2) Dustin Hoffman in "Kramer vs. Kramer," (3) Sally Field in "Norma Rae," (4) Melvyn Douglas in "Being There," (5) Meryl Streep in "Kramer vs. Kramer," (6) Robert Benton for "Kramer vs. Kramer," (7) Robert S. Benjamin, Hal Elias, Alec Guinness, (8) "The Tin Drum."

1980: (1) "Ordinary People," (2) Robert DeNiro in "Raging Bull," (3) Sissy Spacek in "Coal Miner's Daughter," (4) Timothy Hutton in "Ordinary People," (5) Mary Steenburgen in "Melvin and Howard," (6) Robert Redford for "Ordinary People," (7) Henry Fonda, (8) "Moscow Does Not Believe in Tears."

1981: (1) "Chariots of Fire," (2) Henry Fonda in "On Golden Pond," (3) Katharine Hepburn in "On Golden Pond," (4) John Gielgud in "Arthur," (5) Maureen Stapleton in "Reds," (6) Warren Beatty for "Reds," (7) Fuji Photo Film Co., Barbara Stanwyck, (8) "Mephisto."

1982: (1) "Gandhi," (2) Ben Kingsley in "Gandhi," (3) Meryl Streep in "Sophie's Choice," (4) Louis Gossett, Jr. in "An Officer and a Gentleman," (5) Jessica Lange in "Tootsie," (6) Richard Attenborough for "Gandhi," (7) Mickey Rooney, (8) "Volver a Empezar" (To Begin Again).

1983: (1) "Terms of Endearment," (2) Robert Duvall in "Tender Mercies," (3) Shirley MacLaine in "Terms of Endearment," (4) Jack Nicholson in "Terms of Endearment," (5) Linda Hunt in "The Year of Living Dangerously," (6) James L. Brooks for "Terms of Endearment," (7) Hal Roach, (8) "Fanny and Alexander."

FOREIGN FILMS RELEASED IN U.S. DURING 1984

CONFIDENTIALLY YOURS

(INTERNATIONAL SPECTRAFILM) Director, Francois Truffaut; Screenplay, Francois Truffaut, Suzanne Schiffman, Jean Aurel; From "The Long Saturday Night" by Charles Williams; Music, Georges Delerue; Photography, Nestor Almendros, Florent Bazin, Tessa Racine; Sound, Pierre Gamet; Costumes, Michele Cerf; Editors, Martine Barraque, Marie-Aimee Debril; Production Manager, Jean-Francois Lentretien; In black and white, and French with English subtitles; Rated PG; 111 minutes; January release.

CAST

Barbara Becker	Fanny Ardant
Julien Vercel	Jean-Louis Trintignant
M. Clement	Philippe Laudenbach
Marie-Christine Vercel	Caroline Sihol
Commissioner	Philippe Morier-Genoud
Bertrand Fabre, photographer	Xavier Saint Macary
Jacques Massoulier	Jean-Pierre Kalfon
Eden Cinema cashier	Anik Belaubrie
Louison	Jean-Louis Richard
Angelface	Yann Dedet
Female Slasher	Nicole Felix
Detective Lablache	Georges Koulouris
Policeman Jambrau	Roland Thenot
Inspector Poivert	Pierre Gare
Slavic Reveller	Jean-Pierre Kohut-Svelko
Secretary	Pascale Pellegrin

Right: Fanny Ardant
© International Spectrafilm

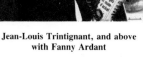

Jean-Louis Trintignant, and above with Fanny Ardant

Jean-Louis Trintignant, Fanny Ardant

NOSTALGHIA

(GRANGE COMMUNICATIONS) Director, Andrei Tarkovsky; Screenplay, Andrei Tarkovsky, Tonino Guerra; Photography, Giuseppe Lanci; Art Director, Andrea Krisanti; Editors, Amedeo Salfa, Erminia Marani; Costumes, Lina Nerli Taviani; Production Manager, Francesco Casati; Assistant Directors, Norman Mozzato, Larissa Tarkovsky; Sound, Remo Ugolinelli; Musical Director, Gino Peguri; Special Effects, Paolo Ricci; In Italian with English subtitles; In color, black and white; Not rated; 120 minutes; January release.

CAST

Gortchkov	Oleg Yankovsky
Eugenia	Domiziana Giordano
Domenico	Erland Josephson
Gortchakov's wife	Patrizia Terreno
Chambermaid	Laura DeMarchi
Domenico's wife	Delia Boccardo
Civil Servant	Milena Vukotic
Farmer	Alberto Canepa

Right: Domiziana Giordano
© *Grange Communications*

Oleg Yankovsky, Domiziana Giordana

159

AND THE SHIP SAILS ON

(TRIUMPH FILMS) Producer, Franco Cristaldi; Director, Federico Fellini; Screenplay, Federico Fellini, Tonino Guerra; Photography, Giuseppe Rotunno; Music, Gianfranco Plenizio; Art Director, Dante Ferretti; Costumes, Maurizio Millenotti; Assistant Directors, Giovanni Arduini, Andrea DeCarlo; Editor, Ruggero Mastroianni; Lyrics, Andrea Zanzotto; Production Manager, Lucio Orlandini; Production Supervisor, Pietro Notarianni; Italian with English subtitles; Associate Producer, Aldo Nemni; In color; Rated PG; 130 minutes; January release

CAST

Orlando	Freddie Jones
Ildebranda Cuffari	Barbara Jefford
Aureliano Fuciletto	Victor Poletti
Sir Reginald J. Dongby	Peter Cellier
Teresa Valegnani	Elisa Mainardi
Lady Dongby Albertini	Norma West
Dorothy	Sarah Jane Varley
Grand Duke Harzock	Fiorenzo Serra
Princess Lherimia	Pina Bausch
Count Bassano	Pasquale Zito
Ines Ruffo Saltini Ione	Linda Polan
Prime Minister	Philip Locke
Ricotin	Jonathan Cecil
U. O. Ziloev	Maurice Barrier
Orchestra Conductor	Paolo Paoloni
Sabatino Lepori	Fred Williams
Film Producer	Elizabeth Kaza
Police Chief	Colin Higgins
Edmea Tetua	Janet Suzman
Ship's Captain	Antonio Vezza
Ship's Officer	Alessandro Partexano
First Mate	Claudio Ciocca
Edmea's Cousin	Ginestra Spinola
Dorothy's Father	Roberto Caponali
Dorothy's Mother	Franca Maresa

and Umberto Zuanelli, Vittorio Zarfati, Domenico Pertica, Franco Ressel, Aisha Bragadin, Ugo Fangareggi, Jean Schlegel, Roger De-Bellegarde, Wolf Gaudlitz, Salvatore Omnis, Cecilia Cerocchi, John Mancini, Salvatore Calabrese, Francesco Maselli, Umberto Barone, Luigi Uzzo, Julian Jenkins, Adam Kotwizky

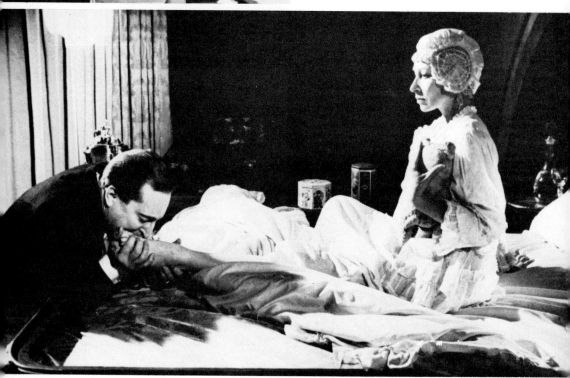

Peter Cellier, Norma West
Freddie Jones, Sarah Jane Varley
Left Center: © *Columbia Pictures*

EL NORTE
(The North)

** (CINECOM INTERNATIONAL/ISLAND ALIVE)** Producer, Anna Thomas; Director, Gregory Nava; Screenplay, Gregory Nava, Anna Thomas; Photography, James Glennon; Sound, Robert Yerington; Editor, Betsy Blankett; Music, Folkloristas, Melecio Martinez, Emil Richards, Linda O'Brien, Samuel Barber, Giuseppe Verdi, Gustav Mahler; In color; Not rated; 139 minutes; January release.

CAST

Rosa Xuncax	Zaide Silvia Gutierrez
Enrique Xuncax	David Villalpando
Arturo Xuncax	Ernesto Gomez Cruz
Lupe Xuncax	Alicia del Lago
Pedro	Eraclio Zepeda
Josefita	Stella Quan
Ramon	Rodolfo Alejandre
Truck Driver	Emilio del Haro
Puma	Rodrigo Puebla
Monty	Trinidad Silva
Raimundo	Abel Franco
Jaime	Mike Gomez
Nacha	Lupe Ontiveros
Ed	John Martin
Joel	Ron Joseph
Bruce	Larry Cedar
Karen	Sheryl Bernstein
Len	Gregory Enten
Carlos	Tony Plana
Jorge	Enrique Castillo
Alice	Diane Civita
Man in bus	Jorge Moreno

Top: (L) David Villalpando, Ernesto Gomez Cruz
(R) Zaide Silvia Gutierrez, Lupe Ontiveros
Center: (L) Zaide Silvia Gutierrez, Alicia del Lago,
David Villalpando (R) Villalpando, Gutierrez
© Cinecom International

Zaide Silvia Gutierrez

161

THE RIDDLE OF THE SANDS

(SATORI) Producer, Drummond Challis; Director, Tony Maylam; Screenplay, Tony Maylam, John Bailey; Based on book by Erskine Childers; Photography, Christopher Challis; Editor, Peter Hollywood; Music, Howard Blake; Art Director, Terry Pritchard; Sound, Rene Borisewitz; Production Associate, Michael York; Production Manager, Aivar Kaulins; In color and Panavision; Not rated; 98 minutes; January release.

CAST

Charles Carruthers	Michael York
Clara	Jenny Agutter
Arthur Davies	Simon MacCorkindale
Dollmann	Alan Badel
Von Bruning	Jurgen Andersen
Frau Dollmann	Olga Lowe
Grimm	Hans Meyer
Bohme	Michael Sheard
The Kaiser	Wolf Kahler
Withers	Ronald Markham

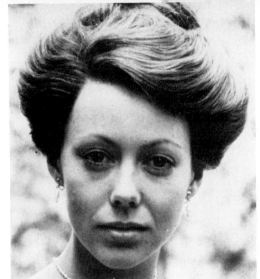

Right: Jenny Agutter
© *Santori Entertainment*

**Michael York, and above
with Simon MacCorkindale**

ENTRE NOUS

(UNITED ARTISTS CLASSICS) Producer, Ariel Zeltoun; Direction and Screenplay, Diane Kurys; Photography, Bernard Lutic; Editor, Joele Van Effenterre; Music, Luis Bacalof; In Panavision and color; French with English subtitles; Not rated; 110 minutes; January release.

CAST

Madeleine	Miou Miou
Lena	Isabelle Huppert
Michel	Guy Marchand
Costa	Jean-Pierre Bacri
Raymond	Robin Renucci
Carlier	Patrick Bauchau
Monsieur Vernier	Jacques Airic
Madame Vernier	Jacqueline Doyen
Florence	Patricia Champane
Sophie	Saga Blanchard
Rene	Guillaume de Guellec
Sarah	Christine Pascal

THE REVOLT OF JOB

(TELECULTURE) Directors, Imre Gyongyossy, Barna Kabay; Screenplay, Imre Gyongyossy, Barna Kabay, Katalin Petenyi; Photography, Gabor Szabo; Editor, Katalin Petenyi; Music, Zoltan Jeny; Hungarian with English subtitles; In Eastmancolor; Not rated; 98 minutes; January release

CAST

Job	Ferenc Zenthe
Roza	Hedi Temessy
Lacko	Gabor Feher
Jani	Peter Rudolf
Ilka	Leticia Caro

Right: Gabor Feher, Ferenc Zenthe
Below: Ferenc Zenthe, Hedi Temessy
© *TeleCulture Inc.*

Ferenc Zenthe, Gabor Feher

Ferenc Zenthe, Hedi Temessy

THAT SINKING FEELING

(SAMUEL GOLDWYN) Producer-Director-Screenwriter, Bill Forsyth; Photography, Michael Coulter; Editor, John Gow; Music, Colin Tully; Designer, Adrienne Atkinson; Assistant Directors, Ian Madden, Sitan Rose; Associate Producer/Production Manager, Paddy Higson; In Fujicolor Negative; Rated PG; 82 minutes; February release (1979 in Scotland).

CAST

Ronnie	Robert Buchanan
Vic	John Hughes
Wal	Billy Greenlees
Simmy	Douglas Sannachan
Alec	Alan Love
The Wee Man	Eric Joseph
Eddie the Driver	Eddie Burt
Policeman	Danny Benson
Mary	Janette Rankin
Bobbie	Derek Miller
Andy	Gordon John Sinclair
Pete	Drew Burnt
Alan	James Ramsey
Watchman	Gerry Clark
Gan Girls	Kim Masterton, Margaret Adams
Doctor	Tom Mannion
Ward Nurse	Margaret McTear
Computer Nurse	Anne Graham
Hi-Fi Salesman	David Scott
Tramp	Alex Mackenzie
Richard DeMarco	Himself
Boy in Daimler	Tony Whitemore

Left: Gordon John Sinclair
© *Samuel Goldwyn Co.*

Gordon John Sinclair (L)

Ana Belen, Eusebio Lazaro, Encarna Paso,
Alvaro Sanchez-Prieto, Imanol Arias,
Angela Molina

DEMONS IN THE GARDEN

(INTERNATIONAL SPECTRAFILM) Director, Manuel Gutierrez Aracon; Screenplay, Manuel Gutierrez, Luis Megino; Producer, Luis Megino; Photography, Jose Luis Alcaine; Editor, Jose Salcedo; Art Director, Andrea D'Odorico; Music, Javer Iturralde; Soloist, Pedro Iturralde; Assistant Director, Josecho San Mateo; Production Director, Jose G. Jacoste; Costumes, Flora Salamero; In color; 1982 release in Spain; Rated R; In Spanish with English subtitles; 100 minutes; February release

CAST

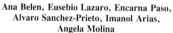

The Family:
Angela	Angela Molina
Ana	Ana Belen
Gloria	Encarna Paso
Juan	Imanol Arias
Oscar	Eusebio Lazaro
Juanito	Alvaro Sanchez-Prieto

Friends:
Traveling Salesman	Francisco Merino
Osorio	Rafael Diaz
Projectionist	Pedro Del Rio
Family Doctor	Eduardo McGregor
Clerk	Luis Lemos
Street Vendor	Francisco Catala
Specialist	Pedro Basanta
Maid	Amparo Climent
Tono	Jorge Roelas

**Top Right: Angela Molina, Encarna Paso,
Ana Belen**
© *International Spectrafilm*

Alvaro Sanchez-Prieto, Angela Molina

INVESTIGATION

(QUARTET FILMS) Director, Etienne Perier; Screenplay, Andre G. Brunelin; Photography, Jean Charvein; Music, Paul Misraki; Based on novel "The Lesser of Two Evils" by Jean Laborde; Producer, Adolphe Viezzi; Executive Producer, Dominique Antoine; Presented by Robert A. McNeil; 1979 release in France; In French with English subtitles; Rated R; 116 minutes; February release

CAST

Stephane Bertin	Victor Lanoux
The Judge	Jean Carmet
Muriel Olivier	Valerie Mairesse
Gaspard	Michel Robin

Left: Valerie Mairesse, Victor Lanoux
© *Robert A. McNeil Movies*

Victor Lanoux, Jean Carmet

Andie MacDowell, Christopher Lambert
Top: Christopher Lambert, Ian Holm, Ralph Richardson

LE BAL

(ALMI CLASSICS) Producer, Giorgio Silvagni; Director, Ettore Scola; From the stage work of the Theatre du Campagnol; Based on an original idea by Jean-Claude Penchenat, Furio Scarpelli, Ettore Scola; Photography, Ricardo Aronovich; Music, Vladimir Cosma; Set Decoration, Luciano Ricceri; Editor, Raimondo Crociani; Performed without dialogue; Not rated; 112 minutes; March release

CAST

Christophe Allwright, Aziz Arbia, Marc Berman, Regis Bouquet, Chantal Capron, Martine Chauvin, Liliane Delval, Francesco DePosa, Etienne Guichard, Raymonde Heudeline, Arnault LeCarpentier, Olivier Loiseau, Nani Noel, Jean-Claude Penchenat, Jean-Francois Perrier, Anita Picchiarini, Francois Pick, Genevieve Rey-Penchenat, Danielle Rochard, Monica Scattini, Michel Toty, Michel Van Speybroeck, Rossana DiLorenzo

**Right: Genevieve Rey-Penchenat,
Marc Berman**
© *Almi Classics*

PRIVATES ON PARADE

(ORION CLASSICS) Executive Producers, George Harrison, Denis O'Brien; Producer, Simon Relph; Director, Michael Blakemore; Screenplay and Lyrics, Peter Nichols; Music, Denis King; Photography, Ian Wilson; Editor, Jim Clark; Production and Costume Designer, Luciana Arrighi; Choreographer, Gillian Gregory; Production Manager, Redmond Morris; Assistant Directors, Jake Wright, Michael Zimbrich, Christopher Figg; Assistant Director, Bryan Oates; Art Directors, Michael White, Andrew Sanders; A Handmade Films production in color; Rated R; 96 minutes; April release

CAST

Maj. Giles Flack	John Cleese
Acting Capt. Terri Dennis	Denis Quilley
Sgt. Maj. Reg Drummond	Michael Elphick
Acting Lt. Sylvia Morgan	Nicola Pagett
Flight Sgt. Kevin Artwright	Bruce Payne
Sgt. Len Bonny	Joe Melia
Sgt. Charles Bishop	David Bamber
Sgt. Eric Young-Love	Simon Jones
Sgt. Steven Flowers	Patrick Pearson
Lee	Phil Tan
Cheng	Vincent Wong
Band Pianist	Neil Pearson
Capt. Sholto Savory	John Standing
Armoury Indian	Talat Hussain
Capt. Henry Cox	John Quayle
Mrs. Reg	Brigitte Kahn
Sikh Doorman	Ishaq Bux
Electrician	Robin Langford
Commanding Officer	Tim Barlow
Armed Escorts	William parker, Mark Elliot, Tim Sinclair
Infantry Officer in the bush	David Griffin
Sailor	Julian Sands

Top: Denis Quilley, Joe Melia, Simon Jones
Below: Bruce Payne, Quilley, Melia
Right: John Cleese, Quilley Top: Michael
Elphick, Cleese, John Standing
© Orion Classics

Joe Melia, Denis Quilley, Simon Jones
Above: Nicola Pagett

Darling Legitimus, Garry Cadenat

SUGAR CANE ALLEY

(ORION CLASSICS) Executive Producer, Jean-Luc Ormieres; Producers, Michel Loulergue, Alix Regis; Direction and Screenplay, Euzhan Palcy; Based on novel "La Rue Cases Negres" by Joseph Zobel; Photography, Dominique Chapuis; Editor, Marie-Joseph Yoyotte; Costumes, Isabelle Filleul; Associate Producer, Claude Nedjar; French with English subtitles; In color; Not rated; 103 minutes; April release

CAST

Jose	Garry Cadenat
M'Man Tine	Darling Legitimus
Medouze	Douta Seck
Monsieur Saint-Louis	Joby Bernabe
Le Gereur	Francisco Charles
La Mere de Leopold	Marie-Jo Descas
Madame Saint-Louis	Marie-Ange Farot
Monsieur Roc	Henri Melon
Douze Orteils	Eugene Mona
Carmen	Joel Palcy

Top: Garry Cadenat, Henri Melon
© *Orion Classics*

BIQUEFARRE

(NEW YORKER) Producers, Marie-Francoise Mascaro/Midas S. A., Bertrand van Effenterre/Mallia Films; Associate Producer, William Gilcher; Direction and Screenplay, Georges Rouquier; Photography, Andre Villard; Editor, Genevieve Louveau; Music, Yves Gilbert; Assistant Director, Alain Peyrollaz; Production Manager, Baba Gamet; Art Director, Geoffrey Larcher; French with English subtitles; In color; Not rated; 90 minutes; April release

CAST

Henri	Henri Rouquier
Maria	Maria Rouquier
Raoul Pradal	Roger Malet
Lucien	Marius Benaben
Hortense	Helene Benaben
Marcel	Andre Benaben
Martine	Francine Benaben
Genevieve	Marie-Helene Benaben
Roch	Roch Rouquier
Raymond	Raymond Rouquier
Jeanette	Georgette Rouquier
Christophe	Christian Viguier
Bernard	Michel Bras
Cecile	Colette Bras
Isabelle Combes	Isabelle Bras
Denise Combes	Reine-Marie Duluc-Ducombs
Dr. Vermillat	Rene Gouzenne
Jeannot Lafeuille	Andre Greffeuille
Annie	Annie Viguier
Jules	Didier Trebosc
Monsieur Testu	Christian Valayer
Albertine	Marie-Francoise Bedel
Leon	Michel Bedel
Pierre	Pierre Rouquier
Albert	Albert Rouquier
Philippe	Philippe Bras

© New Yorker Films

Maria Rouquier, Henri Rouquier

PHAR LAP

(20th CENTURY-FOX) Producer, John Sexton; Director, Simon Wincer; Executive Producer, Richard Davis; Screenplay, David Williamson; Photography, Russell Boyd; Designer, Laurence Eastwood; Music, Bruce Rowland; Editor, Tony Paterson; Costumes, Anna Senior; Assistant Directors, Murray Newey, Michael Bourchier, Deuel Droogan, Christopher Walker; Production Manager, Paula Gibbs; Production Coordinator, Peta Lawson; Art Director, David Bowden; In Panavision, color, and Dolby Stereo; Rated PG; 107 minutes; April release

CAST

Tommy Woodcock	Tom Burlinson
Dave Davis	Ron Leibman
Harry Telford	Martin Vaughan
Bea Davis	Judy Morris
Vi Telford	Celia DeBurgh
"Cashy" Martin	Richard Morgan
William Neilsen	Robert Grubb
Emma	Georgia Carr
Jim Pike	James Steele
Lachlan McKinnon	Vincent Ball
Bert Wolfe	Peter Whitford
Eric Connolly	John Stanton
James Crofton	Roger Newcombe
Baron Long	Len Kaserman
Trainer	Tom Woodcock

Right: Tom Burlinson, Georgia Carr
© *John Sexton*

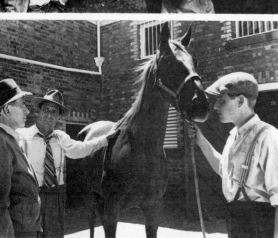

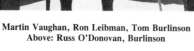

Martin Vaughan, Ron Leibman, Tom Burlinson
Above: Russ O'Donovan, Burlinson

Tom Burlinson racing Phar Lap
Above: Ron Leibman, Judy Morris

ZAPPA

(INTERNATIONAL SPECTRAFILM) Director, Bille August; Screenplay, Bille August, Bjarne Reuter; Based on novel by Bjarne Reuter; Photography, Jan Weincke; Production Manager, Ib Tardini; Production Coordinator, Janne Find; Costumes, Gitte Kolvig; Editor, Janus Billeskov Jansen; Producer, Per Holst Filmproduktion; Danish with English subtitles; Not rated; 103 minutes; May release

CAST

Bjorn	Adam Tonsberg
Mulle	Morton Hoff
Sten	Peter Reichhardt
Bjorn's Mother	Lone Lindorff
Bjorn's Father	Arne Hansen
Henning, Bjorn's younger brother	Thomas Nielsen
Sten's Mother	Solbjorg Hojfeldt
Bjorn's Grandfather	Willy Jacobsen
Kirsten	Rikke Bondo
Sisse	Mette Knudsen
Asger	Michael Shomacker
Folke	Jonas Elmer
Kalormen, teacher	Soren Frolund

© *International Spectrafilm*

HEAT OF DESIRE

(TRIUMPH) Producers, Lise Fayolle, Giorgio Silvagni; Director, Luc Beraud; Screenplay, Luc Beraud, Claude Miller; Photography, Bernard Lutic; Music, Éric Demarsan; Editor, Joelle Van Effenterre; French with English subtitles; Rated R; 90 minutes; May release

CAST

Serge Laine	Patrick Dewaere
Carol	Clio Goldsmith
Helene	Jeanne Moreau
Max	Guy Marchand
Rognon	Pierre Dux
Martinez	Jose-Luis Lopez Vasquez

Patrick Dewaere, Jeanne Moreau
Above: Clio Goldsmith, Patrick Dewaere
© *Columbia Pictures*

DANNY BOY

(TRIUMPH) Executive Producer, John Boorman; Producer, Barry Blackmore; Direction and Screenplay, Neil Jordan; Photography, Chris Menges; Art Director, John Lucas; Editor, Pat Duffner; Music, Paddy Meegan; Costumes, Janet O'Leary; Production Manager, Seamus Byrne; 1982 release in Ireland; In Technicolor; Rated R; 92 minutes; May release

CAST

Annie	Veronica Quilligan
Danny	Stephen Rea
Bill	Alan Devlin
Ray	Peter Caffrey
Deirdre	Honor Heffernan
Bride	Lise-Ann McLaughlin
Groom	Ian McElhinney
Best Man	Derek Lord
Bloom	Ray McAnally
Bonner	Donal McCann
Aunt Mae	Marie Kean
Bouncer	Don Foley
Assistant	Gerald McSorley
Female Assistant	Liz Bono
Photographer	Tom Collins
George	Tony Rohr
Beth	Anita Reeves
Mary	Sorcha Cusack
Uncle	Michael Lally
Francie	Macrea Clarke
Young Female Patient	Sally Friel

© *Columbia Pictures*

Stephen Rea, and above with
Veronica Quilligan

ANOTHER TIME, ANOTHER PLACE

(SAMUEL GOLDWYN) Producer, Simon Perry; Direction and Screenplay, Michael Radford; Based on novel by Jessie Kesson; Associate Producer, Paul Cowan; Executive Producer, Timothy Burrill; Editor, Tom Priestley; Music, John McLeod; Art Director, Hayden Pearce; Costumes, Louise Frogley; In color; Rated R; 101 minutes; May release

CAST

Janie	Phyllis Logan
Luigi	Giovanni Mauriello
Umberto	Gian Luca Favilla
Paolo	Claudio Rosini
Dougal	Paul Young
Beel	Gregor Fisher
Finlay	Tom Watson
Kirsty	Jennifer Piercey
Meg	Denise Coffey
Jess	Yvonne Gilan
Else	Carol Ann Crawford
Alick	Ray Jeffries
Jeems	Scott Johnston
Raffaello	Corrado Sfogli
Antonio	Nadio Fortune
Officer	Peter Finlay
Randy Bob	David Mowat
P.O.W.	Stephen Gressieux

Right: Phyllis Logan, also below
© *Samuel Goldwyn Co.*

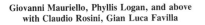

Giovanni Mauriello, Phyllis Logan, and above with Claudio Rosini, Gian Luca Favilla

Phyllis Logan, Giovanni Mauriello

THE BOUNTY

(ORION) Producer, Bernard Williams; Director, Roger Donaldson; Screenplay, Robert Bolt; Based on "Captain Bligh and Mr. Christian" by Richard Hough; Photography, Arthur Ibbetson; Music, Vangelis; Designer, John Graysmark; Editor, Tony Lawson; Costumes, John Bloomfield; Assistant Directors, David Tringham, Michael Stevenson, Debbie Vertur; Special Effects, John Stears; Production Supervisor, Douglas Twiddy; Production Coordinator, Loretta Ordewer; Art Director, Tony Reading; Choreographer, Terry Gilbert; In J-D-C Widescreen, Technicolor and Dolby Stereo; Rated PG; 132 minutes; May release

CAST

Fletcher Christian	Mel Gibson
Lt. William Bligh	Anthony Hopkins
Admiral Hood	Laurence Olivier
Capt. Greetham	Edward Fox
Fryer	Daniel Day-Lewis
Cole	Bernard Hill
Young	Philip Davis
Churchill	Liam Neeson
King Tynah	Wi Kuki Kaa
Mauatua	Tevaite Vernette
Adams	Philip Martin Brown
Nelson	Simon Chandler
Dr. Huggan	Malcolm Terris
Heywood	Simon Adams
Smith	John Sessions
McCoy	Andrew Wilde
Quintal	Neil Morrissey
Mills	Richard Graham
Ellison	Dexter Fletcher
Purcell	Pete Lee-Wilson
Norton	Jon Gadsby
Lamb	Brendan Conroy
Blind Fiddler	Barry Dransfield
Valentine	Steve Fletcher
Prosecuting Captain	Jack May
Queen Tynah	Mary Kauila
Mrs. Bligh	Sharon Bower
King Tynah's Councillor	Tavana

Left: Laurence Olivier, Edward Fox
Above: Liam Neeson, Anthony Hopkins, Philip Davis,
Mel Gibson, Dexter Fletcher Top: Gibson, Hopkins
© Orion Pictures

Mel Gibson

Mel Gibson, Tevaite Vernette

THE GUEST

(RM PRODUCTIONS) Producer, Gerald Berman; Director, Ross Devenish; Screenplay, Athol Fugard; Photography, Rod Stewart; Editor, Lionel Selwyn; Designer, Jeni Halliday; In color; Not rated; 114 minutes; June release

CAST

Eugene Marais	Athol Fugard
Dr. A. G. Visser	Marius Weyers
Oom Doors, the farmer	Gordon Vorster
Tant Corrie, his wife	Wilma Stockenstrom

Left: Athol Fugard

MARIGOLDS IN AUGUST

(RM PRODUCTIONS) Producers, Jonathan Cohen, Mark Forstater; Screenplay, Athol Fugard; Director, Ross Devenish; Photography, Michael Davis; Editor, Lionel Selwyn; Not rated; 87 minutes; June release.

CAST

Daan	Winston Ntshona
Melton	John Kani
Paulus Olifant	Athol Fugard

Center: Athol Fugard, Winston Ntshona

Athol Fugard

THE FOURTH MAN

(SPECTRAFILM) Producer, Rob Houwer; Director, Paul Verhoeven; Screenplay, Gerard Soeteman; Based on novel by Gerard Reve; Photography, Jan De Bont; Music, Loek Dikker; Editor, Ine Schenkkan; Art Director, Roland De Groot; Costumes, Elly Claus; Assistant Director, Jindra Markus; Assistant Producers, Ineke Van Wezel, Jelte Velzen; Production Manager, Remmelt Remmelts; Dutch with English subtitles; In color and Dolby Stereo; 104 minutes; June release

CAST

Gerard Reve	Jeroen Krabbe
Christine Halsslag	Renee Soutendijk
Herman	Thom Hoffman
Dr. DeVries	Dolf De Vries
Ria (Lady in Blue)	Geert De Jong
Funeral Director	Hans Veerman
Josefs	Hero Muller
Adrienne	Caroline De Beus
First Husband	Reinout Bussemaker
Second Husband	Erik J. Meijer
Third Husband	Ursul De Geer
Surfer	Filip Bolluyt
Sales Clerk in bookstore	Hedda Lornie
Gerard's Boyfriend	Paul Nygaard
Waiter on train	Guus van der Made
Nurse	Pamela Teves
Woman at lecture	Hella Faassen
AKO Sales Clerk	Helen Hedy

Right: Jeroen Krabbe, and below
with Renee Soutendijk
© *International Spectrafilm*

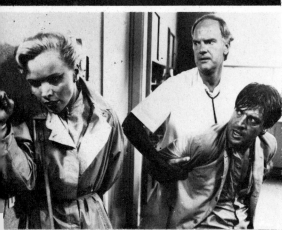

Renee Soutendijk, Dolf DeVries, Jeroen Krabbe
Above: Jeroen Krabbe

Thom Hoffman, Jeroen Krabbe

180

CAREFUL HE MIGHT HEAR YOU

(20th CENTURY-FOX) Producer, Jill Robb; Director, Carl Schultz; Screenplay, Michael Jenkins; Based on novel by Sumner Locke Elliott; Photography, John Seale; Designer, John Stoddart; Editor, Richard Francis-Bruce; Music, Ray Cook; Production Manager, Greg Ricketson; Assistant Director, Colin Fletcher; Costumes, Bruce Finlayson; Art Director, John Carroll; A Syme International Production in association with the N.S.W. Film Corporation; In Panavision, Dolby Stereo and color; Rated PG; 116 minutes; June release

CAST

PS	Nicholas Gledhill
Vanessa	Wendy Hughes
Lila	Robyn Nevin
George	Peter Whitford
Logan	John Hargreaves
Agnes	Isabelle Anderson
Vere	Geraldine Turner
Ettie	Colleen Clifford
Diana	Julie Nihill
Mrs. Grindel	Beth Child
Winnie Grindel	Pega Williams
Chauffeur	Steven Fyfield
Miss Pile	Jacqueline Kott
Cynthia	Kylie Burgess
Ian	Toby Blanchard
Miss Golden	Virginia Portingale
Mr. Hood	Michael Long
Judge	Edward Howell
Mr. Gentle	Len London
Magician	Colin Croft

Right: Nicholas Gledhill, Robyn Nevin
© *20th Century-Fox*

Wendy Hughes, Nicholas Gledhill
Above: Gledhill, Peter Whitford, Robyn Nevin

Wendy Hughes, Nicholas Gledhill,
Robyn Nevin

ANOTHER COUNTRY

(ORION CLASSICS) Producer, Alan Marshall; Director, Marek Kanievska; Executive Producers, Robert Fox, Julian Seymour; Editor, Gerry Hambling; Designer, Brian Morris; Photography, Peter Biziou; Screenplay by Julian Mitchell from his stage play; Production Manager, Simon Bosanquet; Assistant Directors, Andy Armstrong, Christopher Figg, Michael Zimbrich, Christopher Knowles; Art Director, Clinton Cavers; In color; Rated PG; 90 minutes; June release

CAST

Guy Bennett	Rupert Everett
Tommy Judd	Colin Firth
Barclay	Michael Jenn
Delahay	Robert Addie
Imogen Bennett	Anna Massey
Julie Schofield	Betsy Brantley
Devenish	Rupert Wainwright
Fowler	Tristan Oliver
Harcourt	Cary Elwes
Menzies	Frederick Alexander
Wharton	Adrian Ross-Magenty
Yevgeni	Geoffrey Bateman
Martineau	Philip Dupuy
Head Boy	Guy Henry
Arthur	Jeffrey Wickham
Best Man	John Line
Trafford	Gideon Boulting
Senior Chaplain	Llewelyn Rees
Waiter	Arthur Howard
Chief Judge	Ivor Roberts
Prefect	Crispin Redman
Spungin	Nick Rowe
Ivy	Kathleen St. John
Batsmen	Martin Wenner, Christopher Milburn
Nicholson	Tristram Jellinek
Henderson	Tristram Wymark

© *Orion Classics*

Rupert Everett (C)
Top Left: Rupert Everett, Colin Firth

AFTER THE REHEARSAL

(TRIUMPH) Producer, Jorn Donner; Direction and Screenplay, Ingmar Bergman; Photography, Sven Nykvist; Editor, Sylvia Ingemarsson; Art Director, Anna Asp; Costumes, Inger Pehrsson; Assistant Director, Eva Bergman; Production Manager, Katinka Farag; Produced by Cinematograph for Personafilm/Munich; Swedish with English Subtitles; In color; Rated R; 72 minutes; June release

CAST

Henrik Vogler	Erland Josephson
Rakel	Ingrid Thulin
Anna Egerman	Lena Olin
Anna at 12	Nadja Palmstjerna-Weiss
Henrik at 12	Bertil Guve

Top: Erland Josephson, Ingrid Thulin
© *Triumph Films*

Lena Olin, Erland Josephson

SKYLINE

(KINO INTERNATIONAL) Direction and Screenplay, Fernando Colomo; Photography, Angel Luis Fernandez; Production Director, Antonio Isasi; Associate Producer, Ana Huete; Editor, Miguel Angel Santamaria; Music, Manzanita; Spanish and English with subtitles; In color; Not rated; 83 minutes; July release

CAST

Gustavo Fernandez	Antonio Resines
Pat	Beatriz Perez-Porro
Jaime Bos	Jaime Nos
Roy	Roy Hoffman
Elizabeth	Patricia Cisarano
Irene	Irene Stillman
Thornton	Whit Stillman

Top: Antonio Resines, Roy Hoffman,
Beatriz Perez-Porro Below: Resines,
Patricia Cisarano © *Kino International*

Antonio Resines (also top)
Above: with Jaime Nos

THE GODS MUST BE CRAZY

(20th CENTURY-FOX) Executive Producer, Boet Troskie; Produced, Directed and Written by Jamie Uys; Assistant Director, Kobus Kruger; Music, John Boshoff; Editor, Jamie Uys; Photography, Buster Reynolds, Robert Lewis; Costumes, Gail Grobbelaar, Mij Reynolds; In Widescreen and color; Rated PG; 109 minutes; July release

CAST

Andrew Steyn	Marius Weyers
Kate Thompson	Sandra Prinsloo
Xi	N!Xau
Sam Boga	Louw Verwey
Reverend	Jamie Uys
Mpudi	Michael Thys
Jack Hind	Nic De Jager
First Card Player	Fanyana Sidumo
Second Card Player	Joe Seakatsie
President	Ken Gampu
Narrator	Paddy O'Byrne

© *20th Century-Fox*
Top Right: Michael Thys

THE BOSTONIANS

(ALMI) Producer, Ismail Merchant; Director, James Ivory; Screenplay, Ruth Prawer Jhabvala; Based on novel by Henry James; Photography, Walter Lassally; Music, Richard Robbins; Executive Producers, Michael Landes, Albert Schwartz; Designer, Leo Austin; Costumes, Jenny Beavan, John Bright; Editors, Katherine Wenning, Mark Potter; Assistant Directors, David Appleton, Ron Peck; Associate Producers, Connie Kaiserman, Paul Bradley; Production Manager, Ted Morley; Production Coordinator, Lorraine Goodman; Art Directors, Tom Walden, Don Carpentier; A Merchant Ivory production in Dolby Stereo and color; Not rated; 120 minutes; July release

CAST

Basil Ransom	Christopher Reeve
Olive Chancellor	Vanessa Redgrave
Verena Tarrant	Madeleine Potter
Miss Birdseye	Jessica Tandy
Mrs. Burrage	Nancy Marchand
Dr. Tarrant	Wesley Addy
Mrs. Tarrant	Barbara Bryne
Dr. Prance	Linda Hunt
Adeline Luna	Nancy New
Henry Burrage	John Van Ness Philip
Mr. Pardon	Wallace Shawn
Henrietta Stackpole	Maura Moynihan
Mrs. Farrinder	Martha Farrar
Mr. Gracie	Peter Bogyo
Newton	Dusty Maxwell
Music Hall Policeman	Charles McCaughan
Music Hall Official	J. Lee Morgan
Mr. Filer	Lee Doyle
Patient	De French
Maid	Jane Manners
Irish Washerwoman	Janet Cicchese
Tough Boy	Scott Kradolfer
Party Guest	June Mitchell

Left: Vanessa Redgrave, Madeleine Potter, Barbara Bryne Top: Vanessa Redgrave, Madeleine Potter
© *Almi Pictures*

Linda Hunt, Christopher Reeve

Christopher Reeve, Madeleine Potter

FIRST NAME: CARMEN

(INTERNATIONAL SPECTRAFILM) Executive Producer, Alain Sarde; Director, Jean-Luc Godard; Screenplay, Anne-Marie Mieville; Adapted from novel "Carmen" by Prosper Merimee; Photography, Raoul Coutard; Editor, Suzanne Lang-Willar; Music, Beethoven; Song "Ruby's Arms" by Tom Waits; Costumes, Renee Renard; Production Director, Bernard Bouix; In Eastmancolor; French with English subtitles; Not rated 85 minutes; July release

CAST

Carmen X	Maruschka Detmers
Joseph Bonnaffe	Jacques Bonnaffe
Claire	Myriem Roussel
The Boss	Christophe Odent
Uncle Jean	Jean-Luc Godard
Fred	Hyppolite Girardot
Carmen's Bodyguard	Bertrand Liebert
Hotel Worker	Alain Bastien-Thiry

**Top: Jacques Bonnaffe and below
with Maruschka Detmers
© *International Spectrafilm***

Jean-Luc Godard

CAL

(WARNER BROS.) Producers, Stuart Craig, David Puttnam; Director, Pat O'Connor; Screenplay, Bernard MacLaverty; Executive Producer, Terence A. Clegg; Editor, Michael Bradsell; Designer, Stuart Craig; Production Manager, Dominic Fulford; Assistant Directors, Bill Craske, Christopher Thompson, John Phelan, Nick Daubeny; Art Director, Josie MacAvin; Costumes, Penny Rose; Production Coordinator, Mo Coppitters; An Enigma production in color; Rated R; 102 minutes; August release.

CAST

Marcella	Helen Mirren
Cal	John Lynch
Shamie	Donal McCann
Skeffington	John Kavanagh
Cyril Dunlop	Ray McAnally
Crilly	Stevan Rimkus
Mrs. Morton	Kitty Gibson
Dermot Ryan	Louis Rolston
Preacher	Tom Hickey
Arty	Gerard Mannix Flynn
Old Mr. Morton	Seamus Ford
Skeffington Senior	Edward Byrne
Man in library	J. J. Murphy
Lucy	Audrey Johnston
Robert Morton	Brian Munn
Scar-faced Policeman	Daragh O'Malley
Second Policeman	George Shane
Shop Assistant	Julia Dearden
Neighbor	Yvonne Adams
Soldier at roadblock	Lawrence Foster
Soldiers at farm	Scott Frederick, Gerard O'Hagan

John Lynch, Helen Mirren
© *Warner Bros.*

Anna Campbell Jones, Jane Briers Above:
Rebecca Johnson, Daisy Cockburn, Jones

SECRETS

(SAMUEL GOLDWYN) Executive Producer, David Puttnam; Producer, Chris Griffin; Director, Gavin Millar; Screenplay, Noella Smith; Photography, Christopher Challis; Associate Producer, David Bill; Editor, Eric Boyd Perkins; Music, Guy Woolfenden; Art Director, Jeffrey Woodbridge; In color; Rated R; 153 minutes; August release

CAST

Mother	Helen Lindsay
Dr. Jefferies	John Horsley
Louise	Anna Campbell Jones
Sydney	Daisy Cockburn
Trottie	Rebecca Johnson
Jane	Lucy Goode
Paul	Richard Tolan
Miss Quick	Carol Gillies
Miss Strickland	Jane Briers
Elderly Teacher	Judith Fellows
Matron	Georgine Anderson
Miss Johnson	Cynthia Grenville
Miss Jones Wallace	Elizabeth Choice
Miss Lane	Matyelock Gibbs
Miss Lightfoot	Nancy Manningham
Boys on train	Peter Scott Harrison, Craig Stokes, Robert Stagg, Paul Gamble

Above: Helen Lindsay, Anna Campbell Jones
© *Samuel Goldwyn Co.*

THE BALLAD OF NARAYAMA

(KINO INTERNATIONAL) Producers, Goro Kusakabe, Jiro Tomoda; Director, Shohei Imamura; Screenplay, Shohei Imamura from the story of the same title and "Men of Tohoku" both by Shichiro Fukazawa; Photography, Masao Tochizawa; Music, Shinichiro Ikebe; Art Director, Nobutaka Yoshino; Editor, Hajime Okayasu; Japanese with English subtitles; In color; Not rated; 128 minutes; September release

CAST

Tatsuehi	Ken Ogata
Orin, his mother	Sumiko Sakamoto
Tamayan, his wife	Takejo Aki
Risuke, his brother	Tonpei Hidari
Kesakichi, older son	Seiji Kurasaki
Tomekichi, younger son	Kaoru Shimamori
Matayan, old neighbor	Ryutaro Tatsumi
Matsu, Kesakichi's girlfriend	Junko Takada
Okane, old widow	Nijiko Kiyokawa
Oei, young widow	Mitsuko Baisho
Katsuzo, Oei's husband	Shoichi Ozawa
Tadayan, Matayan's son	Mitsuaki Fukamizu
Old Salt Dealer	Norihei Miki
Amaya, Matsu's father	Akio Yokoyama
Amaya's wife	Sachie Shimura
Amaya's son	Masami Okamoto
Jinsaku, a villager	Fujio Tsumeda
Teruyan, another villager	Taiji Tonoyama

Right: Ken Ogata, Sumiko Sakamoto
© *Toei Co.*

Thommy Berggren and above with
Gunilla Nyroos (also right)

A HILL ON THE DARK SIDE OF THE MOON

(CRYSTAL PICTURES) Director, Lennart Hjulstrom; Screenplay, Agneta Pleijel; Photography, Sten Holmberg, Rolf Lindstrom; Music, Lars-Erik Brossner; Editor, Lasse Lundberg; In Eastmancolor; Swedish with English subtitles; Not rated; 101 minutes; September release

CAST

Sonya Kovalevsky	Gunilla Nyroos
Maxim Kovalevsky	Thommy Berggren
Foufa	Lina Pleijel
Ann-Charlotte Leffler	Bibi Andersson
Gustaf Edgren	Ingvar Hirdwell

© *Crystal Pictures*

CARMEN

(TRIUMPH) Producer, Patrice Ledoux; Director, Francesco Rosi; From the opera by Georges Bizet; Libretto, Henri Meilhac, Ludovic Halevy; Based on novella by Prosper Merimee; Screen Adaptation, Francesco Rosi, Tonino Guerra; Photography, Pasqualino De Santis; Sets and Costumes, Enrico Job; Editors, Ruggero Mastroianni, Colette Semprun; Choreography, Antonio Gades; Production Manager, Alessandro Von Normann; Assistant Director, Giovanni Arduini; In Panavision, Eastmancolor, Dolby Stereo; French with English subtitles; Rated PG; 152 minutes; September release.

CAST

Carmen	Julia Migenes-Johnson
Don Jose	Placido Domingo
Escamillo	Ruggero Raimondi
Micaela	Faith Esham
Dancairo	Jean-Philippe Lafont
Remendado	Gerard Garino
Mercedes	Susan Daniel
Frasquita	Lilian Watson
Zuniga	John Paul Bogart
Morales	Francois Le Roux
Lillas Pastia	Julien Guiomar
Guide	Accursio Di Leo
Manuelita	Maria Campano
Court Dancers	Cristina Hoyos, Juan Antonio Jimenez
Old Dancer (Innkeeper)	Enrique El Cojo
Escamillo's double	Santiago Lopez

Antonio Gades Dance Company

**Left: John Paul Bogart, Julia Migenes-Johnson
Above: Julia Migenes-Johnson (C)
© Columbia Pictures**

**Placido Domingo,
Julia Migenes-Johnson**

Ruggero Raimondi

SWANN IN LOVE

(ORION CLASSICS) Director, Volker Schlondorff; Screenplay, Peter Brook, Jean-Claude Carriere, Marie-Helene Estienne; Adaptation, Volker Schlondorff; Based on novel "Un Amour de Swann" by Marcel Proust; Photography, Sven Nykvist; Music, Hans-Werner Henze; Sets, Jacques Saulnier; Costumes, Yvonne Sasinot De Nesle; French with English subtitles; Rated R; 110 minutes; September release

CAST

Swann	Jeremy Irons
Odette de Crecy	Ornella Muti
Baron de Charlus	Alain Delon
Duchesse de Guermantes	Fanny Ardant
Madame Verdurin	Marie-Christine Barrault
Madame Cottard	Nathalie Juvet
Sous-maitresse	Charlotte Kerr
Madame de Gallardon	Philippine Pascale
Madame de Cambremer	Charlotte De Turckheim
Monsieur Cottard	Jean-Francois Balmer
Monsieur Verdurin	Jean-Louis Richard
Duc de Guermantes	Jacques Boudet
Forcheville	Roland de Chaudenay
Saniette	Bruno Thost
Biche	Roland Topor
Chloee	Ann Bennent
Young Man	Nicolas Baby
Madame Verdurin's Guest	Catherine Lachens
Head of Protocole	Humbert Balsan
Monsieur Vinteuil	Jean Aurenche
Mademoiselle Vinteuil	Veronique Dietschy
Aime	Jean-Pierre Kopf

Top: Jeremy Irons, Ornella Muti (also below)
© *Orion Classics*

**Alain Delon Top: Ornella
Muti, Jeremy Irons**

191

SHIVERS

(NEW YORKER) Direction and Screenplay, Wojciech Marczewski; Photography, Jerzy Zielinski; Music, Andrzej Trzaskowski; Design, Anna Jekielek; Editor, Irena Chorynska; Production Manager, Zbibniew Tolloczko; Assistant Directors, Aleksander Sajkow, Wieslaw Saniewski, Krzysztof Maj; Produced by The Polish Corporation for Film Production; Polish with English subtitles; In color; Not rated; 106 minutes; October release

CAST

Tomasz	Tomasz Hudziec
Pathfinder Camp Counselor	Teresa Marczewska
School Teacher	Marek Kondrat
Supervisor	Zdzislaw Wardejn
Tomasz' Mother	Teresa Sawicka
Tomasz' Father	Wladyslaw Kowalski
Tutor	Bogdan Koca
School Director	Zygmunt Bielawski

Top: Teresa Marczewska
Below and Right: Tomasz Hudziec
© *New Yorker Films*

Tomasz Hudziec

A NOS AMOURS

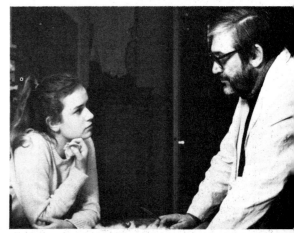

(TRIUMPH) Director, Maurice Pialat; Story and Screenplay, Arlette Langmann, Maurice Pialat; Assistant Directors, Florence Quentin, Cyril Collard, Christian Argentino; Executive Producer, Micheline Pialat; Associate Producer, Emmanuel Schlumberger; Photography, Jacques Loiseleux; Production Managers, Sylvie Danton, Herve Austen; Music Henry Purcell's "The Cold Song" performed by Klaus Nomi; Sets, Jean-Paul Camail, Arlette Langmann; Costumes, Valerie Schlumberger, Martha De Villalonga; Editors, Yann Dedet, Sophie Coussein, Valerie Condroyer, Corinne Lazare, Jean Gargonne, Nathalie Letrosne, Catherine Legault; French with English subtitles; In color; Rated R; 102 minutes; October release

CAST

Suzanne	Sandrine Bonnaire
Robert	Dominique Besnehard
The Father	Maurice Pialat
The Mother	Evelyne Ker
Anne	Anne-Sophie Maille
Michel	Christophe Odent
Luc	Cyr Boitard
Martine	Maite Maille
Bernard	Pierre-Loup Rajot
Jean-Pierre	Cyril Collard
Nathalie	Nathalie Gureghian
Instructor	Guenole Pascal
Charline	Caroline Cibot
Jacques	Jacques Fieschi
Marie-France	Valerie Schlumberger
American	Tom Stevens
Fanny	Tsilka Theodorou
Claude	Vanghel Theodorou
Freddy	Herve Austen
Henri	Eric Viellard

Right: Sandrine Bonnaire, Evelyne Ker Above: Bonnaire, Maurice Pialat
© *Columbia Pictures*

Sandrine Bonnaire (R) and above with Dominique Besnehard

Sandrine Bonnaire

COMFORT AND JOY

(UNIVERSAL) Producers, Davina Belling, Clive Parsons; Direction and Screenplay, Bill Forsyth; Associate Producer, Paddy Higson; Music, Mark Knopfler; Photography, Chris Menges; Designer, Adrienne Atkinson; Editor, Michael Ellis; Assistant Director, Ian Madden; Production Manager, David Brown; Art Director, Andy Harris; In Technicolor; Rated PG; 106 minutes; October release

CAST

Alan	Bill Paterson
Maddy	Eleanor David
Charlotte	C. P. Grogan
Trevor	Alex Norton
Colin	Patrick Malahide
Hilary	Rikki Fulton
Mr. McCool	Roberto Bernardi
Bruno	George Rossi
Paolo	Peter Rossi
Renato	Billy McElhaney
Rufus	Gilly Gilchrist
Gloria	Caroline Guthrie
Nancy	Ona McCracken
Fiona	Elizabeth Sinclair
Sarah	Katy Black
Lily	Robin Black
George	Ron Donachie
Psychiatrist	Arnold Brown
Archie	Iain McColl
Amos	Billy Johnstone
Keith	Alistair Campbell
Mrs. Wilson	Elspet Cameron
Maria	Pearl Deans

Left: Alex Norton, Bill Paterson, Billy McElhaney, C. P. Grogan, Roberto Bernardi
Top: Bill Paterson
© *Universal*

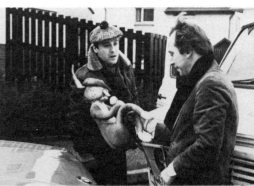

Bill Paterson,
Eleanor David

C. P. Grogan, Bill Paterson
Above: Alex North, Paterson

DIARY FOR MY CHILDREN

(NEW YORKER) Produced by Mafilm/Budapest; Directed and Written by Marta Meszaros; Photography, Miklos Jancso, Jr.; Music, Zsolt Dome; Hungarian with English subtitles; Black and white; Not rated; 106 minutes; October release

CAST

Juli .... Zsuzsa Czinkoczi
Magda .... Anna Polony
Janos .... Jan Nowicki
Janos' Son .... Tamas Toth
Grandpa .... Pal Zolnay
Grandma .... Mari Szemes

Top: Jan Nowicki, Zsuzsa Czinkoczi
© *New Yorker Films*

Ildiko Bansagi, Zsuzsa Czinkoczi

THE PLOUGHMAN'S LUNCH

(SAMUEL GOLDWYN) Producers, Simon Relph, Ann Scott; Director, Richard Eyre; Screenplay, Ian McEwan; Music, Dominic Muldowney; Photography, Clive Tickner; Editor, David Martin; Designer, Luciana Arrighi; Production Manager, Redmond Morris; Assistant Director, Simon Relph; Art Director, Michael Pickwoad; Costumes, Luciana Arrighi; A Goldcrest and Michael White production in color; Rated R; 107 minutes; October release

CAST

James Penfield	Jonathan Pryce
Jeremy Hancock	Tim Curry
Susan Barrington	Charlie Dore
Ann Barrington	Rosemary Harris
Matthew Fox	Frank Finlay
Edward	Simon Stokes
Lecturer	Bill Paterson
Bob Tuckett	Peter Walmsley
Editor	Bob Cartland
Mr. Penfield	Nat Jackley
Mrs. Penfield	Pearl Hackney
Edward	Simon Stokes
Tom Fox	Orlando Wells
Betty	Libba Davies
Carmen	Sandra Voe
Pete	Andrew Norton
Jill	Clare Sutcliffe
Carol	Cecily Hobbs

Right: Jonathan Pryce, below with
Tim Curry, Charlie Dore
© *Samuel Goldwyn Co.*

Jonathan Pryce, also above
with Rosemary Harris

Charlie Dore, Jonathan Pryce

A LOVE IN GERMANY

(TRIUMPH) Producer, Artur Brauner; Director, Andrzej Wajda; Screenplay, Boleslaw Michalek, Agnieszka Holland, Andrzej Wajda; From novel "Eine Liebe in Deutschland" by Rolf Hochhuth; Photography, Igor Luther; Music, Michel Legrand; Executive Producer, Peter Hahne; Designers, Allan Starski, Gotz Heymann, Jurgen Henze; Assistant Director, Gunter Kraa; Costumes, Ingrid Zore, Krystyna Zachwatowicz-Wajda; Editor, Halina Prugar-Ketling; Production Managers, Jurgen von Kornatzki, Gunther Russ; Associate Producer, Emmanuel Schlumberger; In color; Rated R; 110 minutes; November release

CAST

Paulina Kropp	Hanna Schygulla
Maria Wyler	Marie-Christine Barrault
Mayer	Armin Mueller-Stahl
Elsbeth Schnittgens	Elisabeth Trissenaar
Wiktorczyk	Daniel Olbrychski
Stanislaw Zasada	Piotr Lysak
Karl Wyler	Gerard Desarthe
Dr. Borg	Bernhard Wicki
Schulze	Ralf Wolter
Narrator	Otto Sander
Klaus	Ben Becker
Herbert, Paulina's son	Thomas Ringelmann
Zinngruber, the mayor	Friedrich G. Beckhaus
Stackmann	Gernot Duda
Melchior	Sigfrit Steiner
Mrs. Melchior	Erika Wackernagel
Alker	Serge Merlin
Stackmann's son	Rainer Basedow
Stepdaughter	Jutta Kloppel
Mrs. Zinngruber	Heidi Joschko

Right: Piotr Lysak, Hanna Schygulla
© Columbia Pictures

Daniel Olbrychski, Armin Mueller-Stahl
Above: Hanna Schygulla

Elisabeth Trissenaar, Marie-Christine Barrault

THE KILLING FIELDS

(WARNER BROS.) Producer, David Puttnam; Director, Rolan
Joffe; Screenplay, Bruce Robinson; Based on article "The Death an
Life of Dith Pran" by Sydney Schanberg; Photography, Chris Menges
Editor, Jim Clark; Music, Mike Oldfield; Designer, Roy Walker; A
Directors, Roger Murray Leach, Steve Spence; Costumes, Judy Moor
croft; Special Effects, Fred Cramer; Associate Producer, Iain Smith
Assistant Director, Bill Westley; In Kay Labs color and Dolby Stereo
Rated R; 141 minutes; November release

CAST

Sydney Schanberg	Sam Watersto
Dith Pran	Dr. Haing S. Ngo
Al Rockoff	John Malkovic
Jon Swain	Julian Sand
Military Attache	Craig T. Nelso
U. S. Consul	Spalding Gra
Dr. Macentire	Bill Paterso
Dr. Sundesval	Athol Fugar
Dougal	Graham Kenned
Ser Moeun	Katherine Krapum Che
Titonel	Oliver Pierpao
Sarun	Edward Entero Che

Left: Sam Waterston
© *Warner Bros.*

*1984 Academy Awards for Supporting Actor
(Haing S. Ngor), Cinematography, Film Editing*

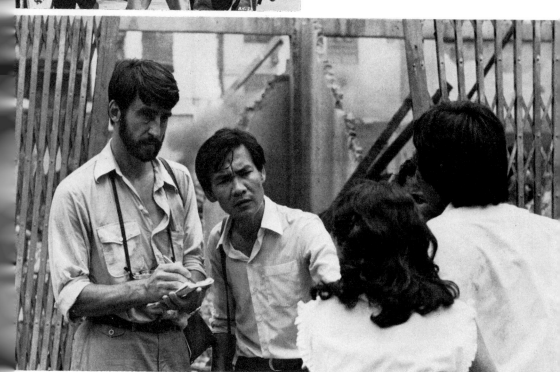

Sam Waterston, Dr. Haing S. Ngor

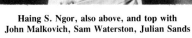

Haing S. Ngor, also above, and top with
John Malkovich, Sam Waterston, Julian Sands

John Malkovich, Haing S. Ngor, Sam Waterston
Above: Julian Sands, Waterston, Malkovich

199

A SUNDAY IN THE COUNTRY

(MGM/UA CLASSICS) Producer, Alain Sarde; Director, Bertrand Tavernier; Screenplay (French with English subtitles), Mr. Tavernier, Colo Tavernier; Based on novel "Monsieur Ladmiral Va Vientot Mourir" by Pierre Bost; Photography, Bruno De Keyzer; Editor, Armand Psenny; Music, Gabriel Faure; In color; Not rated; 94 minutes; November release

CAST

Monsieur Ladmiral	Louis Ducreux
Irene	Sabine Azema
Gonzague (Edouard)	Michel Aumont
Marie-Therese	Genevieve Mnich
Mercedes	Monique Chaumette
Madame Ladmiral	Claude Winter
Emile	Thomas Duval
Lucien	Quentin Ogier
Mireille	Katia Wostrikoff
First Little Girl	Valentine Suard
Second Little Girl	Erika Faivre
Accordionist	Marc Perrone
Dance Hall Servant	Pascale Vignal
Hector	Jacques Poitrenaud

Left: Sabine Azema, Michel Aumont, Genevieve Mnich
© MGM/UA Entertainment

Sabine Azema, Louis Ducreux

Sabine Azema, Louis Ducreux (also at top)

A PASSAGE TO INDIA

(COLUMBIA) Producers, John Brabourne, Richard Goodwin; Directed, Written and Edited by David Lean; Designer, John Box; Music, Maurice Jarre; Photography, Ernest Day; Costumes, Judy Moorcroft; Associate Editor, Eunice Mountjoy; Production Supervisor, Barrie Melrose; Production Managers, Jim Brennan, Shama Habibullah; Based on novel by E. M. Forster and play by Santha Rama Rau; Assistant Directors, Patrick Cadell, Christopher Figg, Nick Laws, Arundhati Rao, Ajit Kumar; Art Directors, Leslie Tomkins, Clifford Robinson, Ram Yedekar, Herbert Westbrook; In Metrocolor and Dolby Stereo; Rated PG; 163 minutes; December release

CAST

Adela Quested	Judy Davis
Dr. Aziz	Victor Banerjee
Mrs. Moore	Peggy Ashcroft
Richard Fielding	James Fox
Godbole	Alec Guinness
Ronny Heaslop	Nigel Havers
Turton	Richard Wilson
Mrs. Turton	Antonia Pemberton
McBryde	Michael Culver
Mahmoud Ali	Art Malik
Hamidullah	Saeed Jaffrey
Major Callendar	Clive Swift
Mrs. Callendar	Anne Firbank
Amritrao	Roshan Seth
Stella	Sandra Hotz
Mr. Das	Rashid Karapiet
Hassen	H. S. Krishnamurthy
Selim	Ishaq Bux
Guide	Moti Makan
Haq	Mohammed Ashiq
Mrs. Leslie	Phyllis Bose
Ingenue	Sally Kinghorne
Clerk of the Court	Paul Anil
Dr. Pana Lal	Z. H. Khan
Anthony	Ashok Mandanna
Begum Hamidullah	Dina Pathak
Mr. Hadley	Adam Blackwood
Indian Businessman	Mellan Mitchell
P. and O. Manager	Peter Hughes

Left: Judy Davis, Nigel Havers, Peggy Ashcroft
Top: Nigel Havers, Judy Davis
© *Columbia Pictures*

1984 Academy Awards for Supporting Actress
(Peggy Ashcroft), and for Original Score

Peggy Ashcroft

Alec Guinness

Victor Banerjee, and above
with Judy Davis

Victor Banerjee (C) Above: James Fox,
Judy Davis Top: Davis, Nigel Havers

Nina Knapskog as "Kamilla"
© *New Line*

Harvey Keitel, Nicole Garcia
in "Corrupt" © *New Line*

ENTER THE FAT DRAGON (World Northal) No credits available; In color; Rated R; January release. CAST: Samo Hung

THE JADE WARRIORS (World Northal) No credits available. In color; Rated R; January release. CAST: Samo Hung, Juan Biao

THE PIT (New World) Executive Producer, John C. Bassett; Producer, Bennet Fode; Director, Lew Lehman; Screenplay, Ian A. Stuart; Photography, Fred Guthe; Editor, Riko Morden; Music, Victor Davies; Art, Peter E. Stone; Production Manager, Donna Smith; Assistant Director, Christopher Danton; In Medallion Color; Rated R; 96 minutes; January release. CAST: Sammy Snyders (Jamie), Jeannie Elias (Sandra), Laura Hollingsworth (Marg), Sonja Smits (Mrs. Lynde), Laura Press (Mrs. Benjamin), Andrea Swartz (Abergail)

THE PLAGUE DOGS (United International) Producer-Director, Martin Rosen; Screenplay by Rosen based on novel by Richard Adams; Production Manager, Judy Hayward; Production Coordinators, Grodon Clark, Robert Graham; Design, Gordon Harrison; Music, Patrick Gleeson, Alan Price; In color and animation; Not rated; 103 minutes; January release. Voices of John Hurt, Christopher Benjamin, Barbara Leigh-Hunt, Judy Geeson, Tony Church, Dandy Nichols, Rosemary Leach, Patrick Stewart and others.

WHEN THE MOUNTAINS TREMBLE (Skylight) Producer-Editor, Peter Kinoy; Directors, Pamela Yates, Thomas Sigel; Music, Ruben Blades; Production Manager, Ntathu Mbatha; Spanish with English subtitles; Not rated; 83 minutes; January release. A documentary with Rigoberta Menchu about the 30 year war between the poor people of Guatamala and the government that oppresses them. Shown with **NICARAGUA: REPORT FROM THE FRONT (First Run Features)** Producers, Deborah Shaffer, Pamela Yates; Co-producers, Ana Maria Garcia, Glenn Silber; Directors, Deborah Shaffer, Thomas Sigel; A Skylight Production; Not rated; 32 minutes. A documentary on U.S. foreign policy toward Nicaragua as it is being enacted along the border between Nicarauga and Honduras.

THE HORSE (Asaya Film/Kentel Film) Director, Ali Ozgenturk; Screenplay, Isil Ozgenturk; Photography, Kenan Ormanlar; Music, Okay Temiz; In Turkish with English subtitles; 1982 film; 116 minutes; January release. CAST: Genco Erkal (Father), Harun Yesilyurt (Son), Ayberk Colok (Merchant), Yaman Okay (Remzi), Guler Okten (Foolish Woman)

CORRUPT (New Line Cinema) Producer, Elda Ferri; Director, Roberto Faenza; Screenplay, Ennio De Concini, Roberto Faenza; Hugh Fleetwood; Based on novel "The Order of Death" by Hugh Fleetwood; Photography, Giuseppe Pinori; Music, Ennio Morricone; In color; Rated R; 99 minutes; January release. CAST: Harvey Keitel (Lt. Fred O'Connor), John Lydon (Leo Smith), Sylvia Sidney (Margaret Smith), Nicole Garcia (Lenore), Leonard Mann (Bob)

KAMILLA (New Line) also released as "Betrayal: The Story of Kamilla"; Direction, Vibeke Lokkeberg; Screenplay, Vibeke Lokkeberg, Terje Kristiansen; Producer, Terje Kristiansen; Editor, Edith Toreg; Norwegian with English subtitles; In color; Not rated; 100 minutes; January release. CAST: Nina Knapskog (Kamilla), Vibeke Lokkeberg (Kamilla's Mother), Helge Jordal (Kamilla's Father), Kenneth Johansen (Svein), Karin Setlitz Haerem, Renie Kleivdal Thorleifsson, Klaus Hagerup, Marie Takvam, Johnny Bergh, Per Jansen, Kjell Pettersen

WARRIORS OF THE WASTELAND (New Line) Producer, Fabrizio De Angelis; Director, Enzo Castellari; Screenplay, Tito Carpi, Enzo Girolami; In color; Rated R; 92 minutes; January release. CAST: Fred Williamson, Timothy Brent, George Eastman, Anna Kanakis, Thomas Moore

BACKSTAGE AT THE KIROV (Armand Hammer) Producers, Gregory Saunders, Kenneth Locker; Written and Directed by Derek Hart; Photography, Ivan Strasburg; Editor, Kenneth Levis; In color; Not rated; 78 minutes; January release. A documentary on the Kirov Theatre, its dancers, and its orchestra.

JUPITER'S THIGH (Quartet/Films) Producers, Alexandre Mnouchkine, George Dancigers, Robert Amon; Director, Philippe de Broca; Screenplay, Mr. de Broca, Michel Audiard; Photography, Jean-Paul Schwartz; Editor, Henri Lanoe; Music, Georges Hatzinassio; French with English subtitles; In color; Rated PG; 96 minutes; January release. CAST: Annie Girardot (Lise), Philippe Noiret (Antoine), Francis Perrin (Hubert), Catherine Alric (Agnes)

BASILEUS QUARTET (Libra/Cinema 5) Direction and Screenplay, Fabio Carpi; Photography, Dante Spinotti; Editor, Massimo Latini; Produced by C.E.P.; In color; Not rated; 118 minutes; January release. CAST: Pierre Malet (Edo), Hector Alterio (Alvaro), Omero Antonutti

Genco Erkal, Harun Yesilyurt
in "The Horse" © *Asaya/Kentel*

Annie Girardot, Philippe Noiret; Catherine
Alric in "Jupiter's Thigh" © *Quartet Films*

(Diego), Francois Simon (Oscar), Michel Vitoid (Guglielmo), Alain Cuny (Finkel), Gabrielle Ferzetti (Mario), Veronique Genest (Sophia), Lisa Kreuzer (Lotte)

THE DEADLY MANTIS (World Northal) Director, Liu Chia-Liang; In color; Rated R; January release. CAST: David Chiang, Huang Hsing-Hsiu, Lily Li, Liu Chia-Hui

LE CRABE TAMBOUR (Interama) Producer, Georges de Beauregard; Director, Pierre Schoendoerffer; Screenplay, Jean-Francois Chauvel, Pierre Schoendoerffer; Based on Schoendoerffer's novel of same name; Photography, Raoul Coutard; Music, Philippe Sarde; Sound, Raymond Adam; Editor, Nguyen Long; In French and color; 1977 release in France; Not rated; 120 minutes; February release. CAST: Jean Rochefort (Captain), Claude Rich (Doctor), Jacques Dufilho (Chief Engineer), Jacques Perrin (Willsdorff, le Crabe Tambour), Odile Versois (Bar Hostess), Aurore Clement (Francine), Morgan-Jones (Lt.), Hubert Laurent (Fishing Fleet Officer), Joseph Momo (Bongo-Ba), Pierre Rousseau (Babourg), Fred Personne (Bar Owner/Gendarme), Francois Landoit (Bochau), Bernard Lajarrige (Rector)

THE SPEARMAN OF DEATH (World Northal) Producer, Run Run Shaw; Director, Chang Chen; In color; Rated R; February release. CAST: Kuo Chue, Chiang Sheng, Wang Li, Lu Feng

SCRUBBERS (Orion Classics) Executive Producers, George Harrison, Denis O'Brien; Producer, Don Boyd; Director, Mai Zetterling; Screenplay, Roy Minton, Jeremy Watt, Mai Zetterling; Associate Producers, David Barber, Jill Gutteridge; Photography, Ernest Vincze; Editor, Rodney Holland; Art Director, Celia Barnett; Assistant Director, Roger H. Lyons; Costumes, Susannah Buxton; Musical Score, Michael Hurd, Ray Cooper; Assistant Directors, Melvin Lind, Timothy Gibbs; Rated R; 90 minutes; In color; February release. CAST: Amanda York (Carol), Chrissie Cotterill (Annetta), Elizabeth Edmonds (Kathleen), Kate Ingram (Eddie), Amanda Symonds (Mac), Kathy Burke (Glennis), Debbie Bishop (Doreen), Eva Notley (Pam), Imogen Bain (Sandy), Honey Bane (Molly), Camille Davis (Sharon), Rachael Weaver (Gwen), Dawn Archibald (Mary), Faith Tingle (Hilary), Lilian Rostkowska (Phyllis), Anna Mackeown (Eva)

JAZZMAN (International Film Exchange) Director, Karen Shakhnazarov; Screenplay, Alexander Borodyansky, Karen Shakhnazarov; Music, Anatoly Kroll; Photography, Vladimir Shevtsik; Art Director, Konstantin Forostenko; In Russian with English subtitles; A Mosfilm production in color; Not rated; 80 minutes; February release. CAST: Igor Sklyar (Konstantine), Alexander Chorny (Stefan), Nikolai Averyuskin (George), Pyotr Shcherbakov (Ivan), Elena Tsiplakova (Katie), Larissa Dolina (Clementine)

DEAR MAESTRO (New Line Cinema) Direction and Screenplay, Luciano Odorisio; Photography, Nando Forni; Editor, Antonio Uterzi; Art Director, Nicola Rubartelli; Costumes, Maria Rosaria Donadio; Assistant Producer, Gaetano Stucchi for RAI; Italian with English subtitles; In color; Not rated; 100 minutes; February release. CAST: Michele Placido (Francesco Maria Vitale), Adalberto Maria Merli (Andrea Serano), Tino Schirinzi (Nicolino), Giuliana DeSio (Marta Vitale), Lino Troisi (Gianni D'Angelo), Fabio Traversa (Vittorio), Guido Celano (Uncle Caesarino), Anna Bonaiuto (Laura (Serano)

SLAYGROUND (Universal) Producers, John Dark, Gower Frost; Director, Terry Bedford; Screenplay, Trevor Preston; Based on novel by Richard Stark; Production Supervisor, Ron Fry; Designer, Keith Wilson; Editor, Nicolas Gaster; Photography, Stephen Smith; Music, Colin Towns; Executive Producer, Bob Mercer; Assistant Director, Steve Lanning; Clothes, Carlo Manzi; Art Directors, Dennis Bosher, Edward Pisoni; In color; Rated R; 89 minutes; February release. CAST: Peter Coyote (Stone), Mel Smith (Abbatt), Billie Whitelaw (Madge), Philip Sayer (Costello), Bill Luhrs (Sheer), Marie Masters (Joni), Clarence Felder (Orxel), Ned Eisenberg (Lonzini), David Hayward (Laufman), Michael Ryan (Danard), Barrett Mulligan (Lucy), Kelli Maroney (Jolene), Margareta Arvidssen (Grete), Rosemary Martin (Dr. King), Malcolm Terris (Venner), Jon Morrison (Webb), Cassie Stuart (Fran), Debby Bishop (Beth), Stephen Yardley (Turner), P. H. Moriarty (Seeley), Ziggy Byfield (Sams), Erick Ray Evans (Malpas), Bill Dean (Compere), Ozzie Yue (Waiter)

THE UNAPPROACHABLE (TeleCulture) Executive Producer, Horst Burkhard; Director, Krzysztof Zanussi; Screenplay, Mr. Zanussi, Edward Zebrowski; Editors, Inge Behrens, Karin Nowarra; Music, Wojciech Kilar; Photography Slawomir Idziak; Designers, Jan Schlubach, Albrecht Konrad; Costumes, Anna Biedrzycka-Sheppard; In color; Not rated; 92 minutes; February release. CAST: Leslie Caron (Claudia), Daniel Webb (Photographer), Leslie Malton (Marianne)

Peter Coyote in "Slayground"
© *Universal*

THE LAST HUNTER (World Northal) Formerly "Hunter of the Apocalypse"; Producer, Gianfranco Couyoumdjian; Director, Anthony M. Dawson (Antonio Margheriti); Screenplay, Dardano Sacchetti; Photography, Riccardo Pallottini; Editor, Alberto Moriani; Music, Franco Micalizzi; Assistant Director, Edoardo Margheriti; Design-Costumes, Bartolomeo Scavia; In Technicolor; Not rated; 95 minutes; February release. CAST: David Warbeck (Capt. Harry Morris), Tisa Farrow (Jane), Tony King (Sgt. Washington), Bobby Rhodes (Carlos), Margit Evelyn Newton (Carol), John Steiner (Maj. Cash), Alan Collins (Bartender)

THE BLACK CAT (World Northal) Producer, Giulio Sbarigia; Director, Lucio Fulci; Screenplay, Biagio Proietti, Lucio Fulci; Based on story by Edgar Allan Poe; Photography, Sergio Slavati; Editor, Vincenzo Tomassi; Music, Pino Donaggio; Assistant Director, Victor Tourjansky; Special Effects, Paolo Ricci; In Technovision and Eastmancolor; Rated R; 91 minutes; February release. CAST: Patrick Magee (Mr. Miles), Mimsy Farmer (Jill), David Warbeck (Insp. Gorley), Al Cliver (Policeman), Dagmar Lassander (Mrs. Grayson), Geoffrey Colpeston (Ins. Flynn), Daniela Dorio (Maureen)

ANTARCTICA (20th Century-Fox) Producers, Masaru Kakutani, Koretsudu Kurahara; Director, Koreyoshi Kurahara; Screenplay, Tatsuo Mogami, Kan Saji, Toshiro Ishido, Koreyoshi Kurahara; Photography, Akira Shiizuka; Editors, Akira Suzuki, Koreyoshi Kurahara; Music, Vangelis; In Dolby Stereo and color; Narrated in English; Rated G; 112 minutes; March release. CAST: Ken Takakura, Tsunehiko Watase, Eiji Okada, Masako Natsume, Keiko Oginome, Takeshi Kusaka, Shigeru Koyuma, So Yamamura

GERMANY PALE MOTHER (New Yorker) Direction and Screenplay, Helma Sanders-Brahms; Photography, Jurgen Jurges; Music, Jurgen Knieper; Editors, Elfi Tillack, Ute Periginelli; Assistant Director, Christa Ritter; Costumes, Janken Janssen; Executive Producer, Ursula Ludwig; In color; German with English subtitles; Not rated; 145 minutes; March release; Germany 1980. CAST: Eva Mattes (Lene), Ernst Jacobi (Hans), Elisabeth Stepanek (Hanne), Angelika Thomas (Lydia), Rainer Friedrichsen (Ulrich), Gisela Stein (Aunt Ihmchen), Fritz Lichtenhahn (Uncle Bertrand), Anna Sanders (Anna)

Alexander Chorny, Pyotr Shcherbakov, Nikolai Averiuskin, Igor Sklyar in "Jazzman"
© *IFEX*

205

Eva Mattes in "Germany Pale Mother"
© *New Yorker*

Keith Aberdeen, Robyn Gibbes
in "Wild Horses" © *Satori*

TRIUMPHS OF A MAN CALLED HORSE (Jensen Farley) Producer, Derek Gibson; Executive Producer, Sandy Howard; Director, John Hough; Screenplay, Ken Blackwell, Carlos Aured; Based on story by Jack DeWitt and a character by Dorothy M. Johnson; Photography, John Alcott, John Cabrera; Editor, Roy Watts; Music, George Garvanrentz; Assistant Director, Kuki Lopez; Design, Alan Roderick-Jones; Art, Marilyn Taylor; Production Executive, Keith Rubinstein; Associate Producer, Donald R. Borchers; In CFI Color; Rated PG; 86 minutes; March release. CAST: Richard Harris (Man Called Horse), Michael Beck (Koda), Ana DeSade (Redwing), Vaughn Armstrong (Capt. Cummings), Anne Seymour (Elk Woman), Buck Taylor (Sgt. Bridges), Simon Andreu (Gance), Lautaro Murua (Perkins), Roger Dudney (Durand), Gerry Gatlin (Winslow), John Davis Chandler (Mason), Miguel Angel Fuentes (Big Bear)

LES COMPERES (European International) Direction, Story and Screenplay by Francis Veber; Photography, Claude Agostini; Editor, Marie Sophie Dubus; Music, Vladimir Cosma; French with English subtitles; In color; Not rated; 92 minutes; March release. CAST: Pierre Richard (Francois), Gerard Depardieu (Jean), Anny Duperey (Christine), Michel Aumont (Paul), Stephane Bierry (Tristan), Jean-Jacques Scheffer (Ralph), Philippe Khorsand (Milan), Roland Blanche (Jeannot), Jacques Frantz (Verdler), Maurice Barrier (Raffert), Charlotte Maury (Mme. Raffert), Giselle Pascal (Louise), Patrick Blondel (Stephane), Florence Moreau (Michele)

L'ARGENT (Cinecom) Direction and Screenplay, Robert Bresson; Photography, Pasqualino de Santis, Emmanuel Machuel; Editor, Jean-Francois Naudon; In color; French with English subtitles; Not rated; 90 minutes; March release. CAST: Christian Patey (Yvon), Sylvie van den Elsen (Little Old Lady), Michel Briguet (Father of Old Lady), Caroline Lang (Elise), Jeanne Aptekman (Yvette), Vincent Risterucci (Lucien), Beatrice Tabourin, Didier Baussy (Photographers), Marc Ernest Fourneau (Norbert), Bruno Lapevre (Martial), Andre Cler (Father Norbert), Claude Cler (Mother Norbert)

MY BEST FRIEND'S GIRL (European International) Producer, Alain Sarde; Director, Bertrand Blier; Screenplay (French with English subtitles), Mr. Blier; Gerard Brach; Photography, Jean Penzer; Editor, Claudine Merlin; Music, J. J. Cale; In color; Not rated; 99 minutes; March release. CAST: Coluche (Micky), Isabelle Huppert (Viviane), Thierry Lhermitte (Pascal), Farid Chopel (Hoodlum), Francois Perrot (Doctor), Daniel Colas (Flirt)

TOO SHY TO TRY (Quartet/Films) Producer, Georges Casati; Director, Pierre Richard; Screenplay, Mr. Richard, Jean-Jacques Annaud, Alain Godard; Photography, Claude Agostini; Music, Vladimir Cosma; French with English subtitles; 1978 film; Rated PG; 90 minutes; March release. CAST: Pierre Richard (Pierre), Aldo Maccione (Aldo), Mimi Coutelier (Agnes), Robert Castel (Player), Catherine Lachens (Trucker), Jacques Francois (Manager)

HUNTERS OF THE GOLDEN COBRA (World Northal) Producer, Gianfranco Couyoumdjian; Director, Anthony Dawson (Antonio Margheriti); Screenplay, Tito Carpi; Photography, Sandro Mancori; Editor, Alberto Moriani; Music, Carlo Savina; Special Effects, Apollonio Abadesa; In Eastmancolor; Not rated; 94 minutes; March release. CAST: David Warbeck (Bob), Almanta Suska (June/April), John Steiner (Capt. Bracken), Alan Collins (Uncle), Protacio Dee (Yamato)

THE HOUSE BY THE CEMETERY (Almi) Producer, Fabrizio DeAngelis; Director, Lucio Fulci; Screenplay, Lucio Fulci, Dardano Saccheti, Giorgio Mariuzzio; Story, Elisa Livia Briganti; Photography, Sergio Salvati; Editor, Vincenzo Tomassi; Music, Walter Rizzati; Assistant Director, Roberto Giandalia; In Panavision Widescreen and color; Not rated; 78 minutes; March release. CAST: Catriona MacColl (Lucy), Paolo Malco (Norman), Ania Pieroni (Ann), Giovanni Frezza (Bob), Dagmar Lassander (Mrs. Gittelson), Giovanni de Nari (Dr. Freudstein)

A QUESTION OF SILENCE (Quartet/Films Inc.) Producers, Matthijs Van Heijningen, Sigma Films; Direction and Screenplay, Marleen Gorris; Photography, Frans Bromet; Editor, Hans Van Dongen; Music, Lodewijk De Boer; Designer, Harry Ammerlann; Wardrobe, Jany Hubar; Dutch with English subtitles; In color; Rated R; 92 minutes; April release. CAST: Cox Habbema (Court Appointee), Edda Barends (Christina M.), Nelly Frijda (Waitress), Henriette Tol (Secretary), Edyy Brugman (Rudd), Dolf DeVries (Boutique Manager), Cees Coolen (Police Inspector), Onno Molenkamp (Pathologist), Hans Croiset (Judge)

JUST A GAME (Film Society) Producers, Monique Messier, Yves Michon, Jacques Pettigrew; Director, Brigitte Sauriol; Screenplay, Miss Sauriol, Miss Messier; Photography, Paul van der Linden; Editor, Marcel Pothier; Music, Yves Laferriere; French with English subtitles; Not rated; 101 minutes; April release. CAST: Marie Tito (Mychele), Raymond Cloutier (Andre), Jennifer Grenier (Catherine), Julie Mongeau (Julie), Julie Desjardins (Maude)

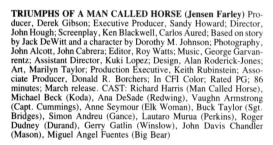

Isabelle Huppert, Thierry Lhermitte, Coluche
in "My Best Friend's Girl"
© *European International*

"A Question of Silence"
© *Quartet/Films Inc.*

Fidel Castro, Martha Frayde
in "Improper Conduct" © *Cinevista*

Andrew Occhipinti, George Rivero
in "Conquest" © *Conquest Films*

WILD HORSES (Satori) Producer, John Barnett; Director, Derek Morton; Executive Producer, Gary Haunan; Screenplay, Kevin Wilson; Photography, Doug Milsome; Production Supervisor, Peter Price; Designer, Joe Bleakley; Editor, Simon Reece; In color; Not rated; 90 minutes; April release. CAST: Keith Aberdein (Mitch), John Bach (Mitch's Friend), Kevin Wilson (Mitch's Friend), Kathy Rawlings (Mitch's Wife), Helena Wilson (Anne), Robyn Gibbes (Sara), Tom Poata (Sam), Marshall Napier (Andy), Matiu Mareikura (Kingi), Martyn Sanderson (Jones), Peter Tait (Joe), Bruno Lawrence (Tyson), Michael Haig (Benson), Richard Poore (Ranger)

IMPROPER CONDUCT (Cinevista) Directed and Written by Nestor Almendros, Orlando Jimenez Leal; Photography, Dominique Merlin; Editors, Michael Pion, Alain Tortevoix; French and Spanish with English subtitles; English narration spoken by Jeoffrey Lawrence Carey; Produced by Les Films du Losange, Margaret Menegoz-Barbet Schroeder, Antenne 2, Michel Thoulouze; In color; 110 minutes; April release. CAST: Reinaldo Arenas, Susan Sontag, Heberto Padilla, Caracol, Cuillermo Cabrera Infante, Armando Valladares, Fidel Castro, Ana Maria Simo, Juan Goytisolo, Carlos Franqui, Martha Frayde, Rene Ariza

KUKURANTUMI: THE ROAD TO ACCRA (Film Society) Producer, Peter Wohigemuth-Reinery; Director, King Ampaw; Screenplay, King Ampaw, Ralf Franz, Thilo Kline; Photography, Eckhard Dorn; Editor, Anja Cox; Not rated; 83 minutes; April release. CAST: Evans Oma Hunter (Addey), Amy Oppiah (Abena), David Dontoh (Bob), Dorothy Ankomah (Mary), George Wilson (Mensah), Ernest Youngman (Kofi), Rose Flynn (Seewaa), Felix Asant Larbi (Boafo), Kwest France (Alhail), Emmi L. Lawson (Old Man)

TURUMBA (Flower Films) Written and Directed by Kidlat Tahimik; In Tagalog with English subtitles; 95 minutes; April release. CAST: Herman Abiad, Katrin Luise

CAGED WOMEN (MPM) Director, Vincent Dawn (Bruno Mattei); Screenplay, P. Molteni, Oliver LeMat; Photography, Luigi Ciccarese; Editor, Bruno Mattei; Music, Luigi Ceccarelli; Art Director, Maurizio Mammi; Production Manager, Sergio Cortona; Assistant Director, Claudio Fragasso; In Telecolor; Rated R; 96 minutes; April release. CAST: Laura Gemser (Laura/Emanuell), Gabriele Tinti (Dr. Moran), Lorraine de Selle (Warden), Maria Romano, Ursula Flores, Raul Cabrera

CONQUEST (UFDC) Producer, Giovanni DiClemente; Director, Lucio Fulci; Screenplay, Gino Capone, Jose Antonio de la Loma, Sr., Carlos Vasallo; From story by DiClemente; Photography, Alejandra Alonso Garcia; Editor, Emilio Rodrigues Oses; Editor, Vincenzo Tomassi; Music, Claudio Simonette; Art Director, Massimo Lentini; In Telecolor; Rated R; 89 minutes; April release. CAST: Jorge Rivero (Max), Andrea Occhipinti (Ilias), Sabrina Siani (Ocron), Conrado San Martin, Violeta Cela, Jose Gras Palau, Maria Scola

HOUSE OF THE LONG SHADOWS (Cannon) Producers, Menahem Golan, Yoram Globus; Director, Pete Walker; Screenplay, Michael Armstrong; Photography, Norman Langley; Music, Richard Harvey; Set Director, Mike Pickwoad; Editor, Robert Dearberg; Assistant Directors, Brian Lawrence, Glynn Purcell, Paul Carnie, Nick Goodden; In color; Rated PG; 96 minutes; April release. CAST: Vincent Price (Lionel), Christopher Lee (Corrigan), Peter Cushing (Sebastian), Desi Arnaz, Jr. (Kenneth), John Carradine (Lord Grisbane), Sheila Keith (Victoria), Julie Peasgood (Mary), Richard Todd (Sam), Louise English (Diana), Richard Hunter (Andrew), Norman Rossington (Stationmaster)

AND NOTHING BUT THE TRUTH (Castle Hill) Producers, Sophie Balhetchet, David Payne; Direction and Screenplay, Karl Francis; Photography, Curtis Clark; Editor, Neil Thomson; Music, Alun Francis; In color; Not rated; 90 minutes; April release. CAST: Glenda Jackson (Sophie), Jon Finch (O'Mally), Kenneth Colley (Martin), James Donnelly (James), Emrys James (Williams), Karen Archer (Brigitte), Simon Jones (Henderson), Huw Ceredig (Elwyn), Alun Lewis (Photographer), Dermot Crowley (Flynne)

CHAMPIONS (Embassy) Producer, Peter Shaw; Director, John Irvin; Screenplay, Evan Jones; Based on book "Champion's Story" by Bob Champion, Jonathan Powell; Editor, Peter Honess; Music, Carl Davis; In color and Dolby Stereo; Rated PG; 115 minutes; April release. CAST: John Hurt (Champion), Gregory Jones (Peter), Mick Dillon (Snowy), Ann Bell (Valda), Jan Francis (Jo), Peter Barkworth (Nick), Edward Woodward (Josh), Ben Johnson (Burly), Kirstie Alley (Barbara), Alison Steadman (Mary), Jonathan Newth (Griffith), Cerl Jackson, Francesca Brill (Nurses), Andrew Wilde (Graham), Judy Parfitt (Dr. Merrow), Carolyn Pickles (Sally), Fiona Victory (Helen), Julie Adams (Emma), Michael Byrne (Richard), Richard Adams (Nicky)

"Turumba"
© *Film Forum/Flower Films*

Sabrina Siani in "Conquest"
© *Conquest Films*

Abigail Cruttenden, John Albasiny
in "Kipperbang" © *United Artists*

Jonathan Segalle (L) in "Drifting"
© *Nu-Image Films*

KIPPERBANG (United Artists Classics) Producer, Chris Griffin; Director, Michael Apted; Executive Producer, David Puttnam; Screenplay, Jack Rosenthal; Photography, Tony Pierce-Roberts; Associate Producer, David Bill; Editor, John Shirley; Music, David Earl; Art Director, Jeffery Woodbridge; Assistant Directors, Dominic Fulford, Andrew Montgomery, Russell Lodge; Costumes, Sue Yelland; Color by Kay Laboratories; An Enigma Production for Goldcrest; Rated PG; 85 minutes; April release. CAST: John Albasiny (Alan), Abigail Cruttenden (Ann), Maurice Dee (Geoffrey), Alison Steadman (Miss Land), Garry Cooper (Tommy), Robert Urquhart (Headmaster), Mark Brailsford (Abbo), Chris Karallis (Shaz), Frances Ruffelle (Eunice), Nicola Prince (Maureen), Richenda Carey (Botany Teacher), Tim Seeley (French Master), Maurice O'Connell (Gym Teacher), Peter Dean (Policeman), Dave Atkins (Fish & Chips Shop), Eric Richard, Arthur Whybrow (Workmen), Philip Edkins (School Boy)

DRIFTING/NAGOOA (Nu-Image) Producer, Kislev Films; Director, Amos Guttman; Screenplay, Amos Guttman, Edna Mazia; Photography, Yossi Wein; Music, Arik Rudich; Editor, Anna Finkelstein; Art Director, Eitan Levi; Production Manager, Oshra Shwartz; Hebrew with English subtitles; In color; Not rated; 80 minutes; April release. CAST: Jonathan Sagalle (Robi), Ami Traub (Han), Ben Levin (Exri), Dita Arel (Rachel), Boaz Torjemann (Baba), Mark Hasmann (Robi's Father)

ERENDIRA (Miramax) Director, Ruy Guerra; Screenplay, Gabriel Garcia Marquez; Photography, Denys Clerval; Editor, Kenout Peltier; Assistant Directors, Felix Martin, Roman Hernandez, Natalie Eckelkamp; Music, Maurice LeCoeur; Art Directors, Pierre Cadiou, Rainer Chaper; Costumes, Alberto Negron; Production Managers, Eduardo Danel, Ginette Mejinsky; Producer, Alain Queffelean; Spanish with English subtitles; In color; Not rated; 103 minutes; April release. CAST: Irene Papas (Grandmother), Claudia Ohana (Erendira), Michael Lonsdale (Senator), Oliver Wehe (Ulysses), Rufus (Photographer), Delia Casanova (Narrator), Blanca Guerra (Ulysses' Mother), Ernesto Gomez Cruz (Grocer), Pierre Vaneck (Ulysses' Father), Carlos Cardan (Smuggler), Humberto Elizondo (Blacaman), Jorge Fegan (Commandant), Francisco Mauri (Postman), Sergio Calderon (Truck Driver), Martin Palomares (Messenger), Salvador Garcini (Juggler), Felix Bussio Madrigal (Fiance), Juan Antonio Ortiz Torres (Musician), Carlos Calderon (Missionary), Rene Barrera (Indian Chief), Gaspar Humberto Mena Escobar (Guard)

THE FAMILY GAME (Film Society) Producers, Shiro Sasaki, Yu Okada; Direction and Screenplay, Yoshimitsu Morita; Based on novel by Yohei Honma; Photography, Yonezo Maeda; Editor, Akimasa Kawashima; Japanese with English subtitles; Not rated; 107 minutes; April release. CAST: Yusaku Matsuda (Yoshimoto), Juzo Itami (Mumata), Saori Yuki (Mother), Junichi Tsujita (Older Brother), Ichirota Miyagawa (Shigeyuki)

THE FIANCEE (Film Society) Directors, Gunter Reisch, Gunther Rucker; Screenplay, Gunther Rucker; Based on trilogy "The House with the Heavy Doors" by Eva Lippold; Photography, Jurgen Brauer; Editor, Erika Lehmphul; Music, Karl-Ernst Sasse; Not rated; German with English subtitles; 105 minutes; April release. CAST: Jutta Wachowiak (Hella), Regimantas Adomaitis (Reimers), Slavka Budinova (Lola), Christine Gloger (Frenzel), Inge Keller (Irene), Kathe Reichel (Olser), Hans-Joachim Hegewald (Hensch)

ANGELA (Embassy) Executive Producer, Zev Braun; Producers, Julian Melzack, Claude Heroux; Director, Boris Sagal; Screenplay, Charles Israel; Photography, Marc Champion; Editor, Yves Langlois; Music, Henry Mancini; Assistant Director, Charles Braive; Designer, Seamus Flannery; Art Director, Keith Pepper; Associate Producers, Alfred Pariser, Leland Nolan; In Bellevue Pathe color; Not rated; 91 minutes; April release. CAST: Sophia Loren (Angela), Steve Railsback (Jean), John Vernon (Ben), John Huston (Hogan), Michelle Rossignol (Coco), Luce Guilbault (Marie)

TREASURE OF THE YANKEE ZEPHYR (Film Ventures) Producers, Antony I. Ginnane, John Barnett, David Hemmings; Director, David Hemmings; Screenplay, Everett DeRoche; Executive Producers, John Daly, Michael Fay, William Fayman; Associate Producer, Brian W. Cook; Music, Brian May; Photography, Vincent Morton; Designer, Bernard Hides; Editor, John Laing; Costumes, Aphrodite Kondos; Assistant Directors, Murray Newey, Chris Kenny, Chris Short; Art Director, Virginia Bieneman; Special Effects, Kevin Chisnall; In color; Rated PG; 91 minutes; April release. CAST: Ken Wahl (Barney), Lesley Ann Warren (Sally), Donald Pleasence (Gibbie), George Peppard (Theo), Bruno Lawrence (Barker), Grant Tilly (Coin Collector), Robert Bruce (Barman), Harry Rutherford-Jones (Harry), Dennis Hunt (Henchman), Dick Jones, Steve Nicolle, Tony Sparks, Francis Taurua, Clark Walkington

Claudia Ohana, Irene Papas
in "Erendira" © *Miramax Films*

Lesley Ann Warren, Donald Pleasence, Ken Wahl
in "Treasure of the Yankee Zephyr" © *ARC*

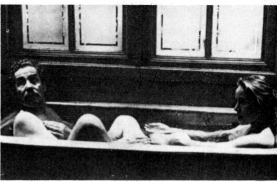

Irene Papas in "Erendira"
© Miramax Films

Erland Josephson, Dominique Sanda
in "Beyond Good and Evil" © Films Inc.

THE PRINCESS (Film Society) Produced by Mafilm; Director, Pai Erdoss; Screenplay (Hungarian with English subtitles), Istvan Kardos; Photography, Lajos Koltai, Ferenc Pap, Gabor Szabo; Not rated; 113 minutes; April release. CAST: Erika Ozsda (Jutka), Andrea Szendrei (Zsuzsa), Denes Diczhazy (Peter), Arpad Toth (Andras), Juli Nyako (Jutka's Sister), Lajos Solfis (Truck Driver)

TUKANA (Film Society) Direction and Screenplay, Chris Owen, Albert Toro; (Tok Pisin with English subtitles); Story, Albert Toro; Photography, Chris Owen; Not rated; 120 minutes; April release. CAST: Albert Toro (Tukana), Francesca Samosa (Josephine), Regina Tulsa (Lucy), Emily Beani (Tukana's Mother), Timothy Harnanin (Tukana's Father), Wenceslas Noruke (Tohiana)

STRAIGHT THROUGH THE HEART (Film Society) Producer, Denyse Noever; Director, Doris Dorrie; Screenplay, Jelena Kristl; In German with English subtitles; Photography, Michael Goebel; Editor, Thomas Wigand; Music, Paul Shigihara; Not rated; 91 minutes; April release. CAST: Beate Jensen (Anna), Sepp Bierbichler (Armin), Gabrielle Litty (Marlies), Nuran Filiz (Marisol), Jens Muller-Rastede (Messenger), Joachim Hoepner (Market Manager)

BIG MEAT EATER (New Line Cinema) Producer, Laurence Keane; Director, Chris Windsor; Screenplay, Laurence Keane, Phil Savath, Chris Windsor; Assistant Director/Production Manager, Dean Stoker; Photography, Doug MacKay; Editors, Laurence Keane, Chris Windsor, Lilla Pederson; Score, J. Douglas Dodd; Choreography, Helen LeCounte; In color; Not rated; 84 minutes; April release. CAST: George Dawson (Bob), Andrew Gillies (Jan), Big Miller (Abdulla), Stephen Dimopoulous (Josef), Georgina Hegedos (Rosa), Ida Carnevali (Babushka), Howard Taylor (Mayor), Heather Smith-Harper (Secretary), Peter Anderson (Alderman), Gillian Neumann (Mrs. Campbell), Sharon Wahl (Nina), Jon Bryden (Ace), Shannon Keane (Kid), Kim Stebner (1st Heavy), Jay Samwald, Neil MacDonald (Meat Carriers), Scott Swanson (Announcer)

TENDERNESS AND ANGER (Cactus Films) Written and Directed by Johannes Flutsch; Photography, Carlo Varini; Editors, Johannes Flutsch, Hannelore Kunzi; German with English subtitles; 90 minutes; May release. CAST: The Cesa family

THE MISSION (New Line Cinema) Produced, Directed, Written and Edited by Parviz Sayyad; Story, Hesam Kowsar, Parviz Sayyad; Co-producer-Photography, Reza Aria; Produced by The New Film Group

and Aria Film Production; Farsi with English subtitles; In color; Not rated; 107 minutes; May release. CAST: Parviz Sayyad (Colonel), Mary Apick (Maliheh), Houshang Touzie, Saeed Rajai (Agents from Teheran), Kamran Nozad (Ghaffar), Mohammad B. Ghaffari (His Eminence), Hatam Anvar (Maziar), Hedyeh Anvar (Farzaneh), Soraya Shayesteh (Woman), Richard Mansfield, David Filinni (Muggers), Liz Jones, John Neil (Passersby), Frank Oddo (Cabbie), Murie Alcid (Cleaning Lady), Aaron Moss, Susan Sands (Couple), Helen Nitsiog (Fabric Seller), James Deenen (Cop), Dalton Alexander (Morgue Attendant)

BEYOND GOOD AND EVIL (Films Inc.) Producer, Robert Gordon Edwards; Director, Liliana Cavani; Screenplay (Italian with English subtitles), Miss Cavani, Franco Arcalli, Italo Moscati; Story, Miss Cavani; Photography, Armando Nannuzzi; Editors, Mr. Arcalli, Robert Jose Pomper; Music, Daniele Paris; In color; Not rated; 106 minutes; May release. CAST: Dominique Sanda (Lou), Erland Josephson (Friedrich), Robert Powell (Paul), Virna Lisi (Elisabeth), Philippe Leroy (Peter), Elisa Cegani (Franziska), Umberto Orsini (Bernard), Michael Degen (Karl), Amedeo Amodio (Dr. Dulcamara), Carmen Scarpitta (Malvida), Nicoletta Macchiavelli (Amanda)

GABRIELA (MGM/UA Classics) Producers, Harold Nebenzal, Ibrahim Moussa; Director, Bruno Barreto; Screenplay, (Portugese with English subtitles), Leopoldo Serran, Bruno Barreto; Based on novel "Gabriela, Clove and Cinnamon" by Jorge Amado; Photography, Carlo di Palma; Editor, Emmanuelle Castro; Music, Antonio Carlos Jobim, Gal Costan; In color and Dolby Stereo; Rated R; 104 minutes; May release. CAST: Sonia Braga (Gabriela), Marcello Mastroianni (Nacib), Antonio Cantafora (Tonico), Paulo Goulart (Colonel), Nelson Xavier (Capitao), Nuno Leal Maia (Engineer), Fernando Ramos (Tuisca), Nicole Puzzi (Malvina), Tania Boscoli (Gloria), Jofre Soares (Ramiro), Paulo Pilia (Prince)

IREZUMI: THE SPIRIT OF TATTOO (Almi Classics) Producers, Yasuyoshi Tokuma, Masumi Kanamaru; Director, Yoichi Takabayashi; Screenplay (Japanese with English subtitles), Chiho Katsura; Based on novel by Baku Akae; Photography, Hideo Fujii; Music, Masaru Sato; In color; Not rated; 88 minutes; May release. CAST: Tomisaburo Wakayama (Kyogoro), Tasayo Utsunomiya (Akane), Yusuke Takita (Fujieda), Masaki Kyomoto (Harutsune), Harue Kyo (Katsuko), Naomi Shiraishi (Haruna), Taiji Tonoyama (Horiatsu)

Bajo Cesa in "Tenderness and Anger"
© Cactus Films

Dominique Sanda, Robert Powell, Erland Josephson in "Beyond Good and Evil"
© Films Inc.

209

Irena Ferris, Jeff Conaway
in "Covergirl" © *New World*

Pierre Jolivet, Jean Reno
in "Le Dernier Combat" © *Columbia*

SPASMS (Producers Distribution Co.) Previously "Death Bite"; Producers, John G. Pozhke, Maurice Smith; Director, William Fruet; Screenplay, Don Enright from novel "Death Bite" by Michael Maryk and Brent Monahan; Photography, Mark Irwin; Editor, Ralph Brunjes; Music, Eric N. Robertson; Assistant Director, David Shepherd; Production Manager/Co-Producer, Gordon Robinson; Co-Producer, John Newton; Art Director, Gavin Mitchell; In Medallion Color; Rated R; 87 minutes; May release. CAST: Peter Fonda (Dr. Brasilian), Oliver Reed (Jason), Kerrie Keane (Susanne), Al Waxman (Crowley), Miguel Fernandes (Mendes), Marilyn Lightstone (Dr. Rothman), Angus MacInnes (Duncan), Laurie Brown (Allison), Gerard Parkes (Capt. Noveck), George Bloomfield (Rev. Thomas)

COVERGIRL (New World) formerly "Dreamworld"; Executive Producers, Pierre David, Victor Solnicki; Producer, Claude Heroux; Director, Jean-Claude Lord; Screenplay, Charles Dennis; Associate Producer, Lawrence Nesis; Photography, Rene Verzier; Music, Christopher L. Stone; Editor, Christopher Holmes; Art Director, Michel Proulx; Costumes, Jean-Claude Poitras; Production Manager, Roger Heroux; Assistant Directors, John Fretz, Frank Ruszcynzki, Michel Sarao; Costumes, Paul Andre Guerin; A Mutual Films Corp., Ltd. Production in color; Rated R; 90 minutes; June release. CAST: Jeff Conaway (T.C.), Irena Ferris (Kit), Cathie Shirriff (Tessa), Roberta Leighton (Dee), Deborah Wakeham (Avril), Kenneth Walsh (Harrison), Charles Dennis (Blitzstein), William Hutt (Alton), Philip Akin (Cairo), Tiiu Leek (Zara), August Schellenberg (Joel), Paulle Clark (Eva), Ian White (Walter), Almaini (Raoul), Samantha Logan (Topsy), Caroline Yeager (Bunny), Charles Jolliffe (Owen), Christopher Newton (Paul), Sandi Ross (Dessie), Stephanie Daniels (Joyce), Henry Ramer (Klaus), Bronwen Mantel (Claire), Arnie Achtman (Taddy), Bernard Hopkins (Priest), Michelle Scarabelli (Snow Queen), Les Rubie (Cabbie), Colin Fox (Maitre d')

EDITH AND MARCEL (Miramax) Produced, Directed and Written by Claude Lelouch; Collaboration on Screenplay and Dialogue, Pierre Uytterhoeven, Gilles Durieux; Music, Francis Lai; Photography, Jean Boffety; Editors, Hugues Darmois, Sandrine Pery; Art Director, Jacques Bufnoir; Costumes, Adrienne Ghenassia; Assistant Directors, Alain Maline, Christine Raspillere; Executive Producer, Tania Zazulinsky; French with English subtitles; In Dolby Stereo and color; Not rated; 140 minutes; June release. CAST: Evelyne Bouix (Edith Piaf/Margot de Villedieu), Marcel Cerdan, Jr. (Marcel Cerdan), Charles Aznavour (Himself), Jacques Villeret (Barbier), Francis Huster (Fran-

cis), Jean-Claude Brialy (Loulou), Jean Bouise (Lucien), Charles Gerard (Charlot), Charlotte de Turkheim (Ginou), Micky Sebastian (Marinette), Maurice Garrel (Margot's Father), Ginette Garcin (Guite), Philippe Khorsand (Jo), Jany Gastaldi (Momone), Candice Patou (Margot's Sister), Tanya Lopert (English Teacher), Jean Rougerie (Theatre Director), Beata Tyszkiewicz

LE DERNIER COMBAT (Triumph) "The Last Battle" Producers, Luc Besson, Pierre Jolivet; Director, Luc Besson; Screenplay, Luc Besson, Pierre Jolivet; Photography, Carlo Varini; Editor, Sophie Schmit; Music, Eric Serra; Art Directors, Christian Grosrichard, Thierry Flamand, Patrick Leberre; Assistant Directors, Patrick Alessandrin, Didier Grousset, Francois Xavier Coutant; Production Managers, Elaine Andre, Alain Floris; Costumes, Martine Rapin, Marie Beau; Presented by Les Films du Loup; French with English subtitles; In Dolby Stereo, Panavision and black and white; Rated R; 90 minutes; June release. CAST: Pierre Jolivet (The Man), Jean Bouise (Doctor), Fritz Wepper (The Captain), Jean Reno (The Brute), Maurice Lamy (Dwarf), Petra Muller (Woman in the cell), Captain's Concubine (Christiane Kruger), Captain's Men: Pierre Carrive, Bernard Havet, Jean-Michel Castanie, Michel Doset, Marcel Berthomier, Garry Jode

ESCAPE FROM SEGOVIA (Grange Communications) Producer, Angel Amigo; Director, Imanol Uribe; Screenplay (Basque and Spanish), Imanol Uribe, Angel Amigo; Photography, Jabler Agirresarobe; Editor, Julio Pena; Music, Amaia Zubiria, Xavier Lasa; In color; Not rated; 98 minutes; June release. CAST: Xabier Elorriaga (Ion), Virginia Mataix (Pxuno), Klara Badiola (Maruja)

IT'S NEVER TOO LATE (Films Inc.) Producer, Francisco Hueva; Director, Jaime de Arminan; Screenplay (Spanish with English subtitles), Jaime de Arminan, Juan Carlos Eguillor; Based on idea by Concha Gregori; Photography, Teo Escamilia; Editor, Jose Luis Matesanz; Music, Jose Nieto; In color; Not rated; 98 minutes; June release. CAST: Jose Luis Gomez (Antonio), Angela Molina (Teresa), Madeleine Christie (Ursula), Maria Silva, Maite Blasco, Eduardo Calvo, Chus Lampreave, Julia Trujillo, Josefina del Cid, Julia Lorente

TIBET: A BUDDHIST TRILOGY (Thread Cross) Direction and Screenplay (Tibetan with English subtitles), Grant Coleman; Producer-Photographer, David Laselles; Photography, Michael Warr; Editor, Pip Heywood; Not rated; 231 minutes; June release. A film on Tibetan culture in exile.

Evelyne Bouix, Marcel Cerdan, Jr.
in "Edith and Marcel" © *Miramax*

Jean Bouise in "Le Dernier Combat"
© *Columbia Pictures*

Noah Hathaway, Moses Gunn
in "The Neverending Story"
© *Neue Constantin Films*

ESCAPE FROM WOMEN'S PRISON (21st Century) Producers, Aldo Baglietta, Bruno Fontana; Director, Conrad Bruegel; Screenplay, Giovanni Brusatori, Bruno Fontana; Photography, Nino Celeste; Editor, Pier Luigi Peonardi; Music, Pippo Caruso; Production Manager, Roberto Carlevari; Assistant Director, Donatelli Batti; In Staco Color; Not rated; 83 minutes; June release. CAST: Lilli Carati (Monica), Ines Pellegrini (Terry), Zora Keer, Franco Ferrer, Patrizia Fonara, Ada Poletta, Angela Doria

BURIED ALIVE (Aquarius) Director Joe D'Amato (Aristide Massaccesi); Screenplay, Ottavio Fabri; Photography, Aristide Massaccesi; Editor, Ornella Michel; Music, The Goblins; Assistant Director, Franco Gandeli; Art Director, Donatella Donati; Production Manager, Oscar Santaniello; In Telecolor; Not rated; 94 minutes; June release. CAST: Kieran Canter, Cinzia Monreale, Franca Stoppi, Sam Modesto, Ana Cardini, Mario Pizzin, Klaus Rainer

AMERICAN NIGHTMARE (Mano) Executive Producers, Anthony Kramreither, Paul Lynch; Producer, Ray Sager; Director, Don McBrearty; Screenplay, John Sheppard from story by John Gault, Steven Blake; Photography, Daniel Hainey; Editor, Ian McBride; Music, Paul Zaza; Art Director, Andrew Deskin; Assistant Director, David Pamplin; Production Manager, Bob Wertheimer; Associate Producer, Derrett Lee; In color; Not rated; 87 minutes; June release. CAST: Lawrence S. Day (Eric), Lora Staley (Louise), Neil Dainard (Tony), Lenore Zann (Tina), Michael Ironside (Skylar), Paul Bradley (Manager), Claudia Udy (Andrea), Larry Aubrey (Dolly), Mike Copeman (Fixer), Alexandra Paul (Isabel)

DEADLINE (New Image) Previously "Anatomy of a Horror"; Executive Producer, Gregory Earls; Producer, Henry Less; Director, Mario Azzopardi; Screenplay, Azzopardi, Dick Oleksiak; Photography, Fred Guthe; Editor, Joseph Ruff, Harvey Zlateratz; Music, Dwayne Ford, Carole Pope, Rough Trade; In Panavision and color; Not rated; 92 minutes; June release. CAST: Stephen Young (Steven), Sharon Masters (Elizabeth), Cindy Hinds (Sharon), Phillip Leonard (Philip), Todd Woodcroft (David), Marvin Goldhar (Burt), Jeannie Elias (Darlene)

TRAP THEM AND KILL THEM (Megastar) Director, Joe D'Amato (Aristide Massaccesi); Screenplay, Romano Scandariato, Massaccesi; Photography, Aristide Massaccesi; Editor, Aldo Moriani; Music, Nico Fidenco; Art Director, Carlo Ferri; Assistant Director, Donatella Donati; Production Manager, Fabrizio Sforza; In Telecolor; Not rated; 92 minutes; June release. CAST: Laura Gemser (Emanuelle), Gabriele

Tinti (Prof. Mark Lester), Susan Scott (Maggie), Donald O'Brien (Donald), Percy Hogan, Monica Zanchi, Anne Marie Clementi, Geoffrey Coplestone

THE NEVERENDING STORY (Warner Bros.) Producers, Bernd Eichinger, Dieter Geissler; Director, Wolfgang Petersen; Screenplay, Wolfgang Petersen, Herman Weigel; Executive Producers, Mark Damon, John Hyde; Co-Producer, Gunther Rohrbach; Associate Producer, Klaus Kahler; Music, Klaus Doldinger, Giorgio Moroder; Photography, Jost Vacano Bvk; Editor, Jane Seitz; Special Effects, Brian Johnson; Designer, Rolf Zehetbauer; Production Manager, Harry Nap; Assistant Directors, Don French, Georg Borgel, Michael Boyadjiew; Art Directors, Gotz Weidner, Herbert Strabel, Johann Iwan Kot; Costumes, Diemut Remy; Scenery, Creature and Costume Designer, Ul De Rico; Designer/Set Decorator, Rolf Zehetbauer; Production Coordinator, Annie Nap-Oleon; Animator, Steve Archer; A Neue Constantin production in collaboration with Bavaria Studios and WDR; In Technivision and Dolby Stereo; Rated PG; 94 minutes; July release. CAST: Barret Oliver (Bastian), Gerald McRaney (Bastian's Father), Drum Garret, Darryl Cooksey, Nicholas Gilbert (Bullies), Thomas Hill (Koreander), Deep Roy (Teeny Weeny), Tilo Pruckner (Night Hob), Moses Gunn (Cairon), Noah Hathaway (Atreyu), Alan Oppenheimer (Falkor's Voice), Sydney Bromley (Engywook), Patricia Hayes (Urgl), Tami Stronach (Empress)

CLASS ENEMY (Teleculture) Producer, Regina Ziegler; Director, Peter Stein; Screenplay, Peter Stein, Juergen Klose; Based on play of same title by Nigel Williams; Photography, Robby Mueller; Costumes, Dorothea Katzer; Designer, Karl-Ernst Herrmann; Editor, Inge Behrens; Assistant Director, Karin Viesel; Production Manager, Carlo Rola; German with English subtitles; In color; Not rated 125 minutes; July release. CAST: Greger Hansen (Angel), Stefan Reck (Pickel), Jean-Paul Raths (Koloss), Udo Samel (Vollmond), Ernst Stoetzner (Fetzer), Tayfun Bademsoy (Kebab)

HEY BABE! (Rafal) Producers, Rafal Zielinski, Arthur Voronka; Executive Producer, Morden Lazarus; Director, Rafal Zienlinski; Screenplay, Edith Rey; Photography, Peter Czerski; Editors, Scott Conrad, Afte Chiriaeff; Music, Gino Soccio, Roger Pilon, Mature Adults; Choreography, Lynn Taylor; Associate Producer, Gilbert; In color; Not rated; 105 minutes; July release. CAST: Buddy Hackett (Sammy), Yasmine Bleeth (Theresa), Marushka Stankova (Miss Wolf), Vlasta Vrana (Roy), Denise Proulx (Miss Dolores)

Tami Stronach, Barret Oliver
in "The Neverending Story"
© *Neue Constantin Films*

"Class Enemy"
© *Teleculture*

211

Jacki Weaver, David Atkins
in "Squizzy Taylor" © *Satori*

Yusuke Kawazu, Miyuki Kuwano
in "Cruel Story of Youth"
© *New Yorker*

THE LAST SEA (Jewish Media Services) A film by Haim Gouri, Jacquot Ehrlich, and David Bergman; Producers, Benny Shilo, Yehezkel Avneri; Editor, Jacquot Ehrlich; Music, Yossi Mar-Hayim; Hebrew, Yiddish and French with English subtitles and voice-over; Not rated; 105 minutes; July release. A tribute to the illegal Jewish immigrants (holocaust survivors) who between 1945 and 1948, overcame hardships to get to Palestine; Part two of a trilogy.

HEART OF THE STAG (New World) Producers, Don Reynolds, Michael Firth; Direction and Story, Michael Firth; Screenplay, Neil Illingsworth; Executive Producers, Rowan Chapman, Keith Gosling; Photography, James Bartle; Production Manager, Sue May; Editor, Michael Horton; Music, Leonard Rosenman; Production Designer, Gary Hansen; Assistant Directors, John McKay, Chris Short; Production Coordinator, Lyn Galbraith; In color; Rated R; 94 minutes; July release. CAST: Bruno Lawrence (Peter Daly), Terence Cooper (Robert Jackson), Mary Regan (Cathy Jackson), Anne Flannery (Mary Jackson), Michael Wilson (Jack Bostwick), Susanne Cowie (Young Cathy), Shearing Gang: John Bach, Tim Lee, Greg Naughton, Tania Bristowe

SQUIZZY TAYLOR (Satori) Producer, Roger LeMesurier; Director, Kevin Dobson; Executive Producer/Screenplay, Roger Simpson; Costumes, Jane Hyland; Designer, Logan Brewer; Photography, Dan Burstall; Music, Bruce Smeaton; In color; Not rated; 98 minutes; July release. CAST: David Atkins (Squizzy Taylor), Jacki Weaver (Dolly), Kim Lewis (Ida), Michael Long (Ins. Piggot), Fred Cul Cullen (Henry), Alan Cassell (Det. Brophy), Steve Bisley (Snowy), Peter Paulsen (Harry), John Larking (Superintendent), Terry Trimble (Grazier), Peter Hosking (Angus), Paul Trahair (Detective), Ernie Bourne (Barber), Jenni Caffin (Lorna), Tony Rickards (Dutch), Simon Thorpe (Paddy)

CRUEL STORY OF YOUTH (New Yorker) Producer, Shochiku Films; Direction-Screenplay, Nagisa Oshima; Photography, Takashi Kawamata; Music, Riichiro Manabe; In color and Cinemascope; Japanese with English subtitles; Not rated; 96 minutes; July release. CAST: Yusuke Kawazu (Kiyoshi), Miyuki Kuwano (Makato), Yoshiko Kuga (Yuki), Jun Hamamura (Father), Fumio Watanabe (Doctor), Kei Sato (Gangster), Kan Nihonyanagi (Horio), Toshiko Kobayashi (Teacher)

ELECTRIC DREAMS (MGM/UA) Producers, Rusty Lemorande, Larry DeWaay; Director, Steve Barron; Screenplay, Rusty Lemorande; Photography, Alex Thomson; Editor, Peter Honess; Music, Giorgio Moroder; In color; Rated PG; 96 minutes; July release. CAST: Lenny Von Dohlen (Miles), Virginia Madsen (Madeline), Maxwell Caulfield (Bill), Bud Cort (Edgar), Don Fellows (Riley), Alan Polonsky (Frank)

ORDEAL BY INNOCENCE (MGM/UA) Producer, Jenny Craven; Executive Producers, Menahem Golan, Yoram Globus; Director, Desmond Davis; Screenplay, Alexander Stuart; Based on novel by Agatha Christie; Photography, Billy Williams; Editor, Timothy Gee; Music, Pino Donaggio; Designer, Ken Bridgeman; Assistant Director, David Tringham; In Eastmancolor; Not rated; 87 minutes; July release. CAST: Donald Sutherland (Dr. Calgary), Faye Dunaway (Rachel), Christopher Plummer (Leo), Ian McShane (Philip), Sarah Miles (Mary), Diana Quick (Gwenda), Annette Crosbie (Kirsten), Michael Elphick (Inspector), Phoebe Nicholls (Tina), Michael Maloney (Micky), Cassie Stuart (Maureen), Billy McColl (Jack)

ONE DEADLY SUMMER (Universal Classics) Director, Jean Becker; Executive Producer, Christine Beytout; Adaptation and Dialogue, Sebastien Japrisot; Production Manager, Alain Darbon; Assistant Directors, Stephane Clavier, Daniel Daujon; Photography, Etienne Becker; Costumes, Therese Ripaud; Editor, Jacques Witta; Music, Georges Delerue; French with English subtitles; In Eastmancolor and Panavision; Rated R; 130 minutes; July release. CAST: Isabelle Adjani (She), Alain Souchon (Pin Pon), Suzanne Flon (Cognata), Jenny Cleve (Pin Pon's Mother), Francois Cluzet (Mickey), Manuel Gelin (Boubou), Michel Galabru (Gabriel), Maria Machado (She's Mother), Roger Carel (Henry IV), Jean Gaven (Leballech), Max Morel (Touret), Cecile Vassort (Josette), Martin LaMotte (Georges), Jacques Nolot (Fiero), Raymond Meunier (Brochard), Jacques Dynam (Ferraldo), Evelyne Didi (Calamite), Yves Afonso (Rostollan), Edith Scob (Lady doctor), Daniel Langlet (Maitre), Catherine LeGouey (Mrs. Brochard), Maiwen Lebesco (She as a child)

THE JIGSAW MAN (United Film) Executive Producer, Mahmud A. Sipra; Producer, S. Benjamin Fisz; Co-Producer, Robert Porter; Director, Terence Young; Associate Producer, Ron Carr; Screenplay, Jo Eisinger; Based on novel by Dorothea Bennett; Photography, Freddie Francis; Designer, Michael Stringer; Art Director, John Roberts; Editors, Peter Hunt, Alan Strachan; Assistant Director, Gerry O'Hara; In color; Not rated; 91 minutes; August release. CAST: Michael Caine (Sir Philip Kimberly), Laurence Olivier (Adm. Sir Gerald Scaith), Susan George (Penny), Robert Powell (Jamie), Charles Gray (Sir James Charley), Michael Medwin (Milroy), Anthony Shaw (Matthews), Maureen Bennett (Susan), Patrick Dawson (Ginger), Juliet Nissen (Miss Fortescue), David Kelly (Cameron), Peter Burton (Douglas), Maggie Rennie (Pauline), Peggy Marshall (Polly), David Allister (Sgt. Lloyd), P. G. Stephens (Driver), Richard Borthwick (Plainclothesman), Matthew Scurfield, Robert Austin (KGB Men)

Virginia Madsen, Maxwell Caulfield, Lenny
Von Dohlen in "Electric Dreams"
© *MGM/UA Entertainment*

Michael Caine, Susan George
in "The Jigsaw Man" © *UFD*

Bruno Ganz, Teresa Madruga
in "In the White City" © *Gray City*

Vittorio Gassman, Geraldine Chaplin
in "Life Is a Bed of Roses" © *Spectrafilm*

IN THE WHITE CITY (Gray City) Producers, Paulo Branco, Alain Tanner, Antonio Vaz Da Silva; Direction and Screenplay, Alain Tanner; Photography, Acacio De Almeida; Music, Jean-Luc Barbier; Editor, Laurent Uhler; Assistant Directors, Christiane Cheneviere, Pedro Ruivo, Joao Canijo; Designer, Maria Jose Branco; Produced by Metro Film/Lisbon, Filmograph/Geneva in Eastmancolor; Portugese-Swiss with English subtitles; Not rated; 108 minutes; August release. CAST: Bruno Ganz (Paul), Teresa Madruga (Rosa), Julia Vonderlinn (Elisa), Jose Carvalho (Hotel Owner), Francisco Baiao (Thief with knife), Jose Wallenstein (2nd Thief), Victor Costa (Waiter), Lidia Franco (Woman in bar), Pedro Efe (Friend in tavern), Cecilia Guimaraes (Woman on train), Joana Vicente (Young Woman on train)

HALF A LIFE (New Line Cinema) Producer, Marin Karmitz; Direction-Screenplay, Romain Goupil; Editor, Francoise Prenant; Photography, Sophie Goupil, Jean Chiabaut, Renan Polles; Production Manager, Stephane Bouveron; In black and white; French with English subtitles; Not rated; 95 minutes; August release. CAST: Michel Recanati, Romain Goupil

LA PETITE SIRENE (World Artists) Producer-Director, Roger Andrieux; Screenplay, Mr. Andrieux; based on novel of same title by Yves Dangerfield; Photography, Robert Alazraki; Editor, Kenout Peltier; Music, Alain Maline; Not rated; 104 minutes; August release. CAST: Laura Alexis (Isabelle), Philippe Leotard (Georges), Evelyne Dress (Nelly), Marie Dubois (Benedicte), Marianne Winquist (Veronique), Diane Sorelle (Claire)

OXFORD BLUES (MGM/UA) Producers, Cassian Elwes, Elliott Kastner; Direction and Screenplay, Robert Boris; Photography, John Stanier; Editor, Patrick Moore; Music, John DuPrez; In Dolby Stereo and color; Rated PG, 96 minutes; August release. CAST: Rob Lowe (Nick), Ally Sheedy (Rona), Amanda Pays (Lady Victoria), Julian Sands (Colin), Julian Firth (Geordie), Alan Howard (Simon)

THE LOST ONE (Fred Pressburger) Producer, Arnold Pressburger; Director, Peter Lorre; Screenplay, Peter Lorre, Benno Vigny, Axel Eggebrecht; Photography, Vaclav Vich; Music, Willi Schmidt-Gentner; A 1951 film in German with English subtitles; Not rated; 98 minutes; August release. CAST: Peter Lorre (Dr. Karl Rothe), Karl John (Hoesch/Novak), Renate Mannhardt (Inge Hermann)

LIFE IS A BED OF ROSES (SpectraFilm) Producer, Philippe Dussart; Director, Alain Resnais; Screenplay, Jean Gruault; Photography, Bruno Nuytten; Music, M. Philippe-Gerard; Art Director, Jacques Saulnier; Editors, Albert Jurgenson, Jean-Pierre Besnard; Costumes, Catherine Leterrier; In color; Rated PG; 111 minutes; August release. CAST: Vittorio Gassman (Walter), Ruggero Raimondi (Michel), Geraldine Chaplin (Nora), Fanny Ardant (Livia), Pierre Arditi (Robert), Sabine Azema (Elizabeth), Robert Manuel (Georges), Martine Kelly (Claudine), Samson Fainsilber (Zoltan), Nathalie Holberg (Veronique), Raoul Vandamme (Andre)

FULL MOON IN PARIS (Orion Classics) Producer, Margaret Menegoz; Direction and Screenplay, Eric Rohmer; Photography, Renato Berta; Editor, Cecile Decligis; Music, Elli and Jacno; In color; Rated R; 102 minutes; September release. CAST: Pascale Ogier (Louise), Fabrice Luchini (Octave), Tcheky Karyo (Remi), Christian Vadim (Bastien), Virginie Thevenet (Camille), Anne-Severine Liotard (Marianne)

EXTERMINATOR 2 (CANNON) Director, Mark Buntzman; Produced and Written by Mark Buntzman, William Sachs; Executive Producers, Menahem Golan, Yoram Globus; Editors, George Norris, Marcus Manton; Photography, Bob Baldwin, Joseph Mangine; Music, David Spear; Additional Direction, William Sachs; Production Manager, Jeffrey Silver; Assistant Directors, Kelly Van Horn, Joseph Winogradoff, Richard Whiting, Nathalie Plemiannikov, Hugh Rawson, Jack White, Kristine Peterson; Costumes, Kristin McNiff; Choreographer, Edward Love; Art Director, Mischa Petrow; In color by TVC; Rated R; 88 minutes; September release. CAST: Robert Ginty (Johnny), Mario Van Peebles (X), Deborah Geffner (Caroline), Frankie Faison (Be Gee), Scott Randolph (Eyes), Reggie Rock Bythewood (Spider), Bruce Smolanoff (Red Rat), David Buntzman (Head Mafioso), Kenny Marino (Tony), Derek Evans (Squealer), Irwin Keyes (Monster), Robert Louis King (Philo), Ayre Gross (Turbo), Janet Rotblatt (Mom), Steffen Zacharias (Pop), Jennifer Brandon (Lisa), Deanna Crowe (Newscaster), Thomas Calabro (Larry), Jesse Aragon (Crackers), Marc Vahanian (Stich), Jayne Kell (Tina), Jack Meeks (Norman), Edgard Mourino (Guard), Kashka (Gangmember), Stanley Brock (Man), L. Scott Caldwell (Patron), Tom Wright (Youth), Ron Taylor (Dude), Bob Watt, Al Sheppard (Cops), Herb Downer (Dr. Turner), Diane Ketterling (Policewoman), Kim Kahana (Bartender), John Turturro, Paul Bates (Guys).

Ally Sheedy, Rob Lowe in "Oxford Blues"
© *MGM/UA Entertainment*

Mario Van Peebles, David Buntzman,
Kenny Marino in "Exterminator 2"
© *Cannon Films*

Romy Schneider, Max von Sydow
in "Death Watch"
© *Quartet/Films Inc.*

Nora Aunor (L), Philip Salvador
in "Bona" © *Film Forum*

DEATH WATCH (Quartet/Films Inc.) Director, Bertrand Tavernier; Producer, Gabriel Boustani; Executive Producer, Jean Serge Breton; Screenplay, David Rayfiel, Bertrand Tavernier; Based on "The Unsleeping Eye" by David Compton; Photography, Pierre William Glenn; Music, Antoine DuHamel; Editors, Armand Psenny, Michael Ellis; Rated PG; 100 minutes; September release. CAST: Romy Schneider (Katherine Mortenhoe), Harvey Keitel (Roddy), Harry Dean Stanton (Vincent Ferriman), Therese Liotard (Tracey), Max von Sydow (Gerald Mortenhoe)

BONA (Film Forum) Producer, Nora Villamayor; Director, Lino Brocka; Screenplay, Cenen Ramones; Photography, Conrado Balthazar; Tagalog with English subtitles; Not rated; 90 minutes; September release. CAST: Nora Aunor (Bona), Philip Salvador (Gardo), Rustica Carpio (Bona's Father), Venchito Galvez (Bona's Mother), Marissa Delgado (Katrina)

A JOKE OF DESTINY (Samuel Goldwyn) Producer, Giuseppe Giovannini; Executive Producer, Manolo Bolognini; Director, Lina Wertmuller; Screenplay, Lina Wertmuller, Age; Story, Ms. Wertmuller, Silvia D'Amico Bendico; Photography, Camillio Bazzoni; Art Director, Enrico Job; Music, Paolo Conte; In color; Italian with English subtitles; Rated PG; 105 minutes; September release. CAST: Ugo Tognazzi (Vincenzo DeAndreliis), Piera Degli Esposti (Maria Theresa), Gastone Moschin (Minister of the Interior), Roberto Herlitzka (Minister's Assistant), Renzo Montagnani (Capt. of the Digos), Enzo Jannacci (Terrorist/Gigi), Valeria Golino (Adalgisa), Massimo Wertmuller (Beniamino), Livia Cerini (Grandmother), Antonella D'Agostino (Wife of Minister), Pina Cei (Maria's Sister), Pierluigi Misasi (Driver)

THE HOLY INNOCENTS (Samuel Goldwyn) Producer, Julian Mateos; Director, Mario Camus; Screenplay (Spanish with English subtitles), Antonio Larreta, Manuel Matji, Mario Camus; Based on novel by Miguel Delibes; Photography, Hans Burmann; Editor, Jose Maria Biurrun; Music, Anton Garcia Abril; In color; Not rated; 108 minutes; September release. CAST: Alfredo Landa (Paco), Francisco Rabal (Azarias), Terele Pavez (Regula), Belen Bailesteros (Nievas), Juan Sanchez (Quirce), Susana Sanchez (Little One), Agata Lys (Dona Purita), Agustin Gonzalez (Don Pedro), Juan Diego (Master Ivan), Mary Carillo (Marchioness), Maribel Martin (Miriam), Jose Guardiola (Senorito de la Jara), Manuel Zarzo (Physician)

NINJA MISSION (New Line) Executive Producers, Charles Aperia, Guy Collins; Director, Mats Helge; Photography, Peter Stevenson; Editor, David Gilbert; Music, Danny Young; In color and widescreen; Rated R; 104 minutes; September release. CAST: Christopher Kohlberg, Hanna Pola, Bo F. Munthe

THE LAST WINTER (Tri-Star) Executive Producers, Avi Lerner, Mota Gorfung; Producer, Jacob Kotzky; Director, Riki Shelach Missimoff; Photography, Amnon Salomon; Art Director, Ofer Lalush; Script, Riki Shelach, Yona Elian, Nava Semel, Dror Schwartz; Based on idea by Dan Wolman from a short script by Ruth Epstein; Screenplay, John Herzfeld; Assistant Directors, David Lipkind, Dror Schwartz; In color; Rated R; 92 minutes; September release. CAST: Yona Elian (Maya), Kathleen Quinlan (Joyce), Michael Schnider (Col. Rosenfeld), Zipora Peled (Sara), Michael Shilo (Unit Commander), Avi Uria (Aaron), Brian Aaron (Michael), Michael Shilo (Unit Commander), Yossi Werzanski (David), Yehuda Fux (Levi), Naomi Sharon (Judith), Zafrir Kochonovsky (Corporal) Lennie Ravitz (Consulate), Herzel Yaakobi (Soldier), Saray Zuriel (Wounded's Wife), Kavin Shepherd (Ilan), Jerry Hyman (Guard)

AMERICAN PICTURES (American Pictures Foundation) Directed, Written and Photographed by Jacob Holdt; Not rated; 115 minutes; September release. Mr. Holdt narrates his odyssey of 100,000 miles across the United States in the 1970's.

NINJA III: THE DOMINATION (Cannon) Producers, Menahem Golan, Yoram Globus; Director, Sam Firstenberg; Screenplay, James R. Silke; Associate Producer, David Womark; Synthesizer Score, Udi Harpaz, Misha Segal; Orchestral Score, Arthur Kempel; Editor, Michael J. Duthie; Photography, Hanania Baer; Production Manager, Rami Alon; Assistant Directors, Irving Schwartz, Anne Cavilier; Art Director, Elliott Ellentuck; Costumes, Nancy Cone; In Metrocolor; Rated R; 95 minutes; September release. CAST: Sho Kosugi (Yamada), Lucinda Dickey (Christie), Jordan Bennett (Secord), David Chung (Black Ninja), Dale Ishimodo (Okuda), James Hong (Miyashima), Bob Craig (Netherland), Pamela Ness (Alana), Roy Padilla (Winslow), Moe Mosley (Pickwick), John LaMotta (Case), Ron Foster (Jimenez), Alan Amiel (Black Ninja Double), Steve Lambert (Pilot), Earl Smith (Jefferson), Carver Barnes (Nicholson), Karen Petty (Tracy), Randy Mulkey (Thug), James Maher (Frankel), Judy Starr (Doctor), Cheryl Van Cleve (Stacy), Suzanne Collins (Patty), Rosemary Ono (Megumi), Janet Marie Heil (Lucy), Charly Harroway (Chang), John Perryman (Tom)

Ugo Tognazzi, Piera Degli Esposti
in "A Joke of Destiny"
© *Samuel Goldwyn Co.*

Yona Elian, Kathleen Quinlan, Stephen
Macht in "The Last Winter"
© *Lerko Productions*

Tracey Ullman, Paul McCartney
in "Give My Regards to Broad Street"
© *MPL Communications*

John Thaw, Karen Black
in "Killing Heat" © *Satori*

HIGHPOINT (New World) Executive Producers, William J. Immerman, Jerry Pam; Producer, Daniel Fine; Associate Producer, Robert J. Opekar; Screenplay, Richard A. Guttman; Director, Peter Carter; Photography, Bert Dunk; Production Managers, Marilyn Stonehouse, Mitch Gamson; Editor, Eric Wrate; Costumes, Patti Unger; Production Designer, Seamus Flannery; Art Director, Rose Marie McSherry; Special Effects, Cliff Wenger, Jr.; Assistant Director, Tony Thatcher; In color; Rated PG; 88 minutes; October release. CAST: Richard Harris (Kinney), Christopher Plummer (James Hatcher), Beverly D'Angelo (Lise), Kate Reid (Mrs. Hatcher), Peter Donat (Don), Robin Gammell (Banner), Maury Chaykin (Falco), Saul Rubinek (Centino), George Buza (Alex), Louis Negin (Molotov), Bill Lynn (Deitrich), David Calderisi (Prisoner/Agent), Eric House (Henchman), Lynda Mason Green (Model), Ken James (Briefcase Man), Frank Gibbs, Trent Dolan (Guards), Ardon Bess, Steve Pernie (Freightmen), Bill Starr, Jack Van Evera (Patrolmen), Susan Connors (Dancer), Roger Periard (Dr. Dumont), Girls at pool: Devon Britton, Kathy Deckard, Sallianne Spence, Margaret Doty

TOY SOLDIERS (New World) Producer, E. Darrell Hallenbeck; Director, David A. Fisher; Screenplay, David A. Fisher, Walter Fox; Photography, Francisco Bojorquez; Editor, Geoffrey Rowland; Associate Producer, Kevin Finnegan; Music, Leland Bond; In color; Rated R; 91 minutes; October release. CAST: Jason Miller (Sarge), Cleavon Little (Buck), Rodolfo De Anda (Col. Lopez), Terri Garber (Amy), Tracy Scoggins (Monique), Willard Pugh (Ace), Jim Greenleaf (Tom), Mary Beth Evans (Buffy), Tim Robbins (Boe), Jay Baker (Jeff), Larry Poindexter (Trevor), Alejandro Arroyo (Rafael), Douglas Warhit (Larry)

GIVE MY REGARDS TO BROAD STREET (20th Century-Fox) Producer, Andros Epaminondas; Director, Peter Webb; Screenplay and Music, Paul McCartney; Designer, Anthony Pratt; Photography, Ian McMillan; Costumes, Milena Canonero; Editor, Peter Beston; Choreographer, David Toguri; Associate Producer, Peter Manley; Production Manager, Charles Salmon; Assistant Director, Selwyn Roberts; Art Director, Adrian Smith; Special Effects, Ian Wingrove; In color and Dolby Stereo; Rated PG; 108 minutes; October release. CAST: John Burgess (Chauffeur), Bryan Brown (Steve), Philip Jackson (Alan), Ian Hastings (Harry), Marie Collett (Valerie), Paul McCartney (Paul), Graham Dene (D. J. Voice), Anthony Bate (Banker), Leonard Fenton (Accountant), Jeremy Child, Richard Kane (Record Executives), Anthony Brown (Inspector), Donald Douglas (Detective), Alison McGuire, Rosin Stewart (Blue-rinse Ladies), John Salthouse (Tom), Amanda Redman (Receptionist), John Bennett (Rath), Christopher Ellison (Rath's Minder), Ringo Starr (Ringo), George Martin (Producer), Geoff Emerick (Engineer), Robert Longden (Tape Operator), Leslie Sarony (Gatekeeper), Barbara Bach (Journalist), Linda McCartney (Linda), Gordon Rollings (Monster), Tracey Ullman (Sandra), John Harding (Ernest), Mark Kingston (Terry) Frank Duncan (William), Ralph Richardson (Jim), John Murphy (Wino), Ruby Buchanan (Bag Lady)

MAN OF FLOWERS (Spectrafilm) Producers, Jane Ballantyne, Paul Cox; Director, Paul Cox; Associate Producer, Tony Llewellyn-Jones; Screenplay, Paul Cox, Bob Ellis; Photography, Yuri Sokol; Art Director, Asher Bilu; Editor, Tim Lewis; Music, Donizetti's "Lucia di Lammermoor"; Sung by Montserrat Caballe, Jose Carreras; In color; Not rated; 91 minutes; October release. CAST: Norman Kaye (Charles), Alyson Best (Lisa), Chris Haywood (David), Sarah Walker (Jane), Julia Blake (Art Teacher), Bob Ellis (Psychiatrist), Barry Dickins (Postman), Patrick Cook (Coppershop Man), Victoria Eagger (Angela), Werner Herzog (Father), Hilary Kelly (Mother), James Stratford (Young Charles), Eileen Joyce, Marianne Baillieu (Aunts), Lirit Bilu, Juliet Bacskai (Florists), Dawn Klingberg (Cleaning Lady), Tony Llewellyn-Jones (Church Warden)

GHOST DANCE (Film Forum) Written, Produced and Directed by Ken McMullen; Photography, Peter Harvey; Editor, Robert Hargreaves; Music, David Cunningham, Michael Giles, Janie Muir; In English and French with English subtitles; A Looseyard production; Not rated; 100 minutes; October release. CAST: Pascale Ogier (Pascale), Leonie Mellinger (Marianne), Jacques Derrida (Himself), Stuart Brisley, Robbie Coltrane, Dominique Pinon

EUREKA (UA Classics) Producer, Jeremy Thomas; Director, Nicolas Roeg; Screenplay, Paul Mayersberg; Based on novel by Marshall Houts; Photography, Alex Thomson; Music, Stanley Myers; Design, Michael Seymour; Art Director, Les Dilley; Editor, Tony Lawson; In color; Rated R; 129 minutes; October release. CAST: Gene Hackman (Jack), Theresa Russell (Tracy), Rutger Hauer (Maillot van Horn), Jane Lapotaire (Helen), Ed Lauter (Perkins), Mickey Rourke (Aurelio), Joe Pesci (Mayakofsky), Helen Kallianiotis (Freda), Corin Redgrave (Worsley), James Faulkner (Roger), Tim Scott (Webb)

WITHOUT WITNESS (International Film Exchange) A Mosfilm production; Director, Nikita Mikhalkov; Screenplay, Nikita Nikhalkov, Sofia Prokofyeva, Ramiz Fataliyev; Photography, Pavel Lebeshev; Art Directors, Alexander Adabashyan, Igor Nakarov, Alexander Samulekin; Music, Edward Artyemiev; In color; Not rated; 97 minutes; October release. CAST: Irina Kupchenko, Mikhail Ulyanov

KILLING HEAT (Satori) Producer, Mark Forstater; Director, Michael Raeburn; Photography, Bille August, Fritz Schroder; Designer, Disley Jones; Editors, Thomas Schwalm, Lasse Dahlberg; Music, Bjorn Isfalt, Temba Tana; Based on novel "The Grass Is Singing" by Doris Lessing; In color; Not Rated; 104 minutes; October release. CAST: Karen Black (Mary Turner), John Thaw (Dick Turner), John Kani (Moses), John Moulder-Brown (Tony Marston)

RUSH (Cinema Shares International) Producer, Marcello Romeo; Director, Anthony Richmond (Tonino Ricci); Screenplay and story, Tito Carpi; Photography, Giovanni Bergmanini; Editor, Vincenzo Tomassi; Music, Francesco De Masi; Production Manager, Romualdo Buzzanca; In color; Not rated; 77 minutes; October release. CAST: Conrad Nichols (Rush), Gordon Mitchell (The Ruler), Laura Trotter, Rita Furlan, Bridgit Pelz, Richard Pizzuti, Osiride Pevarello, Paolo Celli, Luigi Filippo Lodoli, Daniel Stroppa

Alyson Best, Norman Kaye
in "Man of Flowers"
© *International Spectrafilm*

Silvana Mangano, Franco Citti
in "Oedipus Rex" © *Horizon Films*

"Snowdrop Festival"
© *IFEX*

OEDIPUS REX (Horizon Films) Directed and Written by Pier Paolo Pasolini; Based on "Oedipus Rex" and "Oedipus at Colonus" by Sophocles; Producer, Alfredo Bini; Photography, Giuseppe Ruzzolini; Editor, Nino Baragli; Art Directors, Andrea Fantacci, Luigi Scaccianoce; Assistant Director, Jean-Claude Biette; Costumes, Danilo Donati; Music, Rumanian and Japanese Folk; A 1967 film in Italian with English subtitles; In Technicolor; Not rated; 110 minutes; November release. CAST: Franco Citti (Oedipus), Silvana Mangano (Jocasta), Alida Valli (Merope), Carmelo Bene (Creon), Julian Beck (Tiresias), Luciano Bartoli (Laius), Francesco Leonetti (Servant), Ahmed Bellashmi (Polybus), Ninetto Davoli (Messenger/Angelo), Pier Paolo Pasolini (High Priest), Jean-Claude Biette (Priest)

THE CASE IS CLOSED (Neelkanth Films) Screenplay and Direction, Mrinal Sen; Based on story by Ramapada Chowdhury; Photography, K. K. Mahajan; Editor, Gangadhar Naskar; Music, B. V. Karanth; Art Direction, Nitish Roy; Bengali with English subtitles; Not rated; In color; 95 minutes; November release. CAST: Mamata Shankar (Mamata/Wife), Anjan Dutt (Anjan Sen/Husband), Sreela Majumber (Sreela), Indranil Moitra (Pupai), Debapratim Das Gupta (Hari), Nilotpal Dey (Police Inspector)

SNOWDROP FESTIVAL (International Film Exchange) Director, Jiri Menzel; Screenplay, Bohumil Hrabal, Jiri Menzel; Photography, Jiri Macak; Music, Jiri Sust; Czechoslovak with English subtitles; Not rated; 95 minutes; November release. CAST: Rudolf Hrusinsky, Jaromir Hanzlik, Jiri Schmitzer, Petr Cepek, Zdena Hadrbolcova, Josef Somr, Libuse Safrankova, Miloslav Stibich, Eugen Jegorov, Bork Prochazka

LA PETITE BANDE (Triumph) Executive Producer, Bob Kellett; Director, Michel Deville; Story, Gilles Perrault; Screen Adaptation, Gilles Perrault, Michel Deville; Music, Edgar Cosma; Photography, Claude Lecomte; Editor, Raymonde Guyot; Assistant Director, Rosalinde Damamme; Costumes, Muriel Ghene; Special Effects, Michel Francois; Production Managers, Franz Damamme, Roger Fleytoux; French with English subtitles; In color; Rated PG; 91 minutes; November release. CAST: Yveline Ailhaud (Female Cooper), Michel Amphoux (Circus Director), Roland Amstutz (from Bavaria), Pierre Ascaride (Nasty Father), Jean-Pierre Bagot (Man with red car), Nathalie Becue (From Bavaria), Didier Benureau (2nd Policeman), Liliane Bertrand (Woman with red car), Jean Bois (Psychiatrist), Jacques Blot,

Jacques Cancelier, Georges Carmier, Marie-Pierre Casey, Pierre Chevalier, Francois Clavier, Josine Comellas, Dominique Constantin, Roger Cornillac, Monique Couturier, Roger Desmare, Claude Dobrinski, Yves Elliot, Pierre Forget, Mireille Franchino, Jean-Louis Grinfeld, Bernard Hocine

JUNGLE WARRIORS (Aquarius) Executive Producers, Monika Teuber, Francisco Araiz-Condoy; Producer-Director, Ernst R. von Theumer; Screenplay, Robert Collector, von Theumer; Photography, Nicholas von Sternberg; Editors, Juan Jose Marino, Warren Chadwick; Music, Roland Baumgartner; Art, Richard McGuire; Assistant Director, Barbara Schubert; In CFI Color; Not rated; 93 minutes; November release. CAST: Nina Van Pallandt (Joanna), Paul L. Smith (Cesar), John Vernon (Vito), Alex Cord (Nicky), Sybil Danning (Angel), Woody Strode (Luther), Kai Wulff (Ben), Dana Elcar (Michael), Suzi Horne (Pam), Mindy Iden (Marci), Kari Lloyd (Brie), Ava Cadell (Didi), Myra Chason (Cindy), Angela Robinson (Monique), Louisa Moritz (Laura), Marjoe Gortner (Larry).

SWORD OF THE VALIANT (Cannon) Producers, Menahem Golan, Yoram Globus; Director, Stephen Weeks; Screenplay, Stephen Weeks, Philip M. Breen, Howard C. Pen; Executive Producers, Michael Kagan, Philip M. Breen; Music, Ron Geesin; Photography, Freddie Young, Peter Hurst; Editors, Richard Marden, Barry Peters; Designers, Maurice Fowler, Derek Nice; Costumes, Shuna Harwood; Associate Producers, Sture Rydman, Basil Keys; Production Manager, Adam Kempton; Assistant Directors, David Brackwell, Ken Tuohy, Richard Hoult; Special Effects, Nobby Clarke; Visual Effects, Cliff Culley, Niel Culley; In J-D-C Widescreen, FujiColor and Dolby Stereo; Rated PG; 102 minutes; November release. CAST: Miles O'Keeffe (Gawain), Cyrielle Claire (Linet), Leigh Lawson (Humphrey), Sean Connery (Green Knight), Trevor Howard (King), Peter Cushing (Seneschal), Ronald Lacey (Oswald), Lila Kedrova (Lady of Lyonesse), John Rhys-Davies (Baron Fortinbras), Wilfrid Brambell (Porter), Brian Coburn (Friar), Bruce Lidington (Bertilak), David Rappaport (Sage), Douglas Wilmer (Black Knight), Emma Sutton (Morgan LaFay), John Serret (Priest), Thomas Heathcote (Armourer), Mike Edmonds (Tiny Man), John Pierce-Jones (Sgt.), James Windsor, Ric Morgan, Peter MacKriel (Recruits), Jerold Wells, Harry Jones (Torturers), John J. Carney (Messenger)

"Le Petite Band"
© *Triumph Films*

Sean Connery, Miles O'Keeffe
in "Sword of the Valiant"
© *Cannon Films*

Brenda Vaccaro, Faye Dunaway, Helen Slater
in "Supergirl" © *Tri-Star Pictures*

Anjan Dutt, Nilotpal Dey
in "The Case Is Closed"

CHINA 9, LIBERTY 37 (Lorimar) Producers, Gianni Bozzacchi, Valerio de Paolis, Monte Hellman; Director, Monte Hellman; Story and Screenplay, Jerry Harvey, Douglas Venturelli; Photography, Giuseppe Rotunno; Editor, Cesare d'Amico; Music, Pina Donaggio; In color and Widescreen; Rated R; 105 minutes; November release. CAST: Warren Oates (Matthew), Fabio Testi (Clayton), Jenny Agutter (Catherine), Sam Peckinpah (Wilbur), Isabel Mestres (Barbara), Gianrico Tondinelli (Johnny), Carlos Bravo (Duke), Paco Benlloch (Virgil), Yvonne Sentis (Prostitute)

LE VIEUX PAYS OU RIMBAUD EST MORT (Thalia) Producer, Cinak/Montreal; Director, Jean Pierre Lefebvre; Screenplay (French with English subtitles), Mr. Lefebvre, Mireille Amiel; Photography, Guy DuFaux; Editor, Marguerite Duparc; Music, Claude Fonfrede; Not rated; 113 minutes; November release. CAST: Marcel Sabourin (Abel), Anouk Ferjac (Anne), Myriam Boyer (Jeanne), Roger Blin (Jeanne's Father), Germaine Delbat (Anne's Mother), Francois Perrot (Anne's Husband), Mark Lesser (Yves), Jean-Francois Stevenin (Taxi Driver/ Painter/Art Dealer), Viviane Lesser (Viviane), Jean Turlier (Mr. de Cassant), Michel Delahaye (Professor), Rita Maiden (Mrs. de Cassant)

LES FLEURS SAUVAGES (Thalia) Direction and Screenplay (French with English subtitles), Photography, Guy DuFaux; Produced and Edited by Marguerite Duparc; Not rated; 152 minutes; November release. CAST: Marthe Nadeau (Simone), Michele Megny (Michele), Pierre Curzi (Pierre), Eric Beausejour (Eric), Claudia Aubin (Claudia)

SUPERGIRL (Tri-Star) Producer, Timothy Burrill; Director, Jeannot Szwarc; Screenplay, David Odell; Photography, Alan Hume; Editor, Malcolm Cooke; Music, Jerry Goldsmith; In Panavision Widescreen, Dolby Stereo and color; Rated PG; 114 minutes; November release. CAST: Faye Dunaway (Selena), Helen Slater (Supergirl/Linda Lee), Peter O'Toole (Zeitar), Mia Farrow (Alura), Brenda Vaccaro (Bianca), Peter Cook (Nigel), Simon Ward (Zor-El), Marc McClure (Jimmy), Hart Bochner (Ethan), Maureen Teefy (Lucy), David Healy (Mr. Danvers)

NUTCRACKER (Almi) Producer, Panos Nicolaou; Director, Anwar Kawadri; Screenplay, Raymond Christodoulou; Associate Producer, George Pavlou; Production Manager, Paul Sparrow; Photography, Peter Jessop; Editor, Max Benedict; Composer-Arranger, Simon Park; In color; Rated R; 105 minutes; November release. CAST: Joan Collins (Mme. Carrere), Carol White (Margaux), Paul Nicolas (Mike), Finola Hughes (Nadia), William Franklyn (Sir Arthur), Murray Melvin

(Leopood), Leslie Ash (Sharon), Fran Fullenwider (Vi), Gess Whitfield (Gus), Dan Meaden (Edwin), Debbie Goodman (Evelyn), Raymond Christodoulou (Drummer), Cherry Gillespie (Mireille), Jane Wellman (Grace), John Vye (Jules), Patrick Wood (Andrew), Patti Hammond (Sue), Liz Green (Jakki), Anita Mahadervan (Paulette), Victoria Shellard (Mandy), Stephen Beagley (Stephen), Ed Bishop (Sam), Martin Burrows (Tom)

THE CLAW AND THE TOOTH (Nicole Jouve Interama) Producer, Les Cineastes Animaliers Associes; Direction and Photography, Francois Bel and Gerard Vienne; Editor, Jacqueline Lecompte; A 1970 film in color; Not rated; 98 minutes; December release. A documentary on wild animals.

MEMOIRS (Chbib) Producer-Director, Bachar Chbib; Screenplay, John B. Wimbs, Mr. Chbib; Based on play "Memoirs of Johnny Daze" by Mr. Wimbs; Editors, Bachar Chbib, Amy Webb; Photography, Cristian Duguay, Bill Kerrigan; Music, Julia Gilmore, Edward Strawiak; Performed by Condition; Not rated; 91 minutes; December release. CAST: Philip Baylaucq (Johnny Daze), Norma Jean Sanders (Ida Rage), Julia Gilmore (Lotta Lov), Rotwang

DON'T OPEN TILL CHRISTMAS (21st Century) Producers, Dick Randall, Steve Minasian; Director, Edmund Purdom; Screenplay, Derek Ford; Additional Scenes written and directed by Al McGoohan; Photography, Alan Pudney; Editor, Ray Selfe; Music, Des Dolan; Special Effects, Coast to Coast Ltd.; In color; Not rated; 86 minutes; December release. CAST: Edmund Purdom (Inspector Harris), Alan Lake (Giles), Belinda Mayne (Kate), Gerry Sundquist (Cliff), Mark Jones (Sgt. Powell), Caroline Munro (Herself), Kevin Lloyd (Gerry), Kelly Baker (Experience Girl), Pat Astley (Sharon), Des Dolan (Detective Constable)

ANNIE'S COMING OUT (Film Australia) Producer, Don Murray; Director, Gil Brealey; Screenplay, John Patterson, Chris Borthwick; Based on book of same title by Rosemary Crossley; Photography, Mick von Bornemann; Editor, Lindsay Frazer; Music, Simon Walker; Art Director, Mike Hudson; Executive Producer, Don Harley; In color; 93 minutes; December release. CAST: Angela Punch McGregor (Jessica), Drew Forsythe (David), Tina Arhonis (Annie), Charles Tingwell (Judge), Monica Maughan (Vera), Mark Butler (Dr. Monroe), Philippa Baker (Sister Waterman), Liddy Clark (Sally), Wallas Eaton (Dr. Rowell), John Frawley (Harding), Alistair Duncan (Hopgood), Simon Chilvers (Metcalf)

Joan Collins in "Nutcracker"
© *Almi*

"The Claw and the Tooth"
© *Film Forum*

| Eddie
Albert | Karen
Allen | Woody
Allen | Eve
Arden | Desi
Arnaz, Jr. | Elizabeth
Ashley |

BIOGRAPHICAL DATA

(Name, real name, place and date of birth, school attended)

AAMES, WILLIE (William Upton): 1961.

ABBOTT, DIAHNNE: NYC, 1945.

ABBOTT, JOHN: London, June 5, 1905.

ABEL, WALTER: St. Paul, MN, June 6, 1898, AADA.

ABRAHAM, F. MURRAY: Pittsburgh, PA, Oct. 24, 1939. UTx.

ADAMS, BROOKE: NYC, 1949. Dalton.

ADAMS, DON: NYC, 1927.

ADAMS, EDIE (Elizabeth Edith Enke): Kingston, PA, Apr. 16, 1929. Juilliard, Columbia.

ADAMS, JULIE (Betty May): Waterloo, Iowa, Oct. 17, 1928. Little Rock Jr. College.

ADAMS, MAUD (Maud Wikstrom): Lulea, Sweden.

ADDAMS, DAWN: Felixstowe, Suffolk, Eng., Sept. 21, 1930. RADA.

ADDY, WESLEY: Omaha, NB, Aug. 4, 1913. UCLA.

ADJANI, ISABELLE: Paris, 1955.

ADRIAN, IRIS (Iris Adrian Hostetter): Los Angeles, May 29, 1913.

AGAR, JOHN: Chicago, Jan. 31, 1921.

AGUTTER, JENNY: London, 1953.

AHERNE, BRIAN: Worcestershire, Eng., May 2, 1902. Malvern College, U. of London.

AIELLO, DANNY: June 20, 1935, NYC.

AIMEE, ANOUK: Paris, Apr. 27, 1934. Bauer-Therond.

AKINS, CLAUDE: Nelson, GA, May 25, 1936. Northwestern U.

ALBERGHETTI, ANNA MARIA: Pesaro, Italy, May 15, 1936.

ALBERT, EDDIE (Eddie Albert Heimberger): Rock Island, IL, Apr. 22, 1908. U. of Minn.

ALBERT, EDWARD: Los Angeles, Feb. 20, 1951. UCLA.

ALBRIGHT, LOLA: Akron, OH, July 20, 1925.

ALDA, ALAN: NYC, Jan. 28, 1936. Fordham.

ALDA, ROBERT (Alphonso D'Abruzzo): NYC, Feb. 26, 1914. NYU.

ALDERSON, BROOKE: Dallas, Tx.

ALEJANDRO, MIGUEL: NYC, Feb. 21, 1958.

ALEXANDER, JANE (Quigley): Boston, MA, Oct. 28, 1939. Sarah Lawrence.

ALLEN, KAREN: Carrollton, IL. Oct. 5, 1951. UMd.

ALLEN, NANCY: NYC 1950.

ALLEN, REX: Wilcox, AZ, Dec. 31, 1922.

ALLEN, STEVE: New York City, Dec. 26, 1921.

ALLEN, WOODY (Allen Stewart Konigsberg): Brooklyn, Dec. 1, 1935.

ALLYSON, JUNE (Ella Geisman): Westchester, NY, Oct. 7, 1917.

ALONSO, MARIA CONCHITA: Cuba 1957.

ALVARADO, TRINI: NYC, 1967.

AMECHE, DON (Dominic Amichi): Kenosha, WI, May 31, 1908.

AMES, ED: Boston July 9, 1929.

AMES, LEON (Leon Wycoff): Portland, IN, Jan. 20, 1903.

AMOS, JOHN: Newark, NJ, Dec. 27, 1940. Colo. U.

ANDERSON, JUDITH: Adelaide, Australia, Feb. 10, 1898.

ANDERSON, LONI: St. Paul, Mn., Aug. 5, 1946.

ANDERSON, LYNN: Grand Forkes, ND; Sept. 26, 1947. UCLA.

ANDERSON, MELODY: Canada 1955, Carlton U.

ANDERSON, MICHAEL, JR.: London, Eng., 1943.

ANDERSSON, BIBI: Stockholm, Nov. 11, 1935. Royal Dramatic Sch.

ANDES, KEITH: Ocean City, NJ, July 12, 1920. Temple U., Oxford.

ANDRESS, URSULA: Switz., Mar. 19, 1936.

ANDREWS, ANTHONY: London, 1948.

ANDREWS, DANA: Collins, MS, Jan. 1, 1909. Sam Houston Col.

ANDREWS, HARRY: Tonbridge, Kent, Eng., Nov. 10, 1911.

ANDREWS, JULIE (Julia Elizabeth Wells): Surrey, Eng., Oct. 1, 1935.

ANGEL, HEATHER: Oxford, Eng., Feb. 9, 1909. Wycombe Abbey.

ANN-MARGRET (Olsson): Valsjobyn, Sweden, Apr. 28, 1941. Northwestern U.

ANSARA, MICHAEL: Lowell, MA, Apr. 15, 1922. Pasadena Playhouse.

ANTHONY, TONY: Clarksburg, WV, Oct. 16, 1937. Carnegie Tech.

ANTON, SUSAN: Yucaipa, CA. Oct. 12, 1950. Bernardino Col.

ANTONELLI, LAURA: Pola, Italy.

ARCHER, JOHN (Ralph Bowman): Osceola, NB, May 8, 1915. USC.

ARDEN, EVE (Eunice Quedens): Mill Valley, CA, Apr. 30, 1912.

ARKIN, ALAN: NYC, Mar. 26, 1934. LACC.

ARNAZ, DESI: Santiago, Cuba, Mar. 2, 1915. Colegio de Dolores.

ARNAZ, DESI, JR.: Los Angeles, Jan. 19, 1953.

ARNAZ, LUCIE: Hollywood, July 17, 1951.

ARNESS, JAMES (Aurness): Minneapolis, MN, May 26, 1923. Beloit College.

ARTHUR, BEATRICE: NYC, May 13, 1926. New School.

ARTHUR, JEAN: NYC, Oct. 17, 1905.

ARTHUR, ROBERT (Robert Arthaud): Aberdeen, WA, June 18, 1925. U. Wash.

ASHLEY, ELIZABETH (Elizabeth Ann Cole): Ocala, FL, Aug. 30, 1939.

ASSANTE, ARMAND: NYC, Oct. 4, 1949. AADA.

ASTAIRE, FRED (Fred Austerlitz): Omaha, NB, May 10, 1899.

ASTIN, JOHN: Baltimore, MD, Mar. 30, 1930. U. Minn.

ASTIN, PATTY DUKE: (see Patty Duke)

ASTOR, MARY (Lucile V. Langhanke): Quincy, IL, May 3, 1906. Kenwood-Loring School.

ATHERTON, WILLIAM: Orange, CT, July 30, 1947. Carnegie Tech.

ATKINS, CHRISTOPHER: Rye, NY, Feb. 21, 1961.

ATTENBOROUGH, RICHARD: Cambridge, Eng., Aug. 29, 1923. RADA.

AUBERJONOIS, RENE: NYC, June 1, 1940. Carnegie Tech.

AUDRAN, STEPHANE: Versailles, Fr., 1933.

AUGER, CLAUDINE: Paris, Apr. 26, 1942. Dramatic Cons.

AULIN, EWA: Stockholm, Sweden, Feb. 14, 1950.

AUMONT, JEAN PIERRE: Paris, Jan. 5, 1909. French Nat'l School of Drama.

AUTRY, GENE: Tioga, TX, Sept. 29, 1907.

AVALON, FRANKIE (Francis Thomas Avallone): Philadelphia, Sept. 18, 1939.

AYKROYD, DAN: Ottawa, Can., 1952.

AYRES, LEW: Minneapolis, MN, Dec. 28, 1908.

AZNAVOUR, CHARLES (Varenagh Aznourian): Paris, May 22, 1924.

BACALL, LAUREN (Betty Perske): NYC, Sept. 16, 1924. AADA.

BACH, BARBARA: Aug. 27, 1946.

Scott Baio	Blanche Baker	Martin Balsam	Adrienne Barbeau	Steven Bauer	Candice Bergen

BACKUS, JIM: Cleveland, Ohio, Feb. 25, 1913. AADA.

BACON, KEVIN: Philadelphia, PA., July 8, 1958.

BADDELEY, HERMIONE: Shropshire, Eng., Nov. 13, 1906 Margaret Morris School.

BAILEY, PEARL: Newport News, VA, March 29, 1918.

BAIN, BARBARA: Chicago, Sept. 13, 1934. U. ILL.

BAIO, SCOTT: Brooklyn, NY, Sept. 22, 1961.

BAKER, BLANCHE: NYC Dec. 20, 1956.

BAKER, CARROLL: Johnstown, PA, May 28, 1931. St. Petersburg Jr. College.

BAKER, DIANE: Hollywood, CA, Feb. 25, 1938. USC.

BAKER, KATHY WHITTON: Midland, TX., June 8, 1950. UCBerkley.

BALABAN, ROBERT; Chicago, Aug. 16, 1945. Colgate.

BALDWIN, ADAM: Chicago, IL. 1962.

BALIN, INA: Brooklyn, Nov. 12, 1937. NYU.

BALL, LUCILLE: Celaron, NY, Aug. 6, 1910. Chatauqua Musical Inst.

BALSAM, MARTIN: NYC, Nov. 4, 1919. Actors Studio.

BANCROFT, ANNE (Anna Maria Italiano): Bronx, NY, Sept. 17, 1931. AADA.

BANNEN, IAN: Airdrie, Scot., June 29, 1928.

BARBEAU, ADRIENNE: Sacramento, CA. June 11, 1945. Foothill Col.

BARDOT, BRIGITTE: Paris, Sept. 28, 1934.

BARKIN, ELLEN: Bronx, NY, 1959. Hunter Col.

BARRAULT, MARIE-CHRISTINE: Paris, 1946.

BARRETT, MAJEL (Hudec): Columbus, OH, Feb. 23. Western Reserve U.

BARRON, KEITH: Mexborough, Eng., Aug. 8, 1936. Sheffield Playhouse.

BARRY, GENE (Eugene Klass): NYC, June 14, 1921.

BARRYMORE, DREW: Los Angeles, Feb. 22, 1975.

BARRYMORE, JOHN BLYTH: Beverly Hills, CA, June 4, 1932. St. John's Military Academy.

BARTHOLOMEW, FREDDIE: London, Mar. 28, 1924.

BARYSHNIKOV, MIKHAIL: Riga, Latvia, Jan. 27, 1948.

BASINGER, KIM: Athens, GA. 1954. Neighborhood Playhouse.

BATES, ALAN: Allestree, Derbyshire, Eng., Feb. 17, 1934. RADA.

BAUER, STEVEN: (Steven Rocky Echevarria): Havana, Cuba, Dec. 2, 1956. UMiami.

BAXTER, ANNE: Michigan City, IN, May 7, 1923. Ervine School of Drama.

BAXTER, KEITH: South Wales, Apr. 29, 1933. RADA.

BEAL, JOHN (J. Alexander Bliedung): Joplin, MO, Aug. 13, 1909. PA. U.

BEATTY, NED: Louisville, KY. 1937.

BEATTY, ROBERT: Hamilton, Ont., Can., Oct. 19, 1909. U. of Toronto.

BEATTY, WARREN: Richmond, VA, March 30, 1937.

BECK, MICHAEL: Horseshoe Lake, AR, 1948.

BEDELIA, BONNIE: NYC, Mar. 25, 1948. Hunter Col.

BEDI, KABIR: India, 1945.

BEERY, NOAH, JR.: NYC, Aug. 10, 1916. Harvard Military Academy.

BELAFONTE, HARRY: NYC, Mar. 1, 1927.

BELASCO, LEON: Odessa, Russia, Oct. 11, 1902.

BEL GEDDES, BARBARA: NYC, Oct. 31, 1922.

BELL, TOM: Liverpool, Eng., 1932.

BELLAMY, RALPH: Chicago, June 17, 1904.

BELLER, KATHLEEN: NYC, 1957.

BELMONDO, JEAN PAUL: Paris, Apr. 9, 1933.

BENEDICT, DIRK (Niewoehner): White Sulphur Springs, MT. March 1, 1945. Whitman Col.

BENJAMIN, RICHARD: NYC, May 22, 1938. Northwestern U.

BENNENT, DAVID: Lausanne, Sept. 9, 1966.

BENNETT, BRUCE (Herman Brix): Tacoma, WA, May 19, 1909. U. Wash.

BENNETT, JILL: Penang, Malay, Dec. 24, 1931.

BENNETT, JOAN: Palisades, NJ, Feb. 27, 1910. St. Margaret's School.

BENSON, ROBBY: Dallas, TX, Jan 21, 1957.

BERENSON, MARISSA: NYC, Feb. 15, 1947.

BERGEN, CANDICE: Los Angeles, May 9, 1946. U. PA.

BERGEN, POLLY: Knoxville, TN, July 14, 1930. Compton Jr. College.

BERGER, HELMUT: Salzburg, Aus., 1945.

BERGER, SENTA: Vienna, May 13, 1941. Vienna Sch. of Acting.

BERGER, WILLIAM: Austria, Jan. 20, 1928. Columbia.

BERGERAC, JACQUES: Biarritz, France, May 26, 1927. Paris U.

BERLE, MILTON (Milton Berlinger): NYC, July 12, 1908. Professional Children's School.

BERLIN, JEANNIE: Los Angeles, Nov. 1, 1949.

BERLINGER, WARREN: Brooklyn, Aug. 31, 1937. Columbia.

BERNARDI, HERSCHEL: NYC, 1923.

BERNHARD, SANDRA: Arizona 1956.

BERRI, CLAUDE (Langmann): Paris, July 1, 1934.

BERTO, JULIET: Grenoble, France, Jan. 1947.

BEST, JAMES: Corydon, IN, July 26, 1926.

BETTGER, LYLE: Philadelphia, Feb. 13, 1915. AADA.

BEYMER, RICHARD: Avoca, IA, Feb. 21, 1939.

BIEHN, MICHAEL: Ariz. 1957.

BIKEL, THEODORE: Vienna, May 2, 1924. RADA.

BIRNEY, DAVID: Washington, DC, Apr. 23, 1939. Dartmouth, UCLA.

BIRNEY, REED: Alexandria, VA., Sept. 11, 1954. Boston U.

BISHOP, JOEY (Joseph Abraham Gottlieb): Bronx, NY, Feb. 3, 1918.

BISHOP, JULIE (formerly Jacqueline Wells): Denver, CO, Aug. 30, 1917. Westlake School.

BISSET, JACQUELINE: Waybridge, Eng., Sept. 13, 1944.

BIXBY, BILL: San Francisco, Jan. 22, 1934. U. CAL.

BLACK, KAREN (Ziegler): Park Ridge, IL, July 1, 1942. Northwestern.

BLAINE, VIVIAN (Vivian Stapleton): Newark, NJ, Nov. 21, 1923.

BLAIR, BETSY (Betsy Boger): NYC, Dec. 11, 1923.

BLAIR, JANET (Martha Jane Lafferty): Blair, PA, Apr. 23, 1921.

BLAIR, LINDA: Westport, CT, Jan. 22, 1959.

BLAKE, AMANDA (Beverly Louise Neill): Buffalo, NY, Feb. 20, 1921.

BLAKE, ROBERT (Michael Gubitosi): Nutley, NJ, Sept. 18, 1933.

BLAKELY, SUSAN: Frankfurt, Germany 1950. U. TEX.

BLAKLEY, RONEE: Stanley, ID, 1946. Stanford U.

BLOOM, CLAIRE: London, Feb. 15, 1931. Badminton School.

BLYTH, ANN: Mt. Kisco, NY, Aug. 16, 1928. New Wayburn Dramatic School.

Hart	Judi	James	Coral	Rory	Virginia
Bochner	Bowker	Brolin	Browne	Calhoun	Capers

BOCHNER, HART: Toronto, 1956. U. San Diego.

BOGARDE, DIRK: London, Mar. 28, 1918. Glasgow & Univ. College.

BOLGER, RAY: Dorchester, MA, Jan. 10, 1903.

BOLKAN, FLORINDA (Florinda Soares Bulcao): Ceara, Brazil, Feb. 15, 1941.

BOND, DEREK: Glasgow, Scot., Jan. 26, 1920. Askes School.

BONO, SONNY (Salvatore): Feb. 16, 1935.

BOONE, PAT: Jacksonville, FL, June 1, 1934. Columbia U.

BOOTH, SHIRLEY (Thelma Ford): NYC, Aug. 30, 1907.

BORGNINE, ERNEST (Borgnino): Hamden, CT, Jan. 24, 1918. Randall School.

BOSTWICK, BARRY: San Mateo, CA., Feb. 24, 1945. NYU.

BOTTOMS, JOSEPH: Santa Barbara, CA, Aug. 30, 1954.

BOTTOMS, TIMOTHY: Santa Barbara, CA, Aug. 30, 1951.

BOULTING, INGRID: Transvaal, So. Africa, 1947.

BOVEE, LESLIE: Bend, OR, 1952.

BOWIE, DAVID: (David Robert Jones) Brixton, South London, Eng. Jan. 8, 1947.

BOWKER, JUDI: Shawford, Eng., Apr. 6, 1954.

BOXLEITNER, BRUCE: Elgin, IL., 1950.

BOYLE, PETER: Philadelphia, PA, 1937. LaSalle Col.

BRACKEN, EDDIE: NYC, Feb. 7, 1920. Professional Children's School.

BRAGA, SONIA: Maringa, Brazil, 1951.

BRAND, NEVILLE: Kewanee, IL, Aug. 13, 1920.

BRANDO, JOCELYN: San Francisco, Nov. 18, 1919. Lake Forest College, AADA.

BRANDO, MARLON: Omaha, NB, Apr. 3, 1924. New School.

BRANDON, CLARK: NYC 1959.

BRANDON, HENRY: Berlin, Ger., June 18, 1912. Stanford.

BRANTLEY, BETSY: Rutherfordton, NC, 1955. London Central Sch. of Drama.

BRAZZI, ROSSANO: Bologna, Italy, Sept. 18, 1916. U. Florence.

BRENNAN, EILEEN: Los Angeles, CA., Sept. 3, 1935. AADA.

BRIAN, DAVID: NYC, Aug. 5, 1914. CCNY.

BRIDGES, BEAU: Los Angeles, Dec. 9, 1941. UCLA.

BRIDGES, JEFF: Los Angeles, Dec. 4, 1949.

BRIDGES, LLOYD: San Leandro, CA, Jan. 15, 1913.

BRISEBOIS, DANIELLE: Brooklyn, June 28, 1969.

BRITT, MAY: (Maybritt Wilkins): Sweden, March 22, 1936.

BRITTANY, MORGAN: (Suzanne Caputo): Los Angeles, 1950.

BRODIE, STEVE (Johnny Stevens): Eldorado, KS, Nov. 25, 1919.

BROLIN, JAMES: Los Angeles, July 18, 1940. UCLA.

BROMFIELD, JOHN (Farron Bromfield): South Bend, IN, June 11, 1922. St. Mary's College.

BRONSON, CHARLES (Buchinsky): Ehrenfield, PA, Nov. 3, 1920.

BROSNAN, PIERCE: Ireland, 1952.

BROWN, BLAIR: Washington, DC, 1948; Pine Manor.

BROWN, BRYAN: Panania, Aust., 1947.

BROWN, GEORG STANFORD: Havana, Cuba, June 24, 1943. AMDA.

BROWN, JAMES: Desdemona, TX, Mar. 22, 1920. Baylor U.

BROWN, JIM: St. Simons Island, NY, Feb. 17, 1935. Syracuse U.

BROWN, TOM: NYC, Jan. 6, 1913. Professional Children's School.

BROWNE, CORAL: Melbourne, Aust., July 23, 1913.

BROWNE, LESLIE: NYC, 1958.

BRYNNER, YUL: Sakhalin Island, Japan, July 11, 1915.

BUCHHOLZ, HORST: Berlin, Ger., Dec. 4, 1933. Ludwig Dramatic School.

BUCKLEY, BETTY: Big Spring, TX., July 3, 1947. TxCU.

BUETEL, JACK: Dallas, TX, Sept. 5, 1917.

BUJOLD, GENEVIEVE: Montreal, Can., July 1, 1942.

BURKE, PAUL: New Orleans, July 21, 1926. Pasadena Playhouse.

BURNETT, CAROL: San Antonio, TX, Apr. 26, 1933. UCLA.

BURNS, CATHERINE: NYC, Sept. 25, 1945. AADA.

BURNS, GEORGE (Nathan Birnbaum): NYC, Jan. 20, 1896.

BURR, RAYMOND: New Westminster, B.C., Can., May 21, 1917. Stanford, U. CAL., Columbia.

BURSTYN, ELLEN (Edna Rae Gillooly): Detroit, MI, Dec. 7, 1932.

BURTON, LeVAR: Los Angeles, CA. Feb. 16, 1958. UCLA.

BUSEY, GARY: Tulsa, OK, 1944.

BUTTONS, RED (Aaron Chwatt): NYC, Feb. 5, 1919.

BUZZI, RUTH: Wequetequock, RI, July 24, 1936. Pasadena Playhouse.

BYGRAVES, MAX: London, Oct. 16, 1922. St. Joseph's School.

BYRNES, EDD: NYC, July 30, 1933. Haaren High.

CAAN, JAMES: Bronx, NY, Mar. 26, 1939.

CABOT, SUSAN: Boston, July 6, 1927.

CAESAR, SID: Yonkers, NY, Sept. 8, 1922.

CAGNEY, JAMES: NYC, July 17, 1899. Columbia.

CAINE, MICHAEL (Maurice Michelwhite): London, Mar. 14, 1933.

CAINE, SHAKIRA (Baksh): Guyana, Feb. 23, 1947. Indian Trust Col.

CALHOUN, RORY (Francis Timothy Durgin): Los Angeles, Aug. 8, 1922.

CALLAN, MICHAEL (Martin Calinieff): Philadelphia, Nov. 22, 1935.

CALVERT, PHYLLIS: London, Feb. 18, 1917. Margaret Morris School.

CALVET, CORRINE (Corrine Dibos): Paris, Apr. 30, 1925. U. Paris.

CAMP, COLLEEN: San Francisco, 1953.

CAMPBELL, GLEN: Delight, AR, Apr. 22, 1935.

CANALE, GIANNA MARIA: Reggio Calabria, Italy, Sept. 12.

CANNON, DYAN (Samille Diane Friesen): Tacoma, WA, Jan. 4, 1935.

CANTU, DOLORES: 1957, San Antonio, TX.

CAPERS, VIRGINIA: Sumter, SC, 1925. Juilliard.

CAPSHAW, KATE: Ft. Worth, TX. 1953. UMo.

CAPUCINE (Germaine Lefebvre): Toulon, France, Jan. 6, 1935.

CARA, IRENE: NYC, Mar. 18, 1958.

CARDINALE, CLAUDIA: Tunis, N. Africa, Apr. 15, 1939. College Paul Cambon.

CAREY, HARRY, JR.: Saugus, CA, May 16, 1921. Black Fox Military Academy.

CAREY, MACDONALD: Sioux City, IA, Mar. 15, 1913. U. of Wisc., U. Iowa.

CAREY, PHILIP: Hackensack, NJ, July 15, 1925. U. Miami.

CARMEN, JULIE: Mt. Vernon, NY, Apr. 4, 1954.

CARMICHAEL, IAN: Hull, Eng., June 18, 1920. Scarborough Col.

CARNE, JUDY (Joyce Botterill): Northampton, Eng., 1939. Bush-Davis Theatre School.

CARNEY, ART: Mt. Vernon, NY, Nov. 4, 1918.

CARON, LESLIE: Paris, July 1, 1931. Nat'l Conservatory, Paris.

CARPENTER, CARLETON: Bennington, VT, July 10, 1926. Northwestern.

| Carleton Carpenter | Nell Carter | Richard Chamberlain | Julie Christie | Stephen Collins | Ellen Corby |

CARR, VIKKI (Florence Cardona): July 19, 1942. San Fernando Col.
CARRADINE, DAVID: Hollywood, Dec. 8, 1936. San Francisco State.
CARRADINE, JOHN: NYC, Feb. 5, 1906.
CARRADINE, KEITH: San Mateo, CA, Aug. 8, 1951. Colo. State U.
CARRADINE, ROBERT: San Mateo, CA, 1954.
CARREL, DANY: Tourane, Indochina, Sept. 20, 1936. Marseilles Cons.
CARRIERE, MATHIEU: West Germany 1950.
CARROLL, DIAHANN (Johnson): NYC, July 17, 1935. NYU.
CARROLL, MADELEINE: West Bromwich, Eng., Feb. 26, 1902. Birmingham U.
CARROLL, PAT: Shreveport, LA, May 5, 1927. Catholic U.
CARSON, JOHN DAVID: 1951, Calif. Valley Col.
CARSON, JOHNNY: Corning, IA, Oct. 23, 1925. U. of Neb.
CARSTEN, PETER (Ransenthaler): Weissenberg, Bavaria, Apr. 30, 1929. Munich Akademie.
CARTER, NELL: Birmingham, AL., Dec. 13.
CASH, ROSALIND: Atlantic City, NJ, Dec. 31, 1938. CCNY.
CASON, BARBARA: Memphis, TN, Nov. 15, 1933. U. Iowa.
CASS, PEGGY (Mary Margaret): Boston, May 21, 1925.
CASSAVETES, JOHN: NYC, Dec. 9, 1929. Colgate College, AADA.
CASSEL, JEAN-PIERRE: Paris, Oct. 27, 1932.
CASSIDY, DAVID: NYC, Apr. 12, 1950.
CASSIDY, JOANNA: Camden, NJ, 1944. Syracuse U.
CASSIDY, SHAUN: Los Angeles, CA., Sept. 27, 1958.
CASTELLANO, RICHARD: Bronx, NY, Sept. 3, 1934.
CAULFIELD, JOAN: Orange, NJ, June 1, 1922. Columbia U.
CAULFIELD, MAXWELL: Glasgow, Scot., Nov. 23, 1959.
CAVANI, LILIANA: Bologna, Italy, Jan. 12, 1937. U. Bologna.
CELI, ADOLFO: Sicily, July 27, 1922. Rome Academy.
CHAKIRIS, GEORGE: Norwood, OH, Sept. 16, 1933.
CHAMBERLAIN, RICHARD: Beverly Hills, CA, March 31, 1935. Pomona.
CHAMPION, MARGE: Los Angeles, Sept. 2, 1925.
CHANNING, CAROL: Seattle, Jan. 21, 1921. Bennington.
CHANNING, STOCKARD (Susan Stockard): NYC, 1944. Radcliffe.

CHAPIN, MILES: NYC, Dec. 6, 1954. HB Studio.
CHAPLIN, GERALDINE: Santa Monica, CA, July 31, 1944. Royal Ballet.
CHAPLIN, SYDNEY: Los Angeles, Mar. 31, 1926. Lawrenceville.
CHARISSE, CYD (Tula Ellice Finklea): Amarillo, TX, Mar. 3, 1922. Hollywood Professional School.
CHASE, CHEVY (Cornelius Crane Chase): NYC, Oct. 8, 1943.
CHER (Cherlin Sarkesian): May 20, 1946, El Centro, CA.
CHIARI, WALTER: Verona, Italy, 1930.
CHRISTIAN, LINDA (Blanca Rosa Welter): Tampico, Mex., Nov. 13, 1923.
CHRISTIE, JULIE: Chukua, Assam, India, Apr. 14, 1941.
CHRISTOPHER, DENNIS (Carelli): Philadelphia, PA, 1955. Temple U.
CHRISTOPHER, JORDAN: Youngstown, OH, Oct. 23, 1940. Kent State.
CILENTO, DIANE: Queensland, Australia, Oct. 5, 1933. AADA.
CLAPTON, ERIC: London, Mar. 30, 1945.
CLARK, DANE: NYC, Feb. 18, 1915. Cornell, Johns Hopkins U.
CLARK, DICK: Mt. Vernon, NY, Nov. 30, 1929. Syracuse U.
CLARK, MAE: Philadelphia, Aug. 16, 1910.
CLARK, PETULA: Epsom, England, Nov. 15, 1932.
CLARK, SUSAN: Sarnid, Ont., Can., Mar. 8, 1940. RADA.
CLAYBURGH, JILL: NYC, Apr. 30, 1944. Sarah Lawrence.
CLERY, CORRINNE: Italy, 1950.
CLOONEY, ROSEMARY: Maysville, KY, May 23, 1928.
CLOSE, GLENN: Greenwich, CT., Mar. 19, 1947. William & Mary Col.
COBURN, JAMES: Laurel, NB, Aug. 31, 1928. LACC.
COCA, IMOGENE: Philadelphia, Nov. 18, 1908.
COCO, JAMES: NYC, Mar. 21, 1929.
CODY, KATHLEEN: Bronx, NY, Oct. 30, 1953.
COLBERT, CLAUDETTE (Lily Chauchoin): Paris, Sept. 15, 1903. Art Students League.
COLE, GEORGE: London, Apr. 22, 1925.
COLEMAN, GARY: Zion, IL., 1968.
COLEMAN, JACK: Easton, PA., 1958. Duke U.

COLLETT, CHRISTOPHER: NYC, Mar. 13, 1968. Strasberg Inst.
COLLINS, JOAN: London, May 21, 1933. Francis Holland School.
COLLINS, STEPHEN: Des Moines, IA, Oct. 1, 1947. Amherst.
COLON, MIRIAM: Ponce, PR., 1945. UPR.
COMER, ANJANETTE: Dawson, TX, Aug. 7, 1942. Baylor, Tex. U.
CONANT, OLIVER: NYC, Nov. 15, 1955. Dalton.
CONAWAY, JEFF: NYC, Oct. 5, 1950. NYC.
CONNERY, SEAN: Edinburgh, Scot., Aug. 25, 1930.
CONNORS, CHUCK (Kevin Joseph Connors): Brooklyn, Apr. 10, 1921. Seton Hall College.
CONNORS, MIKE (Krekor Ohanian): Fresno, CA, Aug. 15, 1925. UCLA.
CONRAD, WILLIAM: Louisville, KY, Sept. 27, 1920.
CONVERSE, FRANK: St. Louis, MO, May 22, 1938. Carnegie Tech.
CONVY, BERT: St. Louis, MO, July 23, 1935. UCLA.
CONWAY, KEVIN: NYC, May 29, 1942.
CONWAY, TIM (Thomas Daniel): Willoughby, OH, Dec. 15, 1933. Bowling Green State.
COOK, ELISHA, JR.: San Francisco, Dec. 26, 1907. St. Albans.
COOPER, BEN: Hartford, CT, Sept. 30, 1932. Columbia U.
COOPER, JACKIE: Los Angeles, Sept. 15, 1921.
CORBETT, GRETCHEN: Portland, OR, Aug. 13, 1947. Carnegie Tech.
CORBY, ELLEN (Hansen): Racine, WI, June 13, 1913.
CORCORAN, DONNA: Quincy, MA, Sept. 29, 1942.
CORD, ALEX (Viespi): Floral Park, NY, Aug. 3, 1931. NYU, Actors Studio.
CORDAY, MARA (Marilyn Watts): Santa Monica, CA, Jan. 3, 1932.
COREY, JEFF: NYC, Aug. 10, 1914. Fagin School.
CORLAN, ANTHONY: Cork City, Ire., May 9, 1947. Birmingham School of Dramatic Arts.
CORLEY, AL: Missouri, 1956. Actors Studio.
CORNTHWAITE, ROBERT: St. Helens, OR. Apr. 28, 1917. USC.
CORRI, ADRIENNE: Glasgow, Scot., Nov. 13, 1933. RADA.
CORTESA, VALENTINA: Milan, Italy, Jan. 1, 1925.
COSBY, BILL: Philadelphia, July 12, 1937. Temple U.
COSTER, NICOLAS: London, Dec. 3, 1934. Neighborhood Playhouse.

| Ben Cross | Blythe Danner | Tony Danza | Ruby Dee | Charles Denner | Colleen Devine |

COTTEN, JOSEPH: Petersburg, VA, May 13, 1905.

COURTENAY, TOM: Hull, Eng., Feb. 25, 1937. RADA.

COURTLAND, JEROME: Knoxville, TN, Dec. 27, 1926.

CRAIG, JAMES (James H. Meador): Nashville, TN, Feb. 4, 1912. Rice Inst.

CRAIG, MICHAEL: India, Jan. 27, 1929.

CRAIN, JEANNE: Barstow, CA, May 25, 1925.

CRAWFORD, BRODERICK: Philadelphia, Dec. 9, 1911.

CREMER, BRUNO: Paris, 1929.

CRENNA, RICHARD: Los Angeles, Nov. 30, 1926. USC.

CRISTAL, LINDA (Victoria Moya): Buenos Aires, Feb. 25, 1934.

CROSBY, HARRY: Los Angeles, CA, Aug. 8, 1958.

CROSBY, KATHRYN GRANT: (see Kathryn Grant)

CROSBY, MARY FRANCES: Calif., Sept. 14, 1959.

CROSS, BEN: London, 1948. RADA.

CROSS, MURPHY (Mary Jane): Laurelton, MD, June 22, 1950.

CROUSE, LINDSAY ANN: NYC, May 12, 1948. Radcliffe.

CROWLEY, PAT: Olyphant, PA, Sept. 17, 1932.

CRUISE, TOM: Syracuse, NY, 1962.

CRYSTAL, BILLY: NYC, 1948.

CULLUM, JOHN: Knoxville, TN, Mar. 2, 1930. U. Tenn.

CULP, ROBERT: Oakland, CA., Aug. 16, 1930. U. Wash.

CULVER, CALVIN: Canandaigua, NY, 1943.

CUMMINGS, CONSTANCE: Seattle, WA, May 15, 1910.

CUMMINGS, QUINN: Hollywood, Aug. 13, 1967.

CUMMINGS, ROBERT: Joplin, MO, June 9, 1910. Carnegie Tech.

CUMMINS, PEGGY: Prestatyn, N. Wales, Dec. 18, 1926. Alexandra School.

CURTIN, JANE: Cambridge, MA; Sept. 6, 1947.

CURTIS, JAMIE LEE: Los Angeles, CA., Nov. 21, 1958.

CURTIS, KEENE: Salt Lake City, UT, Feb. 15, 1925. U. Utah.

CURTIS, TONY (Bernard Schwartz): NYC, June 3, 1924.

CUSACK, CYRIL: Durban, S. Africa, Nov. 26, 1910. Univ. Col.

CUSHING, PETER: Kenley, Surrey, Eng., May 26, 1913.

DAHL, ARLENE: Minneapolis, Aug. 11, 1928. U. Minn.

DALLESANDRO, JOE: Pensacola, FL, Dec. 31, 1948.

DALTON, TIMOTHY: Wales, 1945. RADA.

DALTREY, ROGER: London, Mar. 1, 1945.

DALY, TYNE: NYC, 1947. AMDA.

DAMONE, VIC (Vito Farinola): Brooklyn, June 12, 1928.

D'ANGELO, BEVERLY: Columbus, OH., 1954.

DANIELS, WILLIAM: Bklyn, Mar. 31, 1927. Northwestern.

DANNER, BLYTHE: Philadelphia, PA. Bard Col.

DANO, ROYAL: NYC, Nov. 16, 1922. NYU.

DANSON, TED: Flagstaff, AZ, 1949. Stanford, Carnegie Tech.

DANTE, MICHAEL (Ralph Vitti): Stamford, CT, 1935. U. Miami.

DANTON, RAY: NYC, Sept. 19, 1931. Carnegie Tech.

DANZA, TONY: Brooklyn, NY., 1951. UDubuque.

DARBY, KIM: (Deborah Zerby): North Hollywood, CA, July 8, 1948.

DARCEL, DENISE (Denise Billecard): Paris, Sept. 8, 1925. U. Dijon.

DARREN, JAMES: Philadelphia, June 8, 1936. Stella Adler School.

DARRIEUX, DANIELLE: Bordeaux, France, May 1, 1917. Lycee LaTour.

DA SILVA, HOWARD: Cleveland, OH, May 4, 1909. Carnegie Tech.

DAVIDSON, JOHN: Pittsburgh, Dec. 13, 1941. Denison U.

DAVIES, RUPERT: Liverpool, Eng., 1916.

DAVIS, BETTE: Lowell, MA, Apr. 5, 1908. John Murray Anderson Dramatic School.

DAVIS, BRAD: Fla., 1950. AADA.

DAVIS, MAC: Lubbock, TX, 1942.

DAVIS, NANCY (Anne Frances Robbins): NYC July 8, 1921. Smith Col.

DAVIS, OSSIE: Cogdell, GA, Dec. 18, 1917. Howard U.

DAVIS, SAMMY, JR.: NYC, Dec. 8, 1925.

DAVIS, SKEETER (Mary Frances Penick): Dry Ridge, KY. Dec. 30, 1931.

DAY, DENNIS (Eugene Dennis McNulty): NYC, May 21, 1917. Manhattan College.

DAY, DORIS (Doris Kappelhoff): Cincinnati, Apr. 3, 1924.

DAY, LARAINE (Johnson): Roosevelt, UT, Oct. 13, 1917.

DAYAN, ASSEF: Israel, 1945. U. Jerusalem.

DEAN, JIMMY: Plainview, TX, Aug. 10, 1928.

DeCARLO, YVONNE (Peggy Yvonne Middleton): Vancouver, B.C., Can., Sept. 1, 1922. Vancouver School of Drama.

DEE, FRANCES: Los Angeles, Nov. 26, 1907. Chicago U.

DEE, JOEY (Joseph Di Nicola): Passaic, NJ, June 11, 1940. Patterson State College.

DEE, RUBY: Cleveland, OH, Oct. 27, 1924. Hunter Col.

DEE, SANDRA (Alexandra Zuck): Bayonne, NJ, Apr. 23, 1942.

DeFORE, DON: Cedar Rapids, IA, Aug. 25, 1917. U. Iowa.

DeHAVEN, GLORIA: Los Angeles, July 23, 1923.

DeHAVILLAND, OLIVIA: Tokyo, Japan, July 1, 1916. Notre Dame Convent School.

DELL, GABRIEL: Barbados, BWI, Oct. 7, 1930.

DELON, ALAIN: Sceaux, Fr., Nov. 8, 1935.

DELORME, DANIELE: Paris, Oct. 9, 1927. Sorbonne.

DeLUISE, DOM: Brooklyn, Aug. 1, 1933. Tufts Col.

DEMONGEOT, MYLENE: Nice, France, Sept. 29, 1938.

DeMORNAY, REBECCA: 1963.

DENEUVE, CATHERINE: Paris, Oct. 22, 1943.

DeNIRO, ROBERT: NYC, Aug. 17, 1943, Stella Adler.

DENISON, MICHAEL: Doncaster, York, Eng., Nov. 1, 1915. Oxford.

DENNER, CHARLES: Tarnow, Poland, May 29, 1926.

DENNIS, SANDY: Hastings, NB, Apr. 27, 1937. Actors Studio.

DEPARDIEU, GERARD: Chateauroux, Fr., Dec. 27, 1948.

DEREK, BO (Mary Cathleen Collins): Long Beach, CA, Oct. 1956.

DEREK, JOHN: Hollywood, Aug. 12, 1926.

DERN, BRUCE: Chicago, June 4, 1936. U PA.

DeSALVO, ANNE: Philadelphia, PA., Apr. 3.

DEVINE, COLLEEN: San Gabriel, CA, June 22, 1960.

DEWHURST, COLLEEN: Montreal June 3, 1926. Lawrence U.

DEXTER, ANTHONY (Walter Reinhold Alfred Fleischmann): Talmadge, NB, Jan. 19, 1919. U. Iowa.

DeYOUNG, CLIFF: Los Angeles, CA, Feb. 12, 1945. Cal State.

DHIEGH, KHIGH: New Jersey, 1910.

DIAMOND, NEIL: NYC, Jan. 24, 1941. NYU.

DICKINSON, ANGIE: Kulm, ND, Sept. 30, 1932. Glendale College.

| Troy Donahue | Patty Duke | Erik Estrada | Linda Evans | James Farentino | Conchata Ferrell |

DIETRICH, MARLENE (Maria Magdalene von Losch): Berlin, Ger., Dec. 27, 1901. Berlin Music Academy.

DILLER, PHYLLIS: Lima, OH, July 17, 1917. Bluffton College.

DILLMAN, BRADFORD: San Francisco, Apr. 14, 1930. Yale.

DILLON, MATT: Larchmont, NY., Feb. 18, 1964. AADA.

DILLON, MELINDA: Hope, AR, Oct. 13, 1939. Goodman Theatre School.

DIVINE (Glenn) Baltimore, MD, 1946.

DOBSON, TAMARA: Baltimore, MD, 1947. MD. Inst. of Art.

DOMERGUE, FAITH: New Orleans, June 16, 1925.

DONAHUE, TROY (Merle Johnson): NYC, Jan. 27, 1937. Columbia U.

DONAT, PETER: Nova Scotia, Jan. 20, 1928. Yale.

DONNELL, JEFF (Jean Donnell): South Windham, ME, July 10, 1921. Yale Drama School.

DOOHAN, JAMES: Vancouver, BC, Mar. 3, Neighborhood Playhouse.

DOOLEY, PAUL: Parkersburg, WV, Feb. 22, 1928. U. WV.

DOUGLAS, DONNA (Dorothy Bourgeois): Baton Rouge, LA, 1935.

DOUGLAS, KIRK (Issur Danielovitch): Amsterdam, NY, Dec. 9, 1916. St. Lawrence U.

DOUGLAS, MICHAEL: New Brunswick, NJ, Sept. 25, 1944. U. Cal.

DOUGLASS, ROBYN: Japan, 1953.

DOURIF, BRAD: Huntington, WV, Mar. 18, 1950. Marshall U.

DOVE, BILLIE: NYC, May 14, 1904.

DOWN, LESLEY-ANN: London, Mar. 17, 1954.

DRAKE, BETSY: Paris, Sept. 11, 1923.

DRAKE, CHARLES (Charles Rupert): NYC, Oct. 2, 1914. Nichols College.

DREW, ELLEN (formerly Terry Ray): Kansas City, MO, Nov. 23, 1915.

DREYFUSS, RICHARD: Brooklyn, NY, Oct. 19, 1947.

DRIVAS, ROBERT: Chicago, Oct. 7, 1938. U. Chi.

DRU, JOANNE (Joanne LaCock): Logan, WV, Jan. 31, 1923. John Robert Powers School.

DUBBINS, DON: Brooklyn, NY, June 28.

DUFF, HOWARD: Bremerton, WA, Nov. 24, 1917.

DUFFY, PATRICK: Montana, 1949. U. Wash.

DUKE, PATTY: NYC, Dec. 14, 1946.

DULLEA, KEIR: Cleveland, NJ, May 30, 1936. Neighborhood Playhouse, SF State Col.

DUNAWAY, FAYE: Bascom, FL, Jan. 14, 1941. Fla. U.

DUNCAN, SANDY: Henderson, TX, Feb. 20, 1946. Len Morris Col.

DUNNE, IRENE: Louisville, KY, Dec. 20, 1898. Chicago College of Music.

DUNNOCK, MILDRED: Baltimore, Jan. 25, 1900. Johns Hopkins and Columbia U.

DUPEREY, ANNY: Paris, 1947.

DURBIN, DEANNA (Edna): Winnipeg, Can., Dec. 4, 1921.

DURNING, CHARLES: Highland Falls, NY, Feb. 28, 1933. NYU.

DUSSOLLIER, ANDRE: Annecy, France, Feb. 17, 1946.

DUVALL, ROBERT: San Diego, CA, 1930. Principia Col.

DUVALL, SHELLEY: Houston, TX, July 7, 1949.

EASTON, ROBERT: Milwaukee, Nov. 23, 1930. U. Texas.

EASTWOOD, CLINT: San Francisco, May 31, 1930. LACC.

EATON, SHIRLEY: London, 1937. Aida Foster School.

EBSEN, BUDDY (Christian, Jr.): Belleville, IL, Apr. 2, 1910. U. Fla.

ECKEMYR, AGNETA: Karlsborg, Swed., July 2. Actors Studio.

EDEN, BARBARA (Moorhead): Tucson, AZ, Aug. 23, 1934.

EDWARDS, VINCE: NYC, July 9, 1928. AADA.

EGAN, RICHARD: San Francisco, July 29, 1923. Stanford U.

EGGAR, SAMANTHA: London, Mar. 5, 1939.

EICHHORN, LISA: Reading, PA, 1952. Queens Ont. U. RADA.

EILBER, JANET: Detroit, MI, July 27, 1951. Juilliard.

EKBERG, ANITA: Malmo, Sweden, Sept. 29, 1931.

EKLAND, BRITT: Stockholm, Swed., 1942.

ELIZONDO, HECTOR: NYC, Dec. 22, 1936.

ELLIOTT, DENHOLM: London, May 31, 1922. Malvern College.

ELLIOTT, SAM: Sacramento, CA, 1944. U. Ore.

ELY, RON (Ronald Pierce): Hereford, TX, June 21, 1938.

ERDMAN, RICHARD: Enid, OK, June 1, 1925.

ERICKSON, LEIF: Alameda, CA, Oct. 27, 1911. U. Calif.

ERICSON, JOHN: Dusseldorf, Ger., Sept. 25, 1926. AADA.

ESMOND, CARL: Vienna, June 14, 1906. U. Vienna.

ESTRADA, ERIK: NYC, Mar. 16, 1949.

EVANS, DALE (Francis Smith): Uvalde, TX, Oct. 31, 1912.

EVANS, GENE: Holbrook, AZ, July 11, 1922.

EVANS, LINDA (Evanstad): Hartford, CT., Nov. 18, 1942.

EVANS, MAURICE: Dorchester, Eng., June 3, 1901.

EVERETT, CHAD (Ray Cramton): South Bend, IN, June 11, 1936.

EVERETT, RUPERT: Norfolk, Eng., 1959.

EWELL, TOM (Yewell Tompkins): Owensboro, KY, Apr. 29, 1909. U. Wisc.

FABARES, SHELLEY: Los Angeles, Jan. 19, 1944.

FABIAN (Fabian Forte): Philadelphia, Feb. 6, 1940.

FABRAY, NANETTE (Ruby Nanette Fabares): San Diego, Oct. 27, 1920.

FAIRBANKS, DOUGLAS JR.: NYC, Dec. 9, 1907. Collegiate School.

FAIRCHILD, MORGAN: (Patsy McClenny) Dallas, TX., 1950. UCLA.

FALK, PETER: NYC, Sept. 16, 1927. New School.

FARENTINO, JAMES: Brooklyn, Feb. 24, 1938. AADA.

FARINA, SANDY (Sandra Feldman): Newark, NJ, 1955.

FARR, DEREK: London, Feb. 7, 1912.

FARR, FELICIA: Westchester, NY, Oct. 4, 1932. Penn State Col.

FARRELL, CHARLES: Onset Bay, MA, Aug. 9, 1901. Boston U.

FARROW, MIA: Los Angeles, Feb. 9, 1945.

FAULKNER, GRAHAM: London, Sept. 26, 1947. Webber-Douglas.

FAWCETT, FARRAH: Corpus Christie, TX. Feb. 2, 1947. TexU.

FAYE, ALICE (Ann Leppert): NYC, May 5, 1912.

FEINSTEIN, ALAN: NYC, Sept. 8, 1941.

FELDON, BARBARA (Hall): Pittsburgh, Mar. 12, 1941. Carnegie Tech.

FELLOWS, EDITH: Boston, May 20, 1923.

FERRELL, CONCHATA: Charleston, WV, Mar. 28, 1943. Marshall U.

FERRER, JOSE: Santurce, P.R., Jan. 8, 1909. Princeton U.

FERRER, MEL: Elberon, NJ, Aug. 25, 1917. Princeton U.

| Rochelle Firestone | Peter Fonda | Sheila Frazier | Boyd Gaines | Betty Garrett | Paul Michael Glaser |

FERRIS, BARBARA: London, 1943.

FERZETTI, GABRIELE: Italy, 1927. Rome Acad. of Drama.

FIELD, SALLY: Pasadena, CA, Nov. 6, 1946.

FIGUEROA, RUBEN: NYC 1958.

FINNEY, ALBERT: Salford, Lancashire, Eng., May 9, 1936. RADA.

FIRESTONE, ROCHELLE: Kansas City, MO., June 14, 1949. NYU.

FIRTH, PETER: Bradford, Eng., Oct. 27, 1953.

FISHER, CARRIE: Los Angeles, CA, Oct. 21, 1956. London Central School of Drama.

FISHER, EDDIE: Philadelphia, Aug. 10, 1928.

FITZGERALD, GERALDINE: Dublin, Ire., Nov. 24, 1914. Dublin Art School.

FLANNERY, SUSAN: Jersey City, NJ, July 31, 1943.

FLAVIN, JAMES: Portland, ME, May 14, 1906. West Point.

FLEMING, RHONDA (Marilyn Louis): Los Angeles, Aug. 10, 1922.

FLEMYNG, ROBERT: Liverpool, Eng., Jan. 3, 1912. Haileybury Col.

FLETCHER, LOUISE: Birmingham, AL, July 1934.

FOCH, NINA: Leyden, Holland, Apr. 20, 1924.

FOLDI, ERZSEBET: Queens, NY, 1967.

FONDA, JANE: NYC, Dec. 21, 1937. Vassar.

FONDA, PETER: NYC, Feb. 23, 1939. U. Omaha.

FONTAINE, JOAN: Tokyo, Japan, Oct. 22, 1917.

FORD, GLENN (Gwyllyn Samuel Newton Ford): Quebec, Can., May 1, 1916.

FORD, HARRISON: Chicago, IL, July 13, 1942. Ripon Col.

FOREST, MARK (Lou Degni): Brooklyn, Jan. 1933.

FORREST, STEVE: Huntsville, TX, Sept. 29, 1924. UCLA.

FORSLUND, CONNIE: San Diego, CA, June 19, 1950, NYU.

FORSTER, ROBERT (Foster, Jr.): Rochester, NY, July 13, 1941. Rochester U.

FORSYTHE, JOHN: Penn's Grove, NJ, Jan. 29, 1918.

FOSTER, JODIE (Ariane Munker): Bronx, NY, Nov. 19, 1962. Yale.

FOX, EDWARD: London, 1937, RADA.

FOX, JAMES: London, 1939.

FOXWORTH, ROBERT: Houston, TX, Nov. 1, 1941. Carnegie Tech.

FOXX, REDD: St. Louis, MO, Dec. 9, 1922.

FRANCIOSA, ANTHONY (Papaleo): NYC, Oct. 25, 1928.

FRANCIS, ANNE: Ossining, NY, Sept. 16, 1932.

FRANCIS, ARLENE (Arlene Kazanjian): Boston, Oct. 20, 1908. Finch School.

FRANCIS, CONNIE (Constance Franconero): Newark, NJ, Dec. 12, 1938.

FRANCISCUS, JAMES: Clayton, MO, Jan. 31, 1934. Yale.

FRANCKS, DON: Vancouver, Can., Feb. 28, 1932.

FRANK, JEFFREY: Jackson Heights, NY, 1965.

FRANKLIN, PAMELA: Tokyo, Feb. 4, 1950.

FRANZ, ARTHUR: Perth Amboy, NJ, Feb. 29, 1920. Blue Ridge College.

FRAZIER, SHEILA: NYC, 1949.

FREEMAN, AL, JR.: San Antonio, TX, 1934. CCLA.

FREEMAN, MONA: Baltimore, MD, June 9, 1926.

FREY, LEONARD: Brooklyn, Sept. 4, 1938. Neighborhood Playhouse.

FULLER, PENNY: Durham, NC, 1940. Northwestern U.

FURNEAUX, YVONNE: Lille, France, 1928. Oxford U.

GABEL, MARTIN: Philadelphia, June 19, 1912. AADA.

GABOR, EVA: Budapest, Hungary, Feb. 11, 1920.

GABOR, ZSA ZSA (Sari Gabor): Budapest, Hungary, Feb. 6, 1918.

GAINES, BOYD: Atlanta, GA., May 11, 1953. Juilliard.

GALLAGHER, PETER: Armonk, NY, 1956, Tufts U.

GAM, RITA: Pittsburgh, PA, Apr. 2, 1928.

GARBER, VICTOR: Montreal, Can., Mar. 16, 1949.

GARBO, GRETA (Greta Gustafson): Stockholm, Sweden, Sept. 18, 1905.

GARDENIA, VINCENT: Naples, Italy, Jan. 7, 1922.

GARDNER, AVA: Smithfield, NC, Dec. 24, 1922. Atlantic Christian College.

GARFIELD, ALLEN: Newark, NJ, Nov. 22, 1939. Actors Studio.

GARLAND, BEVERLY: Santa Cruz, CA, Oct. 17, 1930. Glendale Col.

GARNER, JAMES (James Baumgarner): Norman, OK, Apr. 7, 1928. Okla. U.

GARR, TERI: Lakewood, OH, 1952.

GARRETT, BETTY: St. Joseph, MO, May 23, 1919. Annie Wright Seminary.

GARRISON, SEAN: NYC, Oct. 19, 1937.

GARSON, GREER: Ireland, Sept. 29, 1906.

GASSMAN, VITTORIO: Genoa, Italy, Sept. 1, 1922. Rome Academy of Dramatic Art.

GAVIN, JOHN: Los Angeles, Apr. 8, 1935. Stanford U.

GAYNOR, MITZI (Francesca Marlene Von Gerber): Chicago, Sept. 4, 1930.

GAZZARA, BEN: NYC, Aug. 28, 1930. Actors Studio.

GEARY, ANTHONY: Utah, 1948.

GEESON, JUDY: Arundel, Eng., Sept. 10, 1948. Corona.

GEORGE, SUSAN: West London, Eng. July 26, 1950.

GERARD, GIL: Little Rock, AR, 1940.

GERE, RICHARD: Philadelphia, PA, Aug. 29, 1949. U. Mass.

GERROLL, DANIEL: London, Oct. 16, 1951. Central.

GHOLSON, JULIE: Birmingham, AL, June 4, 1958.

GHOSTLEY, ALICE: Eve, MO, Aug. 14, 1926. Okla U.

GIANNINI, CHERYL: Monessen, PA., June 15.

GIANNINI, GIANCARLO: Spezia, Italy, Aug. 1, 1942. Rome Acad. of Drama.

GIBSON, MEL: Oneonta, NY., Jan. 1951. NIDA.

GIELGUD, JOHN: London, Apr. 14, 1904. RADA.

GILFORD, JACK: NYC, July 25.

GILLIS, ANNE (Alma O'Connor): Little Rock, AR, Feb. 12, 1927.

GILLMORE, MARGALO: London, May 31, 1897. AADA.

GILMORE, VIRGINIA (Sherman Poole): Del Monte, CA, July 26, 1919. U. Calif.

GINGOLD, HERMIONE: London, Dec. 9, 1897.

GIROLAMI, STEFANIA: Rome, Italy, 1963.

GISH, LILLIAN: Springfield, OH, Oct. 14, 1896.

GLASER, PAUL MICHAEL: Boston, MA, 1943. Boston U.

GLASS, RON: Evansville, IN, 1946.

GLEASON, JACKIE: Brooklyn, Feb. 26, 1916.

GLENN, SCOTT: Pittsburgh, PA, Jan. 26, 1942; William and Mary Col.

GLOVER, JOHN: Kingston, NY, Aug. 7, 1944.

GODDARD, PAULETTE (Levy): Great Neck, NY, June 3, 1911.

GOLDBLUM, JEFF: Pittsburgh, PA, Oct. 22, 1952. Neighborhood Playhouse.

GOLDEN, ANNIE: NYC, 1952.

Dody Goodman	Peter Graves	Lee Grant	Dorian Harewood	Eileen Heckart	John Heard

GONZALES-GONZALEZ, PEDRO: Aguilares, TX, Dec. 21, 1926.

GOODMAN, DODY: Columbus, OH, Oct. 28, 1915.

GORDON, GALE (Aldrich): NYC, Feb. 2, 1906.

GORDON, KEITH: NYC, Feb. 3, 1961.

GORDON, RUTH: (Jones): Wollaston, MA, Oct. 30, 1896. AADA.

GORING, MARIUS: Newport Isle of Wight, 1912. Cambridge, Old Vic.

GORMAN, CLIFF: Jamaica, NY, Oct. 13, 1936. NYU.

GORSHIN, FRANK: Apr. 5, 1933.

GORTNER, MARJOE: Long Beach, CA, 1944.

GOSSETT, LOUIS: Brooklyn, May 27, 1936. NYU.

GOULD, ELLIOTT (Goldstein): Brooklyn, Aug. 29, 1938. Columbia U.

GOULD, HAROLD: Schenectady, NY, Dec. 10, 1923. Cornell.

GOULET, ROBERT: Lawrence, MA, Nov. 26, 1933. Edmonton.

GRANGER, FARLEY: San Jose, CA, July 1, 1925.

GRANGER, STEWART (James Stewart): London, May 6, 1913. Webber-Douglas School of Acting.

GRANT, CARY (Archibald Alexander Leach): Bristol, Eng., Jan. 18, 1904.

GRANT, DAVID MARSHALL: Westport, CT, 1955. Yale.

GRANT, KATHRYN (Olive Grandstaff): Houston, TX, Nov. 25, 1933. UCLA.

GRANT, LEE: NYC, Oct. 31, 1930. Juilliard.

GRANVILLE, BONITA: NYC, Feb. 2, 1923.

GRAVES, PETER (Aurness): Minneapolis, Mar. 18, 1926. U. Minn.

GRAY, CHARLES: Bournemouth, Eng., 1928.

GRAY, COLEEN (Doris Jensen): Staplehurst, NB, Oct. 23, 1922. Hamline U.

GRAY, LINDA: Santa Monica, CA; Sept. 12, 1940.

GRAYSON, KATHRYN (Zelma Hedrick): Winston-Salem, NC, Feb. 9, 1922.

GREENE, ELLEN: NYC, Feb. 22, Ryder Col.

GREENE, LORNE: Ottawa, CAN., Feb. 12, 1915. Queens U.

GREENE, RICHARD: Plymouth, Eng., Aug. 25, 1914. Cardinal Vaughn School.

GREENWOOD, * JOAN: London, Mar. 4, 1919. RADA.

GREER, JANE: Washington, DC, Sept. 9, 1924.

GREER, MICHAEL: Galesburg, IL, Apr. 20, 1943.

GREGORY, MARK: Rome, Italy. 1965.

GREY, JOEL (Katz): Cleveland, OH, Apr. 11, 1932.

GREY, VIRGINIA: Los Angeles, Mar. 22, 1917.

GRIEM, HELMUT: Hamburg, Ger. U. Hamburg.

GRIFFITH, ANDY: Mt. Airy, NC, June 1, 1926. UNC.

GRIFFITH, MELANIE: NYC, Aug. 9, 1957 Pierce Col.

GRIMES, GARY: San Francisco, June 2, 1955.

GRIMES, TAMMY: Lynn, MA, Jan. 30, 1934. Stephens Col.

GRIZZARD, GEORGE: Roanoke Rapids, NC, Apr. 1, 1928. UNC.

GRODIN, CHARLES: Pittsburgh, PA, Apr. 21, 1935.

GROH, DAVID: NYC, May 21, 1939. Brown U., LAMDA.

GUARDINO, HARRY: Brooklyn, Dec. 23, 1925. Haaren High.

GUINNESS, ALEX: London, Apr. 2, 1914. Pembroke Lodge School.

GUNN, MOSES: St. Louis, MO, Oct. 2, 1929. Tenn. State U.

GUTTENBERG, STEVEN: Brooklyn, NY, Aug. 1958. UCLA.

GWILLIM, DAVID: Plymouth, Eng., Dec. 15, 1948. RADA.

HACKETT, BUDDY (Leonard Hacker): Brooklyn, Aug. 31, 1924.

HACKMAN, GENE: San Bernardino, CA, Jan. 30, 1931.

HADDON, DALE: Montreal, CAN., May 26, 1949. Neighborhood Playhouse.

HAGMAN, LARRY (Hageman): Weatherford, TX., Sept. 21, 1931. Bard.

HALE, BARBARA: DeKalb, IL, Apr. 18, 1922. Chicago Academy of Fine Arts.

HALEY, JACKIE EARLE: Northridge, CA, 1963.

HALL, ALBERT: Boothton, AL, Nov. 10, 1937. Columbia.

HALL, ANTHONY MICHAEL: NYC, 1968.

HAMILL, MARK: Oakland, CA, Sept. 25, 1952. LACC.

HAMILTON, GEORGE: Memphis, TN, Aug. 12, 1939. Hackley.

HAMILTON, MARGARET: Cleveland, OH, Dec. 9, 1902. Hathaway-Brown School.

HAMLIN, HARRY: Pasadena, CA, Oct. 30, 1951. Yale.

HAMPSHIRE, SUSAN: London, May 12, 1941.

HANKS, TOM: Oakland, CA., 1957.

HANNAH, DARYL: Chicago, IL., 1960, UCLA.

HARDIN, TY (Orison Whipple Hungerford II): NYC, June 1, 1930.

HAREWOOD, DORIAN: Dayton, OH, Aug. 6. U. Cinn.

HARMON, MARK: Los Angeles, CA, 1951; UCLA.

HARPER, VALERIE: Suffern, NY, Aug. 22, 1940.

HARRINGTON, PAT: NYC, Aug. 13, 1929. Fordham U.

HARRIS, BARBARA (Sandra Markowitz): Evanston, IL, 1937.

HARRIS, ED: Tenafly, NJ, Nov. 28, 1950. Col.

HARRIS, JULIE: Grosse Point, MI, Dec. 2, 1925. Yale Drama School.

HARRIS, RICHARD: Limerick, Ire., Oct. 1, 1930. London Acad.

HARRIS, ROSEMARY: Ashby, Eng., Sept. 19, 1930. RADA.

HARRISON, GREG: Catalina Island, CA, 1950; Actors Studio.

HARRISON, NOEL: London, Jan. 29, 1936.

HARRISON, REX: Huyton, Cheshire, Eng., Mar. 5, 1908.

HARROLD, KATHRYN: Tazewell, VA. 1950. Mills Col.

HARTMAN, DAVID: Pawtucket, RI, May 19, 1935. Duke U.

HARTMAN, ELIZABETH: Youngstown, OH, Dec. 23, 1941. Carnegie Tech.

HASSETT, MARILYN: Los Angeles, CA, 1949.

HAUER, RUTGER: Amsterdam, Hol. 1944.

HAVER, JUNE: Rock Island, IL, June 10, 1926.

HAWN, GOLDIE: Washington, DC, Nov. 21, 1945.

HAYDEN, LINDA: Stanmore, Eng. Aida Foster School.

HAYDEN, STERLING (John Hamilton): Montclair, NJ, March 26, 1916.

HAYES, HELEN: (Helen Brown): Washington, DC, Oct. 10, 1900. Sacred Heart Convent.

HAYS, ROBERT: Bethesda, MD., 1948; SD State Col.

HAYWORTH, RITA: (Margarita Cansino): NYC, Oct. 17, 1918.

HEARD, JOHN: Washington, DC, Mar. 7, 1946. Clark U.

HEATHERTON, JOEY: NYC, Sept. 14, 1944.

HECKART, EILEEN: Columbus, OH, Mar. 29, 1919. Ohio State U.

HEDISON, DAVID: Providence, RI, May 20, 1929. Brown U.

HEGYES, ROBERT: NJ, May 7, 1951.

HEMINGWAY, MARIEL: Nov. 22, 1961.

HEMMINGS, DAVID: Guilford, Eng. Nov. 18, 1941.

HENDERSON, MARCIA: Andover, MA, July 22, 1932. AADA.

HENDRY, GLORIA: Jacksonville, FL. 1949.

HENNER, MARILU: Chicago, IL. Apr. 4, 1952.

Celeste Holm	Robert Hooks	Kim Hunter	Zeljko Ivanek	Glynis Johns	Page Johnson

HENREID, PAUL: Trieste, Jan. 10, 1908.

HENRY, BUCK (Zuckerman): NYC, 1931. Dartmouth.

HENRY, JUSTIN: Rye, NY, 1971.

HEPBURN, AUDREY: Brussels, Belgium, May 4, 1929.

HEPBURN, KATHARINE: Hartford, CT, Nov. 8, 1907. Bryn Mawr.

HERRMANN, EDWARD: Washington, DC, July 21, 1943. Bucknell, LAMDA.

HERSHEY, BARBARA: see Seagull, Barbara Hershey.

HESTON, CHARLTON: Evanston, IL, Oct. 4, 1922. Northwestern U.

HEWITT, MARTIN: Claremont, CA, 1960; AADA.

HEYWOOD, ANNE (Violet Pretty): Birmingham, Eng., Dec. 11, 1932.

HICKMAN, DARRYL: Hollywood, CA, July 28, 1930. Loyola U.

HICKMAN, DWAYNE: Los Angeles, May 18, 1934. Loyola U.

HILL, ARTHUR: Saskatchewan, CAN., Aug. 1, 1922. U. Brit. Col.

HILL, STEVEN: Seattle, WA, Feb. 24, 1922. U. Wash.

HILL, TERENCE (Mario Girotti): Venice, Italy, Mar. 29, 1941. U. Rome.

HILLER, WENDY: Bramhall, Cheshire, Eng., Aug. 15, 1912. Winceby House School.

HILLIARD, HARRIET: (See Harriet Hilliard Nelson.)

HINGLE, PAT: Denver, CO, July 19, 1923. Tex. U.

HIRSCH, JUDD: NYC, Mar. 15, 1935. AADA.

HODGE, PATRICIA: Lincolnshire, Eng., 1946. LAMDA.

HOFFMAN, DUSTIN: Los Angeles, Aug. 8, 1937. Pasadena Playhouse.

HOLBROOK, HAL (Harold): Cleveland, OH, Feb. 17, 1925. Denison.

HOLLIMAN, EARL: Tennesas Swamp, Delhi, LA, Sept. 11, 1928. UCLA.

HOLM, CELESTE: NYC, Apr. 29, 1919.

HOMEIER, SKIP (George Vincent Homeier): Chicago, Oct. 5, 1930. UCLA.

HOOKS, ROBERT: Washington, DC, Apr. 18, 1937. Temple.

HOPE, BOB: London, May 26, 1903.

HOPPER, DENNIS: Dodge City, KS, May 17, 1936.

HORNE, LENA: Brooklyn, June 30, 1917.

HORTON, ROBERT: Los Angeles, July 29, 1924. UCLA.

HOUGHTON, KATHARINE: Hartford, CT, Mar. 10, 1945. Sarah Lawrence.

HOUSEMAN, JOHN: Bucharest, Sept. 22, 1902.

HOUSER, JERRY: Los Angeles, July 14, 1952. Valley Jr. Col.

HOUSTON, DONALD: Tonypandy, Wales, 1924.

HOVEY, TIM: Los Angeles, June 19, 1945.

HOWARD, KEN: El Centro, CA, Mar. 28, 1944. Yale.

HOWARD, RON: Duncan, OK, Mar. 1, 1954. USC.

HOWARD, RONALD: Norwood, Eng., Apr. 7, 1918. Jesus College.

HOWARD, TREVOR: Kent, Eng., Sept. 29, 1916. RADA.

HOWELLS, URSULA: London, Sept. 17, 1922.

HOWES, SALLY ANN: London, July 20, 1930.

HUDDLESTON, MICHAEL: Roanoke, VA., AADA.

HUDSON, ROCK (Roy Scherer Fitzgerald): Winnetka, IL, Nov. 17, 1924.

HUGHES, BARNARD: Bedford Hills, NY, July 16, 1915. Manhattan Col.

HUGHES, KATHLEEN (Betty von Gerkan): Hollywood, CA, Nov. 14, 1928. UCLA.

HULCE, THOMAS: Plymouth, MI, Dec. 6, 1953. N.C.Sch. of Arts.

HUNNICUT, GAYLE: Ft. Worth, TX, Feb. 6, 1943. UCLA.

HUNT, LINDA: Morristown, NJ, Apr. 2, 1945. Goodman Theatre.

HUNT, MARSHA: Chicago, Oct. 17, 1917.

HUNTER, KIM (Janet Cole): Detroit, Nov. 12, 1922.

HUNTER, TAB (Arthur Gelien) NYC, July 11, 1931.

HUPPERT, ISABELLE: Paris, Fr., Mar. 16, 1955.

HURT, MARY BETH (Supinger): Marshalltown, IA., 1948. NYU.

HURT, WILLIAM: Washington, D.C., Mar. 20, 1950. Tufts, Juilliard.

HUSSEY, RUTH: Providence, RI, Oct. 30, 1917. U. Mich.

HUSTON, JOHN: Nevada, MO, Aug. 5, 1906.

HUTTON, BETTY (Betty Thornberg): Battle Creek, MI, Feb. 26, 1921.

HUTTON, LAUREN (Mary): Charleston, SC, Nov. 17, 1943. Newcomb Col.

HUTTON, ROBERT (Winne): Kingston, NY, June 11, 1920. Blair Academy.

HUTTON, TIMOTHY: Malibu, CA, Aug. 16, 1960.

HYDE-WHITE, WILFRID: Gloucestershire, Eng., May 13, 1903. RADA.

HYER, MARTHA: Fort Worth, TX, Aug. 10, 1924. Northwestern U.

INGELS, MARTY: Brooklyn, NY, Mar. 9, 1936.

IRELAND, JOHN: Vancouver, B.C., CAN., Jan. 30, 1914.

IRONS, JEREMY: Cowes, Eng. Sept. 19, 1948. Old Vic.

IVANEK, ZELJKO: Lujubljana, Yugo., Aug. 15, 1957. Yale, LAMDA.

IVES, BURL: Hunt Township, IL, June 14, 1909. Charleston ILL. Teachers College.

JACKSON, ANNE: Alleghany, PA, Sept. 3, 1926. Neighborhood Playhouse.

JACKSON, GLENDA: Hoylake, Cheshire, Eng., May 9, 1936. RADA.

JACKSON, KATE: Birmingham, AL. Oct. 29, 1948. AADA.

JACKSON, MICHAEL: Gary, Ind., Aug. 29, 1958.

JACOBI, DEREK: Leytonstone, London, Eng. Oct. 22, 1938. Cambridge.

JACOBI, LOU: Toronto, CAN., Dec. 28, 1913.

JACOBS, LAWRENCE-HILTON: Virgin Islands, 1954.

JACOBY, SCOTT: Chicago, Nov. 19, 1956.

JAECKEL, RICHARD: Long Beach, NY, Oct. 10, 1926.

JAGGER, DEAN: Lima, OH, Nov. 7, 1903. Wabash College.

JAGGER, MICK: July 26, 1943.

JAMES, CLIFTON: NYC, May 29, 1921. Ore. U.

JARMAN, CLAUDE, JR.: Nashville, TN, Sept. 27, 1934.

JASON, RICK: NYC, May 21, 1926. AADA.

JEAN, GLORIA (Gloria Jean Schoonover): Buffalo, NY, Apr. 14, 1927.

JEFFREYS, ANNE (Carmichael): Goldsboro, NC, Jan. 26, 1923. Anderson College.

JEFFRIES, LIONEL: London, 1927, RADA.

JERGENS, ADELE: Brooklyn, Nov. 26, 1922.

JETT, ROGER (Baker): Cumberland, MD., Oct. 2, 1946. AADA.

JOHN, ELTON: (Reginald Dwight) Middlesex, Eng., Mar. 25, 1947. RAM.

JOHNS, GLYNIS: Durban, S. Africa, Oct. 5, 1923.

JOHNSON, CELIA: Richmond, Surrey, Eng., Dec. 18, 1908. RADA.

JOHNSON, PAGE: Welch, WV, Aug. 25, 1930. Ithaca.

JOHNSON, RAFER: Hillsboro, TX, Aug. 18, 1935. UCLA.

JOHNSON, RICHARD: Essex, Eng., 1927. RADA.

Katy Jurado **William Katt** **Lilia Kedrova** **Aron Kincaid** **Doris Kuntsman** **Burt Lancaster**

JOHNSON, ROBIN: Brooklyn, NY: May 29, 1964.

JOHNSON, VAN: Newport, RI, Aug. 28, 1916.

JONES, CHRISTOPHER: Jackson, TN, Aug. 18, 1941. Actors Studio.

JONES, DEAN: Morgan County, AL, Jan. 25, 1936. Actors Studio.

JONES, JACK: Bel-Air, CA, Jan. 14, 1938.

JONES, JAMES EARL: Arkabutla, MS, Jan. 17, 1931. U. Mich.

JONES, JENNIFER (Phyllis Isley): Tulsa, OK, Mar. 2, 1919. AADA.

JONES, SAM J.: Chicago, IL, 1954.

JONES, SHIRLEY: Smithton, PA, March 31, 1934.

JONES, TOM (Thomas Jones Woodward): Pontypridd, Wales, June 7, 1940.

JONES, TOMMY LEE: San Saba, TX, Sept. 15, 1946. Harvard.

JORDAN, RICHARD: NYC, July 19, 1938. Harvard.

JOURDAN, LOUIS: Marseilles, France, June 18, 1920.

JULIA, RAUL: San Juan, PR, Mar. 9, 1940. U PR.

JURADO, KATY (Maria Christina Jurado Garcia): Guadalajara, Mex., 1927.

KAHN, MADELINE: Boston, MA, Sept. 29, 1942. Hofstra U.

KANE, CAROL: Cleveland, OH, 1952.

KAPLAN, JONATHAN: Paris, Nov. 25, 1947. NYU.

KAPOOR, SHASHI: Bombay 1940.

KAPRISKY, VALERIE: Paris, 1963.

KATT, WILLIAM: Los Angeles, CA, 1955.

KAUFMANN, CHRISTINE: Lansdorf, Graz, Austria, Jan. 11, 1945.

KAYE, DANNY: (David Daniel Kominski): Brooklyn, Jan. 18, 1913.

KAYE, STUBBY: NYC, Nov. 11, 1918.

KEACH, STACY: Savannah, GA, June 2, 1941. U. Cal., Yale.

KEATON, DIANE (Hall): Los Angeles, CA, Jan. 5, 1946. Neighborhood Playhouse.

KEATS, STEVEN: Bronx, NY, 1945.

KEDROVA, LILA: Greece, 1918.

KEEL, HOWARD (Harold Keel): Gillespie, IL, Apr. 13, 1919.

KEELER, RUBY (Ethel): Halifax, N.S., Aug. 25, 1909.

KEITH, BRIAN: Bayonne, NJ, Nov. 15, 1921.

KEITH, DAVID: Knoxville, Tn., 1954. UTN.

KELLER, MARTHE: Basel, Switz., 1945. Munich Stanislavsky Sch.

KELLERMAN, SALLY: Long Beach, CA, June 2, 1938. Actors Studio West.

KELLEY, DeFOREST: Atlanta, GA, Jan. 20, 1920.

KELLY, GENE: Pittsburgh, Aug. 23, 1912. U. Pittsburgh.

KELLY, JACK: Astoria, NY, Sept. 16, 1927. UCLA.

KELLY, NANCY: Lowell, MA, Mar. 25, 1921. Bentley School.

KEMP, JEREMY: Chesterfield, Eng., 1935. Central Sch.

KENNEDY, ARTHUR: Worcester, MA, Feb. 17, 1914. Carnegie Tech.

KENNEDY, GEORGE: NYC, Feb. 18, 1925.

KENNEDY, LEON ISAAC: Cleveland, OH., 1949.

KERR, DEBORAH: Helensburg, Scot., Sept. 30, 1921. Smale Ballet School.

KERR, JOHN: NYC, Nov. 15, 1931. Harvard, Columbia.

KHAMBATTA, PERSIS: Bombay, Oct. 2, 1950.

KIDDER, MARGOT: Yellow Knife, CAN., Oct. 17, 1948. UBC.

KIER, UDO: Germany, Oct. 14, 1944.

KILEY, RICHARD: Chicago, Mar. 31, 1922. Loyola.

KINCAID, ARON (Norman Neale Williams III): Los Angeles, June 15, 1943. UCLA.

KING, ALAN (Irwin Kniberg): Brooklyn, Dec. 26, 1927.

KING, PERRY: Alliance, OH, Apr. 30, 1948. Yale.

KINGSLEY, BEN (Krishna Bhanji): Snaiton, Yorkshire, Eng., Dec. 31, 1943.

KINSKI, NASTASSJA: Germany, Jan. 24, 1960.

KITT, EARTHA: North, SC, Jan. 26, 1928.

KLEMPERER, WERNER: Cologne, Mar. 22, 1920.

KLUGMAN, JACK: Philadelphia, PA, Apr. 27, 1925. Carnegie Tech.

KNIGHT, ESMOND: East Sheen, Eng., May 4, 1906.

KNIGHT, SHIRLEY: Goessel, KS, July 5, 1937. Wichita U.

KNOWLES, PATRIC (Reginald Lawrence Knowles): Horsforth, Eng., Nov. 11, 1911.

KNOX, ALEXANDER: Strathroy, Ont., CAN., Jan. 16, 1907.

KNOX, ELYSE: Hartford, CT, Dec. 14, 1917. Traphagen School.

KOENIG, WALTER: Chicago, IL, Sept. 14. UCLA.

KOHNER, SUSAN: Los Angeles, Nov. 11, 1936. U. Calif.

KORMAN, HARVEY: Chicago, IL, Feb. 15, 1927. Goodman.

KORVIN, CHARLES (Geza Korvin Karpathi): Czechoslovakia, Nov. 21. Sorbonne.

KOSLECK, MARTIN: Barkotzen, Ger., Mar. 24, 1907. Max Reinhardt School.

KOTTO, YAPHET: NYC, Nov. 15, 1937.

KREUGER, KURT: St. Moritz, Switz., July 23, 1917. U. London.

KRISTEL, SYLVIA: Amsterdam, Hol., Sept. 28, 1952.

KRISTOFFERSON, KRIS: Brownsville, TX, June 22, 1936, Pomona Col.

KRUGER, HARDY: Berlin Ger., April 12, 1928.

KULP, NANCY: Harrisburg, PA, 1921.

KUNTSMANN, DORIS: Hamburg, 1944.

KWAN, NANCY: Hong Kong, May 19, 1939. Royal Ballet.

LACY, JERRY: Sioux City, IA, Mar. 27, 1936. LACC.

LADD, CHERYL: (Stoppelmoor): Huron, SD, July 12, 1951.

LADD, DIANE: (Ladnier): Meridian, MS, Nov. 29, 1932. Tulane U.

LaGRECA, PAUL: Bronx, NY, June 23, 1962. AADA.

LAHTI, CHRISTINE: Detroit, MI, Apr. 4, 1950; U. Mich.

LAMARR, HEDY (Hedwig Kiesler): Vienna, Sept. 11, 1913.

LAMAS, LORENZO: Los Angeles, Jan. 1958.

LAMB, GIL: Minneapolis, June 14, 1906. U. Minn.

LAMBERT, CHRISTOPHER: NYC, 1958.

LAMOUR, DOROTHY (Mary Dorothy Slaton): New Orleans, LA.; Dec. 10, 1914. Spence School.

LANCASTER, BURT: NYC, Nov. 2, 1913. NYU.

LANCHESTER, ELSA (Elsa Sullivan): London, Oct. 28, 1902.

LANDAU, MARTIN: Brooklyn, NY, 1931. Actors Studio.

LANDON, MICHAEL (Eugene Orowitz): Collingswood, NJ, Oct. 31, 1936. USC.

LANDRUM, TERI: Enid, OK., 1960.

LANE, ABBE: Brooklyn, Dec. 14, 1935.

LANE, DIANE: NYC, Jan. 1963.

LANGAN, GLENN: Denver, CO, July 8, 1917.

LANGE, HOPE: Redding Ridge, CT, Nov. 28, 1933. Reed Col.

LANGE, JESSICA: Minnesota, Apr. 20, 1949. U. Minn.

LANGTON, PAUL: Salt Lake City, UT, Apr. 17, 1913. Travers School of Theatre.

| Robert Lansing | Cloris Leachman | Perry Lopez | Gina Lollobrigida | Kurt Mann | Mary Martin |

LANSBURY, ANGELA: London, Oct. 16, 1925. London Academy of Music.

LANSING, ROBERT (Brown): San Diego, CA, June 5, 1929.

LAURE, CAROLE: Montreal, Can., 1951.

LAURIE, PIPER (Rosetta Jacobs): Detroit, MI, Jan. 22, 1932.

LAW, JOHN PHILLIP: Hollywood, Sept. 7, 1937. Neighborhood Playhouse, U. Hawaii.

LAWRENCE, BARBARA: Carnegie, OK, Feb. 24, 1930. UCLA.

LAWRENCE, CAROL (Laraia): Melrose Park, IL, Sept. 5, 1935.

LAWRENCE, VICKI: Inglewood, CA, 1949.

LAWSON, LEIGH: Atherston, Eng., July 21, 1945. RADA.

LEACHMAN, CLORIS: Des Moines, IA, Apr. 30, 1930. Northwestern U.

LEAUD, JEAN-PIERRE: Paris, 1944.

LEDERER, FRANCIS: Karlin, Prague, Czech., Nov. 6, 1906.

LEE, CHRISTOPHER: London, May 27, 1922. Wellington College.

LEE, PEGGY (Norma Delores Egstrom): Jamestown, ND, 1920.

LEE, MARK: Australia, 1958.

LEE, MICHELE (Dusiak): Los Angeles, June 24, 1942. LACC.

LEIBMAN, RON: NYC, Oct. 11, 1937. Ohio Wesleyan.

LEIGH, JANET (Jeanette Helen Morrison): Merced, CA, July 6, 1926. College of Pacific.

LEMMON, JACK: Boston, Feb. 8, 1925. Harvard.

LENZ, RICK: Springfield, IL, Nov. 21, 1939. U. Mich.

LEONARD, SHELDON (Bershad): NYC, Feb. 22, 1907, Syracuse U.

LEROY, PHILIPPE: Paris, Oct. 15, 1930. U. Paris.

LESLIE, BETHEL: NYC, Aug. 3, 1929. Brearley School.

LESLIE, JOAN (Joan Brodell): Detroit, Jan. 26, 1925. St. Benedict's.

LESTER, MARK: Oxford, Eng., July 11, 1958.

LEVELS, CALVIN: Cleveland, OH., Sept. 30, 1954. CCC.

LEWIS, JERRY: Newark, NJ, Mar. 16, 1926.

LIGON, TOM: New Orleans, LA, Sept. 10, 1945.

LILLIE, BEATRICE: Toronto, Can., May 29, 1898.

LINCOLN, ABBEY (Anna Marie Woolridge): Chicago, Aug. 6, 1930.

LINDFORS, VIVECA: Uppsala, Sweden, Dec. 29, 1920. Stockholm Royal Dramatic School.

LISI, VIRNA: Rome, 1938.

LITHGOW, JOHN: Rochester, NY, Oct. 19, 1945. Harvard.

LITTLE, CLEAVON: Chickasha, OK, June 1, 1939. San Diego State.

LOCKE, SONDRA: Shelbyville, TN, 1947.

LOCKHART, JUNE: NYC, June 25, 1925. Westlake School.

LOCKWOOD, GARY: Van Nuys, CA, Feb. 21, 1937.

LOCKWOOD, MARGARET: Karachi, Pakistan, Sept. 15, 1916. RADA.

LOGGIA, ROBERT: Staten Island, NY., Jan. 3, 1930. UMo.

LOLLOBRIGIDA, GINA: Subiaco, Italy, July 4, 1927. Rome Academy of Fine Arts.

LOM, HERBERT: Prague, Czechoslovakia, 1917. Prague U.

LOMEZ, CELINE: Montreal, Can., 1953.

LONDON, JULIE (Julie Peck): Santa Rosa, CA, Sept. 26, 1926.

LONG, SHELLEY: Indiana, 1950. Northwestern U.

LONOW, MARK: Brooklyn, NY.

LOPEZ, PERRY: NYC, July 22, 1931. NYU.

LORD, JACK (John Joseph Ryan): NYC, Dec. 30, 1928. NYU.

LOREN, SOPHIA (Sofia Scicolone): Rome, Italy, Sept. 20, 1934.

LOUISE, TINA (Blacker): NYC, Feb. 11, 1934, Miami U.

LOVELACE, LINDA: Bryan, TX, 1952.

LOWE, ROB: Ohio, 1964.

LOWITSCH, KLAUS: Berlin, Apr. 8, 1936. Vienna Academy.

LOY, MYRNA (Myrna Williams): Helena, MT, Aug. 2, 1905. Westlake School.

LUCAS, LISA: Arizona, 1961.

LULU: Glasglow, Scot., 1948.

LUND, JOHN: Rochester, NY, Feb. 6, 1913.

LUPINO, IDA: London, Feb. 4, 1916. RADA.

LYDON, JAMES: Harrington Park, NJ, May 30, 1923.

LYNLEY, CAROL (Jones): NYC, Feb. 13, 1942.

LYNN, JEFFREY: Auburn, MA, 1909. Bates College.

LYON, SUE: Davenport, IA, July 10, 1946.

LYONS, ROBERT F.: Albany, NY. AADA.

MacARTHUR, JAMES: Los Angeles, Dec. 8, 1937. Harvard.

MACCHIO, RALPH: Huntington, NY., 1962.

MacGINNIS, NIALL: Dublin, Ire., Mar. 29, 1913. Dublin U.

MacGRAW, ALI: NYC, Apr. 1, 1938. Wellesley.

MacLAINE, SHIRLEY (Beatty): Richmond, VA, Apr. 24, 1934.

MacMAHON, ALINE: McKeesport, PA, May 3, 1899. Barnard College.

MacMURRAY, FRED: Kankakee, IL, Aug. 30, 1908. Carroll Col.

MACNEE, PATRICK: London, Feb. 1922.

MacNICOL, PETER: Dallas, TX, Apr. 10, UMN.

MacRAE, GORDON: East Orange, NJ, Mar. 12, 1921.

MADISON, GUY (Robert Moseley): Bakersfield, CA, Jan. 19, 1922. Bakersfield Jr. College.

MAHARIS, GEORGE: Astoria, NY, Sept. 1, 1928. Actors Studio.

MAHONEY, JOCK (Jacques O'Mahoney): Chicago, Feb. 7, 1919. U. of Iowa.

MAJORS, LEE: Wyandotte, MI, Apr. 23, 1940. E. Ky. State Col.

MAKEPEACE, CHRIS: Toronto, Can., 1964.

MALDEN, KARL. (Mladen Sekulovich): Gary, IN, Mar. 22, 1914.

MALET, PIERRE: St. Tropez, Fr., 1955.

MALONE, DOROTHY: Chicago, Jan. 30, 1925. S. Methodist U.

MANN, KURT: Roslyn, NY, July 18, 1947.

MANOFF, DINAH: NYC, Jan. 25, 1958. CalArts.

MANZ, LINDA: NYC, 1961.

MARAIS, JEAN: Cherbourg, France, Dec. 11, 1913. St. Germain.

MARGO (Maria Marguerita Guadalupe Boldoay Castilla): Mexico City, May 10, 1917.

MARGOLIN, JANET: NYC, July 25, 1943. Walden School.

MARIN, JACQUES: Paris, Sept. 9, 1919. Conservatoire National.

MARINARO, ED: NYC, 1951. Cornell.

MARSHALL, BRENDA (Ardis Anderson Gaines): Isle of Negros, P.I., Sept. 29, 1915. Texas State College.

MARSHALL, E. G.: Owatonna, MN, June 18, 1910. U. Minn.

MARSHALL, KEN: NYC, 1953. Juilliard.

MARSHALL, PENNY: Bronx, NY, Oct. 15, 1942. U. N. Mex.

MARSHALL, WILLIAM: Gary, IN, Aug. 19, 1924. NYU.

MARTIN, DEAN (Dino Crocetti): Steubenville, OH, June 17, 1917.

MARTIN, DEAN PAUL: Los Angeles, CA, 1952. UCLA.

MARTIN, MARY: Weatherford, TX, Dec. 1, 1914. Ward-Belmont School.

MARTIN, STEVE: Waco, TX, 1946. UCLA.

Lee Marvin	Lonette McKee	Doug McKeon	Mariangela Melato	Barry Miller	Liza Minnelli

MARTIN, TONY (Alfred Norris): Oakland, CA, Dec. 25, 1913. St. Mary's College.

MARVIN, LEE: NYC, Feb. 19, 1924.

MASON, MARSHA: St. Louis, MO, Apr. 3, 1942. Webster Col.

MASON, PAMELA (Pamela Kellino): Westgate, Eng., Mar. 10, 1918.

MASSEN, OSA: Copenhagen, Den., Jan. 13, 1916.

MASSEY, DANIEL: London, Oct. 10, 1933. Eton and King's Col.

MASTERSON, PETER: Angleton, TX, June 1, 1934. Rice U.

MASTRANTONIO, MARY ELIZABETH: Chicago, Il., Nov. 17, 1958. UIll.

MASTROIANNI, MARCELLO: Fontana Liri, Italy, Sept. 28, 1924.

MATHESON, TIM: Glendale, CA, Dec. 31, 1947. CalState.

MATTHAU, WALTER (Matuschanskayasky): NYC, Oct. 1, 1920.

MATTHEWS, BRIAN: Philadelphia, PA, Jan. 24, 1953. St. Olaf.

MATURE, VICTOR: Louisville, KY, Jan. 29, 1915.

MAY, ELAINE (Berlin): Philadelphia, Apr. 21, 1932.

MAYEHOFF, EDDIE: Baltimore, July 7. Yale.

MAYO, VIRGINIA (Virginia Clara Jones): St. Louis, MO, Nov. 30, 1920.

McCALLUM, DAVID: Scotland, Sept. 19, 1933. Chapman Col.

McCAMBRIDGE, MERCEDES: Jolliet, IL, Mar. 17, 1918. Mundelein College.

McCARTHY, ANDREW: NYC, 1963, NYU.

McCARTHY, KEVIN: Seattle, WA, Feb. 15, 1914. Minn. U.

McCLORY, SEAN: Dublin, Ire., Mar. 8, 1924. U. Galway.

McCLURE, DOUG: Glendale, CA, May 11, 1935. UCLA.

McCOWEN, ALEC: Tunbridge Wells, Eng., May 26, 1925. RADA.

McCREA, JOEL: Los Angeles, Nov. 5, 1905. Pomona College.

McDERMOTT, HUGH: Edinburgh, Scot., Mar. 20, 1908.

McDOWALL, RODDY: London, Sept. 17, 1928. St. Joseph's.

McDOWELL, MALCOLM (Taylor): Leeds, Eng., June 15, 1943. LAMDA.

McENERY, PETER: Walsall, Eng., Feb. 21, 1940.

McFARLAND, SPANKY: Dallas, TX, 1936.

McGAVIN, DARREN: Spokane, WA, May 7, 1922. College of Pacific.

McGILLIS, KELLY: Newport Beach, CA, 1958. Juilliard.

McGOVERN, ELIZABETH: Evanston, IL, July 18, 1961. Juilliard.

McGUIRE, BIFF: New Haven, CT, Oct. 25, 1926. Mass. State Col.

McGUIRE, DOROTHY: Omaha, NE, June 14, 1918.

McHATTIE, STEPHEN: Antigonish, NS, Feb. 3. AcadiaU, AADA.

McKAY, GARDNER: NYC, June 10, 1932. Cornell.

McKEE, LONETTE: Detroit, MI, 1954.

McKELLEN, IAN: Burnley, Eng., May 25, 1939.

McKENNA, VIRGINIA: London, June 7, 1931.

McKEON, DOUG: New Jersey, 1966.

McKUEN, ROD: Oakland, CA, Apr. 29, 1933.

McLERIE, ALLYN ANN: Grand Mere, Can., Dec. 1, 1926.

McNAIR, BARBARA: Chicago, Mar. 4, 1939. UCLA.

McNALLY, STEPHEN (Horace McNally): NYC, July 29, 1913. Fordham U.

McNICHOL, KRISTY: Los Angeles, CA, Sept. 11, 1962.

McQUEEN, ARMELIA: North Carolina, Jan. 6, 1952. Bklyn Consv.

McQUEEN, BUTTERFLY: Tampa, FL, Jan. 8, 1911. UCLA.

McQUEEN, CHAD: Los Angeles, CA, 1961. Actors Studio.

MEADOWS, AUDREY: Wuchang, China, 1919. St. Margaret's.

MEADOWS, JAYNE (formerly, Jayne Cotter): Wuchang, China, Sept. 27, 1920. St. Margaret's.

MEARA, ANNE: Brooklyn, NY, Sept. 20, 1929.

MEDWIN, MICHAEL: London, 1925. Instut Fischer.

MEEKER, RALPH (Ralph Rathgeber): Minneapolis, Nov. 21, 1920. Northwestern U.

MEISNER, GUNTER: Bremen, Ger., Apr. 18, 1926. Municipal Drama School.

MEKKA, EDDIE: Worcester, MA, 1932. Boston Cons.

MELATO, MARIANGELA: Milan, Italy, 1941. Milan Theatre Acad.

MELL, MARISA: Vienna, Austria, Feb. 25, 1939.

MERCADO, HECTOR JAIME: NYC, 1949. HB Studio.

MERCOURI, MELINA: Athens, Greece, Oct. 18, 1915.

MEREDITH, BURGESS: Cleveland, OH, Nov. 16, 1908. Amherst.

MEREDITH, LEE (Judi Lee Sauls): Oct., 1947. AADA.

MERKEL, UNA: Covington, KY, Dec. 10, 1903.

MERRILL, DINA (Nedinia Hutton): NYC, Dec. 9, 1925. AADA.

MERRILL, GARY: Hartford, CT, Aug. 2, 1915. Bowdoin, Trinity.

METZLER, JIM: Oneonda, NY. Dartmouth Col.

MICHELL, KEITH: Adelaide, Aus., Dec. 1, 1926.

MIDLER, BETTE: Honolulu, HI., Dec. 1, 1945.

MIFUNE, TOSHIRO: Tsingtao, China, Apr. 1, 1920.

MILES, SARAH: Ingatestone, Eng., Dec. 31, 1941. RADA.

MILES, SYLVIA: NYC, Sept. 9, 1932.

MILES, VERA (Ralston): Boise City, OK, Aug. 23, 1929. UCLA.

MILFORD, PENELOPE: Winnetka, IL.

MILLAND, RAY (Reginald Truscott-Jones): Neath, Wales, Jan. 3, 1908. King's College.

MILLER, ANN (Lucille Ann Collier): Chireno, TX, Apr. 12, 1919. Lawler Professional School.

MILLER, BARRY: NYC, 1958.

MILLER, JASON: Long Island City, NY, Apr. 22, 1939. Catholic U.

MILLER, LINDA: NYC, Sept. 16, 1942. Catholic U.

MILLER, MARVIN: St. Louis, July 18, 1913. Washington U.

MILLS, HAYLEY: London, Apr. 18, 1946. Elmhurst School.

MILLS, JOHN: Suffolk, Eng., Feb. 22, 1908.

MILNER, MARTIN: Detroit, MI, Dec. 28, 1931.

MIMIEUX, YVETTE: Los Angeles, Jan. 8, 1941. Hollywood High.

MINNELLI, LIZA: Los Angeles, Mar. 12, 1946.

MIOU-MIOU: Paris, Feb. 22, 1950.

MITCHELL, CAMERON: Dallastown, PA, Nov. 4, 1918. N.Y. Theatre School.

MITCHELL, JAMES: Sacramento, CA, Feb. 29, 1920. LACC.

MITCHUM, JAMES: Los Angeles, CA, May 8, 1941.

MITCHUM, ROBERT: Bridgeport, CT, Aug. 6, 1917.

MONTALBAN, RICARDO: Mexico City, Nov. 25, 1920.

MONTAND, YVES (Yves Montand Livi): Mansummano, Tuscany, Oct. 13, 1921.

MONTGOMERY, BELINDA: Winnipeg, Can., July 23, 1950.

MONTGOMERY, ELIZABETH: Los Angeles, Apr. 15, 1933. AADA.

MONTGOMERY, GEORGE (George Letz): Brady, MT, Aug. 29, 1916. U. Mont.

Mary Tyler Moore	Tony Musante	Patricia Neal	Don Nute	Nancy Olson	Michael O'Keefe

MOOR, BILL: Toledo, OH, July 13, 1931. Northwestern.

MOORE, CONSTANCE: Sioux City, IA, Jan. 18, 1919.

MOORE, DEMI (Guines): Roswell, NMx, Nov. 11, 1962.

MOORE, DICK: Los Angeles, Sept. 12, 1925.

MOORE, DUDLEY: London, Apr. 19, 1935.

MOORE, FRANK: Bay-de-Verde, Newfoundland, 1946.

MOORE, KIERON: County Cork, Ire., 1925. St. Mary's College.

MOORE, MARY TYLER: Brooklyn, Dec. 29, 1936.

MOORE, ROGER: London, Oct. 14, 1927. RADA.

MOORE, TERRY (Helen Koford): Los Angeles, Jan. 7, 1929.

MOREAU, JEANNE: Paris, Jan. 23, 1928.

MORENO, RITA (Rosita Alverio): Humacao, P.R., Dec. 11, 1931.

MORGAN, DENNIS (Stanley Morner): Prentice, WI, Dec. 10, 1910. Carroll College.

MORGAN, HARRY (HENRY) (Harry Bratsburg): Detroit, Apr. 10, 1915. U. Chicago.

MORGAN, MICHELE (Simone Roussel): Paris, Feb. 29, 1920. Paris Dramatic School.

MORIARTY, CATHY: Bronx, NY, 1961.

MORIARTY, MICHAEL: Detroit, MI, Apr. 5, 1941. Dartmouth.

MORISON, PATRICIA: NYC, 1915.

MORLEY, ROBERT: Wiltshire, Eng., May 26, 1908. RADA.

MORRIS, GREG: Cleveland, OH, Sept. 27, 1934. Ohio State.

MORRIS, HOWARD: NYC, Sept. 4, 1919. NYU.

MORSE, DAVID: Hamilton, MA, 1953.

MORSE, ROBERT: Newton, MA, May 18, 1931.

MOSS, ARNOLD: NYC, Jan. 28, 1910. CCNY.

MOYA, EDDY: El Paso, TX, Apr. 11, 1963. LACC.

MULLIGAN, RICHARD: NYC, Nov. 13, 1932.

MURPHY, EDDIE: Brooklyn, NY, Apr. 3, 1961.

MURPHY, GEORGE: New Haven, CT, July 4, 1902. Yale.

MURPHY, MICHAEL: Los Angeles, CA, 1949.

MURRAY, BILL: Evanston, IL, Sept. 21, 1950. Regis Col.

MURRAY, DON: Hollywood, July 31, 1929. AADA.

MURRAY, KEN (Don Court): NYC, July 14, 1903.

MUSANTE, TONY: Bridgeport, CT, June 30, 1936. Oberlin Col.

NABORS, JIM: Sylacauga, GA, June 12, 1932.

NADER, GEORGE: Pasadena, CA, Oct. 19, 1921. Occidental College.

NADER, MICHAEL: Los Angeles, CA, 1945.

NAPIER, ALAN: Birmingham, Eng., Jan. 7, 1903. Birmingham University.

NATWICK, MILDRED: Baltimore, June 19, 1908. Bryn Mawr.

NAUGHTON, JAMES: Middletown, CT, Dec. 6, 1945. Yale.

NAVIN, JOHN P., JR.: Philadelphia, PA, 1968.

NEAL, PATRICIA: Packard, KY, Jan. 20, 1926. Northwestern U.

NEFF, HILDEGARDE (Hildegard Knef): Ulm, Ger., Dec. 28, 1925. Berlin Art Academy.

NELL, NATHALIE: Paris, Oct. 1950.

NELLIGAN, KATE: London, Ont., Can., 1951. U Toronto.

NELSON, BARRY (Robert Nielsen): Oakland, CA, 1920.

NELSON, DAVID: NYC, Oct. 24, 1936. USC.

NELSON, GENE (Gene Berg): Seattle, WA, Mar. 24, 1920.

NELSON, HARRIET HILLIARD (Peggy Lou Snyder): Des Moines, IA, July 18, 1914.

NELSON, LORI (Dixie Kay Nelson): Santa Fe, NM, Aug. 15, 1933.

NELSON, RICK (Eric Hilliard Nelson): Teaneck, NJ, May 8, 1940.

NELSON, WILLIE: Texas, Apr. 30, 1933.

NETTLETON, LOIS: Oak Park, IL. Actors Studio.

NEWHART, BOB: Chicago, IL, Sept. 5, 1929. Loyola U.

NEWLEY, ANTHONY: Hackney, London, Sept. 21, 1931.

NEWMAN, BARRY: Boston, MA, Mar. 26, 1938. Brandeis U.

NEWMAN, PAUL: Cleveland, OH, Jan. 26, 1925. Yale.

NEWMAR, JULIE (Newmeyer): Los Angeles, Aug. 16, 1935.

NEWTON-JOHN, OLIVIA: Cambridge, Eng., Sept. 26, 1948.

NICHOLAS, PAUL: London, 1945.

NICHOLS, MIKE (Michael Igor Peschkowsky): Berlin, Nov. 6, 1931. U. Chicago.

NICHOLSON, JACK: Neptune, NJ, Apr. 22, 1937.

NICKERSON, DENISE: NYC, 1959.

NICOL, ALEX: Ossining, NY, Jan. 20, 1919. Actors Studio.

NIELSEN, LESLIE: Regina, Saskatchewan, Can., Feb. 11, 1926. Neighborhood Playhouse.

NIMOY, LEONARD: Boston, MA, Mar. 26, 1931. Boston Col., Antioch Col.

NOLAN, KATHLEEN: St. Louis, MO, Sept. 27, 1933. Neighborhood Playhouse.

NOLAN, LLOYD: San Francisco, Aug. 11, 1902. Stanford U.

NOLTE, NICK: Omaha, NE, 1941. Pasadena City Col.

NORRIS, CHRISTOPHER: NYC, Oct. 7, 1943. Lincoln Square Acad.

NORRIS, CHUCK (Carlos Ray): Ryan, OK, 1939.

NORTH, HEATHER: Pasadena, CA, Dec. 13, 1950. Actors Workshop.

NORTH, SHEREE (Dawn Bethel): Los Angeles, Jan. 17, 1933. Hollywood High.

NORTON, KEN: Aug. 9, 1945.

NOURI, MICHAEL: Washington, DC, Dec. 9, 1945.

NOVAK, KIM (Marilyn Novak): Chicago, Feb. 18, 1933. LACC.

NUREYEV, RUDOLF: Russia, Mar. 17, 1938.

NUTE, DON: Connellsville, PA, Mar. 13, Denver U.

NUYEN, FRANCE (Vannga): Marseilles, France, July 31, 1939. Beaux Arts School.

O'BRIAN, HUGH (Hugh J. Krampe): Rochester, NY, Apr. 19, 1928. Cincinnati U.

O'BRIEN, CLAY: Ray, AZ, May 6, 1961.

O'BRIEN, EDMOND: NYC, Sept. 10, 1915. Fordham, Neighborhood Playhouse.

O'BRIEN, MARGARET (Angela Maxine O'Brien): Los Angeles, Jan. 15, 1937.

O'CONNELL, ARTHUR: NYC, Mar. 29, 1908. St. John's.

O'CONNOR, CARROLL: Bronx, NY, Aug. 2, 1925. Dublin National Univ.

O'CONNOR, DONALD: Chicago, Aug. 28, 1925.

O'CONNOR, GLYNNIS: NYC, Nov. 19, 1956. NYSU.

O'CONNOR, KEVIN: Honolulu, HI, May 7, U. Hi.

O'HANLON, GEORGE: Brooklyn, NY, Nov. 23, 1917.

O'HARA, MAUREEN (Maureen FitzSimons): Dublin, Ire., Aug. 17, 1920. Abbey School.

O'HERLIHY, DAN: Wexford, Ire., May 1, 1919. National U.

O'KEEFE, MICHAEL: Paulland, NJ, 1955, NYU, AADA.

OLIVIER, LAURENCE: Dorking, Eng., May 22, 1907. Oxford.

O'LOUGHLIN, GERALD S.: NYC, Dec. 23, 1921. U. Rochester.

OLSON, NANCY: Milwaukee, WI, July 14, 1928. UCLA.

O'NEAL, GRIFFIN: Los Angeles, 1965.

| Tricia O'Neil | Peter O'Toole | Janis Paige | Gregory Peck | Suzanne Pleshette | Sidney Poitier |

O'NEAL, PATRICK: Ocala, FL, Sept. 26, 1927. U. Fla.

O'NEAL, RON: Utica, NY, Sept. 1, 1937. Ohio State.

O'NEAL, RYAN: Los Angeles, Apr. 20, 1941.

O'NEAL, TATUM: Los Angeles, Nov. 5, 1963.

O'NEIL, TRICIA: Shreveport, LA, Mar. 11, 1945. Baylor U.

O'NEILL, JENNIFER: Rio de Janeiro, Feb. 20, 1949. Neighborhood Playhouse.

O'SULLIVAN, MAUREEN: Byle, Ire., May 17, 1911. Sacred Heart Convent.

O'TOOLE, ANNETTE: Houston, TX, 1953. UCLA.

O'TOOLE, PETER: Connemara, Ire., Aug. 2, 1932. RADA.

PACINO, AL: NYC, Apr. 25, 1940.

PAGE, GERALDINE: Kirksville, MO, Nov. 22, 1924. Goodman School.

PAGE, TONY (Anthony Vitiello): Bronx, NY, 1940.

PAGET, DEBRA (Debralee Griffin): Denver, Aug. 19, 1933.

PAIGE, JANIS (Donna Mae Jaden): Tacoma, WA, Sept. 16, 1922.

PALANCE, JACK (Walter Palanuik): Lattimer, PA, Feb. 18, 1920. UNC.

PALMER, BETSY: East Chicago, IN, Nov. 1, 1929. DePaul U.

PALMER, GREGG (Palmer Lee): San Francisco, Jan. 25, 1927. U. Utah.

PALMER, LILLI: Posen, Austria, May 24, 1914. Ilka Gruning School.

PAMPANINI, SILVANA: Rome, Sept. 25, 1925.

PAPAS, IRENE: Chiliomodion, Greece, Mar. 9, 1929.

PARE, MICHAEL: Brooklyn, NY, 1959.

PARKER, ELEANOR: Cedarville, OH, June 26, 1922. Pasadena Playhouse.

PARKER, FESS: Fort Worth, TX, Aug. 16, 1927. USC.

PARKER, JAMESON: 1947. Beloit Col.

PARKER, JEAN (Mae Green): Deer Lodge, MT, Aug. 11, 1912.

PARKER, SUZY (Cecelia Parker): San Antonio, TX, Oct. 28, 1933.

PARKER, WILLARD (Worster Van Eps): NYC, Feb. 5, 1912.

PARKINS, BARBARA: Vancouver, Can., May 22, 1943.

PARSONS, ESTELLE: Lynn, MA, Nov. 20, 1927. Boston U.

PARTON, DOLLY: Sevierville, TN, Jan. 19, 1946.

PATINKIN, MANDY: Chicago, IL, 1953. Juilliard.

PATRICK, DENNIS: Philadelphia, Mar. 14, 1918.

PATTERSON, LEE: Vancouver, Can., Mar. 31, 1929. Ontario Col.

PAVAN, MARISA (Marisa Pierangeli): Cagliari, Sardinia, June 19, 1932. Torquado Tasso College.

PEACH, MARY: Durban, S. Africa, 1934.

PEARL, MINNIE (Sarah Cannon): Centerville, TN, Oct. 25, 1912.

PEARSON, BEATRICE: Denison, TX, July 27, 1920.

PECK, GREGORY: La Jolla, CA, Apr. 5, 1916. U. Calif.

PELIKAN, LISA: Paris, July 12. Juilliard.

PENHALL, BRUCE: Balboa, CA, 1958.

PENN, SEAN: California, Aug. 17, 1960.

PEPPARD, GEORGE: Detroit, Oct. 1, 1928. Carnegie Tech.

PEREZ, JOSE: NYC 1940.

PERKINS, ANTHONY: NYC, Apr. 14, 1932. Rollins College.

PERREAU, GIGI (Ghislaine): Los Angeles, Feb. 6, 1941.

PERRINE, VALERIE: Galveston, TX, Sept. 3, 1944. U. Ariz.

PESCOW, DONNA: Brooklyn, NY, 1954.

PETERS, BERNADETTE (Lazzara): Jamaica, NY, Feb. 28, 1948.

PETERS, BROCK: NYC, July 2, 1927. CCNY.

PETERS, JEAN (Elizabeth): Canton, OH, Oct. 15, 1926. Ohio State U.

PETERS, MICHAEL: Brooklyn, NY, 1948.

PETTET, JOANNA: London, Nov. 16, 1944. Neighborhood Playhouse.

PFEIFFER, MICHELLE: Santa Ana, CA, 1957.

PHILLIPS, MacKENZIE: Hollywood, CA, 1960.

PHILLIPS, MICHELLE (Holly Gilliam): NJ, June 4, 1944.

PICERNI, PAUL: NYC, Dec. 1, 1922. Loyola U.

PINCHOT, BRONSON: 1959, Yale.

PINE, PHILLIP: Hanford, CA, July 16, 1925. Actors' Lab.

PISIER, MARIE-FRANCE: Vietnam, May 10, 1944. U. Paris.

PLACE, MARY KAY: Port Arthur, TX, Sept., 1947. U. Tulsa.

PLAYTEN, ALICE: NYC, Aug. 28, 1947. NYU.

PLEASENCE, DONALD: Workshop, Eng., Oct. 5, 1919. Sheffield School.

PLESHETTE, SUZANNE: NYC, Jan. 31, 1937. Syracuse U.

PLOWRIGHT, JOAN: Scunthorpe, Brigg, Lincolnshire, Eng., Oct. 28, 1929. Old Vic.

PLUMMER, AMANDA: NYC, Mar. 23, 1957. Middlebury Col.

PLUMMER, CHRISTOPHER: Toronto, Can., Dec. 13, 1927.

PODESTA, ROSSANA: Tripoli, June 20, 1934.

POITIER, SIDNEY: Miami, FL, Feb. 27, 1924.

POLITO, LINA: Naples, Italy, Aug. 11, 1954.

POLLARD, MICHAEL J.: Pacific, NJ, May 30, 1939.

PORTER, ERIC: London, Apr. 8, 1928. Wimbledon Col.

POWELL, JANE (Suzanne Burce): Portland, OR, Apr. 1, 1928.

POWELL, ROBERT: Salford, Eng., June 1, 1944. Manchester U.

POWER, TARYN: Los Angeles, CA, 1954.

POWER, TYRONE IV: Los Angeles, CA, Jan. 1959.

POWERS, MALA (Mary Ellen): San Francisco, Dec. 29, 1921. UCLA.

POWERS, STEFANIE (Federkiewicz): Hollywood, CA, Oct. 12, 1942.

PRENTISS, PAULA (Paula Ragusa): San Antonio, TX, Mar. 4, 1939. Northwestern U.

PRESLE, MICHELINE (Micheline Chassagne): Paris, Aug. 22, 1922. Rouleau Drama School.

PRESNELL, HARVE: Modesto, CA, Sept. 14, 1933. USC.

PRESTON, ROBERT (Robert Preston Meservey): Newton Highlands, MA, June 8, 1913. Pasadena Playhouse.

PRICE, VINCENT: St. Louis, May 27, 1911. Yale.

PRIMUS, BARRY: NYC, Feb. 16, 1938. CCNY.

PRINCE (Rogers Nelson): Minneapolis, MN, 1960.

PRINCE, WILLIAM: Nicholas, NY, Jan. 26, 1913. Cornell U.

PRINCIPAL, VICTORIA: Fukuoka, Japan, Mar. 3, 1945. Dade Jr. Col.

PROCHNOW, JURGEN: Germany, 1941.

PROVAL, DAVID: Brooklyn, NY, 1943.

PROVINE, DOROTHY: Deadwood, SD, Jan. 20, 1937. U. Wash.

PROWSE, JULIET: Bombay, India, Sept. 25, 1936.

PRYOR, RICHARD: Peoria, IL, Dec. 1, 1940.

PURCELL, LEE: Cherry Point, NC, June 15, 1947. Stephens.

PURCELL, NOEL: Dublin, Ire., Dec. 23, 1900. Irish Christian Brothers.

PURDOM, EDMUND: Welwyn Garden City, Eng., Dec. 19, 1924. St. Ignatius College.

PYLE, DENVER: Bethune, CO, 1920.

Aidan Quinn	Gilda Radner	Carl Reiner	Diana Rigg	Cesar Romero	Eva Marie Saint

QUAID, DENNIS: Houston, TX, Apr. 9, 1954.

QUAYLE, ANTHONY: Lancashire, Eng., Sept. 7, 1913. Old Vic School.

QUINE, RICHARD: Detroit, MI, Nov. 12, 1920.

QUINLAN, KATHLEEN: Mill Valley, CA, Nov. 19, 1954.

QUINN, AIDAN: Chicago, IL, 1959.

QUINN, ANTHONY: Chihuahua, Mex., Apr. 21, 1915.

RADNER, GILDA: Detroit, MI, June 28, 1946.

RAFFERTY, FRANCES: Sioux City, IA, June 16, 1922. UCLA.

RAFFIN, DEBORAH: Los Angeles, Mar. 13, 1953. Valley Col.

RAINER, LUISE: Vienna, Aust., 1912.

RAINES, ELLA (Ella Wallace): Snoqualmie Falls, WA, Aug. 6, 1921. U. Wash.

RAMPLING, CHARLOTTE: Surmer, Eng., Feb. 5, 1946. U. Madrid.

RAMSEY, LOGAN: Long Beach, CA, Mar. 21, 1921. St. Joseph.

RANDALL, TONY (Leonard Rosenberg): Tulsa, OK, Feb. 26, 1920. Northwestern U.

RANDELL, RON: Sydney, Australia, Oct. 8, 1920. St. Mary's Col.

RASULALA, THALMUS (Jack Crowder): Miami, FL, Nov. 15, 1939. U. Redlands.

RAY, ALDO (Aldo DeRe): Pen Argyl, PA, Sept. 25, 1926. UCLA.

RAYE, MARTHA (Margie Yvonne Reed): Butte, MT, Aug. 27, 1916.

RAYMOND, GENE (Raymond Guion): NYC, Aug. 13, 1908.

REAGAN, RONALD: Tampico, IL, Feb. 6, 1911. Eureka College.

REASON, REX: Berlin, Ger., Nov. 30, 1928. Pasadena Playhouse.

REDDY, HELEN: Australia, Oct. 25, 1942.

REDFORD, ROBERT: Santa Monica, CA, Aug. 18, 1937. AADA.

REDGRAVE, CORIN: London, July 16, 1939.

REDGRAVE, LYNN: London, Mar. 8, 1943.

REDGRAVE, MICHAEL: Bristol, Eng., Mar. 20, 1908. Cambridge.

REDGRAVE, VANESSA: London, Jan. 30, 1937.

REDMAN, JOYCE: County Mayo, Ire., 1919. RADA.

REED, DONNA (Donna Mullenger): Denison, IA, Jan. 27, 1921. LACC.

REED, OLIVER: Wimbledon, Eng., Feb. 13, 1938.

REED, REX: Ft. Worth, TX, Oct. 2, 1939. LSU.

REEMS, HARRY (Herbert Streicher): Bronx, NY, 1947. U. Pittsburgh.

REEVE, CHRISTOPHER: NJ, Sept. 25, 1952. Cornell, Juilliard.

REEVES, STEVE: Glasgow, MT, Jan. 21, 1926.

REGEHR, DUNCAN: Lethbridge, Can., 1954.

REID, ELLIOTT: NYC, Jan. 16, 1920.

REINER, CARL: NYC, Mar. 20, 1922. Georgetown.

REINER, ROBERT: NYC, 1945. UCLA.

REMICK, LEE: Quincy, MA. Dec. 14, 1935. Barnard College.

RETTIG, TOMMY: Jackson Heights, NY, Dec. 10, 1941.

REVILL, CLIVE: Wellington, NZ, Apr. 18, 1930.

REY, FERNANDO: La Coruna, Spain, 1917.

REYNOLDS, BURT: Waycross, GA, Feb. 11, 1935. Fla. State U.

REYNOLDS, DEBBIE (Mary Frances Reynolds): El Paso, TX, Apr. 1, 1932.

REYNOLDS, MARJORIE: Buhl, ID, Aug. 12, 1921.

RHOADES, BARBARA: Poughkeepsie, NY, 1947.

RICH, IRENE: Buffalo, NY, Oct. 13, 1891. St. Margaret's School.

RICHARDS, JEFF (Richard Mansfield Taylor): Portland, OR, Nov. 1. USC.

RICKLES, DON: NYC, May 8, 1926. AADA.

RIEGERT, PETER: NYC, Apr. 11, 1947. U Buffalo.

RIGG, DIANA: Doncaster, Eng., July 20, 1938. RADA.

RINGWALD, MOLLY: Sacramento, CA, 1968.

RITTER, JOHN: Burbank, CA, Sept. 17, 1948. U.S. Cal.

ROBARDS, JASON: Chicago, July 26, 1922. AADA.

ROBERTS, ERIC: Biloxi, MS, 1956. RADA.

ROBERTS, RALPH: Salisbury, NC, Aug. 17, 1922. UNC.

ROBERTS, TANYA (Leigh): NYC, 1955.

ROBERTS, TONY: NYC, Oct. 22, 1939. Northwestern U.

ROBERTSON, CLIFF: La Jolla, CA, Sept. 9, 1925. Antioch Col.

ROBERTSON, DALE: Oklahoma City, July 14, 1923.

ROBINSON, CHRIS: Nov. 5, 1938, West Palm Beach, FL. LACC.

ROBINSON, JAY: NYC, Apr. 14, 1930.

ROBINSON, ROGER: Seattle, WA, May 2, 1941. USC.

ROCHEFORT, JEAN: Paris, 1930.

ROCK-SAVAGE, STEVEN: Melville, LA, Dec. 14, 1958. LSU.

ROGERS, CHARLES "BUDDY": Olathe, KS, Aug. 13, 1904. U. Kan.

ROGERS, GINGER (Virginia Katherine McMath): Independence, MO, July 16, 1911.

ROGERS, ROY (Leonard Slye): Cincinnati, Nov. 5, 1912.

ROGERS, WAYNE: Birmingham, AL, Apr. 7, 1933. Princeton.

ROLAND, GILBERT (Luis Antonio Damaso De Alonso): Juarez, Mex., Dec. 11, 1905.

ROLLINS, HOWARD E., JR.: 1951, Baltimore, MD.

ROMAN, RUTH: Boston, Dec. 23, 1922. Bishop Lee Dramatic School.

ROME, SIDNE: Akron, OH. Carnegie-Mellon.

ROMERO, CESAR: NYC, Feb. 15, 1907. Collegiate School.

RONSTADT, LINDA: Tucson, AZ, July 15, 1946.

ROONEY, MICKEY (Joe Yule, Jr.): Brooklyn, Sept. 23, 1920.

ROSE, REVA: Chicago, IL, July 30, 1940. Goodman.

ROSS, DIANA: Detroit, MI, Mar. 26, 1944.

ROSS, KATHARINE: Hollywood, Jan. 29, 1943. Santa Rosa Col.

ROSSELLINI, ISABELLA: Rome, June 18, 1952.

ROSSITER, LEONARD: Liverpool, Eng., Oct. 21, 1926.

ROUNDTREE, RICHARD: New Rochelle, NY, Sept. 7, 1942. Southern Ill.

ROURKE, MICKEY: Miami, FL, 1950.

ROWLANDS, GENA: Cambria, WI, June 19, 1936.

RUBIN, ANDREW: New Bedford, MA, June 22, 1946. AADA.

RUDD, PAUL: Boston, MA, May 15, 1940.

RULE, JANICE: Cincinnati, OH, Aug. 15, 1931.

RUPERT, MICHAEL: Denver, CO, Oct. 23, 1951. Pasadena Playhouse.

RUSH, BARBARA: Denver, CO, Jan. 4, 1929. U. Calif.

RUSSELL, JANE: Bemidji, MI, June 21, 1921. Max Reinhardt School.

RUSSELL, JOHN: Los Angeles, Jan. 3, 1921. U. Calif.

RUSSELL, KURT: Springfield, MA, Mar. 17, 1951.

RUTHERFORD, ANN: Toronto, Can., Nov. 2, 1917.

RUYMEN, AYN: Brooklyn, July 18, 1947. HB Studio.

SACCHI, ROBERT: Bronx, NY, 1941. NYU.

John Savage	Diana Scarwid	Max Showalter	Sylvia Sidney	Ron Silver	Maggie Smith

SAINT, EVA MARIE: Newark, NJ, July 4, 1924. Bowling Green State U.

ST. JACQUES, RAYMOND (James Arthur Johnson):CT.

ST. JAMES, SUSAN (Suzie Jane Miller): Los Angeles, Aug. 14. Conn. Col.

ST. JOHN, BETTA: Hawthorne, CA, Nov. 26, 1929.

ST. JOHN, JILL (Jill Oppenheim): Los Angeles, Aug. 19, 1940.

SALDANA, THERESA: Brooklyn, NY, 1955.

SALMI, ALBERT: Coney Island, NY, 1925. Actors Studio.

SALT, JENNIFER: Los Angeles, Sept. 4, 1944. Sarah Lawrence Col.

SANDS, TOMMY: Chicago, Aug. 27, 1937.

SAN JUAN, OLGA: NYC, Mar. 16, 1927.

SARANDON, CHRIS: Beckley, WV, July 24, 1942. U. WVa., Catholic U.

SARANDON, SUSAN (Tomalin): NYC, Oct. 4, 1946. Catholic U.

SARGENT, RICHARD (Richard Cox): Carmel, CA, 1933. Stanford.

SARRAZIN, MICHAEL: Quebec City, Can., May 22, 1940.

SAVAGE, JOHN (Youngs): Long Island, NY, Aug. 25, 1949. AADA.

SAVALAS, TELLY (Aristotle): Garden City, NY, Jan. 21, 1925. Columbia.

SAVOY, TERESA ANN: London, July 18, 1955.

SAXON, JOHN (Carmen Orrico): Brooklyn, Aug. 5, 1935.

SCALIA, JACK: Bensonhurst, NY, 1951.

SCARPELLI, GLEN: Staten Island, NY, July 1966.

SCARWID, DIANA: Savannah, GA. AADA, Pace U.

SCHEIDER, ROY: Orange, NJ, Nov. 10, 1935. Franklin-Marshall.

SCHELL, MARIA: Vienna, Jan. 15, 1926.

SCHELL, MAXIMILIAN: Vienna, Dec. 8, 1930.

SCHNEIDER, MARIA: Paris, Mar. 27, 1952.

SCHRODER, RICKY: Staten Island, NY, Apr. 13, 1970.

SCHWARZENEGGER, ARNOLD: Austria, 1947.

SCHYGULLA, HANNA: Katlowitz, Poland. 1943.

SCOFIELD, PAUL: Hurstpierpoint, Eng., Jan. 21, 1922. London Mask Theatre School.

SCOTT, DEBRALEE: Elizabeth, NJ, Apr. 2.

SCOTT, GEORGE C.: Wise, VA, Oct. 18, 1927. U. Mo.

SCOTT, GORDON (Gordon M. Werschkul): Portland, OR, Aug. 3, 1927. Oregon U.

SCOTT, MARTHA: Jamesport, MO, Sept. 22, 1914. U. Mich.

SCOTT, RANDOLPH: Orange County, VA, Jan. 23, 1903. UNC.

SCOTT-TAYLOR, JONATHAN: Brazil, 1962.

SEAGULL, BARBARA HERSHEY (Herztein): Hollywood, Feb. 5, 1948.

SEARS, HEATHER: London, 1935.

SECOMBE, HARRY: Swansea, Wales, Sept. 8, 1921.

SEGAL, GEORGE: NYC, Feb. 13, 1934. Columbia.

SELLARS, ELIZABETH: Glasgow, Scot., May 6, 1923.

SELWART, TONIO: Watenberg, Ger., June 9, 1906. Munich U.

SERNAS, JACQUES: Lithuania, July 30, 1925.

SEYLER, ATHENE (Athene Hannen): London, May 31, 1889.

SEYMOUR, ANNE: NYC, Sept. 11, 1909. American Laboratory Theatre.

SEYMOUR, JANE (Joyce Frankenberg): Hillingdon, Eng., Feb. 15, 1951.

SHARIF, OMAR (Michel Shalboub): Alexandria, Egypt, Apr. 10, 1932. Victoria Col.

SHARKEY, RAY: Brooklyn, NY, 1952. HB Studio.

SHATNER, WILLIAM: Montreal, Can., Mar. 22, 1931. McGill U.

SHAW, SEBASTIAN: Holt, Eng., May 29, 1905. Gresham School.

SHAW, STAN: Chicago, IL, 1952.

SHAWLEE, JOAN: Forest Hills, NY, Mar. 5, 1929.

SHAWN, DICK (Richard Shulefand): Buffalo, NY, Dec. 1, 1929. U. Miami.

SHEA, JOHN V.: North Conway, NH, Apr. 14, 1949. Bates, Yale.

SHEARER, MOIRA: Dunfermline, Scot., Jan. 17, 1926. London Theatre School.

SHEEDY, ALLY: NYC, June 13, 1962. USC.

SHEEN, MARTIN (Ramon Estevez): Dayton, OH, Aug. 3, 1940.

SHEFFIELD, JOHN: Pasadena, CA, Apr. 11, 1931. UCLA.

SHEPARD, SAM (Rogers): Ft. Sheridan, IL, Nov. 5, 1943.

SHEPHERD, CYBIL: Memphis, TN, Feb. 18, 1950. Hunter, NYU.

SHIELDS, BROOKE: NYC, May 31, 1965.

SHIRE, TALIA: Lake Success, NY. Yale.

SHORE, DINAH (Frances Rose Shore): Winchester, TN, Mar. 1, 1917. Vanderbilt U.

SHOWALTER, MAX (formerly Casey Adams): Caldwell, KS, June 2, 1917. Pasadena Playhouse.

SIDNEY, SYLVIA: NYC, Aug. 8, 1910. Theatre Guild School.

SIGNORET, SIMONE (Simone Kaminker): Wiesbaden, Ger., Mar. 25, 1921. Solange Sicard School.

SILVER, RON: NYC, July 2, 1946. SUNY.

SILVERS, PHIL (Philip Silversmith): Brooklyn, May 11, 1911.

SIMMONS, JEAN: London, Jan. 31, 1929. Aida Foster School.

SIMON, SIMONE: Marseilles, France, Apr. 23, 1910.

SIMPSON, O. J. (Orenthal James): San Francisco, CA, July 9, 1947. UCLA.

SINATRA, FRANK: Hoboken, NJ, Dec. 12, 1915.

SINCLAIR, JOHN (Gianluigi Loffredo): Rome, Italy, 1946.

SINDEN, DONALD: Plymouth, Eng., Oct. 9, 1923. Webber-Douglas.

SINGER, LORI: NYC, 1962, Juilliard.

SKALA, LILIA: Vienna. U. Dresden.

SKELTON, RED (Richard): Vincennes, IN, July 18, 1910.

SKERRITT, TOM: Detroit, MI, 1935. Wayne State U.

SLATER, HELEN: NYC, Dec. 14, 1963.

SMITH, ALEXIS: Penticton, Can., June 8, 1921. LACC.

SMITH, CHARLES MARTIN: Los Angeles, CA, 1954. CalState U.

SMITH, JACLYN: Houston, TX, Oct. 26, 1947.

SMITH, JOHN (Robert E. Van Orden): Los Angeles, Mar. 6, 1931. UCLA.

SMITH, KATE (Kathryn Elizabeth): Greenville, VA, May 1, 1909.

SMITH, KENT: NYC, Mar. 19, 1907. Harvard U.

SMITH, LOIS: Topeka, KS, Nov. 3, 1930. U. Wash.

SMITH, MAGGIE: Ilford, Eng., Dec. 28, 1934.

SMITH, ROGER: South Gate, CA, Dec. 18, 1932. U. Ariz.

SMITHERS, WILLIAM: Richmond, VA, July 10, 1927. Catholic U.

SNODGRESS, CARRIE: Chicago, Oct. 27, 1946. UNI.

SOLOMON, BRUCE: NYC, 1944. U. Miami, Wayne State U.

SOMERS, SUZANNE (Mahoney): San Bruno, CA, Oct. 16, 1946. Lone Mt. Col.

SOMMER, ELKE (Schletz): Berlin, Nov. 5, 1940.

SONDERGAARD, GALE: Litchfield, MN, Feb. 15, 1899. UMn.

| Lewis J. Stadlen | Kim Stanley | Daniel Stern | Beatrice Straight | George Takei | Jessica Tandy |

SORDI, ALBERTO: Rome, Italy, 1919.

SORVINO, PAUL: NYC, 1939. AMDA.

SOTHERN, ANN (Harriet Lake): Valley City, ND, Jan. 22, 1907. Washington U.

SOUL, DAVID: Aug. 28, 1943.

SPACEK, SISSY: Quitman, TX, Dec. 25, 1949. Actors Studio.

SPANO, VINCENT: Brooklyn, NY, Oct. 18, 1962.

SPENSER, JEREMY: Ceylon, 1937.

SPRINGER, GARY: NYC, July 29, 1954. Hunter Col.

SPRINGFIELD, RICK (Richard Springthorpe): Sydney, Aust. Aug. 23, 1949.

STACK, ROBERT: Los Angeles, Jan. 13, 1919. USC.

STADLEN, LEWIS J.: Brooklyn, Mar. 7, 1947. Neighborhood Playhouse.

STAFFORD, NANCY: Ft. Lauderdale, FL.

STALLONE, FRANK: NYC, July 30, 1950.

STALLONE, SYLVESTER: NYC, July 6, 1946. U. Miami.

STAMP, TERENCE: London, 1940.

STANDER, LIONEL: NYC, Jan. 11, 1908. UNC.

STANG, ARNOLD: Chelsea, MA, Sept. 28, 1925.

STANLEY, KIM (Patricia Reid): Tularosa, NM, Feb. 11, 1925. U. Tex.

STANWYCK, BARBARA (Ruby Stevens): Brooklyn, July 16, 1907.

STAPLETON, JEAN: NYC, Jan. 19, 1923.

STAPLETON, MAUREEN: Troy, NY, June 21, 1925.

STEEL, ANTHONY: London, May 21, 1920. Cambridge.

STEELE, TOMMY: London, Dec. 17, 1936.

STEENBURGEN, MARY: Newport, AR, 1953. Neighborhood Playhouse.

STEIGER, ROD: Westhampton, NY, Apr. 14, 1925.

STERLING, JAN (Jane Sterling Adriance): NYC, Apr. 3, 1923. Fay Compton School.

STERLING, ROBERT (William Sterling Hart): Newcastle, PA, Nov. 13, 1917. U. Pittsburgh.

STERN, DANIEL: Bethesda, MD, 1957.

STEVENS, ANDREW: Memphis, TN, June 10, 1955.

STEVENS, CONNIE (Concetta Ann Ingolia): Brooklyn, Aug. 8, 1938. Hollywood Professional School.

STEVENS, FISHER: Chicago, IL, Nov. 27, 1963. NYU.

STEVENS, KAYE (Catherine): Pittsburgh, July 21, 1933.

STEVENS, MARK (Richard): Cleveland, OH, Dec. 13, 1920.

STEVENS, STELLA (Estelle Eggleston): Hot Coffee, MS, Oct. 1, 1936.

STEVENSON, PARKER: CT, 1953.

STEWART, ALEXANDRIA: Montreal, Can., June 10, 1939. Louvre.

STEWART, ELAINE: Montclair, NJ, May 31, 1929.

STEWART, JAMES: Indiana, PA, May 20, 1908. Princeton.

STEWART, MARTHA (Martha Haworth): Bardwell, KY, Oct. 7, 1922.

STIMSON, SARA: Helotes, TX, 1973.

STING (Gordon Matthew Sumner): Wallsend, Eng., 1951.

STOCKWELL, DEAN: Hollywood, Mar. 5, 1935.

STOCKWELL, JOHN: Texas, 1961. Harvard.

STORM, GALE (Josephine Cottle): Bloomington, TX, Apr. 5, 1922.

STRAIGHT, BEATRICE: Old Westbury, NY, Aug. 2, 1916. Dartington Hall.

STRASBERG, SUSAN: NYC, May 22, 1938.

STRASSMAN, MARCIA: New Jersey, 1949.

STRAUD, DON: Hawaii, 1943.

STRAUSS, PETER: NY, 1947.

STREEP, MERYL (Mary Louise): Summit, NJ, June 22, 1949., Vassar, Yale.

STREISAND, BARBRA: Brooklyn, Apr. 24, 1942.

STRITCH, ELAINE: Detroit, MI, Feb. 2, 1925. Drama Workshop.

STRODE, WOODY: Los Angeles, 1914.

STRUTHERS, SALLY: Portland, OR, July 28, 1948. Pasadena Playhouse.

SULLIVAN, BARRY (Patrick Barry): NYC, Aug. 29, 1912. NYU.

SUMMER, DONNA (LaDonna Gaines): Boston, MA, Dec. 31, 1948.

SUTHERLAND, DONALD: St. John, New Brunswick, Can., July 17, 1934. U. Toronto.

SVENSON, BO: Goteborg, Swed., Feb. 13, 1941. UCLA.

SWEET, BLANCHE: Chicago, 1896.

SWINBURNE, NORA: Bath, Eng., July 24, 1902. RADA.

SWIT, LORETTA: Passaic, NJ, Nov. 4. AADA.

SYLVESTER, WILLIAM: Oakland, CA, Jan. 31, 1922. RADA.

SYMS, SYLVIA: London, June 1, 1934. Convent School.

T, MR. (Lawrence Tero): Chicago, 1952.

TABORI, KRISTOFFER (Siegel): Los Angeles, Aug. 4, 1952.

TAKEI, GEORGE: Los Angeles, CA, Apr. 20. UCLA.

TALBOT, LYLE (Lysle Hollywood): Pittsburgh, Feb. 8, 1904.

TALBOT, NITA: NYC, Aug. 8, 1930. Irvine Studio School.

TAMBLYN, RUSS: Los Angeles, Dec. 30, 1934.

TANDY, JESSICA: London, June 7, 1909. Dame Owens' School.

TAYLOR, DON: Freeport, PA, Dec. 13, 1920. Penn State U.

TAYLOR, ELIZABETH: London, Feb. 27, 1932. Byron House School.

TAYLOR, KENT (Louis Weiss): Nashua, IA, May 11, 1906.

TAYLOR, ROD (Robert): Sydney, Aust., Jan. 11, 1929.

TAYLOR-YOUNG, LEIGH: Wash., DC, Jan. 25, 1945. Northwestern.

TEAGUE, ANTHONY SKOOTER: Jacksboro, TX, Jan. 4, 1940.

TEEFY, MAUREEN: Minneapolis, MN, 1954; Juilliard.

TEMPLE, SHIRLEY: Santa Monica, CA, Apr. 23, 1927.

TERRY-THOMAS (Thomas Terry Hoar Stevens): Finchley, London, July 14, 1911. Ardingly College.

TERZIEFF, LAURENT: Paris, June 25, 1935.

THACKER, RUSS: Washington, DC, June 23, 1946, Montgomery Col.

THAXTER, PHYLLIS: Portland, ME, Nov. 20, 1921. St. Genevieve.

THELEN, JODI: St. Cloud, MN., 1963.

THOMAS, DANNY (Amos Jacobs): Deerfield, MI, Jan. 6, 1914.

THOMAS, MARLO (Margaret): Detroit, Nov. 21, 1938. USC.

THOMAS, PHILIP: Columbus, OH, May 26, 1949. Oakwood Col.

THOMAS, RICHARD: NYC, June 13, 1951. Columbia.

THOMPSON, JACK (John Payne): Sydney, Aus., 1940. U. Brisbane.

THOMPSON, MARSHALL: Peoria, IL, Nov. 27, 1925. Occidental.

THOMPSON, REX: NYC, Dec. 14, 1942.

THOMPSON, SADA: Des Moines, IA, Sept. 27, 1929. Carnegie Tech.

THULIN, INGRID: Solleftea, Sweden, Jan. 27, 1929. Royal Drama Theatre.

TICOTIN, RACHEL: Bronx, NY, 1958.

TIERNEY, GENE: Brooklyn, Nov. 20, 1920. Miss Farmer's School.

TIERNEY, LAWRENCE: Brooklyn, Mar. 15, 1919. Manhattan College.

TIFFIN, PAMELA (Wonso): Oklahoma City, Oct. 13, 1942.

John
Travolta

Leslie
Uggams

Peter
Ustinov

Brenda
Vaccaro

James
Victor

Jennifer
Warren

TODD, RICHARD: Dublin, Ire., June 11, 1919. Shrewsbury School.

TOLO, MARILU: Rome, Italy, 1944.

TOMLIN, LILY: Detroit, MI, Sept. 1, 1939. Wayne State U.

TOPOL (Chaim Topol): Tel-Aviv, Israel, Sept. 9, 1935.

TORN, RIP: Temple, TX, Feb. 6, 1931. U. Tex.

TORRES, LIZ: NYC, 1947. NYU.

TOTTER, AUDREY: Joliet, IL, Dec. 20, 1918.

TRAVERS, BILL: Newcastle-on-Tyne, Engl, Jan. 3, 1922.

TRAVIS, RICHARD (William Justice): Carlsbad, NM, Apr. 17, 1913.

TRAVOLTA, JOEY: Englewood, NJ, 1952.

TRAVOLTA, JOHN: Englewood, NJ, Feb. 18, 1954.

TREMAYNE, LES: London, Apr. 16, 1913. Northwestern, Columbia, UCLA.

TREVOR, CLAIRE (Wemlinger): NYC, March 8, 1909.

TRINTIGNANT, JEAN-LOUIS: Pont-St. Esprit, France, Dec. 11, 1930. Dullin-Balachova Drama School.

TRYON, TOM: Hartford, CT, Jan. 14, 1926. Yale.

TSOPEI, CORINNA: Athens, Greece, June 21, 1944.

TUCKER, FORREST: Plainfield, IN, Feb. 12, 1919. George Washington U.

TURNER, KATHLEEN: Springfield, MO, June 19, 1954. UMd.

TURNER, LANA (Julia Jean Mildred Frances Turner): Wallace, ID, Feb. 8, 1921.

TUSHINGHAM, RITA: Liverpool, Eng., 1940.

TUTIN, DOROTHY: London, Apr. 8, 1930.

TUTTLE, LURENE: Pleasant Lake, IN, Aug. 20, 1906. USC.

TWIGGY (Lesley Hornby): London, Sept. 19, 1949.

TYLER, BEVERLY (Beverly Jean Saul): Scranton, PA, July 5, 1928.

TYRRELL, SUSAN: San Francisco, 1946.

TYSON, CICELY: NYC, Dec. 19.

UGGAMS, LESLIE: NYC, May 25, 1943.

ULLMANN, LIV: Tokyo, Dec. 10, 1938. Webber-Douglas Acad.

USTINOV, PETER: London, Apr. 16, 1921. Westminster School.

VACCARO, BRENDA: Brooklyn, Nov. 18, 1939. Neighborhood Playhouse.

VALLEE, RUDY (Hubert): Island Pond, VT, July 28, 1901. Yale.

VALLI, ALIDA: Pola, Italy, May 31, 1921. Rome Academy of Drama.

VALLONE, RAF: Riogio, Italy, Feb. 17, 1916. Turin U.

VAN CLEEF, LEE: Somerville, NJ, Jan. 9, 1925.

VAN DE VEN, MONIQUE: Holland, 1957.

VAN DEVERE, TRISH (Patricia Dressel): Englewood Cliffs, NJ, Mar. 9, 1945. Ohio Wesleyan.

VAN DOREN, MAMIE (Joan Lucile Olander): Rowena, SD, Feb. 6, 1933.

VAN DYKE, DICK: West Plains, MO, Dec. 13, 1925.

VAN FLEET, JO: Oakland, CA, 1922.

VAN PATTEN, DICK: NYC, Dec. 9, 1928.

VAN PATTEN, JOYCE: NYC, Mar. 9, 1934.

VAUGHN, ROBERT: NYC, Nov. 22, 1932. USC.

VEGA, ISELA: Mexico, 1940.

VENNERA, CHICK: Herkimer, NY, Mar. 27, 1952. Pasadena Playhouse.

VENORA, DIANE: Hartford, Ct., 1952. Juilliard.

VENTURA, LINO: Parma, Italy, July 14, 1919.

VENUTA, BENAY: San Francisco, Jan. 27, 1911.

VERDON, GWEN: Culver City, CA, Jan. 13, 1925.

VEREEN, BEN: Miami, FL, Oct. 10, 1946.

VICTOR, JAMES (Lincoln Rafael Peralta Diaz): Santiago, D.R., July 27, 1939. Haaren HS/NYC.

VILLECHAIZE, HERVE: Paris, Apr. 23, 1943.

VINCENT, JAN-MICHAEL: Denver, CO, July 15, 1944. Ventura.

VIOLET, ULTRA (Isabelle Collin-Dufresne): Grenoble, France.

VITALE, MILLY: Rome, Italy, July 16, 1938. Lycee Chateaubriand.

VOHS, JOAN: St. Albans, NY, July 30, 1931.

VOIGHT, JON: Yonkers, NY, Dec. 29, 1938. Catholic U.

VOLONTE, GIAN MARIA: Milan, Italy, Apr. 9, 1933.

VON SYDOW, MAX: Lund, Swed., July 10, 1929. Royal Drama Theatre.

WAGNER, LINDSAY: Los Angeles, June 22, 1949.

WAGNER, ROBERT: Detroit, Feb. 10, 1930.

WAHL, KEN: Chicago, IL, 1957.

WAITE, GENEVIEVE: South Africa, 1949.

WALKEN, CHRISTOPHER: Astoria, NY, Mar. 31, 1943. Hofstra.

WALKER, CLINT: Hartfold, IL, May 30, 1927. USC.

WALKER, NANCY (Ann Myrtle Swoyer): Philadelphia, May 10, 1921.

WALLACH, ELI: Brooklyn, Dec. 7, 1915. CCNY, U. Tex.

WALLACH, ROBERTA: NYC, Aug. 2, 1955.

WALLIS, SHANI: London, Apr. 5, 1941.

WALSTON, RAY: New Orleans, Nov. 22, 1917. Cleveland Playhouse.

WALTER, JESSICA: Brooklyn, NY, Jan. 31, 1940. Neighborhood Playhouse.

WANAMAKER, SAM: Chicago, June 14, 1919. Drake.

WARD, BURT (Gervis): Los Angeles, July 6, 1945.

WARD, RACHEL: London, 1957.

WARD, SIMON: London, 1941.

WARDEN, JACK: Newark, NJ, Sept. 18, 1920.

WARNER, DAVID: Manchester, Eng., 1941. RADA.

WARREN, JENNIFER: NYC, Aug. 12, 1941. U. Wisc.

WARREN, LESLEY ANN: NYC, Aug. 16, 1946.

WARREN, MICHAEL: South Bend, IN, 1946. UCLA.

WARRICK, RUTH: St. Joseph, MO, June 29, 1915. U. Mo.

WASHBOURNE, MONA: Birmingham, Eng., Nov. 27, 1903.

WASHINGTON, DENZEL: Mt. Vernon, NY, Dec. 28, 1954. Fordham.

WASSON, CRAIG: Ontario, OR, Mar. 15, 1954. UOre.

WATERSTON, SAM: Cambridge, MA, Nov. 15, 1940. Yale.

WATLING, JACK: London, Jan. 13, 1923. Italia Conti School.

WATSON, DOUGLASS: Jackson, GA, Feb. 24, 1921. UNC.

WAYNE, DAVID (Wayne McKeehan): Travers City, MI, Jan. 30, 1914. Western Michigan State U.

WAYNE, PATRICK: Los Angeles, July 15, 1939. Loyola.

WEATHERS, CARL: New Orleans, LA, 1948. Long Beach CC.

WEAVER, DENNIS: Joplin, MO, June 4, 1924. U. Okla.

WEAVER, MARJORIE: Crossville, TN, Mar. 2, 1913. Indiana U.

WEAVER, SIGOURNEY (Susan): NYC, 1949. Stanford, Yale.

WEBBER, ROBERT: Santa Ana, CA, Sept. 14, 1925. Compton Jr. Col.

WEDGEWORTH, ANN: Abilene, TX, Jan. 21, 1935. U. Tex.

WELCH, RAQUEL (Tejada): Chicago, Sept. 5, 1940.

Carl Weathers

Raquel Welch

Treat Williams

Debra Winger

WELD, TUESDAY (Susan): NYC, Aug. 27, 1943. Hollywood Professional School.
WELDON, JOAN: San Francisco, Aug. 5, 1933. San Francisco Conservatory.
WELLER, PETER: New Britain, CT., June 24, 1947. AmThWing.
WELLES, GWEN: NYC, Mar. 4.
WELLES, ORSON: Kenosha, WI, May 6, 1915. Todd School.
WESTON, JACK (Morris Weinstein): Cleveland, OH, Aug. 21, 1915.
WHITAKER, JOHNNY: Van Nuys, CA, Dec. 13, 1959.
WHITE, CAROL: London, Apr. 1, 1944.
WHITE, CHARLES: Perth Amboy, NJ, Aug. 29, 1920. Rutgers U.
WHITE, JESSE: Buffalo, NY, Jan. 3, 1919.
WHITMAN, STUART: San Francisco, Feb. 1, 1929. CCLA
WHITMORE, JAMES: White Plains, NY, Oct. 1, 1921. Yale.
WHITNEY, GRACE LEE: Detroit, MI, Apr. 1, 1930.
WIDDOES, KATHLEEN: Wilmington, DE, Mar. 21, 1939.
WIDMARK, RICHARD: Sunrise, MN, Dec. 26, 1914. Lake Forest.
WILCOX-HORNE, COLIN: Highlands, NC, Feb. 4, 1937. U. Tenn.
WILDE, CORNEL: NYC, Oct. 13, 1915. CCNY, Columbia.
WILDER, GENE (Jerome Silberman): Milwaukee, WI, June 11, 1935. U. Iowa.
WILLIAMS, BILLY DEE: NYC, Apr. 6, 1937.
WILLIAMS, CINDY: Van Nuys, CA, Aug. 22, 1947. LACC.
WILLIAMS, DICK A.: Chicago, IL, Aug. 9, 1938.
WILLIAMS, EMLYN: Mostyn, Wales, Nov. 26, 1905. Oxford.

WILLIAMS, ESTHER: Los Angeles, Aug. 8, 1921.
WILLIAMS, GRANT: NYC, Aug. 18, 1930. Queens College.
WILLIAMS, ROBIN: Chicago, IL, July 21, 1952. Juilliard.
WILLIAMS, TREAT (Richard): Rowayton, CT. 1952.
WILLIAMSON, FRED: Gary, IN, Mar. 5, 1938. Northwestern.
WILSON, DEMOND: NYC, Oct. 13, 1946. Hunter Col.
WILSON, FLIP (Clerow Wilson): Jersey City, NJ, Dec. 8, 1933.
WILSON, LAMBERT: Paris, 1959.
WILSON, NANCY: Chillicothe, OH, Feb. 20, 1937.
WILSON, SCOTT: Atlanta, GA, 1942.
WINDE, BEATRICE: Chicago, Jan. 6.
WINDOM, WILLIAM: NYC, Sept. 28, 1923. Williams Col.
WINDSOR, MARIE (Emily Marie Bertelson): Marysvale, UT, Dec. 11, 1924. Brigham Young U.
WINFIELD, PAUL: Los Angeles, 1940. UCLA.
WINGER, DEBRA: Cleveland, OH, May 16, 1955. Cal State.
WINKLER, HENRY: NYC, Oct. 30, 1945. Yale.
WINN, KITTY: Wash., D.C., 1944. Boston U.
WINTERS, JONATHAN: Dayton, OH, Nov. 11, 1925. Kenyon Col.
WINTERS, ROLAND: Boston, Nov. 22, 1904.
WINTERS, SHELLEY (Shirley Schrift): St. Louis, Aug. 18, 1922. Wayne U.
WITHERS, GOOGIE: Karachi, India, Mar. 12, 1917. Italia Conti.
WITHERS, JANE: Atlanta, GA, Apr. 12, 1926.
WOODLAWN, HOLLY (Harold Ajzenberg): Juana Diaz, PR, 1947.
WOODS, JAMES: Vernal, UT, Apr. 18, 1947. MIT.

WOODWARD, JOANNE: Thomasville, GA, Feb. 27, 1930. Neighborhood Playhouse.
WOOLAND, NORMAN: Dusseldorf, Ger., Mar. 16, 1910. Edward VI School.
WOPAT, TOM: Lodi, WI, 1950.
WORONOV, MARY: Brooklyn, Dec. 8, 1946. Cornell.
WORTH, IRENE: (Hattie Abrams) June 23, 1916. Neb. UCLA.
WRAY, FAY: Alberta, Can., Sept. 15, 1907.
WRIGHT, TERESA: NYC, Oct. 27, 1918.
WYATT, JANE: Campgaw, NJ, Aug. 10, 1911. Barnard College.
WYMAN, JANE (Sarah Jane Fulks): St. Joseph, MO, Jan. 4, 1914.
WYMORE, PATRICE: Miltonvale, KS, Dec. 17, 1926.
WYNN, KEENAN: NYC, July 27, 1916. St. John's.
WYNN, MAY (Donna Lee Hickey): NYC, Jan. 8, 1930.
WYNTER, DANA (Dagmar): London, June 8, 1927. Rhodes U.
YORK, DICK: Fort Wayne, IN, Sept. 4, 1928. De Paul U.
YORK, MICHAEL: Fulmer, Eng., Mar. 27, 1942. Oxford.
YORK, SUSANNAH: London, Jan. 9, 1941. RADA.
YOUNG, ALAN (Angus): North Shield, Eng., Nov. 19, 1919.
YOUNG, LORETTA (Gretchen): Salt Lake City, Jan. 6, 1912. Immaculate Heart College.
YOUNG, ROBERT: Chicago, Feb. 22, 1907.
ZACHARIAS, ANN: Stockholm, Sw., 1956.
ZADORA, PIA: Forest Hills, NY. 1954.
ZETTERLING, MAI: Sweden, May 27, 1925. Ordtuery Theatre School.
ZIMBALIST, EFREM, JR.: NYC, Nov. 30, 1918. Yale.

James Woods

Joanne Woodward

Michael York

Ann Zacharias

Efrem Zimbalist, Jr.

| Luther
Adler | Richard
Basehart | Richard
Burton | Jackie
Coogan | Peggy Ann
Garner | Janet
Gaynor |

1984 OBITUARIES

LUTHER ADLER, 81, NYC-born actor on screen and stage, died Dec. 8, 1984 at his home in Kutztown, PA, after a long illness. At the age of 5 he made his acting debut in his parents' Adler Yiddish Theatre Company in NYC, and continued his career for over 70 decades. After his Broadway successes, he made his film debut in 1937's "Lancer Spy," subsequently appearing in such films as "Cornered," "Saigon," "The Loves of Carmen," "Wake of the Red Witch," "House of Strangers," "D.O.A.," "Kiss Tomorrow Goodbye," "M," "The Desert Fox," "Hoodlum Empire," "Miami Story," "Girl in the Red Velvet Swing," "The Last Angry Man," "Cast a Giant Shadow," "The Brotherhood," "Murph the Surf," "Man in the Glass Booth," "Voyage of the Damned" and "The Three Sisters." He had also appeared on tv. Surviving are his second wife, a son, and two sisters, Stella and Julia.

E. J. ANDRE, 76, Detroit-born character actor on film, stage and tv, died of cancer Sept. 6, 1984 in his home in Hollywood, CA. After his film debut in "The Ten Commandments," he appeared in such pictures as "Battle at Bloody Beach," "Magic," "The Dutchess and the Dirtwater Fox," "Papillon" and "Nickelodeon." He is survived by his widow and a son.

RICHARD BASEHART, 70, Ohio-born screen, stage and tv actor, died Sept. 17, 1984 after several strokes in Los Angeles, CA, the first, immediately after narrating the closing ceremonies of the Olympics. After Broadway success, he began his film career in 1947 with "Cry Wolf" and "Repeat Performance." Subsequent film credits include "He Walked by Night," "Roseanna McCoy," "Tension," "Outside the Wall," "Fourteen Hours," "House on Telegraph Hill," "Decision Before Dawn," "Titanic," "Moby Dick," "La Strada," "Time Limit," "Brothers Karamazov," "Portrait in Black," "Passport to China," "Being There." For 4 years he was Admiral Nelson in the tv series "Voyage to the Bottom of the Sea." Surviving are his third wife, two daughters, and a son.

RICHARD BENEDICT, 64, Sicily-born tv director, former actor, died of a heart attack Apr. 25, 1984 in his home in Studio City, CA. At age 7 he came to the U.S. and in his teens became a prizefighter. After appearing on Broadway, he moved to Hollywood in 1945 and subsequently appeared in "See My Lawyer," "A Walk in the Sun," "O.S.S.," "Till the End of Time," "The Guilt of Janet Ames," "Backlash," "Crossfire," "Race Street," "City Across the River," "Scene of the Crime," "Ace in the Hole," "Okinawa," "The Juggler," "Act of Love," "The Shrike," "Monkey on My Back," "Beginning of the End," "Let's Go, Navy!," "Murder without Tears," "Spring Reunion," "He Laughed Last," and "Ocean's Eleven." He turned to directing tv in the early 1960's. He is survived by his widow, a daughter, and an actor son Nick.

SUDIE BOND, 56, Kentucky-born actress on stage, screen and tv, died Nov. 10, 1984 of a respiratory ailment in her NYC apartment, shortly after returning from her performance in an Off-Broadway production of "The Foreigner." Her screen credits include "Guns of the Trees," "Andy," "I Am the Cheese," "The Gold Bug," "Silkwood," "Swingshift," "Love Story," "Come Back to the 5 & Dime, Jimmy Dean," and "Johnny Dangerously." On tv she appeared in "Maude," "Mary Hartman," "The Guiding Light," "Flo," and "Benson." A son survives.

FREDERICK BRISSON, 71, Copenhagen-born stage and film producer, died Oct. 8, 1984 after a stroke in NYC. His screen credits include "Moonlight Sonata," "Never Wave at a Wac," "Five Finger Exercise," "Under the Yum Yum Tree," "The Velvet Touch," "The Pajama Game" and "Damn Yankees." He was married for 35 years to the late actress Rosalind Russell, and was separated from his second wife. A son survives.

PETER BULL, 72, British actor on stage, screen and tv, and a writer, died of a heart attack May 20, 1984 in his native London. He began his career on stage in 1933, and made his Broadway debut in 1935. His first film (1934) was "The Silent Voice," followed by "As You Like It," "Sabotage," "The Ware Case," "The Turners of Prospect Road," "Saraband for Dead Lovers," "African Queen," "Oliver Twist," "The Captain's Progress," "Malta Story," "Beau Brummel," "Footsteps in the Fog," "Three Worlds of Gulliver," "Goodbye Again," "The Old Dark House," "Tom Jones," "Dr. Strangelove," "You Must Be Joking," "Dr. Doolittle," "Lock Up Your Daughters," "The Executioner," "Joseph Andrews" and "Yellowbeard." Two brothers survive.

WALTER BURKE, 75, actor on screen, stage and tv, died Aug. 4, 1984 of emphysema in Woodland Hills, CA. After his film debut in 1949 in "All the King's Men," his credits include "Mystery Street," "M," "The Guy Who Came Back," "Wreck of the Mary Deare," "Let No Man Write My Epitaph," "Jack the Giant Killer," "The President's Analyst," "The Wheeler Dealers," "Double Trouble" and "Support Your Local Sheriff." In the early 1970's he moved to Pennsylvania where he taught. Four daughters survive.

RICHARD BURTON, 58, Wales-born Richard Jenkins, one of the finest actors on stage and screen, died Aug. 5, 1984 of a cerebral hemorrhage in Geneva, Switzerland. He was the most nominated actor who never won an Oscar. His film debut was 1947 in "Last Days of Dolwyn," followed by "Now Barabbas Was a Robber," "Waterfront," "Her Paneled Door," "Green Grow the Rushes," "Woman with No Name," "My Cousin Rachel," "Desert Rats," "The Robe," "Prince of Players," "Rains of Ranchipur," "Alexander the Great," "Sea Wife," "Bitter Victory," "Look Back in Anger," "Bramble Bush," "Ice Palace," "A Midsummer Night's Dream" (narrator), "The Longest Day," "Cleopatra," "The V.I.P.'s," "Becket," "Hamlet," "Night of the Iguana," "Sandpiper," "The Spy Who Came in from the Cold," "Who's Afraid of Virginia Woolf?," "Taming of the Shrew," "The Comedians," "Dr. Faustus," "Boom!," "Where Eagles Dare," "Candy," "Staircase," "The Keep," "Man from Nowhere," "Anne of the Thousand Days," "Guilt Merchants," "Wagner," "Hammersmith Is Out," "Bluebeard," "Raid on Rommel," "Villain," "The Klansman," "Exorcist II," "Equus," "The Wild Geese," "Circle of Two," "Breakthrough," and "1984." He is survived by his fourth wife, and 3 daughters, actress Kate, Jessica and Maria. Interment was in Celigny, Switzerland.

JEANNE CAGNEY, 65, NYC-born actress on stage, screen, tv and radio, died of undisclosed cause on Dec. 7, 1984 in her home in Newport Beach, CA. After her screen debut in "All Women Have Secrets," she appeared in "Rhythm on the River," "Golden Gloves," "Queen of the Mob," "Yankee Doodle Dandy," "The Time of Your Life," "Quicksand," "Don't Bother to Knock," "A Lion Is in the Streets," "Kentucky Rifle," "Man of a 1000 Faces," and "Town Tamer," her last in 1965. Surviving are two daughters, and two brothers, William and actor James.

HOWLAND CHAMBERLIN, 73, screen, stage and tv character actor, died Sept. 1, 1984 of complications from lung and liver problems. In addition to over 100 plays, he appeared in some 40 films, including "The Web," "A Song Is Born," "Force of Evil," "And Baby Makes Three," "Francis," "House by the River," "Edge of Doom," "Mister 880," "Surrender," "Pickup," "The Racket," "The Big Night," "The Best Years of Our Lives," "Force of Evil," "High Noon," "Kramer vs. Kramer," "Barbarosa" and "Electric Dreams." He is survived by his widow, a son and a daughter.

JACKIE COOGAN, 69, Los Angeles-born actor, died Mar. 1, 1984 of a heart attack in Santa Monica, CA. After his film debut at 18 months he later, at the age of 9, became the number one boxoffice star in 1923, earning over $2,000,000. Because his parents had spent his earnings, the publicity forced the passage of the so-called Coogan Law, putting juvenile earnings into trust funds. His many film credits include "The Kid," "Peck's Bad Boy," "Oliver Twist," "Daddy," "Circus Days," "Long Live the King," "Little Robinson Crusoe," "Boy of Flanders," "Old Clothes," "Tom Sawyer," "Huckleberry Finn," "Home on the Range," "College Swing," "The Buster Keaton Story," "Kilroy Was Here," "The Joker Is Wild," "Eighteen and Anxious," "High School Confidential," "Lonelyhearts," "Beat Generation," "Shakiest Gun in the West," "Million Dollar Legs," "Marlowe," "Dr. Heckyl and Mr. Hype," "The Prey," and "The Escape Artist." His greatest success in later years was as Uncle Fester on the tv series "The Addams Family." Surviving are his fourth wife of 30 years, two sons and two daughters.

CLYDE COOK, 92, Australia-born character actor and comedian, died in his sleep Aug. 13, 1984 at his home in Carpenteria, CA. After World War I, he moved to the U.S. and appeared in Ziegfeld Follies, and numerous two-reel comedies. His many feature length films include "He Who Gets Slapped," "Good Time Charley," "The Docks of New York," "Strong Boy," "Dangerous Woman," "Taming of the Shrew," "Dawn Patrol," "Sunny," "Never the Twain Shall Meet," "Blondie of the Follies," "West of Singapore," "Oliver Twist," "Barbary Coast," "Kidnapped," "Bull Dog Drummond," "Sea Hawk," "Ladies in Retirement," "White Cargo," "Forever and a Day," "To Each His Own," "The Verdict," and "Donovan's Reef" his last in 1963. A son and a daughter survive.

ROLAND CULVER, 83, British stage and screen character actor, died of a heart ailment Feb. 29, 1984 in his native London. He had appeared in more than 40 plays and 50 films. His screen credits include "Nell Gwyn," "Love on Wheels," "Accused," "French without Tears," "Night Train to Munich," "Secret Mission," "The Avengers," "Spitfire," "On Approval," "English without Tears," "The Life and Death of Colonel Blimp," "Dear Octopus," "Dead of Night," "Perfect Strangers," "To Each His Own," "Wanted for Murder," "Down to Earth," "Singapore," "The Emperor Waltz," "The Great Lover," "Man Who Loved Redheads," "Betrayed," "The Holly and the Ivy," "Safari," "The Ship That Died of Shame," "Mad Little Island," "Bonjour Tristesse," "The Truth about Women," "The Circle," "Term of Trial," "A Pair of Briefs," "The Yellow Rolls Royce," "Thunderball," "In Search of Gregory," "Fragment of Fear" and "Rough Cut." Surviving are his widow, and two sons, Robin, a painter, and Michael an actor.

RUTH CUMMINGS, 90, stage and screen actress, died Dec. 6, 1984 in Woodland Hills, CA. She began her career as Ruth Sinclair and appeared in such films as "The Heart Line," "Without Benefit of Clergy" and "The Masquerade." After her marriage to director Irving Cummings (he died in 1959), she became Ruth Cummings and was seen in such films as "La Boheme," "In Old Kentucky," "Love," "The Student Prince," "Quality Street," "Annie Laurie," "California," "Lovers?," "Mysterious Lady," "A Woman of Affairs," "Wild Orchids," "Our Dancing Daughters," "A Certain Young Man," "Masks of the Devil," "Wyoming," "Our Modern Maidens," "Bridge of San Luis Rey," and "Redemption." She is survived by her son, tv producer-writer, Irving Cummings, Jr.

RICHARD DEACON, 62, Philadelphia-born screen, stage and tv actor, died of a heart attack Aug. 8, 1984 in Los Angeles, CA. He had appeared in over 1000 tv shows, and 100 films. His screen credits include "Desiree," "My Sister Eileen," "Good Morning, Miss Dove," "Hot Blood," "Francis in the Haunted House," "The Power and the Prize," "Solid Gold Cadillac," "Spring Reunion," "The Remarkable Mr. Pennypacker," "Young Philadelphians," "Dear Hart," "Enter Laughing," "Billie," "Blackbeard's Ghost," "Lady in Cement," "The Happy Hooker Goes to Hollywood." He is probably best remembered for his role of Mel Cooley on the tv series "The Dick Van Dyke Show," but he also appeared as a regular on 14 different series. His father survives.

DIANA DORS, 52, nee Diana Fluck in Swindon, Midlands, Eng., died of cancer May 4, 1984 in London, Eng. She began her career at 17 in "The Shop at Sly Corner," and became England's answer to Marilyn Monroe. Her credits include "Good Time Girl," "The Weak and the Wicked," "A Kid for Two Farthings," "Blonde Sinner," "Value for Money," "An Alligator Named Daisy," "Unholy Wife," "Room 43," "Scent of Mystery," "On the Double," "King of the Roaring 20's," "Berserk!," "Danger Route," "Hammerhead," "Baby Love," "A Girl in My Soup," "Deep End," "Fright," "The Pied Piper," "Nothing but the Night," "Craze," "Tales from beyond the Grave," "What the Swedish Butler Saw," and "Losing" her last film. Surviving are her third husband, Alan Lake, and three sons, two by Richard Dawson, her second husband.

JUNE DUPREZ, 66, stage and screen actress, died Oct. 30, 1984 after a long illness in her native London, Eng. Her career began in 1936 in "The Crimson Circle," followed by "The Cardinal," "The Spy in Black," "The Lion Has Wings," "Thief of Bagdad," "Little Tokyo USA," "They Raid by Night," "Forever and a Day," "None but the Lonely Heart," "Brighton Strangler," "And Then There Were None," "That Brennan Girl," and "One Plus One" (or "Mrs. Kingsley's Report"). She also appeared with the American Repertory Theatre in NYC. Two daughters survive.

MERIE EARLE, 95, Ohio-born character actress, died of uremic poisoning on Nov. 4, 1984 in Glendale, CA. She had appeared in over 50 commercials, and ten feature films including "Going Ape!," "Crazy Ladies" and "Almost Summer." She was probably best known for her role of Maude Gormley on "The Waltons" tv series. No reported survivors.

SAMUEL G. ENGEL, 79, producer-screenwriter, died from a heart condition Apr. 7, 1984 in his home in Santa Cruz, CA. He wrote such films as "Sins of Man," "The Big Shakedown," "Johnny Apollo," "Scotland Yard," "Private Nurse," and "My Darling Clementine." He was a producer on such films as "Crack-up," "Sitting Pretty," "Street with No Name," "Mr. Belvedere Goes to College," "Come to the Stable," "Rawhide," "Belles on Their Toes," "A Man Called Peter," "Daddy Long Legs," "Good Morning, Miss Dove," "Boy on a Dolphin," "Bernardine," "The Story of Ruth" and "The Lion." He was a founder of the Producers Guild, and started the televising of the "Oscar" ceremonies. He is survived by his widow and two sons.

BESS FLOWERS, 85, veteran screen actress, died July 28, 1984 in Woodland Hills, CA. She entered films in the 1920's, and among her many credits are "Irene," "The Ghost Talks," "Bachelor Apartment," "Paid to Dance," "The Shadow," "Lone Wolf in Paris," "Meet John Doe," "Song of the Thin Man," "Born to Be Bad," "It Happened One Night," "Ninotchka," "You Can't Take It with You," "Deception," "The Great Gatsby," "All About Eve," "The View from Pompey's Head," "Pal Joey" and "Good Neighbor Sam." She was married twice. No reported survivors.

CARL FOREMAN, 69, Chicago-born producer and screenwriter, died of cancer June 26, 1984 in his home in Beverly Hills, CA. His scripts for "High Noon," "Champion," "The Men," "The Guns of Navarone" and "Young Winston" were all nominated for Oscars, and "The Bridge on the River Kwai" that he had co-written with Michael Wilson received a 1957 Oscar. Other credits include "Dakota," "Home of the Brave," "Young Man with a Horn," "Cyrano de Bergerac," "The Key," "The Victors," "Born Free," "MacKenna's Gold" and "The Virgin Soldiers." Survivors include his widow and three children.

PEGGY ANN GARNER, 53, Ohio-born film and stage actress, died of cancer Oct. 16, 1984 in Woodland Hills, CA. She began her career as a child and in 1945 received an honorary Oscar as outstanding child actress in "A Tree Grows in Brooklyn." Other credits include "In Name Only," "The Pied Piper," "Jane Eyre," "The Keys of the Kingdom," "Junior Miss," "Nob Hill," "Home Sweet Homicide," "Thunder in the Valley," "Little Miss Thoroughbred," "Daisy Kenyon," "Sign of the Ram," "The Big Cat," "Teresa," "Black Widow," "Eight Witnesses," "The Black Forest," "The Cat," and "A Wedding." She frequently appeared on tv from 1950–67. She had been married and divorced three times. A daughter survives.

JANET GAYNOR, 77, Philadelphia-born Laura Gainor, stage and screen actress, died Sept. 14, 1984 in Palm Springs, CA, of complications from a traffic accident in Sept. 1982 in San Francisco. She began her career as an extra, but quickly became one of the most popular stars of films. In 1928 the Oscars were first presented, and Miss Gaynor received the "Best Actress" award for "Sunrise," "Seventh Heaven" and "Street Angel." Subsequent films include "Four Devils," "Christina," "Lucky Star," "Sunny Side Up," "Happy Days," "High Society Blues," "The Man Who Came Back," "Daddy Long Legs," "Merely Mary Ann," "Delicious," "The First Year," "Tess of the Storm Country," "State Fair," "Adorable," "Paddy the Next Best Thing," "Carolina," "Change of Heart," "Servants' Entrance," "One More Spring," "The Farmer Takes a Wife," "Small Town Girl," "Ladies in Love," "A Star Is Born" (for which she received an Oscar nomination), "Three Loves Has Nancy," "The Young in Heart." She had been starred with Charles Farrell in 12 pictures. In 1939, at the peak of her career, she announced her retirement and married designer Gilbert Adrian. She came out of retirement to appear in 1957's "Bernardine." Shortly after Adrian died in 1959, she made her stage debut. In 1964 she married producer Paul Gregory who survives, as does her son Robin Gaynor Adrian.

GEORGE GIVOT, 81, Omaha-born vaudeville, radio and film actor, died June 7, 1984 in Palm Springs, CA. After his 1933 debut in "The Chief," he appeared in "Hollywood Party," "Riffraff," "Paddy O'Day," "Step Lively, Jeeves," "Wake Up and Live," "The Hit Parade," "Thin Ice," "Conquest," "Beg, Borrow or Steal," "45 Fathers," "Hollywood Cavalcade," "Young as You Feel," "Road to Morocco," "DuBarry Was a Lady," "Behind the Rising Sun," "Government Girl," "April in Paris," "Three Sailors and a Girl," "Miracle in the Rain" and "China Girl." His widow survives.

NED GLASS, 78, Poland-born character actor on stage, screen and tv, died of heart failure June 15, 1984 in Encino, CA. After his picture debut in 1938's "Give Me a Sailor," he had roles in such films as "He's a Cockeyed Wonder," "Storm Warning," "Yellow Tomahawk," "The Steel Cage," "Hot Rod Rumble," "Back from the Dead," "The Rebel Set," "West Side Story," "Experiment in Terror," "Kid Galahad," "The Grip of Fear," "Who's Got the Action?," "Papa's Delicate Condition," "Charade," "A Big Hand for the Little Lady," "Blindfold," "Fortune Cookie," "Never a Dull Moment," "Love Bug," "Lady Sings the Blues," "All-American Boy," "Save the Tiger," "All the Marbles" and "Street Music." He had been a regular on the tv series "Bridget Loves Bernie," and "Julia" as Sol Cooper. A brother survives.

FRANCES GOODRICH, 93, New Jersey-born writer for stage and screen, died of lung cancer Jan. 29, 1984 in New York City. She began her career as an actress in 1916. In 1930 she collaborated with Albert Hackett on a play and they were married the next year. Together they continued to write for both media. Film credits include "Naughty Marietta," "Ah, Wilderness," "Rose Marie," "After the Thin Man," "The Firefly," "Society Lawyer," "Another Thin Man," "Lady in the Dark," "Hitler Gang," "The Virginian," "It's a Wonderful Life," "The Pirate," "Summer Holiday," "Easter Parade," "In the Good Old Summertime," "Father of the Bride," "Father's Little Dividend," "Too Young to Kiss," "The Long, Long Trailer," "Seven Brides for Seven Brothers," "Gaby," "A Certain Smile," "The Diary of Anne Frank," and "Five Finger Exercise." She is survived by her husband, a sister and a brother.

DAVID GORCEY, 63, one of the original "Dead End Kids" of the Bowery Boys film comedies, died after lapsing into a diabetic coma on Oct. 23, 1984 in Los Angeles, CA. He had appeared in more than 100 movies, usually as straight man for his brother Leo who died in 1969. He retired in 1958 to run a halfway house for alcoholics and drug abusers. His credits include "Little Tough Guy," "Juvenile Court," "Newsboys Home," "Sgt. Madden," "The Ghost Creeps," "Pride of the Bowery," "Flying Wild," "Spooks Run Wild," "That Gang of Mine," "Mr. Wise Guy," "Smart Alecks," "In Fast Company," "News Hounds," "Jinx Money," "Trouble Makers," "Hold That Baby," "Angels in Disguise," "Blonde Dynamite," "Lucky Losers," "Let's Go, Navy!," "Up in Smoke," "In the Money." Surviving are a son and a daughter.

LLOYD GOUGH, 77, NYC-born stage, film and tv actor, died of an aortic aneurism July 23, 1984 in Sherman Oaks, CA. After his Broadway success, he appeared in such films as "All My Sons," "River Lady," "Babe Ruth Story," "Southern Yankee," "That Wonderful Urge," "Tulsa," "Roseanna McCoy," "Always Leave Them Laughing," "Tension," "Outside the Wall," "Sunset Boulevard," "Storm Warning," "Valentino," "The Screen," "Rancho Notorious," "Tony Rome," "Madigan," "The Great White Hope," "House Calls" and "The Front." He is survived by his wife, actress Karen Morley, a stepson, and two brothers.

NEIL HAMILTON, 85, Massachusetts-born stage, screen and tv actor, died Sept. 24, 1984 of complications from asthma in his home in Escondido, CA. After his big break in 1923 in "The White Rose," he appeared in over 80 films, including "America," "Men and Women," "Golden Princess," "Desert Gold," "Beau Geste," "The Great Gatsby," "The Music Master," "Ten Modern Commandments," "Shield of Honor," "The Showdown," "Mother Machree," "Don't Marry," "The Grip of the Yukon," "The Patriot," "What a Night!," "Why Be Good?," "A Dangerous Woman," "Studio Murder Mystery," "The Mysterious Dr. Fu Manchu," "Dawn Patrol," "The Cat Creeps," "Widow from Chicago," "Laughing Sinners," "The Great Lover," "This Modern Age," "The Sin of Madelon Claudet," "Tarzan the Ape Man," "What Price Hollywood," "Two Against the World," "Payment Deferred," "Animal Kingdom," "One Sunday Afternoon," "Here Comes the Groom," "Blind Date," "Keeper of the Bees," "Portia on Trial," "Army Girl," "The Saint Strikes Back," "Father Takes a Wife," "Brewster's Millions," "Good Neighbor Sam," "The Family Jewels," "Madam X," and "Batman." In later life he was best known for his Commissioner Gordon on the popular tv series "Batman." His widow survives.

LILLIAN HELLMAN, 79, New Orleans-born playwright and screenwriter, died of cardiac arrest June 30, 1984 at Martha's Vineyard, Mass. In addition to adaptations of her plays, film credits include "The Dark Angel," "These Three," "Dead End," "The Spanish Earth," "The Little Foxes," "The North Star," "Watch on the Rhine," "The Searching Wind," "Another Part of the Forest," "The Children's Hour," "Toys in the Attic," "The Chase," and "Julia." No immediate survivors.

IAN HENDRY, 53, English film and tv actor, died Dec. 24, 1984 in London of undisclosed cause. His pictures include "In the Nick," "Live Now, Pay Later," "The Girl in the Headlines," "This Is My Street," "The Beauty Jungle," "Children of the Damned," "The Model Murder Case," "The Hill," "Repulsion," "Southern Star," "The Intermecine File," "Get Carter," "The Assassin," "The Birch," "Theatre of Blood." He appeared in the tv series "The Avengers" and "Brookside." No reported survivors.

SAM JAFFE, 93, NYC-born character actor on stage, screen and tv, died of cancer Mar. 24, 1984 in his home in Beverly Hills, CA. He began his career on stage, and in 1934 he made his movie debut in "Scarlet Empress," followed by such pictures as "Lost Horizon," "Gunga Din!," "Stage Door Canteen," "We Live Again," "Gentleman's Agreement," "Accused," "Rope of Sand," "Asphalt Jungle" (for which he received an Oscar nomination, and best actor award at the Venice Film Festival), "I Can Get It for You Wholesale," "Day the Earth Stood Still," "The Barbarian and the Geisha," "Ben-Hur," "Guns for San Sebastian," "The Great Bank Robbery," "Kremlin Letter," "Dunwich Horror," "Nothing Lasts Forever," and "On the Lines." He leaves his widow, actress Bettye Ackerman.

J. DELOS JEWKES, 89, singer and actor, died July 17, 1984 of a heart attack in Provo, UT. He had appeared in approximately 300 films, and was featured in all the MacDonald-Eddy musicals. He supplied the voice for God in DeMille's "Ten Commandments." Surviving are a son and two daughters.

SUNNY JOHNSON, 30, California-born actress, died June 20, 1984 after suffering a cerebral hemorrhage in her West Hollywood apartment. She had appeared in "National Lampoon's Animal House," "Almost Summer," "Where the Buffalo Roam," "Why Would I Lie?," "Flashdance," "Dr. Heckyl and Mr. Hype," "The Night the Lights Went Out in Georgia," "The Immoral Minority Picture Show." Her parents and several sisters survive.

WILLIAM KEIGHLEY, 94, Philadelphia-born former actor who became a theatre and film director, and radio producer, died of a stroke on June 24, 1984 in Los Angeles, CA. His many film credits include "Easy to Love," "Dr. Monica," "Big Hearted Herbert," "Babbitt," "Right to Live," "G Men," "Special Agent," "Stars over Broadway," "The Singing Kid," "The Green Pastures," "The Prince and the Pauper," "Varsity Show," "Adventures of Robin Hood," "Valley of the Giants," "Brother Rat," "Yes, My Darling Daughter," "Each Dawn I Die," "Fighting 69th," "Torrid Zone," "No Time for Comedy," "Four Mothers," "The Bride Came C.O.D.," "The Man Who Came to Dinner," "George Washington Slept Here," "Rocky Mountain" and "A Baby for Midge." He had been host and director of the Lux Radio Theatre. He is survived by his widow, former actress Genevieve Tobin.

WALTER WOOLF KING, 88, San Francisco-born former stage and film actor, and singer, died of a heart attack Oct. 24, 1984 in Beverly Hills, CA. Until he became a film actor in the 1930's, he appeared on Broadway as Walter Woolf. His screen credits include "Golden Dawn," "Girl without a Room," "One More Spring," "Ginger," "A Night at the Opera," "Call It a Day," "Swiss Miss," "Big Town Czar," "Balalaika," "Go West," "Taxi," "Tonight We Sing," "The Helen Morgan Story," "The Householder," "Smart Alecks," "Yanks Ahoy," "Bottom of the Bottle," "Kathy O'," "Hong Kong Confidential" and "Rosie." A son and daughter survive.

NORMAN KRASNA, 74, NYC-born screenwriter and playwright, producer and director, died of a heart attack Nov. 1, 1984 in Los Angeles, CA. He received an Oscar in 1943 for his screenplay of "Princess O'Rourke," and was nominated for "The Richest Girl in the World," "Fury," and "The Devil and Miss Jones." Other credits include "Four Hours to Kill," "As Good as Married," "Mr. and Mrs. Smith," "Dear Ruth," "John Loves Mary," "Indiscreet," "Who Was That Lady?," "Sunday in New York," "Flame of New Orleans," "The Devil and Miss Jones," "It Started with Eve," "Practically Yours," "White Christmas," "The Big Hangover," "Ambassador's Daughter," "Let's Make Love," "My Geisha," "I'd Rather Be Rich." Surviving are his second wife and six children.

JACK LaRUE, 83, actor, born Gaspere Biondolillo in NYC, died Jan. 11, 1984 after a heart attack in Santa Monica, CA. He had appeared in over 200 films, often as villain or gangster, after his 1932 screen debut in "The Mouthpiece." Credits include "Radio Patrol," "Virtue," "A Farewell to Arms," "Christopher Strong," "Woman Accused," "Story of Temple Drake," "Gambling Ship," "Good

Dame," "Straight Is the Way," "Times Square Lady," "Special Agent," "His Night Out," "Strike Me Pink," "Her Husband Lies," "Captains Courageous," "Valley of the Giants," "Sea Hawk," "Ringside Maisie," "Swamp Woman," "The Desert Song," "Pistol Packin' Mama," "Dakota," "Murder in the Music Hall," "In Old Sacramento," "My Favorite Brunette," "No Orchids for Miss Blandish" and "Robin and the Seven Hoods." No reported survivors.

PETER LAWFORD, 61, British-born actor, died of cardiac arrest Dec. 24, 1984 in Los Angeles, CA. After his film debut in 1938 in "Lord Jeff," he appeared in more than 30 productions, including "A Yank at Eton," "White Cliffs of Dover," "Picture of Dorian Gray," "Son of Lassie," "Cluny Brown," "Two Sisters from Boston," "It Happened in Brooklyn," "Good News," "Easter Parade," "Little Women," "Red Danube," "Royal Wedding," "You for Me," "Ocean's 11," "Exodus," "Pepe," "Sergeants 3," "Advise and Consent," "The Longest Day," "Harlow," "The Oscar," "That's Entertainment," "Rosebud," and "Where Is Parsifal?" his final picture. Surviving is his third wife, a son and three daughters. After cremation, he was interred in Westwood Village Cemetery.

ANDREA LEEDS, 70, actress, nee Antoinette Lees in Butte, MT, died of cancer May 21, 1984 in Palm Springs, CA. She was nominated for an Oscar for her performance in "Stage Door" in 1937. Other credits include "Come and Get It," "The Goldwyn Follies," "Letter of Introduction," "Youth Takes a Fling," "They Shall Have Music," "The Real Glory," "Swanee River" and "Earthbound." After her marriage in 1939, she retired from film making. She is survived by her son, Robert S. Howard, Jr.

ANN LITTLE, 93, silent film actress, died May 21, 1984 in her home in Los Angeles, CA. After her debut in 1910 she appeared in many westerns with Jack Hoxie, William S. Hart and Wallace Reid. Other credits include "Lightning Bryce" series, "The Roaring Road," "Believe Me, Xantippe," "Firefly of France," "The Squaw Man," "Cradle of Courage," "Chain Lightning," "Hair Trigger" and "The Greatest Menace." She retired in 1923. No reported survivors.

AVON LONG, 73, Baltimore-born dancer, singer and actor on stage, screen and tv, died of cancer Feb. 15, 1984 in NYC. His career began on stage in 1936, and his film appearances were in "Finian's Rainbow," "Ziegfeld Follies," "Centennial Summer," "Romance on the High Seas," "Manhattan Merry-Go-Round," "The Sting," "Harry and Tonto" and "Trading Places." His widow and two daughters survive.

JOSEPH LOSEY, 75, Wisconsin-born director, died June 22, 1984 in his London home. He had left the U.S. after being blacklisted during the McCarthy era. His films include "The Boy with Green Hair," "The Lawless," "M," "The Prowler," "The Big Night," "Time without Pity," "Chance Meeting," "The Servant," "King and Country," "Eva," "These Are the Damned," "Modesty Blaise," "Accident," "Boom!," "Secret Ceremony," "Figures in a Landscape," "The Go-Between," "The Concrete Jungle," "The Assassination of Trotsky," "A Doll's House" with Jane Fonda, "Galileo," "The Romantic Englishwoman," "M. Klein," "Don Giovanni," "The Trout" and "Steaming." He is survived by his fourth wife, and two sons.

JOHN LEE MAHIN, 81, Illinois-born screenwriter, died Apr. 18, 1984 of emphysema in Santa Monica, CA. He wrote or co-wrote more than 35 screenplays, two of which received Oscar nominations: "Captains Courageous" and "Heaven Knows, Mr. Allison." Other credits include "Red Dust," "Beast of the City," "Bombshell," "Mogambo," "Prizefighter and the Lady," "Hell Below," "Treasure Island," "Chained," "Naughty Marietta," "Small Town Girl," "Love on the Run," "Too Hot to Handle," "Boom Town," "Dr. Jekyll and Mr. Hyde," "Johnny Eager," "Tortilla Flat," "Down to the Sea in Ships," "Show Boat," "Quo Vadis," "Elephant Walk," "The Bad Seed," "No Time for Sergeants," "The Horse Soldiers," "North to Alaska," "The Spiral Road" and "Moment to Moment" his last film in 1966. His widow and three children survive.

JOHN MARLEY, 77, NYC-born character actor on stage, screen and tv, died May 22, 1984 after open-heart surgery in Los Angeles. His film credits include "My Six Convicts," "The Joe Louis Story," "The Square Jungle," "Timetable," "I Want to Live," "America America," "Cat Ballou," "Faces" (for which he received the Venice Film Festival Best Actor Award), "Love Story" (for which he received an Oscar nomination), "A Man Called Sledge," "The Dead Are Alive," "Dead of Night," "Blade," "Jory," "Framed," "W.C. Fields and Me," "Kid Vengeance," "The Car," "The Godfather," "Tribute," "Hooper," "The Amateur," "Mother Lode" and "On the Edge." Surviving are his widow, two sons and two daughters.

JUNE MARLOWE, 81, Minnesota-born actress, died Mar. 10, 1984 in Burbank, CA. She was the heroine in Rin-Tin-Tin films and the school teacher in "Our Gang" comedies. Other credits include "Find Your Man," "Man without a Conscience," "Clash of the

Wolves," "Lost Lady," "Pleasure Buyers," "Don Juan," "Night Cry," "Life of Riley," "Free Lips," "Foreign Legion," "Pardon Us," "Riddle Ranch," "Slave Girl." She retired after her marriage to film executive Rodney S. Sprigg.

JAMES MASON, 75, British-born stage and screen actor, died July 27, 1984 after a heart attack in his home in Lausanne, Switzerland. In almost 50 years, he made over 100 films, and was three times nominated for an Oscar for his roles in "The Verdict," "A Star Is Born" and "Georgy Girl." Other credits include "Fire over England," "Mill on the Floss," "Return of the Scarlet Pimpernel," "This Man Is Dangerous," "Secret Mission," "Thunder Rock," "Man in Grey," "The Seventh Veil," "Wicked Lady," "Odd Man Out," "Man of Evil," "The Reckless Moment," "Madame Bovary," "Pandora and the Flying Dutchman," "The Desert Fox," "Five Fingers," "Prisoner of Zenda," "Julius Caesar," "The Trials of Oscar Wilde," "Desert Rats," "Botany Bay," "20,000 Leagues under the Sea," "Forever Darling," "Island in the Sun," "Cry Terror," "North by Northwest," "Lolita," "Torpedo Bay," "Fall of the Roman Empire," "Pumpkin Eater," "Lord Jim," "The Piano Player," "Genghis Khan," "The Blue Max," "Stranger in the House," "Mayerling," "The Sea Gull," "Child's Play," "The Last of Sheila," "The Mackintosh Man," "Heaven Can Wait," "The Boys from Brazil," "Alexandre," "Yellowbeard" and his last film, "The Shooting Party." Surviving are his second wife, Australian actress Clarissa Kay, and a son and a daughter from his first marriage.

EDITH MASSEY, 66, NYC-born character actress, died Oct. 24, 1984 in Los Angeles, CA. She had appeared in "Multiple Maniacs," "Pink Flamingos," "Female Trouble," "Desperate Living," "Polyester" and "Mutants from Space." She is survived by a sister and two brothers.

GEORGE MATHEWS, 73, Brooklyn-born stage, screen and tv character actor, died of a heart disease Nov. 7, 1984 in his home in Caesar's Head, SC, where he had retired. After success on Broadway, he appeared in such films as "Up in Arms," "The Eve of St. Mark," "A Wing and a Prayer," "The Great John L.," "Pat and Mike," "City Beneath the Sea," "Act of Love," "The Man with the Golden Arm," "Proud Ones," "Last Wagon," "Gunfight at O.K. Corral," "The Buccaneer" and "Heller in Pink Tights." His widow survives.

DORIS MAY, 81, silent screen actress, died of heart failure on May 12, 1984 in Camarillo, CA. Her credits include "The Bronze Bell," "Eden and Return," "The Foolish Age," "The Foolish Matrons," "Peck's Bad Boy," "The Rookie's Return," "Boy Crazy," "Gay and Devilish," "The Understudy," "Up and at 'Em," "The Common Law," "The Gunfighter," "Tea with a Kick," "Conductor 1492," "Deadwood Coach," "Faithful Wives," "Mary's Ankle" and "23½ Hours Leave." She was the widow of Western actor Wallace MacDonald. A niece survives.

MAY McAVOY, 82, NYC-born silent screen star, died Apr. 26, 1984 after a heart attack in Sherman Oaks, CA. She dropped out of high school to pursue an acting career, and subsequently appeared in such films as "A Perfect Lady," "Sentimental Tommy," "A Private Scandal," "Clarence," "Kick In," "Grumpy," "Only 38," "Hollywood," "Enchanted Cottage," "Three Women," "Tarnish," "Mad Whirl," "Lady Windemere's Fan," "Matinee Ladies," "The Jazz Singer" (Jolson's leading lady), "If I Were Single," "Caught in the Fog," "Ben Hur," "Stolen Kisses" and "No Defense." She retired in 1929 when she married Maurice G. Cleary, an United Artists and Lockheed Aircraft executive. They were later divorced.

ETHEL MERMAN, 76, musical comedy star on stage and screen, died in her sleep Feb. 15, 1984 in her Manhattan apartment. Born Ethel Zimmerman in Astoria, NY, she became a stenographer before entering show business in the late 1920's, and became an instant star in 1930. Her subsequent film credits include "Follow the Leader," "Big Broadcast of 1932" (also 1936), "Shoot the Works," "We're Not Dressing," "Kid Millions," "Happy Landing," "Strike Me Pink," "Tops Is the Limit," "Alexander's Ragtime Band," "Straight Place and Show," "Stage Door Canteen," "Call Me Madam," "There's No Business Like Show Business," "It's a Mad, Mad World," "The Art of Love" and "Airplane." She was married four times, and is survived by her son, Robert Levitt.

MARY MILES MINTER, 82, silent screen star, died of heart failure Aug. 4, 1984 in Santa Monica, CA. Born Juliet Reilly, she changed her name after making her first film in 1912, subsequently appearing in over 50 films in the next 10 years. A great beauty, she rivaled the popularity of Mary Pickford until at 20 her career was ruined by the unsolved slaying of her lover and director William Desmond Taylor. Her credits include "Always in the Way," "Dimples," "Lovely Mary," "Barbara Frietchie," "Melissa of the Hills," "Her Country's Call," "Bachelor's Wife," "Anne of Green Gables," "Nurse Marjorie," "Little Clown," "Judy of Rogue Harbor," "Don't Call Me Little Girl," "Her Winning Way," "Moonlight and Hon-

| Peter Lawford | James Mason | May McAvoy | Mary Miles Minter | Walter Pidgeon | William Powell |

eysuckle," "Cowboy and the Lady," "Tillie," "The Heart Specialist," "South of Suva," "Drums of Fate" and her last film "Trail of the Lonesome Pine." She was married later to Brandon O'Hildebrandt who died in 1965. There are no known survivors. After cremation, her ashes were scattered at sea.

WOODROW PARFREY, 61, NYC-born film, tv and stage character actor, died of a heart attack July 29, 1984 in his Los Angeles home. Among his screen credits are "Planet of the Apes," "Dirty Harry," "Papillon," "Bronco Billy," "Used Cars," "Frances," "The Seduction." He had appeared in over 100 tv shows. Surviving are his wife of 34 years, two sons and two daughters.

SAM PECKINPAH, 59, director, died of cardiac arrest Dec. 28, 1984 in Inglewood, CA., after having been flown there from Puerto Vallarta, MX. His films include "The Deadly Companions," "Ride the High Country," "Major Dundee," "The Wild Bunch," "The Ballad of Cable Hogue," "Straw Dogs," "The Getaway," "Junior Bonner," "Pat Garrett and Billy the Kid," "The Killer Elite," "Cross of Iron," "Convoy" and "The Osterman Weekend." He had been married and divorced four times. He leaves four daughters and a son.

JAN PEERCE, 80, famed opera tenor whose career spanned 50 years, died after a stroke Dec. 15, 1984 in his native New York City. In addition to performing in opera and theatre, he appeared in such films as "Hymn of the Nations," "Carnegie Hall," "Something in the Wind," and "Of Men and Music." Survivors include his widow, two daughters and a son.

WALTER PIDGEON, 87, Canadian-born stage, screen and tv actor, died after a series of strokes on Sept. 26, 1984 in Santa Monica, CA. He achieved great popularity from the 8 films he made with Greer Garson in the 1940's, and was nominated for an Oscar for "Mrs. Miniver" and "Madame Curie" in which he co-starred. He had appeared in over 100 pictures, during the five decades of his career. Among his credits are "Old Loves and New," "Heart of Salome," "Melody of Love," "Bride of the Regiment," "Kiss Me Again," "Going Wild," "Rockabye," "Gorilla," "Fatal Lady," "As Good as Married," "Saratoga," "Girl of the Golden West," "Shopworn Angel," "Too Hot to Handle," "Listen Darling," "House across the Bay," "It's a Date," "Dark Command," "Sky Murder," "Flight Command," "Blossoms in the Dust," "How Green Was My Valley," "Design for Scandal," "White Cargo," "The Youngest Profession," "Mrs. Parkington," "Week-end at the Waldorf," "Holiday in Mexico," "Secret Heart," "Julia Misbehaves," "Command Decision," "That Forsyte Woman," "Red Danube," "The Miniver Story," "Million Dollar Mermaid," "The Bad and the Beautiful," "Dream Wife," "Executive Suite," "Men of the Fighting Lady," "The Last Time I Saw Paris," "Hit the Deck," "Forbidden Planet," "Advise and Consent," "Funny Girl," "Neptune Factor," and "Sextette" his last cameo role. He leaves his second wife, and a daughter by his first wife who died in childbirth.

WILLIAM POWELL, 91, Pittsburgh-born stage and film actor, died of natural causes Mar. 5, 1984 in Palm Springs, CA, where he had retired in 1956. After appearing in some 200 plays, he entered silent films in 1921 with "Sherlock Holmes," subsequently making 30 others. His first talkie was "Interference" in 1928 followed by over 60 more productions. He was nominated for an Oscar for his roles in "The Thin Man," "My Man Godfrey" and "Life with Father." Other credits include "When Knighthood Was in Flower," "Bright Shawl," "Romola," "Aloma of the South Seas," "Beau Geste," "Nevada," "The Great Gatsby" (1926), sequels to "The Thin Man," "Canary Murder Case," "Four Feathers," "Paramount on Parade," "Dishonored," "Road to Singapore," "One Way Passage," "Private Detective," "Manhattan Melodrama," "The Key," "Evelyn Prentice," "Reckless," "Escapade," "The Great Ziegfeld," "Libeled Lady," "The Last of Mrs. Cheyney," "Double Wedding," "Love Crazy," "Ziegfeld Follies," "Hoodlum Saint," "Mr. Peabody and the Mermaid," "Dancing in the Dark," "How to Marry a Millionaire," "The Senator Was Indiscreet," and his last in 1955 "Mister Roberts." He and Myrna Loy became one of the most popular teams in films and appeared together in 14 pictures, including the "Thin Man"

series. He had been married three times, and is survived by his wife of 44 years, former actress Diane Lewis.

JUNE PREISSER, 61, New Orleans-born dancer and actress, was killed Sept. 19, 1984 in a car collision in Boca Raton, FL. Her only child, J. Moss Terry 4th, was killed also. Before turning 17 she made her Broadway debut in "Ziegfeld Follies," and was signed for her film debut in 1939's "Babes in Arms," followed by "Dancing Coed," "Judge Hardy and Son," "Strike Up the Band," "Gallant Sons," "Henry Aldrich for President," "Sweater Girl," "Merrily We Sing," "Babes on Swing Street," "Murder in the Blue Room," "I'll Tell the World," "Let's Go Steady," "Freddie Steps Out," "High School Hero," "Junior Prom," "Her Sister's Secret," "Sarge Goes to College," "Vacation Days," "Two Blondes and a Redhead," "Campus Sleuth," "Smart Politics" and "The Music Man" (1948). She ended her career in the late 1940's and lived with her son in Boca Raton. Two grandchildren survive.

LEO ROBIN, 84, Pittsburgh-born song lyricist, died of heart failure Dec. 29, 1984 in Woodland Hills, CA. He received 9 Academy Award nominations for best song, and won in 1938 for "Thanks for the Memory." Other well known songs include "Louise," "Love in Bloom," "One Hour with You," "Diamonds Are a Girl's Best Friend," "Beyond the Blue Horizon," "My Ideal," "Blue Hawaii," "Prisoner of Love," "With Every Breath I Take," "If I Should Lose You," "Easy Living" and "For Every Man There's a Woman." His collaboration with composer Ralph Rainger made them one of the most successful Hollywood songwriting teams, mostly for Paramount. He also wrote with Richard Whiting, Harry Warren, Jerome Kern, Arthur Schwartz, Harold Arlen, Jule Styne and Sigmund Romberg. He leaves his widow and a daughter.

FLORA ROBSON, 82, British stage, screen and tv actress, died in her sleep July 7, 1984 in Brighton, Eng. Her long career included 60 films and more than 100 plays. In 1960 Queen Elizabeth made her a Dame Commander of the Order of the British Empire. In 1946 she was nominated for an Oscar for her performance in "Saratoga Trunk." Other film credits include "Catherine the Great," "Fire over England," "Wuthering Heights," "We Are Not Alone," "The Lion Has Wings," "The Sea Hawk," "Bahama Passage," "Caesar and Cleopatra," "The Years Between," "Black Narcissus," "Saraband," "Malta Story," "Romeo and Juliet" (1954), "55 Days at Peking," "The Shuttered Room," "Fragment of Fear," "The Beloved," "Dominique," and her last, "Clash of the Titans." She was never married, and no survivors were reported.

LEONARD ROSSITER, 57, British stage, tv and screen actor, collapsed during a performance in London and died of a heart attack Oct. 5, 1984. He had appeared in such films as "This Sporting Life," "Billy Liar," "They All Died Laughing," "King Rat," "Hotel Paradiso," "Deadlier Than the Male," "The Whisperers," "2001 A Space Odyssey," "Oliver!," and "Britannia Hospital." Surviving are his widow, actress Gillian Raine, and a daughter.

HENRY ROWLAND, 70, Omaha-born film and tv character actor, died Apr. 26, 1984 in Northridge, CA. After his film debut in "Safari" (1940), he appeared in more than 50 pictures, often in Westerns or as a Nazi. His credits include "The Pied Piper," "Berlin Correspondent," "The Moon Is Down," "Paris After Dark," "Winged Victory," "Gallant Journey," "The Showdown," "Wagon Team," "Prince of Pirates," "Topeka," "Rogue's Regiment," "Return to Treasure Island," "Hell on Devil's Island," "Chicago Confidential," "Asphalt Jungle," "All the Brothers Were Valiant," "What a Way to Go," "36 Hours," "Hurry Sundown," "Beyond the Valley of the Dolls," "Super Vixens," "The Last Tycoon," and "The Frisco Kid." He appeared on many tv shows. His widow survives.

EDMON RYAN, 79, stage, film and tv actor, died of a heart attack Aug. 4, 1984 in Louisville, KY. After his 1938 film debut in "Crime over London," his credits include "The Human Monster," "Side Street," "Topaz," "Mystery Street," "The Breaking Point," "Three Secrets," "Undercover Girl," "Highway 301," "The Guy Who Came Back," "Go, Man, Go," "Two for the Seesaw," "The Americanization of Emily," "The Playground," and "Dallas." Surviving is a daughter.

| Flora Robson | Francois Truffaut | Johnny Weissmuller | Oskar Werner | Henry Wilcoxon | Estelle Winwood |

ARTHUR SCHWARTZ, 83, Brooklyn-born composer-producer for stage and films, died after a stroke on Sept. 3, 1984 in his home in Kintnersville, PA. His long-time lyricist collaborator Howard Dietz, died in 1983. Other partners include Ira Gershwin, Frank Loesser, Johnny Mercer, E. Y. Harburg, Oscar Hammerstein 2nd, Dorothy Fields and Leo Robin. Among his memorable songs are "That's Entertainment," "Dancing in the Dark," "I Guess I'll Have to Change My Plan," "You and the Night and the Music," "Alone Together," "If There Is Someone Lovelier Than You," and "They're Either Too Young or Too Old." In 1938, after many Broadway successes, he moved to Hollywood and wrote songs for such movies as "Navy Blues," "Thank Your Lucky Stars," "The Time, the Place and the Girl," "Excuse My Dust," "You're Never Too Young," "The Bandwagon," and "Cover Girl." His widow and two sons survive.

HARRY SUKMAN, Chicago-born composer, died after a heart attack on his 72nd birthday after playing at a benefit for a stroke center in Palm Springs, CA. He received a 1960 Oscar for his score for "Song without End." He also scored "Riders to the Stars," "Fanny," "Madison Avenue," "Screaming Eagles," "Thunder of Drums," and "The Singing Nun." He also worked on many tv shows. No reported survivors.

RUTH TAYLOR, 76, former film actress, died Apr. 12, 1984 in Palm Springs, CA. Among her screen credits are "Gentlemen Prefer Blondes" (1928), "Just Married," "The College Coquette" and "This Thing Called Love." Her son, actor-writer Buck Henry, survives.

FRANCOIS TRUFFAUT, 52, Paris-born critic, director, screenwriter and actor, died of brain cancer on Oct. 21, 1984 in Neuilly, France. He was a leading figure in the French New Wave and one of the most critically acclaimed throughout the world. In 1973 his "Day for Night" received an Oscar for best foreign language film. Other pictures were "The 400 Blows," "Shoot the Piano Player," "Jules and Jim," "Stolen Kisses," "The Wild Child," "The Story of Adele H," "Such a Gorgeous Kid Like Me," "The Soft Skin," "Fahrenheit 451" (his only English-language film), "The Bride Wore Black," "Mississippi Mermaid," "Small Change," "The Man Who Loved Women," "The Green Room" starring himself, "Love on the Run," "The Last Metro," "The Woman Next Door" and "Confidentially Yours." He had appeared in such films as "Le Chateau de Verre," "Le Coup de Berger," "The Waves Are Fine in September," "Close Encounters of the Third Kind," and the documentaries "Langlois," "I'm a Stranger Here Myself," and for tv "A Tribute to Rossellini." He is survived by two daughters from his marriage to Madeleine Morgenstern, and a daughter by actress Fanny Ardant.

CAROL EBERTS VEAZIE, 89, film, stage and tv actress, died July 19, 1984 in Carmel, CA. She had appeared in "The Catered Affair," "A Cry in the Night," "Designing Woman," "Auntie Mame," "Baby, the Rain Must Fall" and "Cat Ballou." Three grandchildren survive.

GEORGE WAGGNER, 90, Philadelphia-born actor, director, producer, screenwriter and songwriter, died of natural causes Dec. 11, 1984 in Woodland Hills, CA. He had roles in numerous silent films, including "The Sheik," "Branded Men," "The Iron Horse," "His Hour" and "Love's Blindness." During the 1930's he became a screenwriter for Monogram, Columbia and Universal, collaborating on such pictures as "Sweetheart of Sigma Chi," "City Limits," "Girl of My Dreams," "Keeper of the Bees," "Three Legionnaires," "Idol of the Crowd," "The Nut Farm," "I Cover the War," "The Fighting Kentuckian," "Operation Pacific" and "Return from the Sea." He produced "Ghost of Frankenstein," "Sin Town," "White Savage," "Phantom of the Opera," "Cobra Woman," "Gypsy Wildcat," "The Climax," "Frisco Sal" and "Shady Lady." A daughter and grandchildren survive.

PAUL FRANCIS WEBSTER, 76, NYC-born song lyricist, died of Parkinson's Disease March 18, 1984 in his home in Beverly Hills, CA. With his frequent collaborator Sammy Fain, he won Oscars for "Secret Love" from "Calamity Jane," and the title tune from "Love Is a Many Splendored Thing." With Johnny Mandel, he won an Oscar

for "The Shadow of Your Smile" from "The Sandpiper." He had been nominated for Academy Awards 16 times. He began his film career in 1935 with "Under the Pampas Moon," "Dressed to Thrill" and "Our Little Girl." "Somewhere My Love" from "Dr. Zhivago" was one of his biggest hits. Others were "Thee I Love," "April Love," "A Certain Smile," "A Very Precious Love," "Tender Is the Night," "So Little Time," "Strange Are the Ways of Love." Surviving are his widow and two sons.

JOHNNY WEISSMULLER, 79, Pennsylvania-born Olympic swimming champion who became a film star as Tarzan, died of a lung blockage Jan. 20, 1984 at his home in Acapulco, Mx. He had been an invalid since suffering a series of strokes in 1977. Beginning his film career in 1932 as "Tarzan, the Ape Man," he made almost 20 Tarzan films, the last in 1949, when he began his "Jungle Jim" series for tv. Other film credits include "Glorifying the American Girl," "Hollywood Party," "Stage Door Canteen," "Combat Correspondent," "Swamp Fire," "Captive Girl," "Mark of the Gorilla," "Pygmy Island," "Jungle Manhunt," "Voodoo Tiger," "Savage Mutiny," "Valley of the Headhunters," "Killer Ape," "Cannibal Attack," "Jungle Moon," "Devil Goddess" and his last "The Phynx" in 1969. He is survived by his fifth wife, a son and a daughter.

OSKAR WERNER, 61, Vienna-born stage and film actor, died Oct. 23, 1984 of a heart attack in Marburg, West Ger., where he was to read for a drama club. Born Oskar Joseph Schliessmayer, he began his career at 18 with Vienna's famous repertory company, and had bit parts in films. His first major film role was in "Angel with a Trumpet" in 1948. Subsequently he appeared in "Decision Before Dawn," "Wonder Boy," "The Last Ten Days," "The Life and Loves of Mozart," "Jules and Jim," "Ship of Fools" for which he received an Oscar nomination, "The Spy Who Came in from the Cold," "Fahrenheit 451," "Interlude," "Lola Montes," "The Shoes of the Fisherman," "A Certain Judas," "So Love Returns" and "Voyage of the Damned." He had been married and divorced twice. He suffered from acute alcoholism and had been a virtual recluse for the last decade. Surviving is a daughter by his first marriage, Eleanore, a violinist.

HENRY WILCOXON, 78, West Indies-born British stage, screen and tv actor-producer, died of leukemia and congestive heart failure on Mar. 6, 1984 in his home in Burbank, CA. After success on the London stage, he went to Hollywood in 1932 for Cecil B. DeMille's "Cleopatra," and became a long-time associate of Mr. DeMille. Subsequent film credits include "The Crusades," "Last of the Mohicans," "Souls at Sea," "If I Were King," "Five of a Kind," "Tarzan Finds a Son," "Free, Blond and 21," "That Hamilton Woman," "Scotland Yard," "South of Tahiti," "The Corsican Brothers," "Mrs. Miniver," "Johnny Doughboy," "Unconquered," "A Connecticut Yankee in King Arthur's Court," "War Lord," "Samson and Delilah," "The Miniver Story," "The Greatest Show on Earth," "Scaramouche," "The Ten Commandments," "Against a Crooked Sky," "F.I.S.T.," "The Man with Bogart's Face," "Caddyshack" and "Sweet Sixteen" (his last in 1983). He was divorced from actress Joan Woodbury. Three daughters survive.

ESTELLE WINWOOD, 101, British-born stage, screen and tv actress, died of a heart attack June 20, 1984 in Woodland Hills, CA. She began her career at the age of 5 and was active on tv until 1983. She made her NY stage debut in 1916, and her film debut in 1933 in "The House of Trent." Among her subsequent screen credits are "Quality Street," "The Glass Slipper," "The Swan," "23 Paces to Baker Street," "This Happy Feeling," "Darby O'Gill and the Little People," "The Misfits," "Notorious Landlady," "The Cabinet of Dr. Caligari," "Alive and Kicking," "Dead Ringer," "Camelot," "Games," "The Producers," "And Jenny Makes Three" and "Murder by Death." She is survived by her fourth husband, English director and teacher Robert Henderson, and a brother.

CORRECTION: Regrettably, in Volume 35 (1984), page 237, the date of death for TENNESSEE WILLIAMS was erroneously recorded, and should read Feb. 25, 1983.

259